TELLING THE NEXT GENERATION

Educational development
in North American
Calvinist Christian Schools

TELLING THE NEXT GENERATION

Educational development in North American Calvinist Christian Schools

HARRO W. VAN BRUMMELEN

UNIVERSITY
PRESS OF
AMERICA

LANHAM • NEW YORK • LONDON

Copyright © 1986 by

University Press of America,® Inc.

4720 Boston Way
Lanham, MD 20706

3 Henrietta Street
London WC2E 8LU England

Printed in the United States of America

Co-published by arrangement with the
Institute for Christian Studies, Ontario, Canada

Library of Congress Cataloging in Publication Data

Van Brummelen, Harro W., 1942-
　Telling the next generation.

　(Christian studies today)
　"Co-published . . . with the Institute for Christian
Studies, Ontario, Canada"—T.p. verso.
　Revision of thesis (Ph.D.)—University of British
Columbia, Vancouver.
　Bibliography: p.
　Includes index.
　1. Reformed Church—Education—Canada—History.
2. Reformed Church—Education—United States—History.
3. Church schools—Canada—History.　4. Church schools—
United States—History.　I. Institute for Christian
Studies.　II. Title.　III. Series.
LC586.R3V36　1986　　377'.8'0973　　86-4056
ISBN 0-8191-5307-9 (alk. paper)
ISBN 0-8191-5308-7 (pbk. : alk. paper)

Things we have heard and known,
    things our fathers have told us—
we will not hide them from their children;
    we will tell the next generation
the praiseworthy deeds of the LORD,
    His power, and the wonders He has done.

—Psalm 78:3-4

ACKNOWLEDGEMENTS

Many individuals and associations helped to make this book possible. The Society of Christian Schools in British Columbia, my employer, graciously allowed me to work on a part-time basis while I researched and wrote this study. The late Dr. George S. Tomkins of the University of British Columbia fostered my interest in curriculum history. I benefited a great deal from his insight. The Drs. Daniel R. Birch, William A. Bruneau, and J. Donald Wilson, also of U.B.C., similarly gave consistently helpful encouragement and advice.

All whom I approached gave ready access to relevant documents. The staff of Heritage Hall Archives at Calvin College in Grand Rapids, Michigan, and especially archivist Mrs. Z. C. (Nettie) Janssens, were exceptionally helpful and pleasant in allowing me access to its centralized collection of Calvinist Christian school documents and materials. Without this collection, this book would not have been possible. Dr. Michael Ruiter made available the records and archives of Christian Schools International. Local school boards in British Columbia and Washington provided minutes and other documents. Many individuals, listed in the footnotes, willingly talked to me about their experiences in and with Christian schools. For Dutch sources and materials I am particularly indebted to Drs. Remmelt de Boer of Wezep, the Netherlands, and René Gortzen of the library of the Free University of Amsterdam.

Mr. Stan Pilon of Lynden's **Wordservice** proved invaluable in transferring my script to computer disk, and bearing with me as revisions needed to be made. Mrs. Mary Kooy of Surrey, B.C., suggested many stylistic improvements.

I obtained most of the photographs from Heritage Hall Archives. Those facing Chapters 3, 6, 7, and 10 are copies of originals, while those facing 4, 5, and 9 were copied from old issues of **The Banner** and **Christian Home and School**. The photograph facing Chapter 2 hails from Den Klokkenberg Archief in the Netherlands, while the one facing Chapter 8 was supplied by Mr. Allan Ramerman of Bellingham, Washington.

Perhaps more than anyone else, my father, a staunch supporter (and loving critic) of Christian schools, wished this study to be written. I worked on some of the last chapters at his deathbed. Both my parents, supportive throughout, passed away several months before the completion of the first draft of the manuscript.

Finally, my deepest thanks are reserved for my loving wife and friend, Wilma. She gave more moral and concrete support than I had a right to expect or receive. Her care and cheerfulness kept our family life on even keel while I was immersed in research and writing.

v

Contents

CONTENTS

CONTENTS

CONTENTS

Preface

This study sets out to do two things. First, it intends to shed new light on the interaction of religion, ethnicity, and education as this came to unique expression in the North American Dutch Calvinist community. Secondly, it holds up a mirror to the Christian school movement rooted in Dutch Calvinism. I consider myself to be a "Kuyperian Calvinist," and as such take a great deal of personal interest in the future of these schools. I hope that the issues discussed and the questions raised in this book will help their leaders and supporters reflect on future initiatives and directions.

I have analyzed the educational thinking and practice that has characterized the North American Calvinist Christian school movement during the past century and a half. To understand the movement, I first had to consider the Dutch educational situation prior to the first wave of Dutch emigration to the U.S. in the middle of the nineteenth century. The Dutch influence with further waves to the U.S. around the turn of the century and to Canada after World War II also proved crucial to the schools' development. My approximate cut-off point is 1977, the year I became personally involved in curriculum development and implementation for Christian schools in British Columbia, and the year before Christian Schools International (formerly the National Union of Christian Schools) established a Canadian Curriculum Council, which I chaired from 1978 to 1984.

This book is a revised version of my doctoral dissertation for the Center for the Study of Curriculum and Instruction at the University of British Columbia in Vancouver, Canada. Interested scholars will find full documentation and a complete bibliography in the original dissertation. Readers not familiar with curriculum theory may wish to skim Chapter 7, the most technical chapter in the book.

Finally, since this is an historical study, this book does not explicate my own views on the role and structure of Christian schooling in North America. Interested readers can find these, for example, in **Shaping School Curriculum: A Biblical View**, edited by Geraldine Steensma and myself.

Harro Van Brummelen

Programme

FRIDAY, OCTOBER 2, 1914
2:00 P. M.
Presiding Officer—Prof. L. Berkhof.

Invocation.

Lecture—"Our Course of Study"........Supt. B. J. Bennink
General Discussion.

Duet—Selected...........Misses Edith and Henrietta Kuiper

Lecture—"Our Teachers, their Opportunities and
Responsibilities"....................Prof. Wm. Rinck
General Discussion.

Soprano Solo—Selected...............Miss Regina Schoonbeek

Closing.

FRIDAY, OCTOBER 2, 1914
7:30 P. M.
Presiding Officer—Prin. G. Bos.

Invocation.

Selection.................................Lagrave Ave. Men's Choir
Mr. J. L. Benjamins, Director

Roundtable discussions on following topics:
(5 minutes for introduction;
10 minutes for general discussion.)

1 "Drop the Dutch from the Curriculum"—
Mr. J. Mulder

2 "I Cannot Teach the Lower Grades"
Miss S. Grevengoed

Pipe Organ Solo—Selected..............Miss Edith Winsemius

3 "Stick-to-it"................................Mr. John De Jager

4 "The Supervising Principal"......Mr. G. J. Heyboer

Selection.................................Lagrave Ave. Men's Choir

5 "Our Mutual Needs"....................Prof. L. Berkhof

Song—"America" and "Blest be the Tie that Binds"—
Audience

Closing.

A page of the program of the 1914 Michigan
Christian Teachers' Institute.

1   Dutch Calvinists and Their North American Christian Schools

During the past decade, non-Catholic private schools in North America have experienced remarkable growth. In the United States, enrollment in such schools increased about 150 percent between 1972 and 1982. Total private school growth in Canada rose 50 percent during the same period while public school enrollment declined fifteen percent. Parents who believe, for one reason or another, that existing public schools are inappropriate for their children, have increasingly established alternative private schools. A large proportion of these schools is an assortment of generally small, locally-controlled, religiously-oriented schools.

Private or non-public schools have been part of a long North American tradition. Until public schools became widely accepted, churches of various denominations operated schools and academies. Roman Catholic parochial or separate schools continued to exist throughout North America even when most other church-controlled schools disappeared. Segments of the Jewish, the German Lutheran, and the Dutch Calvinist communities, among others, have also supported religiously-oriented day school education from their first founding until the present. This study focuses on schools rooted in the Dutch Calvinist tradition.

Just as most American schools were moving out of the church's orbit in the mid-nineteenth century, newly-arrived Calvinists from the Netherlands founded their first schools in Michigan.[1] Their schools remained small in number. Grouped together as the National Union of Christian Schools [NUCS] (since 1978 Christian Schools International), they never attracted much attention. Yet in 1969 eighty percent of all families in the major supporting denomination, the 300 000-member Christian Reformed Church, sent their children to NUCS schools.[2] In Canada, the schools presently form the largest identifiable and cohesive group of Christian schools other than Catholic ones. Thirty percent of the pupils in non-Catholic private schools in Alberta and British

1

CALVINIST CHRISTIAN SCHOOLS

Columbia attend these Calvinist-inspired Christian schools. Ontario's sixty-eight schools, with 9 700 pupils, form the largest concentration of NUCS schools outside of Michigan. Dutch Calvinist persistence in operating these schools, however, has detracted little from the perception that the Dutch assimilate easily into a compatible American or Canadian environment. This conviction has been one reason for the relative paucity of studies about the Dutch in North America. The little existing research has seldom dealt with North American Calvinist schools.

Until the 1970s, Dutch immigrants or their descendants founded most NUCS schools. The first major wave of Dutch settlers to the United States in the 1840s and 1850s migrated for both economic and religious reasons. In the 1830s, groups of mainly rural, orthodox Calvinists (or Seceders, as they came to be called) left the national Dutch Reformed Church, resulting in religious oppression. Intolerance towards them (and towards their attempts to establish parochial schools) worsened their already low socio-economic status. Thus the economic depression of the 1840s affected them more than most. Soon, several of their religious leaders recommended emigration to the New World, and between 1846 and 1857 almost 40 000 Dutch peasants and rural artisans left for America.[3] In 1856 a handful of these settlers began the first Calvinist school in Grand Rapids, Michigan.

Later Dutch immigrants who came to North America between 1880 and World War I and after World War II did not come for religious reasons. Yet these waves also contained a disproportionately large number of Orthodox Calvinists. Most of their leaders encouraged Christian schools, basing their desirability on the perceived Enlightenment and, later, socialist influences on Dutch public schools and their curricula. Successive groups of immigrants brought with them fresh Dutch ideas about the nature and programs of Christian schools—and, often, principals and teachers to implement them. One important theme of this book is that the immigrants' religious and ethnic backgrounds, inextricably intertwined, provided the main contours for the schools and their curricula. The development of North American Calvinist schools cannot be understood without considering their Dutch roots.

The Calvinist schools bolstered the religious and ethnic cohesiveness of the Christian Reformed community. School leaders from time to time avowed their resolve to broaden the ethnic base of the schools. Partly for that reason, since 1910 associations of parents and not church congregations have operated almost all schools. Nevertheless, close if informal liaison with the Christian Reformed

2

Church continued. In contrast, contact with theologically-close but ethnically-distinct Presbyterian groups was almost totally lacking. The schools sustained Dutch Calvinist social patterns and, often against the expressed desires of their proponents, preserved ethnic consciousness, at least until recently.

The schools' founders were unabashedly Calvinistic in their beliefs as well as in their views of society and the role of Christians in it. The leader of the first Dutch settlement in Michigan intended "to found a kingdom of orthodox Christianity in the primeval forests of Western Michigan."[4] Such "orthodox Christianity" held that God ordained persons to both salvation and holiness. Faith involved sound doctrine and godliness based on Biblical precepts. Like the Puritans, these Calvinists believed each person must be educated in order to be able to read and understand the Bible. School instruction had to be carried out "in the nurture and admonition of the Lord." The school principal who more than anyone else shaped America's Dutch Calvinist schools in the early twentieth century defined education as

> that process of development of man's body and soul so that all his faculties may reach a state of perfection which enables him to fulfill his obligations toward God, himself, and his neighbor.[5]

For Dutch Calvinists, one's obligation to God came first. Only Christian schools could be duly concerned with both "body and soul" and properly define a "state of perfection." Supporters considered public schools, often with superior facilities and better qualified teachers, philosophically and religiously incompatible with Calvinistic beliefs.

Two overlapping but distinct strains of Calvinism affected the North American schools. The original nineteenth century pietistic and individualistic supporters emphasized Calvinistic doctrines and strict personal moral uprightness. Children, they believed, must be shielded from their American environment, and consequently they maintained instruction in Dutch until well into the twentieth century. Even today, their modern counterparts send children to Christian schools primarily to isolate children from unhealthy "worldly" influences. The second group has consisted mainly of followers of Abraham Kuyper, the foremost Calvinist leader in the Netherlands from 1880 to 1920. Without denying the doctrinal and moral facets of Calvinism, the "Kuyperians" attached much greater importance to God calling Christians to be actively engaged in politics, commerce, science, education and the arts. Kuyperians wanted Christian school pupils to analyze and respond to societal phenomena and issues. In obedience to God and in a uniquely Christian way, students must be helped to contribute to the growth and

3

development of society. Around the turn of the century newly-arrived Kuyperians in the U.S. opposed Dutch language instruction since children could understand and influence American society only if fluent in English. They also strove for a socially-relevant curriculum broader in scope than the teaching of Biblical concepts and basic skills. One reason that the differences between the two groups have persisted is that each found elements of social and political thought in the United States that supported their views.

Proponents of Calvinist schools have vigorously claimed that Christian beliefs should affect not only the school atmosphere but the total curriculum and its implementation. The Lordship of Jesus Christ over all creation, they asserted, must affect all aspects of human society, and consequently all subject matter. The first Christian textbooks were developed in the Netherlands while the first schools were being established. The school movement in the United States has published a steady though far from profuse flow of textbooks and other curriculum materials, not only for Biblical studies, but also for social studies, language arts and science. Canadian groups supplemented these with their own products in the 1970s. The intent of all publications was that the curriculum would embody Calvinistic conceptions of the nature of human beings and their relationships to God, the character and utilization of physical reality, the Christian's role in society, and the ultimate purpose of human life on earth.

This book considers a number of questions about the history of North American Calvinist school thought and practice, taking into account Dutch developments as they influenced North American schools. In what ways has their curriculum, i.e., the dynamic, ever-changing series of planned learning activities, been distinctive? How far did Calvinistic philosophical and religious views have a bearing on programs and textbooks and their use? How did trends in public education affect curriculum and instruction? To what extent did the schools make decisions without reference to the general political and educational context? Did the cultural background of the school's supporters lead them to favour one particular curriculum orientation over another (e.g., an academic rather than an experiential one)? Who made the key program decisions and on what basis? How was instruction influenced by parental wishes? By general societal expectations of schooling? By educational thinkers like Pestalozzi and Dewey? By government recommendations and stipulations? By the Christian Reformed Church? The investigation of such questions will help determine in what ways the goals of the schools have or have not been realized. More generally, it will give some indications whether non-public schools can

4

institute and maintain distinctive programs when one of their major goals is to enable children to function effectively in society around them.

The ethnic, rural and socio-economic background of supporters had a bearing on the schools' curricular and instructional decisions. In 1963, for example, a long-term American NUCS high school teacher concluded that the students' social background contributed to diligence but also to an all-too-ready acceptance of whatever teachers presented. As a result, he wondered, was the curriculum geared too much to indoctrination rather than education?[6] Whether or not his conclusion was correct, his assumption of the relevance of social background to learning was valid. Societal trends have influenced Christian schools. In the mid-1910s war-generated nativism accelerated the Americanization of the schools, as the schools' readers, social studies publications, and even penmanship samples displayed an uncritical devotion to America as the land of liberty and freedom. As in public schools, the increasing percentage of teenagers completing high school in the 1950s and 1960s led to greater curricular diversity. The swings from 1960s social activism and innovation to the late 1970s retrenchment, with corresponding educational moves from neo-progressivism to "back to the basics," also affected Christian schools, though in muted fashion. The social milieu did not fail to touch the schools and their programs. This study opens the way for a future full social history of this group of schools.

One of the themes that recurred repeatedly in the history of Calvinistic schools was that "Christian principles" and "the teaching of the Lord" must permeate all instruction. The schools strove to make curriculum materials and implementation distinctively Christian. But they have not been united about the meaning of "distinctively Christian." In the Netherlands in the 1840s, Seceder schools saturated the curriculum with religious doctrines and personal moral injunctions. This group also stressed "receptacle" learning, i.e., the memorization and regurgitation of information supplied by the teacher. On the other hand, the start of the first interdenominational, parent-controlled school in the Netherlands in 1844 came in opposition to the mechanical inculcation of information prevalent in public schools. This Christian school was founded so that children would be treated as responsible, individual personalities. Teachers were to model a Christian life rather than hold forth about it, and meet the everyday needs of children at their level of development. Later the Kuyperians also took this view, but, unlike both previous groups, stressed that the curriculum should help children "to become a reforming influence in our society and develop a Christian culture and lifestyle according to the norms of God's Word" [i.e, the Bible].[7]   Curriculum disagreements between the pietistic, protectionistic position and the more socially relevant one have arisen periodically.   Indeed, a recent influx of isolationistic non-Calvinist Christians into many NUCS schools has once again accentuated this difference of approach.

Another prominent theme has been the schools' quest for educational excellence.   Religious perspective and content, many supporters believed, should enhance rather than erode education standards.   Although founded for religious and moral reasons, schools often took pride in exceeding public school norms on examinations and standardized tests.   However, beyond the assumption that such secular standards must be met, little agreement about the characteristics of quality education existed.   For some, it meant exhaustive training in basic skills.   For others, it consisted of a thorough classical education that trained the powers of the mind.   A few believed that excellence would occur only if the structure and content of learning helped children to discover and explore their own particular abilities and identities.   Still others felt excellence was attained when students were able to analyze and respond to societal issues in a Christian manner. Often these diverse views represented Calvinistic adaptations of curriculum orientations prevalent in public education.

An additional thread in this study is how Dutch Calvinists expressed their changing conceptions of their schools' function in their curricula.   Until 1890, parents supported the schools primarily to sustain the religious, moral and cultural tenets of their Dutch Calvinist heritage.   Since they believed the preservation of their convictions to depend on a knowledge of the Dutch language, they considered the schools to be "Dutch schools."   On the other hand, Kuyper's followers saw the schools as instruments in bringing about a new, more Calvinistic social order throughout America.   In the 1930s, leaders of the schools, like those in other segments of society, tried to erect social and ideological bulwarks in the face of social and economic instability and uncertainty.   Schools became safeguards to defend Calvinism against the dangers of modernism and progressivism.   The post-World War II Kuyperians, especially in Canada, looked at the schools once again as possible Christian vanguards benefiting all segments of a pluralistic society.   During the 1970s, Canadian Christian high school teachers developed a **Man in Society** course that emphasized contributions Christians could make to Canadian society.[8]

Long before this, however, most American Christian school supporters had adopted the American civil religion: a faith in the

6

equality of men, in the entrepreneurial spirit and continued progress, in individualism and pragmatism.[9] Dutch Calvinists had become American Calvinists, fitting into the American way of life while continuing to uphold their Calvinist doctrines and morals. Many post-World War II Canadian immigrants suspected this American way of life to be inconsistent with true Christianity. As Kuyperians, they wanted Christians to influence not only personal morals but also legal, political, social and economic decisions and the related societal structures. Working within the Canadian "mosaic," Canadian Calvinists felt positive about working towards the implementation of a Kuyperian vision of society.[10] In the late 1960s and the 1970s, many Canadians, dissatisfied with what they felt to be the shallow Christian perspective of American curriculum materials, began developing their own approaches and writing their own materials. Canadian Christian school leaders—supported by a number of Americans—did not want to train children to fit into the individualistic, pragmatic, materialistic American way of life.

This book, then, considers how religious and moral beliefs, theoretical thought, social and economic influences, and national identities combined to forge school programs that the Dutch Calvinist community deemed to meet its children's needs at various times and in different places. It investigates the extent to which the curriculum has been unique and in what ways it absorbed past or current ideas in general educational thinking or practice. The motives of the supporters of Christian schools remained hidden sometimes even to themselves. Their vision of what Christian day schools should be like was often clouded. Conditions and teacher qualifications frequently left something to be desired. Yet the schools not only survived for more than 125 years, but are still growing today and catering to a wide range of evangelical Christians. This book attempts to answer how the schools' programs have made them attractive alternatives for 80 000 American and Canadian pupils—or whether, indeed, reasons for their popularity must be found outside of their curricula.

NOTES

1. Evangelical Protestants had forged a consensus of faith and ethics and believed that public education would promote such a consensus (Timothy L. Smith, "Protestant Schooling and American Nationality, 1800-1850," **Journal of American History** 53 [March 1967]). Dutch immigrants who promoted parochial schools seemed to give more

consideration to conditions in Dutch public schools than in American ones.

2. Robert P. Swierenga, "The Dutch," in Stephan Thernstrom, ed., **Harvard Enclyclopedia of American Ethnic Groups** (Cambridge, Mass.: Belknap Press of Harvard University Press, 1980), p. 293. In 1978 the NUCS became known as Christian Schools International [CSI]. The organization is not to be confused with the Association of Christian Schools International [ASCI], the 1978 amalgamation of several other regional Christian school association in the United States. CSI, with its roots in Dutch Calvinism, had 400 member schools in 1984-85 with a total enrollment of 77 091 students, of which 113 schools with 16 906 students were in Canada. ACSI represents a broader spectrum of evangelical Protestant schools. In 1984-85 it reported 2150 member schools with an enrollment of 364 000 students. ACSI does not publish separate Canadian figures but in Canada in 1984 was much smaller than CSI. This book will use the name National Union of Christian Schools [NUCS] rather than CSI, since the organization was known by the NUCS name until the 1977 cut-off date of this study.

3. Based on the figures of Robert P. Swierenga, "Dutch International Labour Migration to North America in the Nineteenth Century," in Herman Ganzevoort and Mark Boekelman, eds., **Dutch Immigration to North America** (Toronto: The Multicultural History Society of Ontario, 1983), pp. vii-viii.

4. Albert Hyma to Mark Fakkema, Feb. 15, 1947 (Hyma personal papers, Heritage Hall Archives, Calvin College, Grand Rapids, Michigan).

5. B. J. Bennink, **De Calvinist**, Dec. 30, 1916.

6. **Christian Home and School**, Sept. - Oct. 1963, pp. 12-13.

7. Edmonton Christian High School, **Handbook for Students 1976-77**, p. 1. Such aims are reminiscent of both John Calvin and Abraham Kuyper.

8. Ary De Moor et al., **Man in Society: A Study in Hope** (Grand Rapids: CSI publications, 1980).

9. For a description of the American "faith" that defined its nationhood, see Allan Smith, "Metaphor and Nationality in North America," **Canadian Historical Review** 51 (Sept. 1970): 252-54.

10. For such an optimistic vision, see, for example, John A. Olthuis, "The Wages of Change," in John A. Olthuis et al., **Out of Concern for the Church** (Toronto: Wedge, 1970), especially pp. 20-25. Kuyper had similarly said on his 1898 trip to America that

"Calvinism has yet a blessing to bring and bright hope to unveil for the future" of Western civilization (Abraham Kuyper, **Lectures on Calvinism** [Grand Rapids: Eerdmans, 1931], p. 40).

Entrance of Den Klokkenberg Christian School in Nijmegen, the first Dutch association-controlled Christian School.

2   Christian Schools in the Netherlands to 1848

The First Christian School Operated by an Association of Parents

For the 400 North American member schools of Christian Schools International (formerly the National Union of Christian School [NUCS]), May 6, 1844 is an important date. That day 116 pupils enrolled in a new school in the city of Nijmegen, a few kilometres from the German border in central Holland. The school was unique: the parents not only agreed to uphold the school's regulations, but also became members of an association that operated the school. They committed themselves to running its affairs and giving it adequate support.[1] This was the first Christian school governed by an independent association of parents, a pattern of organization that at present characterizes almost all NUCS schools in North America.

More than the school's organizational structure was unique. The school's main leader was the lawyer Justinus J. L. van der Brugghen, later Prime Minister of the Netherlands. He established the school to teach children the principles of the Christian faith in a vibrant, meaningful way. As chairman of Nijmegen's school commission since 1838, Van der Brugghen had become disillusioned with the city's schools.

However, there had been one exceptional school. In 1840, a group influenced by the Dutch Protestant revival (**het Réveil**) had started a kindergarten for working-class children. Its aims were to improve their physical care, their intellectual growth, and, especially, their religious development. The teacher was "to tell them in a child-like way about Jesus, so that ignorance [would] not prevent them one day from approaching Him." Van der Brugghen, who himself had become part of the revival movement in Nijmegen, was impressed with the kindergarten's program and instructions. Within eighteen months he spearheaded efforts to begin a continuation school.[3]

Those efforts met the stiff resistance of local and provincial authorities. All schools in the Netherlands needed government

11

permission to operate. Such permission could be granted to organizations, to qualified teachers who wanted to operate their own school, and to churches operating free schools for the poor. Early in 1842, Van der Brugghen arranged for the kindergarten graduates to attend a school operated by an approved teacher, Mr. C. F. Gehne. This German "revivalist" simultaneously and in the same location operated a Lutheran school for the poor. Van der Brugghen solicited donations for tuition among the Dutch elite. With this arrangement, Gehne no longer feared a loss of students and income because of parental complaints about his religious beliefs. He now took joy in giving Biblical instruction with "clear blessing and support."[4]

However, in October Gehne left for a position in an Indonesian school for which he had applied several years earlier. The Lutheran congregation decided to close its school for the poor, but agreed to appoint an instructor for three more months while Van der Brugghen sought permission to start a non-public school. Unfortunately, the new teacher had not taken the necessary examination and was not licensed by the national government to operate his own school. Consequently, one Friday the police removed all pupils but the twenty attending as Lutheran school paupers. Van der Brugghen quickly found another teacher permitted to operate his own school and willing to risk the suspension of his license for not remaining religiously neutral in his instruction. As a result, on Monday the other sixty children again received instruction, now in a large house that became known as **Den Klokkenberg** [The Bell Mountain] because of its location.

In the meantime, the city council, advised by the regional school inspector, twice denied Van der Brugghen's request to establish a school. An appeal to the provincial authorities received a favourable answer nine months later, while it took eight more months for the Dutch Minister of the Interior to approve the teacher. Once the school could officially open in 1844, enrollment increased rapidly to 190 students of diverse Protestant as well as Roman Catholic and Jewish backgrounds. Only a minority of these were children who had attended the kindergarten for the working class poor. Thus the school's popularity was not based solely on its Christian emphasis; it was partly due to dissatisfaction with existing schools.

Van der Brugghen's own main motive was to have a school in which teachers and students could freely pray and speak about Christ as the Messiah. He and his fellow revivalists opposed Rousseau's view that religious instruction should wait until the child was able to make independent religious and moral judgments, a view that had gained influence in the Netherlands. In the school, Van der Brugghen believed,

12

the Christian gospel had to be present as a "re-creating power." His intent was to inculcate Christian faith and service. This was not easy. As Van der Brugghen wrote on March 10, 1845,

> Our school continually gives us much difficulty and anxiety. . . it is so difficult in our nation, in all spheres of Christian action, to find suitable and usable people, because there is much orthodoxy and mysticism present, but little, relentlessly little, living faith and true desire to serve the Lord.[5]

Van der Brugghen's views opposed the narrow moralism that prevailed in Dutch schools. For him Christ was not just an excellent teacher of virtue who gave salutary moral prescriptions. Rather, as the Saviour of sinners he was the life breath of true culture through whom knowledge and art would blossom. The school, therefore, was to have no exaggeration of "Christian forms," no display of "insincere affection," and no indoctrination of difficult "truths of faith." Doctrines were to be taught by the church, not the school. The way Biblical history was taught in school, the content of the whole curriculum, the atmosphere that the teacher created—all were to contribute to a living, culture-enriching faith.

These views led Van der Brugghen to search for a "Christian" pedagogy. For this he turned to Franz Ludwig Zahn in Moers, not far across the German border from Nijmegen. Zahn operated the Evangelical Teacher Seminary in the tradition of the German pietist educator August Herman Francke, but tried to avoid Francke's harshness. Van der Brugghen sent Gehne to observe this school so that he could apply its methods.

Van der Brugghen's search for a more Christian pedagogy was related to his dissatisfaction with the receptacle learning in government schools in which, he claimed, children memorized astonishingly much but after they left knew astonishingly little. Van der Brugghen believed that education, to be Christian, had to enable children to think about and apply knowledge as well as to meet high academic standards. Van der Brugghen foreshadowed Herman Bavinck, the Dutch pedagogical thinker often referred to by North American Christian school leaders in the first half of the twentieth century, by insisting that instead of becoming pre-programmed rolls on a barrel organ, pupils must be led to be independent personalities who create and play their own melodies. Further, teachers had to be able to implement the best current educational thinking. To accomplish this, Van der Brugghen started a normal school at **Den Klokkenberg** a few years later. He also continued to be interested in improving government education. In 1857, when

Dutch prime minister, he added five subjects to the elementary school curriculum and strengthened teacher examinations so that all schools would offer a more balanced and significant program.

What was the curriculum of **Den Klokkenberg** school? Daily prayer and hymns were followed by an hour of explanation and discussion of Zahn's German **Biblische Historien** [Biblical Histories]. A group of Holland's religious and political leaders led by Van der Brugghen and Guillaume Groen van Prinsterer soon translated these books into Dutch. Once this was done, pupils read their own copies. Now, Van der Brugghen hoped, Bible instruction would not be tainted with the perceived narrow, rationalistic moralism of the public school curriculum.[6] Van der Brugghen further added general history, French, German, and later, English, subjects not taught in public schools. To complete a well-rounded curriculum, he engaged the city's music master to teach vocal music four times a week. Moreover, he stimulated the writing and publication of suitable reading and song books. Van der Brugghen also visited the school each day to encourage and guide the staff. His stature and impact made the school a popular institution.

The **Den Klokkenberg** school, important mainly for its later influence on the development of Dutch Christian education, was intended to be the harbinger and example of schools established elsewhere. By 1848, however, only three similar schools existed. Yet the **Den Klokkenberg** school and the related publication of the **Nijmeegsch Schoolblad** [Nijmegen's School Journal] from 1844 to 1852 and a number of Christian textbooks put an indelible stamp on Dutch Christian education. Indirectly, Van der Brugghen's thinking also affected much later Christian schools in North America. The seed that Van der Brugghen had sown took root, although it did not germinate fully until the turn of the century. Then the Dutch leaders Abraham Kuyper and Herman Bavinck, this time on more explicitly philosophical grounds, promoted association-controlled Christian schools and developed an outline of a Christian approach to pedagogy. Their ideas influenced North American NUCS schools more directly than Van der Brugghen's. This is best understood in light of the philosophical, religious, and educational context of the first Dutch Christian schools and the factors that led to the **Landverhuizing** [the Migration] to the U.S. between 1846 and 1848. This migration led to the founding of the first Calvinist Christian schools in the New World.

The Philosophical, Religious, and Political
Background of Nineteenth Century
Dutch Education

The overthrow of the Dutch republic by France in 1795 accelerated the effect of Enlightenment rationalism and morality on Dutch society. Also, the Reformed Church lost its status as a state church. The authority of the clergy was minimized in what was now called the Batavian Republic. Cultural and ecclesiastical changes accompanied the establishment of the Kingdom of Holland under the rule of Napoleon's brother in 1806, its annexation as part of the French republic in 1810, and its renewed independence under King William I in 1813.

The eighteenth century **Philosophes** had repudiated basic Christian doctrines, but had often maintained a respectful attitude towards a non-personal Supreme Being or "First Cause." They replaced the authority of the Bible with a faith in Reason, and forged a climate of opinion where grace was transformed into virtue and justification became a human endeavour instead of a divine gift. To be enlightened meant to apply Reason to the book of nature. True religion and morality were founded on natural law revealed to all men. Guided by Reason and experience, humans were able to become free from ignorance and superstition, become virtuous citizens, and perfect the good life. Faith in rationalism replaced faith in the Trinitarian God.

What Carl L. Becker called the heavenly city of the eighteenth-century philosophers soon clashed with traditional Calvinism in post-Napoleonic Holland. The followers of the Enlightenment, who provided religious, cultural, political and educational leadership in early nineteenth century Holland, rejected Calvinist dogmas and faith in divine grace. Jesus was no longer the Son of God and Saviour (a doctrine that could not be brought into agreement with Reason and experience), but a historical human noted for his teaching of virtue and character. Philosophy and science could and should be reconciled with religion. The discord among factions of Christians was to be a thing of the past.[7]

Only Reason could lead to true virtue and break the shackles of an outmoded faith. A thinker such as John Locke, who had lived as a fugitive in Holland from 1683 to 1688, influenced many with his belief in the "natural" religion of God, virtue and immortality. Locke admitted that even though reason was autonomous, man's necessities, passions, vices and mistaken interests got in the way of perfect morality and virtue. These views struck a responsive chord in the Dutch with their

Calvinist background. Complete unbelief was unnecessary; humans could be perfected through their own efforts to live virtuous lives. Such faith replaced Calvinism and dominated Dutch society, but it also led orthodox Calvinists to react by establishing a new church and Christian schools.

In 1816 the King reinstated a government-subsidized national church. He changed its name from **Gereformeerde Kerk** to **Hervormde Kerk,** imposing a hierarchical system of church government with himself as head. At this time, the "Groningen school" of enlightened theology, which included most Dutch leaders, controlled the direction of the church. For this group, doctrine was immaterial since the end of religion was not salvation but the achievement of virtue. Tolerance, love of peace and unity, moral improvement, and the practice of virtue had replaced more traditional Christian dogmas. The church introduced hymns that typified these views, even when parishioners refused to sing them and walked out in protest: "Virtue, oh yes! I find her beautiful,/She stretches herself for the great reward,/I follow her path with joy and courage,/I know that he who does not sin,/Who does not forget his duties,/With reason may be said to be most happy." Similarly the prayers eschewed the key doctrine of the Protestant Reformation, justification through faith, and heralded the rewards of virtuous living. Christianity was reduced to a system of rational, moral rules. Resistance to such thinking crystallized in two religious movements, **het Réveil** [the Awakening] and **de Afscheiding** [the Secession], both of which were closely connected with Christian schooling.[8]

Before 1795, though the government was the official "authority" of most elementary schools, a close bond between the schools and the national church existed. With the new education regulations of 1798, the church's influence on the schools declined. An "agent of national instruction" was given central authority over all elementary and secondary schools. He ensured that not only schools but all cultural institutions would "promote the enlightenment and culture" of all citizens. His duties included "to make such arrangement that [would] positively modify the National Character and promote good morals."[9] The Minister who strengthened centralized control of education in the French-influenced 1806 Act later reflected:

> . . . all legislation with respect to schools and education originates with the principle that the national government is responsible for all opportunities for the education and nurture of youth, no matter of what age or sex, outside of the parental home. . . . Whatever name those opportunities carry—public or non-public—and whatever their inclinations or goals—civic or

religious—this neither can nor may make any difference in the care that the government owes its youth.[10]

Thus, education became a centralized monopoly of the state, and remained so after Holland regained independence in 1813. Teachers were required to instruct children in "all social and Christian virtues" so that they would become "virtuous and useful persons" as well as "rational beings."[11] The 1806 Act also stipulated that non-public schools must obtain permission to operate from municipal governments. Since most school inspectors were clergymen of the liberal "Groningen school" who held that doctrinal discord would undermine the ideals of the Enlightenment, almost all Roman Catholic and orthodox Protestant requests to start non-public schools were denied. Starting in 1834, much frustration and agitation resulted from the vetoed requests to establish such schools. Not until 1848 were non-public schools given the constitutional right to operate freely.

Education in the Netherlands During the First Half of the Nineteenth Century

The Netherlands is at the crossroads of Western Europe. It has been a trading nation both on the seas and on the European rivers. Its ruling House of Orange had its roots in Germany; France ruled Holland from 1795 to 1813; and Belgium was part of Holland until 1830. The main religion of its northern part, Calvinism, had its roots in France and Switzerland. Moreover, Holland provided refuge to such thinkers as Descartes and Locke, as well as to the French Huguenots and English Puritans. Holland was in close touch with the economic and social life of surrounding nations with their philosophical and intellectual milieux, combining, molding, adapting, and extrapolating the various influences to suit the Dutch temperament and conditions.

Thus Dutch education in the early part of the nineteenth century exemplified a unique blending of European educational thought. Locke's thought had a direct impact on Dutch culture whereas Rousseau's influence appears to have been mostly indirect. Pedagogy that harmonized with Enlightenment ideas reached Holland largely through the work of the Germans founding the "Philantropinums," Basedow, Salzmann, and Campe. Especially the last two combined the principles they inherited from Rousseau with strict moralizing and religious tendencies. Friedrich von Rochow worked within their framework, though in addition he strove to provide more educational opportunities for the peasants. The designer of the important 1806 Dutch School Act, Adriaan van den Ende, was an ardent admirer of Von Rochow, and some of his readers were translated into Dutch.

The other thinker whose ideas became popular among Dutch educators was Pestalozzi, who had been influenced by Rousseau's **Emile** but was more acceptable than Rousseau since he favoured non-sectarian Christian moral instruction.   Also, he saw the importance of both liberty and obedience, re-uniting what Rousseau had separated.   His emphasis on the three-fold nature of moral education—the arousing of noble feelings, the exercise of self-control, and the formation of personal standards—had an impact on Dutch education.   A major Dutch pedagogue who popularized Pestalozzi, H. J. Niewold, spoke of eliciting the moral good of which "His Majesty the child" was capable early in life.[12]

The Enlightenment influence of all these educators on Dutch schooling became clear in a number of ways.   The school system promoted the goodness of the child and a "natural" religion rather than a doctrinal, catechetical one.   It also held that the moral and intellectual aspects of education were closely related, and that therefore pupils' readers must stress examples of various social virtues. Further, it emphasized study of the mother tongue, geography, nature study, and physical education, and correspondingly de-emphasized history, Latin and Greek.   This last point explains why Van der Brugghen was said to have "added" history to the curriculum of his Christian school.

When the first Christian schools[13] were started in the 1840s, most Dutch schools taught "common" virtues to all children by means of "natural" religion and morality.   An important intent of learning reading and writing was the cultivation of cleanliness and quickness. Arithmetic similarly not only promoted independent thinking and investigation, but also domesticity, cleanliness and practicality.   The Groningen Normal School director wrote that through education "the human race will eventually stride forward to intellectual and moral perfection." Education would lead children to become more like Jesus, the ideal of human perfection.[14]

A movement that developed a remarkable influence on Dutch society and on education was a private association, **De Maatschappij tot nut van't algemeen** [The Society for Public Welfare].   In 1834, fifty years after it had been founded, the Society had 193 branches with almost 12 000 members throughout the Netherlands. By that time it had established four or five normal schools and a substantial number of model schools for children of its members and for poorer citizens. Moreover, it published forty-five books, including both textbooks and general pedagogical books.   In line with its Enlightenment philosophy it strongly favoured a common program in a system attended by all children, whatever their religious background. The Society formulated most basic concepts contained in Dutch school legislation of the early nineteenth century. Above all, it promoted a virtuous, tolerant, and enlightened nation. The schools were to stimulate within children the love and practice of the "essential abilities," i.e., of the "most noble religious virtues" of love, thankfulness, and trust.[15]

An "enlightened" common religion would be the basis for instilling such virtues. One prescribed textbook published by the Society carried the subtitle, "Which supplies natural and reasoned evidence for the existence of God; the extent to which we can know such a being; and which logical consequences can be concluded." A government catechism answered "Which religion is most suitable?" with "All religions are equal in the eyes of the wise as long as their doctrines and morals are in agreement with the laws of the State." The Society's Christianity was a "bag of virtues" to be accepted by liberal and orthodox Protestants, Catholics, and Jews. In 1846 **Nijmegen's School Journal** protested that "the life wisdom sold by the Society for Public Welfare in no way gives life to its owners."[16] While the Society became influential and raised educational standards, in Enlightenment fashion it did not tolerate education based on principles that differed from its own.

Eventually the Society's vociferous opposition to Christian and Catholic schools contributed to the Dutch **Schoolstrijd** [School Struggle]. Its views led to more secular schooling. The French philosopher and educator Victor Cousin, visiting one of the Society's normal schools, expressed surprise that no positive religious education took place. The director replied that this was in order not to give offense to anyone. Though general school regulations prescribed prayer and authorized "proper" use of the Bible, such practices became more and more constricted. By 1820 the Netherlands Bible Society felt it necessary to investigate the Bible's infrequent use in the schools. Not only the Society for Public Welfare but also most school inspectors and many Catholic priests opposed Bible reading. Teachers were afraid to provoke reactions and therefore avoided its use.

At the same time, religious education exercises differed from one locality to the next. A new Roman Catholic priest, apprehensive of Protestant interpretations of the Bible, might force a reversal of practices. No matter what a teacher did, the inspector might complain that he was not following regulations or was giving offense. The Reverend L. J. Hulst, later involved with Michigan Christian schools, gave this graphic description of his 1830s school experience:

> Education had to be neutral in order not to offend dissentients. We surely still had one of the best teachers, but the poor man

was bound hands and feet. We still read from the Bible every Friday, but that had to happen secretively. As soon as the reading was done, the Bible was put away in the drawer of the school desk. It happened once that a careless boy, after the reading, had left the Bible on the desk. Unexpectedly the school inspector came in, he saw it; opened it up, and it was a prohibited book—a **Bible**! Teacher! he called out, what do I find here? A Bible in school? Don't you know that the law prohibits this, since it offends dissentients? The teacher stood perplexed, muttered something in his beard, was given a sharp rebuke, and that was the end of it that time. The careless boy was rebuked by the teacher, and we were all warned never to display a Bible openly.[17]

Hulst's small northern community had few if any "dissentients." Yet school inspectors prohibited the use of the Bible there as elsewhere. In other communities teachers were eventually dismissed for reading it. The teaching of religion had become an explosive curriculum issue.

In 1840 Van der Brugghen wrote that in Nijmegen, a predominantly Roman Catholic city, teachers did not dare read the story of Joseph or discuss religion for fear of offending Roman Catholics and losing their jobs. Only the Society of Public Welfare school, without Catholic children, taught morality overtly. However, it was a morality, Van der Brugghen concluded, that "at its root is nothing but a **natural** morality which, though illuminated through examples from the gospel, is drawn from motives of pride, earthly gain, social benefit and the pursuit of honour, and results in self-righteousness."[18] The Society's views of an enlightened religion and rational virtues had affected teachers, programs and prescribed textbooks. Consequently, opposition to government schools by orthodox Protestants, and later by Catholics also, steadily gained strength.

Van der Brugghen's **Nijmegen's School Journal** sharply criticized the government's prescribed readers. The Society for Public Welfare promoted its views by publishing many of these books. Van Heijningen Bosch's **The Friend of Small Children** had no fewer than sixty printings. It specialized in the type of moral maxims that angered Van der Brugghen. Rather than encouraging Christian self-denial, the maxims promoted self-benefit: "He, to whom we do good, also does us good later," and "Ah! Ah! what a good name cannot do! I always want to do good, then I will get a good name."[19] Also objectionable were Niewold's readers that preached salvation through good works, on the basis of Jesus' example, rather than through Christ's love and our faith.

The readers that were especially taken to task by **Nijmegen's School Journal** were N. Anslijn's **De brave Hendrik** [Virtuous Henry[20]]

20

and **De brave Maria** [Virtuous Maria]. In Kantian fashion, their principles and practices of morality were held to be completely rational, with the assumptions of God and immortality tacked on. Children read and re-read these booklets until they had memorized them. The first volume began with:

> Dost thou not know Henry, who always so politely takes off his hat when he passes by?
> Many people call him Virtuous Henry, because he is so obedient, and because he behaves so friendly towards everyone.
> He never harms anyone.
> There are some children that do not love him.
> Yes, but those are just naughty children.
> All virtuous children gladly keep company with Henry.
> Children who go around with Henry become even more virtuous since they learn from him how they must act.[21]

Maria was similarly presented as an industrious, friendly, beloved paragon of virtue.[22] Both represented industrious and obedient ideals for which children should strive. When Henry received a prize, he was told, "Always act so virtuously, and you shall be loved by the gentlemen who supervise the school as well as by God." Henry was indeed "a virtuous child who [could] expect the crown of glory from God."[23] Living virtuously would lead to happiness and a life in heaven.

Nijmegen's School Journal unequivocally called these books "unchristian" since a person's virtues rather than Christ's atoning death were held to lead to salvation. It asked, "Is it any wonder that Christian parents want something better?"[24] Many parents indeed **did** want a different religious and pedagogical direction in the schools, but they did not agree on what content or what type of instruction should be offered in alternative schools. Specifically, the two major Protestant dissentient groups viewed Christian school curriculum and instruction quite differently.

"Het Réveil" and "De Afscheiding": The Awakening and the Secession

Two religious movements in the Netherlands in the first half of the nineteenth century set the stage for Christian schools. First was the **Réveil**, the Dutch manifestation of the European religious awakenings in the 1700s. It had dual roots in eighteenth century Dutch pietism and in the later Genevan revival. The **Réveil** consisted mainly of aristocratic and prominent leaders: poets, a major government economist, and jurists and statesmen such as Groen van Prinsterer and

Van der Brugghen. Both of the latter became closely involved in the Christian school movement.

The **Réveil** circle was a relatively small group of people who fought what they perceived to be the superficiality, rigidity and deadness of an unenlightened and enslaved age and sought revival within the national church through personal conversion, warm faith and religious fervor. Like England's Methodists, these revivalists wanted to break the lifeless formalism of the national church; unlike the Methodists, they were mainly upper class and continued to function within the established church. They also met in small groups for Bible study and seminars on Dutch history, literature, and current social problems. The most influential gatherings became those of the Society of Christian Friends which met twice a year for nine years beginning in 1845 and stimulated and supported Christian social activity, including Christian elementary and normal schools.[25]

Groen van Prinsterer was chairman of The Christian Friends but his influence reached far beyond the **Réveil** circles. In his published lectures, **Unbelief and Revolution,** he dealt at some length with Rousseau's views, including the latter's belief that children belonged to the republic before they belonged to their parents. Groen argued that a liberalism that replaced Christian revelation with Reason would eventually result in an atheistic and totalitarian society. Without Biblical roots, morality's only standard would be "enlightened self-interest"; and virtue would be "an affectation, a dupery." Sovereignty of reason would supplant the Gospel with a self-made religion that would despise Christianity as superstitious folly. In the public school, "so-called neutrality grows into the most pernicious partiality favouring unbelief and ends in proselytism for the religion of reason and nature."[26]

Given Groen's beliefs it was little wonder that already at the second meeting of the Society of Friends education was the main topic of discussion. Some members reported that prayer, the singing of psalms and Bible reading took place undisturbed in some schools, but others told the gathering that in some provinces regulations completely forbade the use of the Bible. The members, deeply concerned about the state of education, appointed a committee to seek authorization to start a non-public Christian school in Amsterdam, authorization that was received a year later.

At the time, Van der Brugghen favoured non-public interdenominational schools. Groen, on the other hand, backed the division of public schools into those of different religious persuasions, still controlled by the state. However, all **Réveil** supporters agreed that the public system as it existed undermined Christian faith and praxis. Their call for a different type of education reached all levels of Dutch society.

Groen had already spoken to the joint chambers of the Dutch parliament in 1840, mainly in support of a second, quite different religious movement, **De Afscheiding** [the Secession]:

> Parents who, with or without sufficient grounds, are convinced that the direction of education in existing schools is unchristian, must not be prevented from giving their children such education, directly and indirectly, for which they believe they can give account to God. Coercion—I say it openly—is unbearable and ought to be ended. It is a presumption originating with theories of the revolution [i.e., the ideologies that led to the French revolution] that holds that children are considered to be the property of the State, disregarding the rights of the parents.[27]

The **Afscheiding** supporters were called "Seceders" because they had stepped out of the national church in 1834. Unlike **Réveil** supporters who included poets and jurists, the Seceders were labourers, hired hands, small farmers and tradesmen, led by a handful of young clergy. The national Reformed church had not only become liberal, but it was also controlled by a distant elite. Local congregations had little say in their own affairs. Thus the Secession was stimulated by a sense of deprivation among the lower classes. Like the **Réveil** adherents, the Seceders also felt strongly about starting alternative schools, albeit ones with different emphases. Their quickly growing band was scorned, however, by the leaders of the national church, who in 1836 wrote:

> . . . that the bulk of the group are people of the lowest class and that most belong to the least knowledgeable and least significant of those classes; that only here and there are a few that are more or less well-to-do; that many are far from irreproachable in their moral and social behaviour, and that the Seceders until now cannot boast of any person of note—that is, of acknowledged knowledge and excellent respectability.[28]

The first Secession leader, the Reverend Hendrik de Cock, had rapidly gained large audiences in the northernmost part of the Netherlands as his sermons had shown a deepening piety and an increasing awareness of traditional Calvinist creeds. When two of his ministerial colleagues accused him of being outmoded, De Cock rejoined with a pamphlet provocatively entitled **The Sheepfold of Christ Assailed by Two Wolves.** After he baptized children of parents outside his own

23

parish, the Reformed Church suspended him on grounds of insubordination and disturbing the peace. At that point, De Cock and 144 members of his congregation drew up an **Act of Secession** and left the national church. Within two years the new church counted 108 congregations with six pastors. The Seceders had three basic objections to the state church: (1) the weakening of the authority of the traditional confessional standards, (2) the introduction of hymns (rather than only psalms) into the services, and (3) the central national state control of the church.

The government tried to stop the exodus from the national Reformed Church. It employed a little-used law still in effect from Napoleon's time to prosecute anyone attending an unauthorized gathering of more than twenty persons. The national Reformed Church synod itself in 1835 appealed to the king to act forcefully since the honour of religion, the purity of morals, and the peacefulness of civil society were threatened.[29] The government acted quickly. Gatherings of Seceders were forcibly dispersed. Seceders, including De Cock, were fined and jailed. When they could not pay, their household goods were sold. Also, they were compelled to billet soldiers in their homes. Feelings ran high on both sides. The Seceders called the Reformed Church in De Cock's town "the synagogue of Satan." At the same time, the Seceders were abused, mishandled, and beaten, and often dismissed by their employers. Such oppression continued from 1834 until 1840 when the new King William II distributed a circular stating that the military were not to be used anymore to oppose the Seceders. Two years later the government declared it would not again exercise any influence in the structure and affairs of the church.

The Seceders were united in their exodus from the national Reformed Church. All favoured a strict interpretation of the Bible. This led to a clearer definition of the Christian gospel but also to a degree of puritanical legalism in such things as Sunday observance. Yet different emphases existed among the Seceder leaders. De Cock emphasized doctrinal orthodoxy and the authority of the new denomination's general synod. Albertus Van Raalte, the later leader of the emigration to Michigan, put more emphasis on local control and experiential religion. Hendrik Scholte stressed piety and the need for personal conversion and had little patience with either doctrines or denominationalism. Later, in Iowa, his church did not join any denomination. De Cock's orthodoxy gradually won out in the Netherlands. However, a strong strain of personal piety remained evident among the people of several provinces as well as among the emigrants who followed Van Raalte and Scholte.

Some Seceders immediately started their own schools. The first one was in the town of Smilde. There a school was started the day after it was decided to form a congregation and even before a church council had been installed. A young teacher, Douwe Van der Werp, later theological tutor for Michigan's Christian Reformed Churches, taught forty children. However, less than a week later the authorities closed the school and served Van der Werp with a court warrant. Soon teachers belonging to the Seceder group were fined if they taught religion and some were excluded from public schools.[30]

In 1840 **De Reformatie** [The Reformation], the Seceders' church paper, called for government school teachers to be free to teach in the way they saw fit. Later that year the Seceder synod petitioned the King for freedom to educate children in harmony with the principles of the Word of God. The King appointed Groen van Prinsterer to a royal commission to investigate the thorny problem of religion in education. Groen's view, however, was a solitary one, and in 1842 the King decided not to make any basic changes in the structure of education. One author in **De Reformatie** thereupon stated that many parents would keep their children at home "rather than let the seeds of heathendom be strewn in the hearts of the little ones." For the first time the magazine raised the possibility that the only solution might be the establishment of non-public schools by parents.[31] Two years later an incensed Van Raalte wrote that children were in danger of losing "positive Christianity" and acquiring "the principles of a decayed reason." Using what was to become a stock expression for North American Christian school leaders in the twentieth century, he added that all education must be permeated with the teaching of Jesus Christ. Lord." Also in line with his North American clerical successors, he gave little indication of what that meant for the curriculum.[32]

Two differences between the Réveil-influenced Van der Brugghen and the Seceders should be noted that help to clarify the operation and curricular practices of the Christian schools in North America during the latter half of the nineteenth century. First, Van der Brugghen believed that Christian schools should be operated by groups of parents and remain free of government and denominational control. The Seceders, on the other hand, objected to the "neutral" moralism and liberalism that determined much of the public school curriculum, but had no difficulty accepting either government or church control as long as program content reflected Calvinist beliefs. Second, while Van der Brugghen would have agreed with Van Raalte's view that schooling was to be based on Christian principles, his vision of what that meant was much broader. He wanted to change not only the obvious religious and moral curriculum content, but also sought a more meaningful pedagogy and a more balanced curriculum. Further, the rural, lower class Seceders were suspicious of culture and of all thought and belief other than that found in the traditional Calvinistic creeds.[33] For both groups, a living faith was important. But while Van der Brugghen stimulated that through the school's atmosphere and pedagogy and through the telling of Bible stories in child-like and gripping ways, what was important for the Seceders was the tried-and-true Heidelberg catechism of Reformation times.[34]

The followers of the **Réveil** and the **Afscheiding** also attended different churches. The former felt it was their duty to reform the national Reformed church from within. The Seceders, on the other hand, felt they needed to form a new denomination in order to remain true to the traditional doctrines of the Reformation. The **Réveil** group had misgivings about the drastic views and actions of the Seceders. In 1846 Van der Brugghen wrote, "Alas, there is still so little **faith** among us, and therefore also little **love**! How can we be so afraid of the Seceders?"[35] Scholte, originally from the **Réveil** group and part of The Christian Friends, several months later wrote that a meeting of the association had once again shown that "many do not wish cooperation with the Seceders, and sometimes find their presence awkward."[36]

Nevertheless, the Seceders were extended legal aid by **Réveil** supporters, especially by Groen van Prinsterer. His 1837 widely-discussed book, **The Measures Against the Seceders Tested With Respect to Constitutional Law,** defended the rights of the Seceders and promoted a principle for which Groen fought his whole life: "Freedom of conscience, freedom of worship, freedom of education: among these is an unbreakable link."[37] Groen and some of his **Réveil** colleagues fully supported the Seceders' efforts to be able freely to establish schools. However, the two groups never joined forces. Partly as a result of this, quite diverse types of Christian schools existed in the Netherlands from 1844 on. It was the Seceder schools that gave the initial impetus for the founding of North American Christian schools.

The First Attempts to Establish
Christian Schools

Van der Brugghen had at least three reasons to make his school one controlled by an association. First, he believed that such schools should be interdenominational since small doctrinal differences should not affect curriculum and instruction. Secondly, he felt that parents' involvement in the school would benefit their children's attitude and achievement. Finally, he was convinced that a church operating a school would tend to reduce religious education to the indoctrination of written dogmas.[38]

However, the Seceders at that time understandably did not ponder such theoretical arguments. During the period of their oppression, they simply wanted their children in a different school, no matter how organized. They realized that their children must learn the three R's if they were to serve God in their lives. Yet the public school taught what for them was a false religion. Moreover, many of their children were barred from the schools because they had refused smallpox vaccinations, while tuition fees continued to be levied. The public school in many villages became a symbol of the unjust treatment accorded the Seceders by the "enlightened" majority. They responded vigorously. For example, one church elder wrote a brochure denouncing a theologically liberal picture Bible used by public school teachers as a work of Satan. Already in 1835, a lay preacher wrote in an uneducated but spirited dialect, "The schools are just as corrupt as the churches. And shall we stay out of them, but send our children there?"[39]

Some Seceder parents began to educate their own children. In at least one case, they sent them to a neighbour woman until she was found out, jailed, and fined. Van der Werp's school started in a barn "provided with sods, animals, and children, to give education to the children in Reformed doctrine." Even though the authorities there and elsewhere closed the schools and prosecuted those involved, small clandestine schools continued to operate. In 1845 one mayor raided and closed a school where he found forty-two children seated on low benches without writing tables. The only textbooks available were the Bible, a compendium of the Heidelberg catechism, and a catechism booklet. In several instances the Seceders prevented closure by claiming they gave exclusively religious education for which no license was needed. That children happened also to learn reading and writing in the course of their catechetical and Biblical instruction was a result that the authorities could not prevent. One of the champions of Christian schools in North America in the late nineteenth century, the Reverend K. Kuiper, received his elementary education exclusively at such a school.[40]

The authorities usually denied requests for permission to start a school. They sanctioned several national Reformed churches to start a "school for paupers." On the other hand, they told the Seceder church council in Leeuwarden that such a school would be "in complete violation of the existing regulations governing education."[41] Generally the national Reformed church did not favour Christian day schools. In

1842 Groen van Prinsterer and six of his friends addressed an open letter to the national churches decrying the use of tax money for schools that they deemed "pernicious for public morals and happiness." Christian schools should be established for all children, not just for paupers, they wrote, so that all could be educated "according to the Evangelical principles of our Church." They added that a Christian Normal school as well as Christian textbooks were also required.[42]

Influential as they were, however, Groen and his friends lobbied from 1843 to 1849 before receiving permission to start a school in the Hague. A group led by Van Raalte was denied permission outright. Not until the new Dutch constitution of 1848 guaranteed freedom of education were many more Christian schools established and, by 1864, 267 existed throughout the Netherlands. One hundred and eighty were operated by associations or small groups of individuals; slightly more than forty each by conservative national Reformed and by Seceder church congregations.

The Curriculum in Early Christian Schools

The **Réveil** group was the first to see the need for a distinctive Christian school curriculum. Van der Brugghen himself had been quick to consider a Christian framework for his program of instruction. His school first of all was to acquaint pupils with the "grace of God in our great God and Saviour Jesus Christ":

> If it has to be that way, rather a little less quickness in arithmetic and its theories, a little less acquaintance with the French departments or the cities of North America, and a little more hope **in the living God . . .**[43]

Yet Christian education was not just to consist of employing Bible texts for handwriting practice, nor of using Biblical events and places in history and geography. Rather, students should be taught to search for truth and soundness

> . . . so that the reading that they have learned shall not tempt them to be wise above how wise one ought to be; so that their writing does not become a means in their hands to spread the poison of heresy and lies around them . . . ; so that arithmetic, in their occupation, will not be misused by them for thievery and wicked deeds and attacks with which they gain their neighbours' property.[44]

Thus, as could be expected within revival circles, the first concerns were with the inculcation of piety based on love and service

28

of Christ and the moral use of knowledge. This also came to expression in the regulations of the **Réveil** school for paupers in the Hague:

> . . . all instruction in these various subjects shall be inspired, governed, and directed by the genuine desire and the intelligent design to educate the child's mind to faith in and obedience to God and His Word . . . careful attention shall be given not only to the intelligible and useful in general, but at the same time especially to Biblical content and Christian character. With instruction of Biblical and national history and geography, opportunities shall again and again be sought, and the occasion be used in a simple and understandable as well as a lively and entertaining manner, without exhaustive argumentation and abstract reasoning, in a loving as well as a serious way, to impress Evangelical truths and Christian lessons.[45]

This quote also indicates, however, that the **Réveil** group looked beyond the purely moral aspect of the curriculum. Van der Brugghen, for one, wanted high quality, culture-enriching knowledge to be taught. More importantly, beliefs also were to affect the choice and presentation of content. In 1853, one school wrote two propositions that summarized how its curriculum must emphasize the necessity both of conversion to God and of using all content to understand God's design and will for society and for individuals:

> 3. [A Christian school] is one in which all knowledge is made subservient to the glory of God, Who revealed Himself in Jesus Christ as the Saviour of sinners; and this happens partly through implanting the conviction in young minds of the uselessness, yes, the harm of all knowledge if the heart is not converted to God, and partly through making students take notice of God's hand in all subjects of human knowledge.
> 4. The first aspect is accomplished through the revelation of dependence on God and His Word in which the teacher must stand and in which he must try to educate his pupils, through communal prayer and reading and appropriate discussion of a part of God's Word each day; the second aspect, by pointing to the work and will of God in all educational subjects that are susceptible to such an approach.
> Managed with ease in the most theoretic subjects; difficult but possible in the more mechanistic (**sic**).[46]

The curriculum was to be non-dogmatic but at the same time oppose the prevalent morality "honoured by Kantian philosophy."[47] Christian faith was to affect the whole curriculum, not just Biblical studies, even if this might be difficult to achieve in more practical subjects. Indeed, developing curriculum approaches that took notice of "God's hand in all subjects of human knowledge" in non-superficial ways was a problem for these schools as it has been for Christian schools ever since, both in the Netherlands and in North America. Both then and now, even for "theoretic" subjects the curriculum has been characterized more by the implanting of Christian morality than by more broadly distinctive "Christian" approaches. Subscribing to guidelines such as the above has been easy for Christian schools; matching classroom reality with them has been much more difficult.

One of the difficulties that plagued **Réveil** leaders (as well as North American Christian schools throughout their history) was that almost no suitable curriculum documents or textbooks were available that would implement this framework. Only Zahn's translated **Biblical Histories** existed. They were, of course, used in Van der Brugghen's school in Nijmegen, though with a methodology that left "much, much to be desired."[48] But more materials were needed. One of the first issues of **Nijmegen's School Journal** called for suitable readers that avoided the "insipid whining" and the "virtue noise" of **Virtuous Henry** and **Virtuous Maria** through which "the glad [gospel] message could not be heard, not known, not understood."[49]

The Reverend J. de Liefde, member of The Christian Friends, accepted the challenge and wrote a series of readers and a number of individual books for Christian schools between 1846 and 1851. About the first of these, **Humans and Animals, Nijmegen's School Journal** wrote that the stories were "entertaining, absorbing one's attention, revealing the cheerful and humorous heart of the author, in which the essence [of the Christian faith] was always central in an unaffected way."[50] Hundreds of Dutch Christian schools found his books suitable for their pupils during the next fifty years. De Liefde also wrote children's songs, many of which are still popular in the Netherlands today. His song **The Most Beautiful Treasure** illustrated how he combined a lighthearted tone with making his "essential" point, while avoiding a narrow moralism:

> Even if my marbles were ruby and sapphire;
> Even if my kite was made of silver paper;
> . . . .
> Even if my piggy bank was the richest in the country;
> Even if I were the smartest in knowledge and intelligence;
> None of it would avail me and it would be no treasure

If I didn't have the love of the Lord.

De Liefde also shared Groen and Van der Brugghen's view that the whole curriculum should be imbued with a Christian view of life. The hymn he wrote for the opening exercises at the school on **Den Klokkenberg** made this clear:

> The Lord calls; He wants to teach us all
> About language and writing, number and nation.
> All that exists is the work of the Lord;
> It all carries on by the signs of His hands.
> He gave speech; He is the Lord of composition;
> Arithmetic is the work of His mind.[51]

Such songs impressed children with the sovereignty of God and with his concern for all of life.

Groen himself already in 1841 had written a **Brief Survey of the History of the Fatherland** for instruction in non-public schools and at home. He tried to identify himself with the period and persons at issue and to recount the whole truth, "even when the most cherished Protestant notions are sacrificed to it."[52] At the same time, he held the history of the Dutch nation to be important especially because "God again brought the gospel truth to light" in Christian-Protestant Holland after it had "sunk in superstition."[53] These views became generally accepted by Christian school supporters. Thus an 1879 newspaper article announced a competition to write a student textbook using Groen's interpretation of history. It was to display a love for truth which emphasized "God's guidance, God's blessing and His punishment for our nation."[54] Although no entries were received, Groen's own history books were studied in Dutch Christian normal schools, and some of his themes were later applied to American history by American Christian school educators in the first part of the twentieth century.

At first, Groen's and De Liefde's books were used more in Réveil-influenced schools than in Seceder ones. The broader educational views of the Réveil leaders were also evident from the teacher training program that Van der Brugghen started in 1846, mainly for subsidized poor students. Its curriculum included not only the regular school, but also Biblical and church history, German and French, logical analysis, mythology, and music.

The Seceders, however, did not use this or similar institutions. One of the church's synods recommended that its three seminary professors ought to train teachers. Usually, the teacher in a Seceder school was an ill-prepared male. He might be the village carpenter or a common labourer. Sometimes he was a congregation member whose

31

work gave him time to teach during the five or six winter months, with the local pastor teaching the remainder of the year. The curriculum was limited. A court warrant issued to a teacher who moved to Michigan in 1846 indicated that he used only religious books such as the Bible, the catechism, and the ten commandments. A former pupil of one school recounted that his school read the Bible in every lesson, used some ABC booklets, and emphasized writing, composition, and mental arithmetic. However, geography, history, algebra, and science were totally lacking. Another pupil described how he used the psalms for handwriting practice. But when the school inspector visited the village, no writing took place since the school officially existed to teach religion only.[55]

The Amsterdam Seceder school was authorized to enroll paupers but also admitted other children of its congregation. In what was to become the pattern for nineteenth-century American Christian schools, the subjects of the curriculum were spelling, reading, arithmetic, singing, a few rudiments of history and geography, and catechism and religious instruction. The church council almost immediately expressed its concern that proper textbooks were to be used. The school's first teacher, W. H. van Leeuwen, a future promoter of Christian schools in Michigan, wrote books that Groen in 1848 criticized as unsuitable both for theological and pedagogical reasons. The books stressed obedience to God, but were complex and dull. Their language was difficult and hid the true meaning of the gospel. The author, Groen said, did not understand the minds of children. He added that "people must not confuse the terminology of church assemblies with the vocabulary of small children. When the pupil cannot as yet count to ten, we will let rest the theorem of Pythagoras, no matter how important." Calvinist doctrine was the central curriculum focus in Seceder schools. The memorization of dogmas overshadowed all other pedagogical concerns.[56]

In short, the culturally-sensitive **Réveil** leaders showed a great deal of interest in curriculum and textbook development. They hoped to break the philosophical and religious direction of the public schools, and develop a more effective pedagogy. Many Seceders sensed that public schools undermined what they considered right for their children. However, most struggled long hours just to survive physically, and their handful of ministers were overworked in church affairs. Therefore, few Seceders were interested or able to direct and strengthen the educational programs of Christian schools. Although they did develop a few basic readers stressing doctrinal truths, generally they were satisfied with schools that would teach their catechism and doctrines.

Two of the Seceder clergy interested in Christian schools soon were to lead many followers to the New World. There the emigrants faced quite different social and political circumstances. Also, they left the Netherlands when Dutch Christian schools were at the very beginning of their development and by no means generally accepted. Once in America, most new settlers felt public district schools could be controlled by them and therefore they had little interest in starting non-public Christian schools. The schools that did start reflected the restrictive views of the more conservative of the Seceders.

"De Landverhuizing": The "Great Migration" from the Netherlands to the New World

The tide of emigration that swept Europe in the early 1840s had bypassed Holland. In 1840, for instance, 29 000 persons left Germany, but only 57 Dutchmen emigrated. Yet in 1846 at a meeting of The Christian Friends, textbook author De Liefde declared that the prevailing religious and economic conditions gave occasion for "leaving the country in order to be able to serve God abroad and to give his children instruction in his fear."[57] That year and the next, about 7 000 Dutch emigrants left for the United States of America.[58] This was such a remarkable number for the Dutch that it became known as **De Landverhuizing** [literally: the Nation-move].

What had brought about this interest in emigration? First, the years 1845 to 1849 are sometimes referred to as **de zwarte jaren** [the black years] in the history of the Netherlands. In agriculture, the potato blight destroyed much of the crop in both 1845 and 1846. The rye crop on which the poor depended when potatoes were in poor supply was cut in half because of the weather and crop rust. With severe economic stagnation, many labourers were unemployed and fully one quarter of the population received relief. Even those who were employed worked long hours for little pay. The elite managed to strengthen its economic position, squeezing out the small independent farmers and artisans. The latter found heavy excise and property taxes to be unjust restraints on freedom. There was unrest in the cities and many permanent paupers roamed the countryside.

The lower class Seceders were among the most disadvantaged. Many had lost what little they had through fines. In the years before the "black years" they faced employment discrimination since they were considered narrow-minded and schismatic. Unlike the members of the state-supported national Reformed Church, they also had to pay their own ministers, build their church buildings, and support their own poor.[59]

The migration took place within this oppressive economic and social context. Yet for many of the disproportionately large number of

Dutch emigrants that were Seceders, the motives were not just economic and social improvement but also freedom of worship and education.[60] Scholte wrote on May 15, 1846:

> The stubborn opposition of the government against freedom of religion and education promotes the desire to emigrate. . . . In North America the land is empty, there is complete freedom of religion and education. When the number of those leaving is somewhat large and they stay together with the purchase of some extensive . . . land, then the local government remains in the hands of the colonists. Here during the last weeks we saw the pronouncement of illegal sentences by which the freedom of education and divine service is being suppressed in extreme ways.[61]

Van Raalte several months later wrote that "especially the need for education—besides other urgent reasons—supplies me with a sharp incentive" for emigration.[62] In his diary another minister wrote that many Seceders left because the Netherlands lacked religiously free schools. One church council's minutes in 1846 summed up the various reasons for emigration: (a) to seek Christian schools, (b) to ensure that work resulted in a reasonable existence, and (c) to escape the impossibility of obeying Biblical injunction to render unto Caesar's what belongs to Caesar under the current Dutch conditions.[63] The religious reasons weighed most heavily with the leaders; the economic, with the majority of the emigrants.[64]

Despite some questions about persons leaving their God-appointed place voluntarily for a nation of "adventurers and swindlers,"[65] Van Raalte organized a Society for Dutch Emigration to the U.S.A. He envisioned a colony where a central town would be surrounded by farms and villages, each of the latter with its own church and Christian school. Soon Van Raalte and his group left to establish Holland, Michigan. Scholte followed shortly to begin a colony in Pella, Iowa. Significantly, Scholte, who had become isolated in the Seceder church and whose theological ideas paralleled Van der Brugghen's, convinced the principal of the latter's teacher training classes, James Muntingh, to emigrate with him to establish the first Pella school. Sadly, Scholte's attempts to imbue the schools in the new colonies with sound pedagogy and a curriculum that was broadly based on Christian principles did not affect the first North American Christian schools. Not until the turn of the century did a second wave of Dutch immigrants try to infuse existing and new Christian schools with the legacy of Van der Brugghen's and Groen's educational ideas.

NOTES

1. J. Kuiper, **Geschiedenis van het Christelijk lager onderwijs,** 2nd ed., [History of Christian elementary education] (Amsterdam: H. A. van Bottenburg, 1904), p. 86; F. Kalsbeek, J. Leus, and J. B. Meijnen, **Van strijd en zegen: gedenkboek van het Christelijk onderwijs** [Concerning strife and blessing: remembrance volume of Christian education] (Leiden: Eduard IJdo, 1904), p. 43; P. Oosterlee, **Geschiedenis van het Christelijk onderwijs** [History of Christian education] (Haarlem: De Erven F. Bohn, 1929), p. 15. In the Netherlands, schools such as this as well as church-controlled ones are called **bijzondere scholen** [i.e., special schools]. There is no exact English equivalent, but I will refer to them as "non-public schools" in this book.

2. R. Turksma, **De geschiedenis van de opleiding tot onderwijzer in Nederland aan de openbare, Protestants-Christelijke en bijzondere-neutrale instellingen** [The history of teacher training in the Netherlands in public, Protestant-Christian, and independent-neutral institutions] (Groningen: J. W. Wolters, 1961), p. 5; A. Ponsteen, **Honderd jaar Christelijk onderwijs te Nijverdal** [One hundred years of Christian education in Nijverdal], published by the local Christian school in 1965, pp. 8-9; Oosterlee, pp. 1-2. The quote is from Oosterlee; translations of Dutch quotes in this book are mine unless otherwise indicated.

3. This is evident, for instance, from a letter Van der Brugghen wrote to Guillaume Groen van Prinsterer on December 20, 1841. Groen van Prinsterer (often referred to just as Groen) is the other major figure in the early Christian school movement in mid-nineteenth century Holland. It has taken Dutch scholars since 1925 to collect and publish Groen's correspondence. There are now five volumes available, with a sixth forthcoming. The letter referred to is found in C. Gerretson and A. Goslinga, **Groen van Prinsterer: schriftelijke nalatenschap, derde deel: briefwisseling, tweede deel 1833-1848** [Groen van Prinsterer: literary estate, third volume: correspondence, second volume 1833-1848] (The Hague: Martinus Nijhoff, 1964), p. 427. I will refer to this volume as GSN III.

4. GSN III, p. 431. A balanced account of Van der Brugghen's activities with respect to the school is given by J. Brouwer, **Het binnenste naar buiten: beginselen en activiteiten van Mr. J. J. L. van der Brugghen** [Externalizing the innermost: principles and activities of lawyer J. J. L. van der Brugghen] (Zutphen: De

Walburg Pers, 1981), pp. 109-19. This doctoral dissertation for the Catholic University of Nijmegen also relates how the two main streams in Protestant Christian education in the Netherlands have viewed and interpreted Van der Brugghen's work quite differently. A writer like P. Oosterlee considered him the "father" of Christian education whose work was central for its future development in the Netherlands. Someone like H. Bouma mentioned him only in passing [H. Bouma, **Een vergeten hoofdstuk** [A forgotten chapter] (Enschedé: J. Boersma, 1959). Bouma dealt almost exclusively with Christian schools started by groups of Seceders from the national Reformed Church. The difference between the two groups is described later in this chapter, as it has a bearing on North American developments. The material in the remainder of this section is based on F. Kalsbeek et al., pp. 38-46; Kuiper, pp. 85-87; Oosterlee, pp. 5-29; Ponsteen, pp. 9-10; and Turksma, pp. 66-67.

5. GSN III, p. 657.
6. While Groen and Van der Brugghen's hope that these books might be used by most schools (public and non-public) was never realized, they were still frequently used "with profit" in Dutch Christian schools in 1904 (Kuiper, p. 86).
7. Carl L. Becker, **The Heavenly City of the Eighteenth-Century Philosophers** (New Haven: Yale University Press, 1932; 10th printing, 1955), especially pp. 47-58; Crane Brinton, **The Shaping of the Modern Mind, The Concluding Half of "Ideas and Men"** (New York: New American Library, 1953), pp. 113-14, 143-44; D. Langedijk, **De geschiedenis van het protestants-Christelijk onderwijs** [The history of Protestant-Christian education] (Delft: Van Keulen, 1953), pp. 2-3; Jantje L. van Essen, "Guillaume Groen van Prinsterer and His Conception of History," **Westminster Theological Journal** 44 (Fall 1982): 207; Albert Hyma, "The Survival and Resurgence of Orthodox Calvinism in the Netherlands (1750-1850)," **Annual Report of the American Historical Association** (Washington: AHA, 1942), vol.3, p. 62.
8. Hyma, p. 62; L. Kalsbeek, **Theologische en wijsgerige achtergronden van de verhouding van kerk, staat en school in Nederland** [Theological and philosophical backgrounds of the relation among church, state, and school in the Netherlands] (Kampen: Kok, 1976), pp. 91-96, 128-29; James Donald Bratt, "Dutch Calvinism in Modern America: The History of a Conservative Subculture" (Ph.D. dissertation, Yale University, 1978), p. 8; L. H. Wagenaar, **Het Réveil en de Afscheiding** [The

36

Awakening and the Secession] (Heerenveen: Hepkema, 1880), pp. 7-9. The hymn and others similar to it are found in L. Kalsbeek, pp. 93-96.

9. Remmelt de Boer, "Groen van Prinsterer, Staatspedagoog?" [Groen van Prinsterer, Pedagogue for the state?] (Master's degree major paper [Doctorandus scriptie], University of Groningen, n.d. [ca. 1977]), pp. 10-11, 54.

10. A. van der Ende, **Geschiedkundige schets van Neerlands schoolwetgeving** [Historical sketch of school legislation in the Netherlands] (Deventer, 1846), pp. 58-59, quoted in De Boer, p. 18.

11. The Dutch word I have translated as "virtuous" is "braaf"--which involves a conglomeration of the concepts of honesty, decency, respectability, goodness, and virtue. De Boer quoted these phrases from early 19th century Dutch school laws and book list regulations (pp. 15, 19).

12. P. L. van Eck, **Hoe 't vroeger was: schetsen ter inleiding tot de geschiedenis van onderwijs en opvoeding** [How it was in the past: sketches to introduce the history of education and nurture] (The Hague: Wolters, 1927), pp. 116-17. See also S. J. Curtis and M. E. A. Boultwood, **A Short History of Educational Ideas** (London: University Tutorial Press, 1953); R. Freeman Butts, **The Education of the West: A Formative Chapter in the History of Civilzation** (New York: McGraw Hill, 1973); and James Bowen, **A History of Western Education**, vol. 3: **The Modern West: Europe and the New World** (London: Methuen, 1981). The remainder of this section is based on the books by F. Kalsbeek et al.; L. Kalsbeek; Kuiper; Langedijk; Oosterlee; Ponsteen; Van Eck; S. Rombouts, **Historiese pedagogiek**, derde deel [Historical pedagogy, vol. 3] (Tilbury: Jongensweeshuis, 1928); and Lea Dasberg and and J. W. G. Jansing, "Onderwijs 1844-1875" [Education 1844-1875], in D. P. Blok et al., eds., **Algemene geschiedenis der Nederlanden**, vol. 12 [General history of the Netherlands, vol. 12] (Haarlem: Van Dishoeck, 1977).

13. Throughout this book I use "Christian schools" in reference to schools established by persons of Dutch, Calvinist background. This does not imply that schools operated by other groups of Christians, such as Catholics and Lutherans, should also not be considered "Christian." However, my terminology follows common parlance, and there is no other simple designation.

14. F. Kalsbeek et al., p. 19.

15. Quoted in Van Eck, p. 215.

16. Quoted, respectively, in L. Kalsbeek, p. 138; Kuiper, p. 42;

Rullman, p. 8; and T. M. Gilhuis, **Memorietafel van het Christelijk onderwijs: de geschiedenis van de schoolstrijd** [Memory register of Christian education: the history of the school struggle] (Kampen: Kok, 1974), p. 63.

17. Lammert J. Hulst, **Drie en zestig jaren prediker** [A preacher for sixty-three years] (Grand Rapids, Michigan: Eerdmans-Sevensma, 1913), p. 4.

18. GSN III, p. 353.

19. F. Kalsbeek, p. 21.

20. See note 11 about this translation.

21. N. Anslijn, N. Z., **De brave Hendrik** (Leyden: Du Mortier, fourteenth printing, 1837), p. A3.

22. See, for example, N. Anslijn, N. Z., **De brave Maria** (Leyden: Du Mortier, twelfth printing, 1837), pp. 8-9.

23. Quoted from Anslijn's book in F. Kalsbeek et al., p. 20.

24. Quoted in L. Kalsbeek, pp. 155-156.

25. Wagenaar, p. 57; J. D. Bratt, pp. 20-21; Kuiper, p. 404; Turksma, p. 63; L. Kalsbeek, p. 179. Other activities included Sunday Schools based on the English model, often including the teaching of reading and writing to children not attending regular schools. It also supported schools and homes for neglected children, homes for prostitutes and unmarried women, and so on.

26. Guillaume Groen van Prinsterer, **Unbelief and Revolution**, Lectures Eight and Nine. First published in 1847 by Luchtmans in Leiden, my quotes are from a recent translation by Harry Van Dyke in collaboration with Donald Morton (Amsterdam: The Groen van Prinsterer Fund, 1975), pp. 17-24. See also the editor's foreword, pp. v-vii. The last quote is from an 1861 speech added as an appendix in 1865 (p. 34).

27. Groen's speech is quoted in De Boer, p. 38.

28. H. Algra, **Het wonder van de 19e eeuw: van vrije kerken en kleine luyden** [The wonder of the nineteenth century: of free churches and plain folks] (Franeker: Wever, 2nd edition, 1966), p. 241.

29. A. and H. Algra, **Dispereert niet**, deel 3 [Do not despair, vol. 3] (Franeker: Wever, 1956, Sixth printing, Second revision, 1972), p. 82.

30. Bouma, pp. 14-23; Langedijk, pp. 37-38.

31. Quoted in Langedijk, p. 46 and p. 57.

32. Gilhuis, pp. 66-68.

33. Donald Oppewal, **The Roots of the Calvinistic Day School Movement** (Grand Rapids: Calvin College Monograph Series, 1963),

p. 12. While Van Raalte and Scholte interacted with the
Réveil circles, few of the other Seceders associated with them if
only because of the social class gaps.

34. The **Heidelberg Catechism** is the best known of the three major
doctrinal standards of all Dutch, Reformed denominations. First
published in Heidelberg, Germany, in 1563, its approval by the
Synod of Dort (1618-19) made it become the most widely used of
the Reformed catechisms and confessions. It is still used by
Reformed denominations in North America for doctrinal instruction
in Sunday evening services and in church education classes.
35. GSN III, p. 733.
36. Ibid., p. 750.
37. Guillaume Groen van Prinsterer, **De maatregelen tegen de
Afgescheidenen van het staatsregt getoetst** (Leiden: Luchtmans,
1837, second printing), p. 13.
38. Oosterlee, p. 103; Brouwer, pp. 96, 107.
39. Bouma, p. 13.   The original read, "De schoelen bint net so
bedurven as de karken en zullen wie er uut blieven, maar sturen
onse kienders der henne?"
40. Gilhuis, p. 70; Bouma, pp. 18-23, 39-40, 47-48, 61.
41. Ponsteen, p. 8; F. Kalsbeek et al., p. 112.
42. Kuiper, pp. 82-83.
43. Gilhuis, p. 82.
44. Ibid., pp. 80-81.
45. F. Kalsbeek et al., p. 67.
46. F. Kalsbeek et al., p. 134.   These were two of twelve theses
governing   the   instruction   of   a   **Réveil**-influenced
interdenominational school in Leiden.   The Seceders objected to
the school's interdenominational, non-dogmatic character, and
started their own school one year later.   It foreshadowed
denominationalism affecting Christian schools for non-educational
reasons, something that still occurs today both in the Netherlands,
and, more recently, in North America.
47. Ibid., p. 135.
48. Letter dated February 6, 1843, published in GSN III, p. 504.
49. Oosterlee, pp. 75-76; F. Kalsbeek et al., p. 44.
50. F. Kalsbeek et al., p. 45.
51. The use of these hymns, written in 1848 and 1846 respectively, is
described in Gilhuis, pp. 73-74 and F. Kalsbeek et al., p. 44.
52. Van Essen, p. 245; F. Kalsbeek et al., p. 74.
53. Guillaume Groen van Prinsterer, **Kort overzicht van de geschiedenis
des vaderlands** [Brief survey of the history of the fatherland]

(Leiden: Luchtmans, 1841), p. 1, quoted in Van Essen, p. 247. Groen also wrote a five-volume **Handbook of the History of the Fatherland.** His writings were too difficult for pupils and used more often as teacher resource books.

54. "V. J." in **De Standaard,** April 7, 1879, quoted in Rullmann, pp. 241-42. Also see GSN III, p. 421.

55. Bouma, pp. 33-45, 88, 144.

56. Ibid., pp. 70-71, 152-153; F. Kalsbeek et al., p. 64. The quote is given in Oosterlee, p. 68.

57. J. C. Rullman, **Gedenkboek bij het vijftig-jarig bestaan van de Unie "Een School Met Den Bijbel"** [Remembrance volume for the fiftieth anniversary of the existence of the Union "A School with the Bible"] (Kampen: Kok, 1928), p. 10.

58. Blok et al., eds., 12:147. However, these figures, based on Dutch government statistics, do not match the 3 610 Dutch immigrants that the U.S. Department of Labor claims entered the U.S. in 1846 and 1847. The Dutch government published a detailed chart giving a complete breakdown of all emigrants by provinces and occupations in its **Staatscourant** of September 5, 1848. This showed that a total of 7 084 emigrants left the Netherlands in 1846 and 1847, the vast majority of whom left for the U.S.A. Considering this and the populations of the Dutch settlements in the U.S.A. by 1848, the figures in Blok are likely more accurate than those given by the U.S. Department of Labor, which did not monitor all ports.

59. Calvin Niewenhuis, "Conditions of Emigration," in **Centennial Facts and Background** (Grand Rapids, Michigan: Christian Reformed Church, 1957), pp. 42-43.

60. Niewenhuis, p. 43. Many of the Seceders called themselves **Gereformeerd** (the name of the national church before the 1816 name change). If all the **Gereformeerden** were Seceders, fifty-eight percent of Dutch emigrant heads of households in 1846 and 1847 were Seceders. This figure is close to the sixty-four percent reported by Swierenga for the period 1846-49 (Robert P. Swierenga, "The Impact of Reformed Dutch Immigration on the American Reformed Churches in the Nineteenth Century," unpublished paper presented to the American Society of Church History, Toronto, on April 18, 1975, p. 37). These numbers were remarkable, especially considering that less than two percent of the Dutch population was Seceder at the time. See the government chart in the September 5, 1848 issue of **De Staatscourant,** reproduced by Pieter R. D. Stokvis, **De Nederlandse**

trek naar Amerika 1846-47 [The Dutch migration to America 1846-47], doctoral dissertation, University of Leiden (Leiden: Universitaire Pers, 1977), pp. 208-10.

61. Letter from Scholte to Groen, dated May 15, 1846. The missing word after "extensive" cannot be read because of damage to the letter. GSN III, p. 740.

62. Letter of Van Raalte to Groen, dated September 21, 1846, in GSN III, p. 744.

63. Bouma, pp. 122. Bouma gives more examples on pp. 79-83, 136.

64. Written communications by leaders emphasized religious and educational reasons. However, a Dutch government chart of reasons given by emigrants leaving between 1831 and 1847 (88 percent of these left in 1846 and 1847) presents a different emphasis. It showed that 68 percent of the emigrants listed economic reasons, 19 percent mentioned high taxes, 19 percent religious oppression, and only 2½ percent freedom of education. If somewhat over half of the emigrants and all of those giving religious and educational reasons were Seceders, still only about one third of the Seceders indicated religious oppression as a major reason for emigration, and less than one-tenth, freedom of education. See reproduction of chart in Stokvis, p. 210.

65. Langedijk, p. 64; GSN III, p. 746.

Alpine Avenue, Grand Rapids, Christian School, circa
1890. The teacher on the left is Bertha Kuiper,
daughter of the Reverend R. T. Kuiper.

3 Calvinist Schools in America: Promoting Religious and Cultural Isolation (1848-1890)

Dutch Calvinist Immigrant Life in the Mid-Nineteenth Century

The leaders of the Dutch emigrants to the New World in the mid-nineteenth century were determined to give children an education with a Christian emphasis. The Michigan leader, the Reverend Albertus Van Raalte, had been part of a group denied permission in 1844 to start a Christian school in the Netherlands, and he gave Christian schooling as one of the main reasons for emigration.[1] The constitution of one emigration society stated that Dutch Christian parents could not in good conscience continue to be "without the opportunity to let their children receive instruction according to their religious convictions."[2]

However, once arrived in America, the immigrants quickly realized that private education was expensive and that they would have much more control over local public schools than they had had in the Netherlands. Consequently many thought district schools might well satisfy their children's needs. As it turned out, only a conservative handful of the immigrants established non-public Christian schools. To understand why and how such schools began, this chapter traces the social, religious, and educational developments in the main Dutch colonies of the mid-nineteenth century. It also discusses how the early Christian schools promoted religious and cultural isolation, also through their curricula.

Both their everyday devoutness and their appeal to a religious basis for their strict moral standards indicated that the Dutch Protestants that settled in the American midwest in the late 1840s and the 1850s were deeply religious. Moreover, though not well educated, most could read and write. They daily read their Bibles and possessed a copy of the Dutch Psalter and the Heidelberg catechism. Lucas, the main chronicler of Dutch emigration to the United States, claims that the settlers also widely read the Dutch translation of Franz Ludwig Zahn's **Biblical Histories**, the first textbook developed for Christian schools in the Netherlands. The majority of settlers were poor, rural Seceders. While most initially farmed, the many tailors, weavers, bakers, shoemakers, smiths, and shopkeepers among them enabled the North American settlements to remain self-contained to a remarkable degree.[3]

The new colonies were isolated from American culture for some time. Van Raalte wanted the settlements to be radiating centres for the Christian gospel. However, the struggle to garner even a bare subsistence from virgin lands wrested from the forests led to inevitable isolation and cultural lag. Also, the colonists craved the freedom to worship and to educate their children without outside interference, and were therefore suspicious of intrusions, of things American that might undermine their traditional belief and lifestyle. In the frontier environment they were cut off not only from America's cultural and religious life, but also from the development of their own people in the Netherlands. Such isolationism was also fostered by their natural reserve and by each community administering its own law and order and legal affairs (e.g., the ecclesiastical authorities ensured that civil irregularities such as the accidental killing of a hog or digging up a neighbour's tree were quickly quelled and settled). At the same time, the colonists, as long as they could maintain religious and cultural freedom, had no qualms about becoming American citizens. Already in 1848 four hundred settlers were granted American citizenship in Holland, Michigan. They did not doubt that America was to become their home and native land.[4]

The faith of the colonists was one that stressed personal salvation and obedience to God. The broader Calvinist emphasis that Christian faith should make an impact on all of culture did not reach America with these settlers. America's constitution gave the colonists the freedom to exercise their individualistic faith and to develop their own churches. At this time denominational schools were declining in America, and the ideal of America's educational leaders was a common public school for all children. Nevertheless, self-supported denominational schools, even with instruction in a foreign language, were not prohibited.[5]

The early colonists wanted to preserve the Dutch language. The more progressive believed this was necessary for a few years for "spiritual sustenance," while the more conservative found it unnecessary for anyone to learn English. After all, almost everyone in the settlements spoke Dutch; church services and activities were in Dutch; and various periodicals were published in the Dutch language. The older people feared that a weakening of the community's religious principles and practices would accompany the loss of the Dutch language. Even fifty years after the immigration of 1846-47, leaders within the Christian Reformed Church still felt called to defend their people against the charge that they wanted to sustain a miniature Netherlands in America.[6]

The two most prominent centres of colonization were Holland, Michigan, and Pella, Iowa, each with its own distinctive characteristics. Van Raalte and his group established Holland, Michigan. The people were poor, food was scarce, and sickness and death were commonplace. For Van Raalte and his people, their Dutch Calvinist faith was the central focus of their existence. This bound them together but also isolated them from their American surroundings.

The Pella settlers differed in several respects. Most came from the central part of the Netherlands where religious tensions had not been as severe as in the north-east, and economic advancement was the major reason for their migration. They were reasonably prosperous. Their leader, the Reverend Hendrik Scholte, though a Seceder, had nevertheless had close contact with the **Réveil** movement in the Netherlands. He did not share Seceder concern for fine points of doctrine nor their isolationist tendencies. Once in Iowa, he eschewed any denominational affiliation or even contact with other Dutch settlers, and, unlike Van Raalte, launched himself and the colony into American society. He named two of the first streets in Pella Expectation and Confidence Avenues, likely thinking of the settlement's economic and social as well as its religious future. His activities, among many others, included being Pella's attorney and justice of the peace, weekly newspaper publisher, postmaster, and school inspector. He also became active in national politics, with President Lincoln inviting him to his inaugural ceremonies as a personal friend.[7] Both Scholte and Van Raalte had powerful personalities that dominated the life of the communities, and both also set the tone for early schooling. But the different types of schools they promoted reflected their different orientations.

The Reformed Church in America: Christianizing
the Public Schools

Not only the leaders but also the churches were closely involved in promoting education. Already at its first meeting in 1848, the regional council of immigrant churches around Holland discussed regulations and boundaries for school districts. In the October 1856 session the council referred a minister who complained about lack of instruction for his church's children to the school inspectors to establish a school district. Here the gathering implicitly accepted that a district common school would provide the children with a proper education. However, the churches were also to exercise responsibility for such schools:

> The schools must be promoted and cared for by the churches as being an important part of the Christian calling of God's church on earth. All lukewarmness and coldness toward that cause must be condemned and rebuked.[8]

In the early 1850s the churches discussed the importance of setting up a Christian academy that would train children after graduation from common school. The churches would supervise the academy, especially the purity of the religious principles taught. Such education was important since "as citizens of the United States we shall never be able, without developing in knowledge and science, to exercise our Christian influence, which God demands of us."[9] Both the degree of church supervision and the preparation of children to exercise "Christian influence" later became recurring themes in North American Christian schools.

In the meantime, in 1850 the Michigan churches under Van Raalte's leadership had decided to join the Reformed Church in America as a separate "western" classis [presbytery].[10] They felt that the Reformed denomination, founded in New Amsterdam more than two hundred years earlier, had not been subject to the Enlightenment influences that had affected the national church in the Netherlands. Also, its New York area churches had helped the new colonists begin life in their new environment.

The American Reformed Church earlier had had a history of Christian schools dating back to the seventeenth century in a few states such as New York. Two years after Van Raalte's group joined the church, it appointed a committee to consider once again the establishment of such schools. However, the committee's conclusion one year later reflected the majority view of the church. Common schools were "productive and incalculably good." As such, the church should try

46

to work within them for the good of all American society.[11] Parochial schools would interfere with the role of the common school to mold a better Christian society.

Thus, the church concluded, its educational efforts should be channeled into making the public schools as Christian as possible. For example, the Church's Board of Publication published a series of Christian school books in the 1860s whose frontispiece showed a picture of a "District School," with several churches positioned in the background. The picture symbolized the prevalent belief in the Reformed Church that a public common school was needed in which the church would have a great deal of influence. As the series' introduction stated, the books aimed "to restore vital Christianity to the place it once held in schools and school books; . . . and habitually to direct the attention of the young to the Lord Jesus Christ."[12] Most of the new immigrants accepted that such "vital Christianity" could be maintained in their local schools in America and that costly non-public alternatives were unnecessary.

But Van Raalte himself surmised that attempts to Christianize the common school were doomed once the population became more heterogenous. He did not see a great deal of difference between Dutch and American public schools, and continued to push for parochial ones:

> The district schools impart the character of a **colorless** Protestantism . . . no sacrifice should be regarded too great, to see that the children of the church are trained in the spirit of a positive Protestantism, derived from the Bible.[13]

While in small, homogeneous communities, the spiritual leaders could control the school, Van Raalte fought to maintain "the principle that the fear of God must be the soul of our education; our Christian color must come out everywhere."[14] Such positive Christian instruction, Van Raalte was convinced, could be upheld in the long run only by parochial schools. In an 1862 sermon, he said that true knowledge should lead children to God, and that knowledge of God was the basis of the academic disciplines—rather vague generalities that later became characteristic of the statements of many clergymen advocating Christian schooling. Though short on specifics, Van Raalte nevertheless felt so strongly about Christian schools that once he threatened to move from Michigan to Pella if donations for Holland's Christian academy were not quickly forthcoming.[15]

However, except for this academy, Van Raalte's ideals were not realized within the Reformed Church. The colonists were too concerned about their own material welfare to support parochial schools

47

and believed neighbourhood control of the common schools would enable their children to receive an acceptable education. They no longer experienced the oppression to which they had been subjected in the Netherlands. Nor was there a leader who, like Van der Brugghen in the Netherlands, had a broad educational vision that could articulate and implement a distinctive Christian approach to education. Van Raalte himself saw elementary education narrowly, mainly as a way to transmit the three R's, religious doctrines and moral maxims. Consequently, his limited conception of Christian parochial schools was rejected in favour of the common district school in Reformed Church circles.

The Christian Reformed Church: The Cradle for North American Christian Schools

It was the Christian Reformed Church[16] that came to support the cause of Christian day school education. A group of about 750 Michigan Reformed Church members who had become increasingly dissatisfied with Van Raalte's decision to join the Reformed Church founded this denomination in 1857. Dutch immigrants who had lived in the New York area for a year or two and then moved to Michigan had spoken of tendencies in the New York and New Jersey churches that had earlier caused the Seceders to leave the Dutch national church. For instance, doctrines such as election were not held in high repute; hymns rather than the traditional psalms were sung; and Freemasonry with its secret, semi-religious oaths was condoned. Van Raalte did not join the new denomination and the group was marked by internal dissension and lack of leadership. Even by 1880 the denomination numbered only 39 congregations and 12 000 members, although the next decade saw a tripling of those numbers through renewed Dutch immigration and through membership transfers from the Reformed church in reaction to the Freemasonry issue.

H. Richard Niebuhr has shown that while the explicit issues were doctrinal ones, the implicit background was the issue of adaptation or resistance to native culture.[17] The Christian Reformed Church was established partly because its members felt uneasy with their Americanized brothers and wanted to hold on to the Old World Seceder church and its **modus operandi**. Thus the leaders of the new denomination were recruited from the Netherlands. For example, the Reverend Douwe J. van der Werp, who had been convicted of operating an illegal Seceder school in the Netherlands in the 1830s and had become a zealous Seceder minister, accepted a call to a Christian Reformed Church in Michigan. There he became the mentor of ministerial students as well as editor of the church paper, **De Wachter** [The Guardian].

For at least the first thirty years of its existence, almost all Christian Reformed Church members held that religious orthodoxy depended on a thorough knowledge of the Dutch language. Van der Werp's **De Wachter** emphasized that Dutch instruction for children was essential to preserve the Reformed faith from corrupting, American religious influences.[18] American Protestantism was shallow at best; orthodox writings were found only in Dutch. The Reverend R. T. Kuiper, a proponent of Christian schools who emigrated from the Netherlands in 1879, two years later decried the fact that in the Reformed Church "the Dutch amounts to very little or nothing," and that in centres like Grand Rapids children were drifting away from their parents because of a lack of fluency in Dutch. Kuiper implied that such lack of knowledge of Dutch would lead to a weaker, less orthodox church.[19]

The church's assemblies regularly affirmed "Dutch Christian education." The 1870 synod declared that every congregation should establish a school, or at least find some means to give "Dutch and Christian" instruction. Six years later speakers suggested that articles in **De Wachter** and penny banks in members' homes should be used to promote Christian schools.[20] The church had picked up the torch for Christian education.

However, many persons in the pew continued to prefer the common schools, both for economic reasons and because they did not find them objectionable. The church paper, **De Wachter**, in 1870 complained that with support for only a handful of schools "we painfully feel the serious want and unjustifiable neglect of our children." Even some ministers and church councils opposed the establishment of Christian schools; they felt that the common schools taught a Christian morality and lifestyle and that specific Calvinist beliefs could be taught by the church.[21]

Officially the Christian Reformed Church continued to encourage Christian schools. But did it do so for the sake of a Christian approach to education or for the sake of Dutch language training? On the floor of synod the Reverend Gerrit Boer gave a word of encouragement for **Dutch** education. Columns in **De Wachter** were to promote **Dutch** Christian education—at a time when in rural communities many weeks might pass by without a word of English being heard, and when the church had no English-speaking congregations.[22] The church's retention of Dutch went hand-in-hand with a conservative, isolationistic outlook on life. Its rationale for Christian schools focused on preserving Dutch Calvinism as an enclave in American society. Leaders sensed little of Van der Brugghen and Groen's conception of Christian schools as institutions that enabled children to contribute to society and culture through the exercise of their Christian faith. For Christian Reformed Church members, America would be the land of promise only if the solitary tulip of Dutch Calvinism could bloom because it was connected with its nourishing bulb by the stem of Dutch language. The first Christian schools were founded to strengthen that stem.

Early Schooling: Teaching the Essentials in District Schools

The colonists were plain folks, but as Calvinist Protestants they stressed literacy and the connection between learning and religion. Since everyone should be able to read the Bible, the Heidelberg catechism, and other religious works, some basic education for their children was a necessity. But the colonists needed their children to work on the land, and already in 1848 the churches in Michigan felt moved to warn against lukewarmness towards schooling. In 1850 this was reiterated: the character, the destination and the welfare of the people depended on their education.[23] Particularly Van Raalte encouraged the colonists to cultivate knowledge and to be diligent in educating their children. In 1852 he wrote in still awkwardly phrased English:

> It is a great and difficult work to elevate an ignorant mass of people, a people of the lower class filled with European prejudices . . . . There is more estimation of education than there is usual among the European emigrants. The religion of the people is a sure pledge of the success. One of the greatest obstacles, however, is the poverty.[24]

The school promoters in Holland, including Van Raalte and the lone American resident of the area, organized a public school district. Van Raalte was elected chairman, and, indeed, at first the distinction between the public school district and the church was not clear-cut. There was little outside supervision and the parents through the local board could control teacher hiring, discipline policies, and choice of textbooks. In effect, the district school was a Christian school. Yet most settlers did not accord education high priority. They lacked interest in school meetings, and during the second year of operation only twenty-seven out of a possible 191 children attended the school.[25]

The education of the first schools in Holland and its surrounding villages did not differ all that much from that in the parochial

Christian schools of the 1860s and 1870s. Whether the instruction was in Dutch or in English, the teacher, always a "godly person," saw to it that the children knew and sang the psalms and were "prepared on the catechism." Besides Biblical studies, the three R's were emphasized, most often in Dutch. A number of teachers used a Bible with two adjoining columns of Dutch and English on each page as their main textbook. The first two teachers in Holland were Americans, one of whom had been sent to Michigan by a New England society organized to stimulate schooling in the "western" states. These teachers also used the standard **Webster's Spelling Book** and provided additional reading through a library of English Sunday school books made available by a New York Reformed Church minister who had visited the colony. These American teachers were viewed with some suspicion since, though devout Christians, they were not Dutch Calvinists.[26]

The faith and piety of the teachers were considered more important than their qualifications. One village close to Holland, for example, hired a fruit tree seller whose "very exemplary conduct and humble but at the same time splendid piety" was believed to enable him to give proper, Christian instruction. The community's minister was often closely involved with the school. In Holland, students were sent to Van Raalte's house to be reprimanded or punished when their deportment cards were marked "very bad." At the same time, some colonists left no doubt that theirs were public district schools and not parochial ones. A state politician complimented one village for having always had an "American type" school rather than one that gave Dutch instruction or one that was sectarian or parochial.[27]

Where communities consisted entirely of Dutch settlers, the district schools held fast to the traditional Calvinist faith. How much of the instruction was to be in Dutch and how much in English was not resolved for many years. After the first two American teachers in Holland, most teachers were either members of the Dutch settlements and their churches, or were American teachers used only part of the year. Even in 1880, three of the four school districts in a township next to Holland gave six to nine months of English instruction. In the remaining months those teachers not speaking Dutch were laid off so that Dutch instruction could be given.[28] In the rural areas parents themselves made such decisions. The first calls for parochial schools arose in the larger centres where parents could not control school policies and feared the corrupting influence of city life.

Almost from the start, however, Van Raalte believed that poor school meeting attendance and the Michigan stipulation that public schools must respect all religious convictions would cause the colonists to lose control. Also, some leaders became increasingly critical of school books written to be "equally good" for all faiths. By 1880, one minister expressed concern that public schools legally could do little more about religious instruction than read a Bible passage. Yet the colonists' "public conscience" was "dormant on this point," often even among the more conservative Christian Reformed members. The ideal to establish independent Christian schools had never been a burning question for most immigrants and faded further with time.[29]

A similar picture can be painted for the early schools in Iowa, with two important differences. First, while Scholte, like Van Raalte, was elected school supervisor for the township in 1848, he did not favour parochial schools but concentrated his educational efforts on Christianizing the public district school. In 1857 he wrote that the district school was "the institution for a country where the sovereignty is vested in the people, and where every individual has his share in shaping the course followed in the conduct of public affairs."[30] Because of this, the public school could be the Christian one for his colonists.

Secondly, Scholte had taken with him James Muntingh, the principal of Van der Brugghen's teacher training classes, to establish the Pella school. Muntingh's background led him to establish a well-rounded curriculum. Besides the fundamental three R's, the Pella school also gave instruction in geography, history and music, and devoted much time to learning English through translation exercises. Each day the school was opened with prayer and the singing of a psalm, followed by Biblical history. Both parents and students appreciated the school, especially for its Biblical instruction. Moreover,

> the scholars who received their education under these early, pioneer teachers were so thoroughly grounded in the essential studies, that many of them would have been a credit to the best equipped schools of today.[31]

As a result, Pella during its first years of existence saw little need for parochial Christian schools. Besides, few Iowa settlers had been involved with attempts to establish Christian schools in the Netherlands. Their attitude towards Christian faith was a somewhat fatalistic one: since God had to convert a person to Christianity, and once converted would remain a Christian, education had little influence on faith and therefore Christian schools were not all that necessary. Moreover, these settlers were not as suspicious as their Michigan counterparts of the larger numbers of Americans settling in Pella. Scholte wanted to break down denominational barriers among Christians

52

in the New World, and, therefore, whether a teacher was Baptist or Reformed was not considered all that important. In fact, it was Michigan's Van Raalte who eventually stimulated the establishment of a Christian parochial school in Pella.[32]

The colonists in both Michigan and Iowa did agree that education beyond the grade school should be offered by the church, if only to ensure proper training of future ministers. In Pella, Scholte cooperated closely with a group of Baptists in establishing Central University in 1853, a grandiose name for a small institution that sixty years later became a college of the Reformed Church. Scholte himself donated land and building materials, and for many years the school served as the continuation of the district school.[33] In Holland, plans had already been under way in 1850 to begin an academy to prepare boys for entrance into New Jersey's Rutgers College."[34] This academy grew into the preparatory department of Holland's Hope College, still a Reformed Church college today. Originally, the academy was the educational link between the grade school and theological training, emphasizing instruction in English, the classical languages, and Dutch. Both money and books were scarce during the first few years. The eastern Reformed churches were asked for help since the academy was to stem "the desolating torrent of vice and infidelity which ceaselessly rolls westward across the illimitable prairies."[35] Without an academy, it was believed, such immorality would easily affect students who would have to attend an existing high school in a larger population centre.

Thus most settlers saw the necessity of some basic education for all children, and of advanced education mainly for aspiring ministers. With local control of such decisions as teacher appointment and the opportunity for some religious instruction, they generally felt that district common schools offered satisfactory education. Being from Seceder stock, they had no well-worked-out principles or theories of education. Their main pedagogical concern was that teachers could maintain order. Gradually and inevitably, however, the district schools became part of the Michigan school system, and not only Dutch but also Calvinist religious instruction disappeared. Especially Christian Reformed ministers arriving from the Netherlands after 1860 who had been involved with Dutch Seceder schools became alarmed and picked up the torch for parochial Christian schools.

The First Parochial Christian Schools

By the mid-nineteenth century, America had lost much of the Puritan religious orientation that had put its stamp on early American schooling, though not its substantive moral outlook. It was the time when Horace Mann wanted the Bible to be read without comment in non-sectarian schools, with the churches teaching religion according to the preferences of individual parents. It is possible that Van Raalte was aware of Mann's ideals that, as Ellwood Cubberley later put it, rapidly led to the secularization of American education. If so, he would have been disturbed that Mann's concepts reflected the late eighteenth century Dutch thinking that had later caused much grief for the Seceders in the Netherlands. Certainly soon after his arrival in America, Van Raalte was convinced that its public schools would impart the character of a "colorless" Protestantism.

Van Raalte therefore encouraged parochial schools, establishing one in his own congregation in 1857. His three visits to the Reformed Church in Pella between 1859 and 1861 resulted in a parochial school being started there with three teachers, one of whom was Muntingh's popular colleague Isaac Overkamp. These schools were to promote Biblical, "positive" Protestant education. The Bible was used as the reading book and the Heidelberg Catechism as textbook, with Dutch language being one of the important subjects taught.[36]

However, Van Raalte's efforts in both Holland and Pella ended in failure. Both parochial schools closed after five or six years of operation because almost all parents were satisfied with their district schools. In Pella, Muntingh tried to implement in the district public school the type of Christian education that Van der Brugghen had envisioned: a well-rounded, pedagogically-sound, non-sectarian Christian program that would help children to function in and contribute to society. Although Van Raalte did not explicitly reject this approach, he was more concerned with Calvinist doctrines and believed that only parochial schools could maintain the centrality of Calvinist religion and morality. Most colonists were not convinced by his arguments. Although Van Raalte was a man of religious vision, his inability to build long-term support for parochial schools in the Reformed Church may have been partly due to his much narrower vision of education than that of Van der Brugghen and his North American follower, James Muntingh.

Van Raalte's emphasis on the suitability of the Bible and the catechism as textbooks for young children, for instance, puts the perspicacity of his pedagogical judgment and insight in doubt. In the

54

end, with Van Raalte's own church abandoning his cause, he became a solitary man. Yet there was little sympathy and no contact between Van Raalte and the Christian Reformed denomination which had started to promote parochial Christian schools; he probably considered the new church too isolationistic and schismatic.[37]

The first Christian Reformed school and the first parochial one to exist continuously for many years was founded in the major urban centre of west Michigan, Grand Rapids, in the winter of 1855-56. Parents much more readily supported a private Christian school in that city's diverse religious and cultural environment than in the rural, homogeneous villages. When the church operating the school in 1857 became part of the new Christian Reformed denomination, teacher Adrian Pleune and his twenty-five pupils moved with the church to a new location. Pleune's training consisted of a grade school education and some experience tutoring Seceder children in the Netherlands. In the summer, when public schools were closed, he taught one hundred pupils, with the assistance of his son. He used Dutch to teach the program of reading and writing, arithmetic, and singing of psalms. Pleune's successor was the equally untrained church janitor and handyman. Nevertheless, the school grew and in 1875 expanded into a new 18 by 12 metre brick building.[38]

Other Michigan centres, like Kalamazoo (1857) and Muskegon (1881) also began parochial schools. In Grand Rapids, the East Street Christian Reformed Church put a barber in charge of a school in its church basement in 1880. On the west side of the city a church council began a school in 1883 to keep children off the street during summer vacations. Two years later this became a year-round school. In all cases, the schools were under the close supervision of the church councils, since, as the minutes of one noted, it would be dangerous for the church not to operate the school. A new school in the Chicago area in 1876 immediately taught part of its program in English. On the other hand, new immigrants opened another school not far away in 1883 explicitly to teach Dutch so that children would understand the church's sermons and religious instruction.[39]

Whatever the language(s) of instruction, on the whole the quality of the schools left much to be desired. The Reverend R. T. Kuiper in 1882 wrote that at least seven improvements were needed: (1) more schools were needed so they would be close to the children; (2) teachers should be qualified pedagogically and be able to nurture children in church doctrine and morality; (3) textbooks with "elevating" content and character should be available; (4) both parents and teachers should cooperate to promote thinking and a desire for knowledge;

(5) instruction should be in English, but with enough Dutch language taught to enable children to understand sermons and catechism instruction and to read religious books; (6) parents should keep children in school until they could read and write adequately; and (7) education should be of more import in the communities' social and religious life.[40]   Kuiper was determined to improve both the schools and the people's attitudes to learning and to Christian education.

But while leaders promoted the schools, Christian Reformed adherents often were indifferent to them, especially in rural areas.   Most preferred Dutch instruction a few hours a week in district or Sunday schools, or summer schools.   Not being convinced of the necessity of Christian day school instruction, they were unwilling to pay tuition from their meagre resources.   By 1886 the yearbook of the Christian Reformed Church reported an enrollment of only 471 pupils in six schools, five of which were in Western Michigan.   Not until 1888 did a new wave of immigration cause enrollment to increase rapidly.[41]   These new supporters once again feared American influences on their children and believed that Dutch parochial schools were indispensable for the future of the church.

Curriculum and Instruction in Early Parochial Christian Schools

Conditions in the early Christian schools often were poor, even by public school standards of the time.   Buildings were inadequately heated and lit, sparsely equipped and crowded.   The poorly paid teachers taught with few textbooks, as much as forty-nine weeks per year, often serving as janitor as well.[42]   In 1873 the minister of one church reported to his church council that "the instruction in [our Christian] school is exceedingly lamentable; everything goes on in the greatest confusion."[43]

As in most common schools, memorization and rote learning were the primary means of instruction.   Classes were ungraded, but yet whole-school recitations were sometimes used.   Parents took pride in the memorization facts of children, particularly of the catechism, and in their reading ability.   Unlike in some public schools, pictures and models were seldom available.   Pestalozzi and other nineteenth century pedagogues began to influence the Christian schools only when more qualified teachers came from the Netherlands in the 1880s and 1890s.   One former student reported that though primitive, his school nevertheless had been one where the centrality of the Christian faith had had an impact on him, especially because of the dedication of the teachers. Even where instruction was substandard, supporters were convinced that the schools were preferable to what they saw as the "terrible and discouraging" influences that American public education would have on their children.[44]

Operating a Christian school usually meant, first of all, operating a Dutch school to preserve Dutch Calvinism, to ward off the influence of a secular society, and to prevent the growth of superficial brands of American Protestantism. Only in Dutch Christian schools could "qualified and God-fearing teachers" explain Bible passages and "apply them to the hearts of the children."[45] A knowledge of Dutch was necessary to prevent a generation gap, to enable religious instruction to take place, and to save the mother tongue that embodied Dutch Calvinist ideals and achievements. In the 1870s and 1880s schools typically offered most instruction in Dutch for the first four or six years, after which students transferred to district schools, left school, or, in one case, continued with English instruction. Church leaders like the Reverend G. E. Boer did affirm that some English instruction should complement the Dutch so that children could take on their roles as self-reliant citizens in church and society and be able to contribute to the life of the nation. The necessity of English instruction was not in dispute, but the balance between Dutch and English and their various functions led to endless discussion and a diversity of arrangements.[46]

That the leaders almost from the start expected the schools to do more than teach Dutch can be inferred, for example, from the desire to provide schools with suitable Christian textbooks in both Dutch and English. Already in 1864 there was a question at a church assembly about translating Dutch Christian textbooks into English. The Reverend W. H. Van Leeuwen, the first teacher of Amsterdam's Seceder school and author of the textbooks that Groen van Prinsterer had criticized as pedagogically unsuitable, was instructed to write the Reformed Church whether it knew of "orthodox" books suitable for Christian schools. If not, the church resolved to translate and print some books in Michigan. Neither plan seems to have had concrete results, and no records confirm that the Reformed Church readers published two years earlier were ever used in Christian Reformed schools.[47]

To supplement the high-priced books imported from the Netherlands, the churches did decide to support a Michigan printer in reprinting four Dutch school booklets. Also, Van Leeuwen in 1880 mentioned where his own 1840s school books could still be bought, and recommended Dutch textbooks such as **Signposts for Youth: Reading Exercises for Christian Schools and Families; God's Providence Evident in Conversion: Guidance and Salvation of Distinguished Persons Outlined**

57

in Narratives: A Reading Book for Christian Schools and Families; and Zahn's Biblical Histories. Moreover, he suggested that pupils read from the New Testament and Proverbs, preferably printed in double-column format with English and Dutch side-by-side.[48]

The most commonly used readers appear to have been those of R. Van Mill, Van Leeuwen's successor in Amsterdam's Seceder school. One of these, the Dutch Reader for Schools and Families, was reprinted several times in Holland, Michigan, in the 1860s. Its preface indicated its intent:

> This reader shall—I know—be rejected by many. Not only will those be annoyed who consider the Bible a book totally unsuitable for children, but also many of those who say they are proponents of Biblical, Christian, yes, positive Christian education (as if there could be a negative Christianity!) shall find truths presented in this reader.
>
> I consider Biblical and Reformed as words of one and the same meaning, and I do not have the freedom to hide any of the eternal truths from children just because they cannot understand them.[49]

Van Mill thus not only defended his readers' heavy-handed theological principles, but also answered Groen's criticism that such an approach might be pedagogically unsuitable for young children. He rejected—as did the early parochial schools which used his readers—Van der Brugghen's pleas that a Christian education must use appropriate pedagogical approaches and make Christianity come alive for the child by avoiding doctrinalism.

Most of Van Mill's selections began and ended with a Bible text, and explicitly emphasized a moral or religious principle. They stressed an all-knowing God who called children to account for their deeds and who punished sin unless there was true repentance. Since God determined events, children must be satisfied with their lot. Also, to reflect devotion owed to God, they must be obedient and respectful to their parents. Van Mill did not consider that worthwhile literature could have inherent and motivational value. For him, the purpose of literature was to show that a Christian life meant individualistic obedience to a narrow set of moral rules. Van Mill and those who used his books saw little of what De Liefde portrayed in his readers: that Christianity could also result in a joyful life where God's love was reflected in work and play. De Liefde's books were advertised in De Wachter, but there is no evidence that they were used in American Christian Schools. One school board member in 1876 pointedly wrote that his school used the same books as Dutch Seceder schools, though for English instruction the school was forced to use "the best kind" available.[50]

What the schools emphasized during this period, therefore, were Biblical studies, reading in Dutch, and writing and arithmetic. Singing was taught because it was important for church worship. Pupils were to become literate enough to participate in the life of the church and of society. Little attention was given to history, geography, science, art and physical education. Since for most supporters the life of the church took precedence, they expressed little interest in a balanced, well-rounded education.

Education Beyond the Elementary Grades

Relatively few Christian Reformed children attended school beyond eight years of grade school: boys were needed on the farm or in the shop; girls, at home. A training school for theological students began in 1864 and twelve years later moved to the second floor of the Williams Street Christian School in Grand Rapids. The curriculum for the first four years paralleled that of a traditional academy; the last two years provided a theological training. Until 1894 only pre-theological students were admitted; the few other secondary students attended Hope preparatory school or a public high school.

The general education required of those future theologians included the classical languages of Greek, Latin, and Hebrew; general history, geography, and psychology; logic and rhetoric; and Dutch language and history.[51] While the range of subjects was much broader than that of Christian elementary schools, American history, British and American literature, and the natural sciences were notably excluded. Perhaps at first the one and only Dutch-trained instructor was unable to teach all these subjects. The choice of subjects shows too, however, that the church still saw its heritage and future within the Dutch cultural tradition. Prospective church leaders did not need to know much about the American cultural setting nor about its English-speaking roots.

A Changing Rationale for Christian Schools

Until the 1880s, Christian schools were operated specifically to maintain Dutch Calvinism in North America. Individual Christian Reformed congregations strictly controlled the few existing schools, and school teachers had to give unconditional assent to church creeds. The church considered the bond between religion and the Dutch language so

59

strong that in 1875 its synod, despite the church's strict interpretation of the Sabbath commandment, allowed the teaching of Dutch reading and spelling on Sundays in places where no other opportunity for learning Dutch existed.[52]

On the one hand, the continued emphasis on the Dutch language helped to maintain the religious basis for the community. Most clergy had been trained in Holland, and all religious works were in Dutch. Consequently, the church could not function without its youth knowing some Dutch. Its knowledge prevented communication barriers between the generations that would have threatened the community's cohesiveness. On the other hand, having parochial schools that taught an unusual foreign language prolonged cultural isolation. Parents feared that in public schools their children might be tainted with a corrupted Christianity. Also, they wanted pupils to be kept away from secular English books that the parents were unable to read. At least until the turn of the century Christian Reformed members supporting the schools were quarantined from the suspect mainstream of American society, even in the large centres. Moral corruption and religious alienation appeared inevitable if this isolation broke down.[53]

Yet the existence of the schools cannot be explained exclusively in terms of the longing for linguistic and cultural separation from American society. Van der Werp in 1870 wrote that the schools were necessary because a good education involved not only reading, writing, bookkeeping and geography, but also a daily imprinting of the religious principles that led to salvation and that formed the basis of social and moral virtues. Later, Van Leeuwen added that the schools would nurture pupils to be jewels of God's church as well as useful members of society. The schools' instruction would reveal the way of salvation, show pupils that their sins might be forgiven in Jesus Christ, and help them to lead Christian lives in society. Such a Christian life was interpreted narrowly, however. The emphasis was on adherence to Calvinist doctrines and the exercise of related personal morals.[54]

During the 1880s, with an influx of new supporters from two main sources, the rationale for Christian schools gradually began to change. First, many Reformed Church members joined the Christian Reformed Church because their church refused to take a strong stand against the Freemasons. More importantly, another wave of emigration from the Netherlands had begun, and the Seceder church in the Netherlands now encouraged these emigrants to join the Christian Reformed Church. One of these was F. Kniphuizen, who in 1885 wrote a series of articles on Christian education in **De Wachter**. He emphasized throughout that such education must be Christian, not Dutch. Like Van der Brugghen forty years earlier, he used readers such as **Virtuous Henry** as examples of the type of book that would lead children to adopt an unacceptable liberalism. Christian schools were to be the cradle of God's church, but at the same time Christian education must enable children to function as full citizens of America. Church services and Calvinistic education programs should be held in English as soon as possible. In a thinly veiled criticism of the schools, he added that, besides the three R's, Christian education should also involve subjects such as geography, physical science and history, all taught in a Christian atmosphere.[55]

Newer immigrants like Kniphuizen, aware of more recent Christian school developments in the Netherlands, recognized that there even the Seceder schools had been influenced to some extent by the legacies of Van der Brugghen and Groen. These new immigrants, moreover, were caught up in the excitement that the Dutch leader Abraham Kuyper was generating for Calvinist education at all levels and for Calvinist involvement in political and cultural life. Thus they desired a Christian education that was relevant for life in American society. They espoused broader objectives for the school, to be met through quality instruction by qualified personnel. Christian schools, to be creditable educational alternatives in American society, would have to offer a well-rounded curriculum in the English language. Christian education was to reach beyond the preservation of narrow theological and moral principles and applications.

In 1883 R. T. Kuiper wrote a Dutch poem for the closing exercises of a Dutch Christian School. It summed up the attitude towards parochial schools during this period of transition:

> In this hour we therefore have reason
> To thank the Lord our God with voice and song
> For the good that our school planned for our youth;
> Not only in the feat of reading Dutch,
> But also how our youth already learned to fear the Lord
> And how the way there leads them to the Kingdom of Heaven.
> . . . .
> Continue therefore to train your children Christianly,
> Teach them to speak Dutch as well as English. . . .
> . . . .
> Read often, then,
> In both those languages
> The word of your God;

> But during your learning,
> Covet his blessing
> According to the command of Jesus.[56]

The choice of language was gradually becoming less important than how children in school could be taught "to fear the Lord" and live in American society. The next chapters will relate how the new influx of immigrants and their thinking influenced the schools and their programs.

NOTES

1. H. Bouma, **Een vergeten hoofdstuk** [A forgotten chapter] (Enschedé: J. Boersma, 1959), p. 77.
2. Quoted by Henry J. Kuiper in **The Banner**, April 11, 1947, p. 452.
3. Henry S. Lucas, **Netherlanders in America: Dutch Immigration to the United States and Canada, 1789-1950** (Ann Arbor: University of Michigan Press, 1955), p. 114. Cyrenus Cole's **Souvenir History of Pella** (Pella, Iowa: The Boston Press, 1922) reported that of two hundred men becoming U.S. citizens after their arrival in Pella, only two could not write their signature (p. 11). See also many of the letters of early immigrants in Herbert J. Brinks, **"Schrijf spoedig terug": letters from immigrants in America 1847-1920** (The Hague: Boekencentrum, 1978). A Dutch government chart reproduced on page 209 of Pieter R. D. Stokvis, **De Nederlandse trek naar Amerika 1846-1847** [The Dutch migration to America 1846-47], doctoral dissertation at the University of Leiden (Leiden: Universitaire Pers, 1977), listed the occupations of all emigrants between 1831 and 1847. Only eight were teachers, at least three of whom had taught in Dutch Seceder schools. James Muntingh, who settled in Iowa, was the sole identified follower of Van der Brugghen's approach to education who migrated. The more conservative Seceder influence became the predominant one in early American Christian schools.
4. John H. Bratt, "Dutch Calvinism in America," in W. Stanford Reid, ed., **John Calvin: His Influence in the Western World** (Grand Rapids: Zondervan, 1982), pp. 298-300. John Kromminga described in detail the cultural and ecclesiastical isolation of the colonies in chapter 4 of **The Christian Reformed Church: A Study in Orthodoxy** (Grand Rapids: Baker, 1949). He showed how American revivalism, frontier "activism," and Enlightenment influences on theology bypassed these Dutch Calvinist communities. See also George Goris, "Puritan Legalism as a Method of Moral

and Religious Reform in the Christian Reformed Church" (Th.D. dissertation, Union Theological Seminary, 1932), pp. 14-15; The Christian Reformed Centennial Committee, **Centennial Facts and Background** (Grand Rapids: Christian Reformed Church, 1957), p. 45; and H. Algra, **Het wonder van de 19e eeuw: van vrije kerken en kleine luyden** [The wonder of the nineteenth century: of free churches and plain folks] (Franeker: Wever, 2nd edition, 1966), p. 189.

5. During this time period, the main debate in the U.S. focused on the availability of free common schools for all children, and to what extent religion should be allowed to be taught in such schools, rather than on the right of private schools to exist. See Chapter 5, "The Common School Crusade," in David B. Tyack, **Turning Points in American Educational History** (Waltham, Mass.: Blaisdell, 1967). In Michigan the first free public schools did not exist until four years before Van Raalte's arrival—and then in Detroit only (H. G. Good, **A History of American Education,** Second Edition, [New York: MacMillan, 1962], p. 151.

6. Gerald F. De Jong, **The Dutch in America 1609-1974** (Boston: Twayne Publishers, 1975), p. 135; John Kromminga, pp. 95-97; and **De Gereformeerde Amerikaan** [The Reformed American], 1 (1897): 1-2.

7. De Jong, pp. 140-41; John H. Bratt, pp. 301-02; Arnold Mulder, **Americans from Holland** (Philadelphia and New York: Lippincott, 1947), pp. 152, 184-87; "The Life and Labors of H. P. Scholte," mimeographed article written in 1930 and published by Nederlandsch Archief van Kerkgeschiedenis [Netherlands Archives for Church History], no author given; 1980 translation by Cornelius Witt available in Heritage Hall Archives, Calvin College, Grand Rapids, Michigan, pp. 5-8.

8. **Minutes of Classis Holland 1848-1858,** trans. by a joint committee of the Christian Reformed Church and the Reformed Church of America (Grand Rapids, Michigan: Eerdmans, 1950), September 27, 1848, Article 6. Michigan's 1837 school law, influenced by Victor Cousin's report of the Prussian schools, gave centralized power to the state superintendent of public instruction. However, conditions in the mid-century meant that such control existed much more in law than in actual fact. Especially in rural areas most decisions were made locally.

9. Ibid., April 30, 1851; April 29, 1852; and September 1, 1852.

10. A classis is a regional council of churches, usually consisting of the minister and an elder of each church. Each classis in turn

appoints delegates to the church's synod or general assembly.

11. **Acts and Proceedings of the General Synod of the Reformed Protestant Dutch Church in North America,** convened in the city of Philadelphia, June 1853, p. 360.

12. Thomas C. Strong, **Christian School Books No. 4, Third Reader** (New York: Board of Publications of the Reformed Protestant Dutch Church, 1862), p. 3. The aims of the book were identical to those of Christian schools of the time. The selections included Bible passages and ever-present religious and moral emphases. However, there is no record indicating that Christian schools used these books. Three reasons may be conjectured: (1) the rift between the Reformed Church and the Christian Reformed Church had just occurred, and adherents of the new church would have been suspicious of any Reformed Church publication; (2) in 1862, the few Christian schools that existed used mostly Dutch; and (3) the inclusion of both psalms and hymns to be memorized was unacceptable to the Christian Reformed Church (which sang psalms only).

13. From a report by Van Raalte, on behalf of Classis Holland to the Board of Domestic Missions of the Reformed Church, found, in translation, in the **21st Annual Report of the Board of Domestic Missions,** 1853, p. 78, as quoted by George Stob, "The Christian Reformed Church and Her Schools," (Th.D. dissertation, Princeton Theological Seminary, 1955), p. 42.

14. Quoted by Stob, p. 43, from Preston J. Stegenga, **Anchor of Hope** (Grand Rapids, Michigan: Eerdmans, 1954), p. 38. By "Christian color" Van Raalte referred to Calvinist distinctiveness.

15. See Henry Schultze, **The Educational Vision of Van Raalte** (Grand Rapids, Michigan: Eerdmans, 1947). Van Raalte's sermon was preached on February 23, 1862, and excerpts were printed by H. J. Kuiper in **The Banner,** April 11, 1947, p. 453. His threat was in a letter written in the minute book of the Old First Reformed Church of Holland, Michigan, November 18, 1956, and reproduced in **Religion and Culture,** May 1924, pp. 181-82.

16. Both the Reformed Church in America and the Christian Reformed Church in North America have had several name changes. In the 1860s, for example, the former was known as the Reformed Protestant Dutch Church, while the latter called itself the True Dutch Reformed Church. For ease of reference, I will use the current "Reformed" and "Christian Reformed" designations throughout. The total North American membership of the Christian Reformed Church today almost equals that of the Reformed

Church (300 000 and 307 000, respectively), but in Canada the Christian Reformed Church's 83 000 members far surpass the Reformed Church's 7 000. See the **1982 Directory** of the Reformed Church in America and the **Yearbook 1983** of the Christian Reformed Church.

17. H. Richard Niebuhr, **The Social Sources of Denominationalism** (New York: Henry Holt, 1929), pp. 213-14. See also Kromminga, pp. 103-04. Kromminga alerted me to the fact that Niebuhr used the Christian Reformed Church as a specific example of ecclesiastical isolation that was modified only gradually over a long period of time. For a recent essay on the socioeconomic and religious differences among the Dutch immigrants in the 1840s and 1850s, see Cornelis Smits, "Secession, Quarrels, Emigration and Personalities," in Herman Ganzevoort and Mark Boekelman, **Dutch Immigration to North America** (Toronto: Multicultural History Society of Ontario, 1983), pp. 97-110.

18. See, for example, articles in **De Wachter** [The Guardian], Dec. 9, 1875, p. 3 and March 2, 1876, p. 2.

19. R. T. Kuiper, **A Voice From America About America**, trans. E. R. Post (Grand Rapids, Michigan: Eerdmans, 1970), pp. 67, 72, 81ff. This volume was first published in Dutch in 1881.

20. **Acts of Synod of the Christian Reformed Church 1857-1880**, transcribed and mimeographed by Calvin Seminary, Grand Rapids, in 1937; July 15 and 16, 1870, p. 127; February 2, 1876, p. 172.

21. M. G. Gritters, "History of Christian Education in this Country," **Christian Home and School**, April, 1945, p. 8. Gritters also gave the quote from **De Wachter**. At this time schools existed in only four towns, all in Western Michigan: Grand Rapids, Muskegon, Grand Haven, and Kalamazoo.

22. **Acts of Synod of the Christian Reformed Church 1857-1880**, June 3, 1874, p. 46; June 3, 1875, p. 154; **Acts 1881**, June 15, 1881, p. 17; R. T. Kuiper, p. 67.

23. **Classis Holland Minutes**, September 27, 1848, and October 30, 1850.

24. Albert Hyma, "The Origins of Our Christian Schools," **Christian Home and School**, March 1947, pp. 8-9. Hyma was quoting a letter of Van Raalte to Dr. J. Garretson of the Reformed Church. See also "An Historical Account by a First Settler," Henry S. Lucas, **Dutch Immigrant Memoirs and Related Writings**, Volume 1 (Assen: Van Gorkum, 1955), pp. 500-501.

25. Albert Hyma, "The Origins of Our Christian Schools," **Christian Home and School**, March 1947, pp. 8-9. This article was based mainly on the minutes of the first school board in Holland,

Michigan. For a summary of the development of American common schools, as well as an indication that often there were no clear lines between "sectarian" and "non-sectarian" schools in the U.S. in the first half of the nineteenth century, see Tyack, **Turning Points**, pp. 119-25.

26. Lucas, **Memoirs**, Volume 1, pp. 97-98. 454; Elvira Langdon Cooper, "Interesting School-Reminiscences," **De Grondwet**, December 20, 1910. Langdon took over the Holland school from Mr. Ira Hoyt who taught at the school for three months. In the January 3, 1911 issue of **De Grondwet** one of the first pupils, D. Broek, referred to Ira Hoyt's use of **Webster's Spelling Book**. See also J. Van Hinte, **Nederlanders in Amerika**, Eerste Deel [Netherlanders in America, Volume 1] (Groningen: P. Noordhoff, 1928), p. 270.

27. Lucas, **Memoirs**, Volume 1, pp. 209, 250, 465; James Van der Sluis, "Interesting School-Reminiscences from Old Scholars," **De Grondwet**, January 3, 1911, and Van Hinte, p. 418.

28. R. T. Kuiper, **A Voice From America About America**, pp. 76-77.

29. Van Hinte, p. 418; and R. T. Kuiper, **A Voice From America About America**, pp. 73-74.

30. Quoted in "The Life and Labors of H. P. Scholte," trans. by Cornelius Witt. The original source of the quotation is not indicated.

31. Jacob Vander Zee, **The Hollanders of Iowa** (Iowa City: State Historical Society of Iowa, 1912), pp. 259-61; Cyrenus Cole et al., **Souvenir History of Pella**, Iowa (Pella: The Booster Press, 1922), pp. 63-64; and K. Van Stigt, **Geschiedenis van Pella, Iowa**, Tweede Deel [History of Pella, Iowa, Volume 2] (Pella: Weekblad Drukkerij, 1897), pp. 83-84. James Muntingh gradually left teaching. See Van Stigt, Volume 3, pp. 109-110. Muntingh started writing his memoirs in **De Gereformeerde Amerikaan** [The Reformed American] in 1904. The second installment indicated in a footnote that he had died at a great age, before writing about his school experiences.

32. J. C. Lobbes, "Scholte's Footprints in Pella," unpublished paper, no date, p. 6; and Van Stigt, **Volume 2**, p. 87. Less prominent centres of Dutch settlement were in the Sheboygan, Wisconsin, and Chicago areas. One writer reported that the language problem plagued the South Holland settlement near Chicago for almost ninety years, even though instruction in the first school in 1854 was in English (Richard A. Cook, **A History of South Holland, Illinois** (South Holland: South Holland Trust and Savings Bank, 1966, p. 53). In Roseland, Illinois, a private school was organized

in 1849 by a Peter De Jong, but it soon closed due to financial problems (Simon Dekker papers, Heritage Hall Archives, "History of Roseland and Vicinity," unpublished manuscript, p. 61).

33. Lucas, **Netherlanders in America**, p. 605, and Cole, p. 66.

34. Lucas, **Netherlanders in America**, p. 579.

35. The quote is taken from a May 8, 1856 letter by John Van Vleck, one of the early teachers at the academy, reproduced in an article in the **Christian Intelligencer** found in the Henry Beets scrapbook in Heritage Hall Archives.

36. Lucas, **Netherlanders in America**, p. 601; Stob, pp. 46-54. See also **Classis Holland Minutes**, Article 16, April 11, 1855 and Article 13, Dec. 17, 1856. There also was a parochial school in Grand Haven at this time about which little is known (Van Stigt, Volume 3, p. 108). The Henry Beets scrapbook in Heritage Hall Archives contains several articles from **The Christian Intelligencer** and **De Grondwet** relating to Van Raalte's parochial school. For the Pella developments, see Van Stigt, Volume 3, p. 130; Van Hinte, Volume 1, p. 419; and Vander Zee, p. 266.

37. Hyma, "The Origins of Our Christian Schools," p. 9. This article is based on Hyma's more extensive work, **Dr. A. C. Van Raalte and His Dutch Settlements** (Grand Rapids, Michigan: Eerdmans, 1947).

38. Ryskamp, p. 230; Stob, pp. 71-72; **De Wachter**, Jan. 21, 1875; **The Banner**, May 11, 1911; Stob, pp. 72-73; and Richard Postma, "The Christian School Movement in Michigan," NUCS **Directory 1923-24**, p. 83. Most public school teachers at this time, of course, also had only a few years of education beyond grade school.

39. Postma, pp. 83-85; Z. Z. Lydens, ed., **The Story of Grand Rapids** (Grand Rapids: Kriegel Publishing, 1966), pp. 498-99; Henry Beets, **De Christelijke Gereformeerde Kerk in Noord America: Zestig jaren van strijd en zegen** [The Christian Reformed Church in North America: Sixty years of strife and blessing] (Grand Rapids: Grand Rapids Printing Company, 1918), pp. 413-15; T. Van der Hoek to his relatives, Sept. 5, 1876 (Heritage Hall Archives); and Dekker, p. 64.

40. R. T. Kuiper, **Een tijdwoord betrekkelijk de kerkelijke toestanden in Noord Amerika** [A timely word concerning the church circumstances in North America] (Wildervank: Van Halteren, 1882), pp. 46-47.

41. See **Jaarboekje van de Hollandsche Christelijke Gereformeerde Kerk in Noord Amerika** [Yearbook of the Netherlands Christian Reformed Church in North America], 1886, 1887, 1888, 1889, 1890, 1891. The figures given likely are incomplete. The yearbook enrollment

figures for 1885-86 to 1890-91 respectively are 471, 570, 819, 1065, 1077, and 1482 pupils. However, the Christian Reformed Church's **Centennial Facts and Background** reports 400, 550, 909, 1390, 1217, and 1562 pupils for these years. With no source given for the latter, I was unable to reconcile the differing statistics.

42. B. J. Bennink, "History of the Christian Schools," mimeographed paper, 1939, 4 pages.

43. **Minutes** of the Church Council of the First True Dutch Reformed Church, November 10, 1873, Article 5. Stob in his thesis expands on this incident, showing how the church elders faced frequent difficulties in obtaining adequate teachers (pp. 75ff.).

44. T. Van den Hoek (South Holland, Illinois) to his relatives, Sept. 5, 1876; W. H. Van Leeuwen in **De Wachter**, November 18, 1880; **Christian School Magazine**, December 1928, pp. 609-10; Postma, p. 86; H. J. Kuiper, "Something About Our Church and Our Schools," **The Banner**, Aug. 15, 1947, p. 944; Lydens, p. 499. For a public school comparison, see William R. Stephens and William Van Til, **Education in American Life** (Boston: Houghton Mifflin, 1972), pp. 94-100.

45. D. J. Van der Werp, **De Wachter**, May 6, 1870; W. H. Van Leeuwen, **De Wachter**, Nov. 18, 1880. As former teachers in early Seceder schools in the Netherlands, both continued to give leadership in the development of Christian schools in the U.S.A. In the South Holland school in 1876 one boy reported in a letter to his grandparents that he read the Bible twice a day in school, and that then the "old pious man master Jansen" would talk with them about it (Jan B. Van Den Hoek, Dec. 4, 1876, Heritage Hall Archives).

46. G. E. Boer, "Hollandsch Onderwijs" [Dutch education], **De Wachter**, Sept. 16, 1875; W. D. Ammermann, **De Wachter**, April 13, 1876, pp. 2-3; Lydens, p. 499; J. C. Lobbes, "Our Christian Schools, Then and Now," **The Banner**, Aug. 23, 1935; Stob, p. 74; R. T. Kuiper, pp. 77-78. **The General Regulations of the Holland Christian Reformed Church in America** (1881, p. 24) stated the desirability of both English and Dutch instruction in Christian schools.

47. Beets, **De Christelijke Gereformeerde Kerk**, p. 414. See also footnote 12.

48. Henry Beets, **The Christian Reformed Church** (Grand Rapids: The Christian Reformed Church, 1946), p. 118; Kuiper, p. 103; W. H. Van Leeuwen, **De Wachter**, November 18, 1880.

49. R. Van Mill, **Leesboek van scholen en huisgezinnen**, p. 3. The

edition I had available was printed in Holland, Michigan by J. Binnekant in 1869.

50. T. Van den Hoek in the South Holland, Chicago area to his Dutch relatives, September 5, 1876 (Heritage Hall Archives).

51. Henry Ryskamp, "The History of Calvin College and Seminary," unpublished manuscript, no date, Chapter III, not paginated. Though not published, John J. Timmersmen acknowledged this as one of his main sources for his history of Calvin College and Seminary, **Promises to Keep** (Grand Rapids, Michigan: Eerdmans, 1975).

52. **Acts of Synod of the Christian Reformed Church 1857-1880**, June 3, 1874, Article 10 and June 2, 1875, Article 4.

53. J. B. Hoekstra, **De Wachter**, Nov. 6 and 23, 1882. See also Stob, pp. 80-88.

54. D. J. Van der Werp, **De Wachter**, May 20, 1870; W. H. Van Leeuwen, **De Wachter**, Nov. 18, 1880; and Dekker, p. 66.

55. **De Wachter**, Feb. 4, March 18, May 20, June 3, and June 17, 1885.

56. This poem originally appeared in the **Yearbook of the Holland Christian Reformed Church in North America for the year 1884**, and was reprinted in W. Lagerwey, **Neen Nederland, 'k vergeet U niet** [No, Netherlands, I won't forget you] (Baarn: Bosch en Keuning, 1982), pp. 85-86. The original word for "good" in the third line is "heil" which has the double meaning of good and welfare as well as of salvation.

The Baxter Street, Grand Rapids, Christian School staff,
1890-95. The solitary male was J. Veltkamp, the first
of the Dutch-trained principals to arrive in the U.S.
in 1885.

4 Casting Dutch Calvinist Schools into an American Mold (1890-1920)

The New Wave of Dutch Immigration

The period 1890-1920 saw many changes in America's Calvinist Christian schools. Not only did their number increase rapidly with new immigration, but principals trained in Dutch Christian normal schools assumed the reins of leadership. These dozen or so men, arriving in America between 1885 and 1900, designed and fashioned the developing Christian school movement.[1] They saw the schools as more than a handmaiden to the church and its doctrinal and linguistic concerns. Also, they were influenced by the outstanding Dutch religious, educational and political leader of the times, Abraham Kuyper, who encouraged them to become involved in American society. They wanted the schools to use English instruction and become superior American institutions with a distinctively Christian pedagogy and curriculum. They developed curriculum materials, established support organizations, and provided some initial teacher training programs. In their attempts to make the schools "American" Christian schools, they were helped by the political and social milieu of World War I, when throughout the United States the canter towards Americanization became a gallop.

Timothy L. Smith has shown how three interlocking motives among immigrants propelled them towards growing concern for schooling.[2] These three also applied to the Dutch immigrants arriving in the United States between 1880 and World War I. First was the economic motive, the desire to earn a better living. Education was to help that pursuit. Second, the structure of family and communal life had to fit their new existence while it preserved their beliefs and values. For many Dutch Orthodox Calvinist immigrants, this called for non-public Christian schools that would transmit the religious traditions and ideals and enable youngsters to function in American society. Third, there was a

TABLE I

CHRISTIAN REFORMED CHURCH MEMBERSHIP, DUTCH IMMIGRATION INTO THE U.S.A.,

AND CHRISTIAN SCHOOL ENROLLMENT, 1880-1920

Year	C.R.C. Membership	Increase in C.R.C. Membership	Increase as Percent of Membership at Start of Decade	Dutch Aliens Admitted to U.S.A.	Number of Christian Schools	Estimated Christian School Enrollment	Estimated Percent of C.R.C. School Children Attending Christian Schools
1881	12 001				6	-	-
1881-90		24 048	200	52 715			
1890	36 049				15	1 482	21
1890-00		17 745	49	29 349			
1900	53 794				17	2 750	29
1900-10		24 633	46	42 463			
1910	78 427				35	6 380	40
1910-20		16 416	21	46 065			
1920	94 843				80	10 980	52

quest for an identity that would fulfill a sense of duty to their homeland people while fostering their new allegiance to America. Although these immigrants were quick to become American citizens, they believed they could make a unique contribution as Dutch Calvinists to American society. Particularly in the heterogeneous cities, it was the "Holland" Christian schools that would nurse a patriotism both to Dutch Calvinism and, increasingly, to the American Dream.

The Christian Reformed Church quadrupled its membership between 1881 and 1900 (Table I),[3] largely as a result of immigration. Most orthodox Calvinist immigrants joined the Christian Reformed Church, since it had close theological ties with the Netherlands and maintained the Dutch language and patterns of worship. In it, the new immigrants felt they could maintain their identity.[4]

Though coming from a wider geographical spectrum than the original members, the new immigrants socially and economically still represented the working classes. Their emigration had been a function of modernization, and modernization also affected their view of reality and their values.[5] Social and technological changes resulted in these settlers becoming increasingly nationalistic and materialistic and interacting much more with the rest of American society than the original settlers of the 1840s and 1850s. Consequently, even though these farmers and labourers had supported Christian schools in the Netherlands, not all saw a need for them in the U.S. Some considered their rural public schools to be virtual Christian ones, while others felt the money should be spent on more useful ways to expand "God's Kingdom." Still others were influenced by politicians of Dutch stock who held that Christian schools were "un-American." In some communities hostility between the pro- and anti- camps did not abate until the 1920s.[6]

Yet during this period the church and school leaders managed to convince a majority of the church membership to support the schools, partly because the forces of modernization had also led to the increased secularization of society, particularly in urban centres. In 1914 the church's synod still complained:

> How many Christian Reformed parents don't send their children to the public school. . . . there are still broad multitudes in our circles who do not have sufficient understanding of positive Christian elementary education and even less of secondary and higher education.[7]

Nevertheless, with church leaders strongly advocating the schools and many immigrants wanting to preserve Dutch Calvinist beliefs and values, the percentage of Christian Reformed school children attending the schools grew slowly but steadily from one-fifth in 1890 to more than half by 1920.[8] Because by then the majority of elementary school graduates—both in non-public and in public schools—continued their education, five Christian high schools had also been started.[9]

The foremost leader of this period was B. J. Bennink, the son of a Seceder minister in the poor, rural north-eastern corner of the Netherlands. In 1886 the twenty-two-year-old Bennink joined a number of his villagers emigrating to the United States, immediately becoming principal of a Muskegon, Michigan, Christian school, and subsequently being principal of six other Christian schools until his retirement in 1929. As indefatigable principal, promoter, writer and organizer, he unquestionably was the leader of the Christian school movement for many years. His whirlwind pace of activities included editing Christian school journals, writing books, organizing school and teacher organizations, and giving teacher training courses. Although Bennink sometimes was despondent about his work paying off, the Christian school community admired his persistent efforts to raise educational standards and his pleas and labours for greater religious distinctiveness in the curriculum.[10]

On the one hand, then, the Christian schools during this period were shaped by the religious and educational background of Bennink and his Dutch-trained colleagues. On the other hand, the forces that molded immigrant life in the U.S. at this time provided the framework within which these men had to work. Public commitment of the American people to "Christian" moral standards was high. The rapid transition of America from an agrarian society to a modern urban one was accompanied by efforts of the "progressive movement" to encourage economic individualism, political democracy, and morality and civic purity. Most Americans still believed that Christianity and democracy were "reciprocating cylinders in the engine of progress."[11] Despite some misgivings about both Arminian fundamentalism and liberal social gospel beliefs, the Christian veneer of American society made it easier for Dutch Calvinists to accept America as their adopted land of freedom and progress, i.e., to "Americanize."

By 1920, the year that the National Union of Christian Schools was founded in Chicago, the schools and their communities were well along the road of Americanization. The Dutch language had become used much less in churches and schools. Key leadership roles in the schools were being taken over by a new, American-trained generation. American patriotism was firmly established. This chapter discusses how the movement adapted to its American context, focusing on events and issues that helped to define the direction and nature of education in the schools from 1890 to 1920. The next chapter deals more specifically with program development and implementation during this period.

Dutch Christian School Development
from 1850 to 1890 that Influenced
B. J. Bennink and His Colleagues

J. J. L. van der Brugghen's 1857 Dutch School Act gave all non-public schools the right to exist. This stipulation, the continuing secularization of the public schools, and, especially, the eventual government subsidies for non-public schools increased the percentage of Dutch elementary pupils in non-public schools from twenty-one in 1860 to seventy-three in 1950. Soon after the passing of the 1857 Act, two organizations of Christian schools were founded. Groen van Prinsterer had hesitantly concluded that his dream of government-controlled schools split according to religious persuasion was no longer feasible, and he became leader of the Association of Christian National School Education, founded in 1860. Eight years later, fearing a lack of orthodoxy, the rival Association of Reformed School Education was begun, mainly by the more conservative Seceders. Bennink and most of his teacher colleagues who emigrated to America came from geographical areas where the latter organization had strong representation. Both organizations raised funds to subsidize poor schools, aided the training of teachers, inspected member schools, spread pedagogical literature, and promised financial support for efforts to publish Christian pedagogical books.[12]

In 1878 the budding leader Abraham Kuyper forged an alliance of the two existing Christian school organizations by establishing The Union: "A School with the Bible." This organization of individuals lent political, moral, educational, and financial support to both associations of Christian schools.[13] Kuyper used the Union to launch the Dutch **Schoolstrijd** [School Struggle], setting about to gain government grants for non-public schools. When in 1889 the schools began to receive a tax subsidy for one-third of their costs, a **Schoolraad** [School Advisory Council], consisting of delegates of the two Christian school associations, the Union, and Christian school teachers' associations, was set up to advise the Christian schools about matters such as government relations, school administration and programs.[14] Both the structure and functions of these organizations became models for Bennink and his colleagues in organizing Christian schools in America.

The Dutch Christian school leaders continued, like Van der Brugghen, to discuss methodological and curricular issues. They published a list of recommended textbooks. The "Union" and the Advisory Council discussed the development of a pedagogical handbook, a course of study and literature anthologies. However, that these came about only long after Bennink's emigration was indicative of a lack of consensus about the curriculum and instruction in Christian schools. In 1890 a former "Union" president complained about those who, "shrugging their shoulders," asked, "What can the Bible offer us with respect to education?"[15]

Another writer concluded that the schools were schools with the Bible but not rooted in the Bible. True, Biblical studies was the first subject each morning, a few readers promoting a Christian view of life were used, and here and there the "hand of God" was recognized. But these were "add-ons"; no comprehensive Christian theory to guide pedagogy and curriculum existed. The author accused the schools of adding Christian details and Bible texts to Enlightenment-influenced courses.[16]

Debates at this time, however, centered much less on pedagogy and curriculum than on the doctrinal basis of the constitutions of the schools, the extent of doctrinal instruction, and organizational and financial arrangements. The politically successful **Schoolstrijd** seemed to sap all energy; at least, it was accompanied by a dearth of pedagogical and curricular insights and directions until the turn of the century. Although leaders **believed** that the whole program of the Christian schools could and should be unique, after Van der Brugghen's initial probes almost no writings indicated that such uniqueness might be possible.

Bennink's teacher training took place within this context. After private tutoring by a Christian school principal, he entered the Christian Normal School in Leeuwarden in the northern part of the Netherlands. He was instructed in school subjects that included geography, national history, nature study, and singing, but likely spent little time in physical education, drawing, and agriculture since those subjects were compulsory only for school pupils going beyond the first six years. He was given a thorough grounding in the educational ideas of European educators such as Pestalozzi, Herbart, and Froebel. While most of his training was geared to "the direction of the government final examinations," Bennink also took the "after-examinations" of one of the Christian school associations, likely the ones in the "direction subjects" (pedagogy; Biblical history, geography and archeology; and national history) given by the Association of Reformed School Education.[17]

INTO AN AMERICAN MOLD (1890-1920)

Thus Bennink and his colleagues brought to North America a sound professional training and an awareness of European educational thought. They had some organizational models to help them unite the American Christian schools into a movement. They were able to teach a Calvinistic interpretation of Biblical studies and Dutch history, and were aware of two available types of Christian readers, rooted in either the **Réveil** or in the Seceder tradition—both of which inculcated a Christian lifestyle and morality, though by differing modes and emphases. Besides the three R's, they also believed history and geography to be important, while the fine arts and physical education were frills. However, they had been given little insight into what a Christian pedagogy might entail or how a distinctive Christian curriculum might be structured.

The Thinking of Abraham Kuyper

More than anyone else in modern times, Abraham Kuyper (1837-1920) put his stamp on Dutch Calvinism, including its North American branch. Preacher and theologian, philosopher and politician, newspaper writer and editor: as such, Kuyper was the dominant and unrivalled thinker, organizer and communicator in Dutch society from about 1880 to early in the new century. He founded the Free [Christian] University of Amsterdam in 1880, and led a second movement out of the national state church in 1886, later merging it with the Seceder churches. As leader of the Anti-Revolutionary political party he became Dutch Prime Minister in 1901. He fought for financial equality of non-public schools, and championed and introduced progressive labour and social welfare legislation. Most of all, he revitalized orthodox Dutch Calvinism and molded it into a force that dominated Dutch society and culture for many years though it never included more than about ten per cent of the Dutch population.[18]

Kuyper's overriding concern was that "in the total expanse of human life there is not a single square inch of which Christ, who alone is sovereign, does not declare, 'That is mine.' " Serving Christ was all-encompassing, and no division could be made between the sacred and the secular. Life was a unity, and the Kingship of Christ applied everywhere and at all times. Activities as disparate as cleaning house and setting up a political party party were all to be done in service to God.[19] This meant, Kuyper continued, that children of Christian parents must learn to see Christ not only as their personal Saviour, but as their King who has a great deal to say about affairs in society. Schools for such children, therefore, should not be standard ones with

77

some religion added as a bonus but, rather, "both the spiritual and the civic instruction shall form one unity. Those who are educated there shall find themselves bound to the spirit and word of the Gospel also in societal concerns." In this way the fruits of the Christian school eventually would result in the Kingship of Christ showing to full advantage, and life in society would be enhanced for all.[20]

Within this overall context, two themes in Kuyper's thinking especially affected North American Christian schools. The first were his notions of antithesis and common grace. Kuyper insisted on an antithesis between Christian and non-Christian thought. Christians were to seek their own understanding of God and his world based on God's revelation in the Bible and in nature. No knowledge was value-free and social structures served an ideology—an unpopular notion at the time. This antithesis Kuyper balanced with a belief in God's common grace to all human beings. Such grace meant that truth and benefit was to be found in the work of non-Christians. Kuyper's conception of the antithesis led to a religious pluralism in Dutch society by which Calvinists, Catholics, liberal Protestants, and socialists each set up, for example, their own political parties, labour unions, and media institutions. On the other hand, his doctrine of common grace held that cooperative efforts such as political coalitions could promote the glory of God.[21]

For Kuyper, Christians were "not only to sow the good seed of the gospel but to enrich its life through cultural contributions."[22] St. Paul's "mind of Christ" was not only to lead people to Christianity but it was also to be brought to bear on all areas of human endeavour. In trying to do so, however, Christian school supporters both in the Netherlands and in North America have often had difficulty keeping the conceptions of the antithesis and of common grace in balance. Tipping the balance towards the antithesis resulted in an avoidance of society and "worldly pursuits," a position close to the individualistic moralism of American fundamentalism. Common grace, on the other hand, bestowed God's blessing to persons without necessarily "saving" them. Its forceful emphasis easily produced social gospel thinking. Therefore, the two conceptions were difficult to harmonize.[23] Recurring controversies about the choice of reading books, for instance, show that Christian schools have often found the task of resolving the implications of Kuyper's two basic conceptions a troublesome one.

Kuyper's second theme that guided his thought and action was "sphere sovereignty," i.e., that each sphere of life (church, state, family, school, industry, etc.) had its own area of responsibility derived directly from God. Neither the churches nor the government, as "spheres" distinct from education, should operate schools. Like Van der Brugghen, Kuyper proposed independent organizations to direct Christian schools, limiting the role of the state in education to protecting the interest of the nation as a whole and providing education for children who otherwise would not get it. As a result of Kuyper's thinking, American Calvinist Christian schools moved from church to association control while accepting government regulations with respect to teacher certification and educational standards.[24]

Early in his career Kuyper did not yet clearly expound either of these two themes. In 1875 he said that with its required Bible reading "the American public school has what we miss and **is a school with the Bible.**" He also quoted laws in various parts of the world (e.g., Upper Canada's 1843 and 1850 School Acts) to show that many government schools were permeated with Christian principles.[25] Here he still believed that government schools, perhaps split along confessional lines, could serve society well. Later, however, he no longer strove for the Christianization of the public school. By the time he visited the United States in 1898 he was convinced that the government should not be involved directly in schooling, and that association-controlled Christian schools were a necessity also in America.[26]

Abraham Kuyper's Influence on American Christian Schools

Kuyper's most visible influence on Christian schools in the United States was that between 1891 and 1911 all but one changed from being church schools to ones operated by independent associations of parents. B. J. Bennink, using Kuyper's reasoning, argued that parents had the "undeniable right to educate their own children," and should therefore operate the schools and determine the quality and quantity of instruction.[27] Associations were established to govern the schools and set their policies, as is still the case for almost all CSI schools today.

What such parental control meant in practice was often not all that clear. In 1914 the chairman of Michigan's Advisory Council of Christian schools, Louis Berkhof, worried that parents tried to regulate teachers directly, and pointed out that teachers were accountable to the board of the school, not to individual parents. Also, in practice close contact and "harmonized cooperation" between the schools and the Christian Reformed Church continued. Often, a school's constitution stipulated that its education was to be in agreement with the church's creeds, and the minister would serve on the school board. Advertisements for teachers specified that applicants should be members of the Christian Reformed Church. A committee of a regional council of congregations in 1907 recommended "better supervision [by church councils] of existing Christian schools" since church elders also were "shepherds of the children." The schools had become separate institutions, but not independent ones.[28]

Some leaders advanced the notion of the "sphere sovereignty" of the schools because they feared that continued church control meant that the schools would focus on narrow theological concerns and not move beyond a Christian Reformed clientele.[29] Perhaps to appease the traditionalists opposed to the separation of church and school, Bennink wrote that

> education does not belong to the State (it's too good for that), but it doesn't belong to the Church either (it's not good enough for that). It belongs to the parents! That is natural, that is American, that is Reformed.[30]

Bennink's comment also indicates, however, that he did not understand Kuyper's sphere sovereignty principle completely. He created a hierarchy of societal institutions, while Kuyper's point was that these institutions coexisted without one being higher than another. This was one of the first indications that Bennink's thinking, despite his enthusiasm for Kuyper, might be on a diverging path.

In 1898 Kuyper spent several months in the United States in order to give a series of Stone Foundation lectures at Princeton Theological Seminary and to receive an honourary doctorate from Princeton University. On this trip, Kuyper was enthusiastically received among Michigan's Dutch immigrants, even though he felt called to enjoin them to become real Americans and learn English as well as any Americans. Their task, Kuyper added, was to apply Calvinistic principles to the already powerful and morally sensitive New World. Kuyper's visit enhanced the belief of his American followers that the Dutch people, including those that had emigrated to the United States, would be in the vanguard of making the future a brighter one through the application of Calvinistic principles to political, social, and economic life and to the world of scholarship and the arts.[31]

But Kuyper's influence on the programs of the schools was limited. As Bennink pointed out, many supporters were caught up in the popularity of the man Kuyper without understanding the principles he set forth.[32] Those who understood Kuyper's call for cultural involvement did accelerate the Americanization process, though natural acculturation and feelings aroused by World War I played roles at least as important. One scholar has contended that Kuyper's thinking caused

Christian schools to be "organized according to the most progressive ideas" and "provided with the best instruction in accordance with the teachings of the Christian faith as set forth in the Reformed Confession."[33] However, men like Bennink who gave educational vigor to the schools did so mainly because of their Dutch professional training and their understanding of current educational thought and practice, not because of a well-developed Kuyperian theory of instruction. At the same time, Kuyper's positive attitude towards the world of scholarship and Christian involvement in the arts and sciences was a major positive shift from the much narrower attitudes of the Seceders, broadening the scope of education for a few of the movement's leaders around the turn of the century.

Kuyper's view of Christianity and culture had great potential impact on the Dutch Calvinist community and its Christian schools. H. Richard Niebuhr has delineated five different approaches that Christians have taken vis-à-vis culture.[34] Like Augustine and Calvin, Kuyper took the view that Christ, as King of all of life, is the transformer of culture in the sense that He redirects, reinvigorates, and regenerates a culture marred by personal and social sin. Only later in his life did Kuyper work out how he believed humans could develop and apply this in and through their vocations and societal structures. Bennink and his colleagues were more influenced by the young Kuyper who had stressed basic principles and spent much of his efforts in building organizational structures. The next chapter shows that the view of Christ as the transformer of culture by and large did not find its way into the Christian school curriculum. Later chapters will show how Kuyper's followers emigrating to Canada after World War II clashed with their American counterparts about curriculum issues.

What Kuyper did help to instill in the Christian school movement was a faith that God guided the destiny of those holding onto and applying Calvinistic principles to areas such as education. The resulting commitment gave supporters the determination to continue to operate Christian schools even when the linguistic reasons became unimportant.

Towards Professionalization and Organization

When the Dutch-trained principals arrived in the 1880s and 1890s, conditions in existing Christian schools were primitive. Classrooms might be church basements with sandy floors and black partitions that doubled as blackboards. Class enrollments were as high as seventy. In one case 120 pupils were crowded into a room built for eighty-five, with one teacher and an assistant. The smaller schools were still ungraded, and sometimes subjects other than Biblical studies were "not taught too thoroughly." Schools constantly faced shortages of money and books, and therefore reading material sometimes was anything that came to hand: an old reader, a book of sermons, or pieces of Scripture "with the binding in tatters, and the print dim, and the paper brown." Around 1900 most schools gave only two or three weeks of summer vacation, partly because additional summer enrollment of public school children kept the schools afloat financially.[35]

Understandably, some church members criticized the schools. In particular, they claimed, pupils were unruly and poorly disciplined, and graduates did "not excel in wisdom or exemplary living." However, supporters replied that the pupils' rowdiness reflected conditions within the families or bad environments, and that the schools did not exist long enough for valid judgments to be made. Further, Christian school graduates did well in county examinations. What clinched the argument was that support for Christian schools was not to depend on "our insight into the results, but on the will of God." And with the battle being the Lord's, some day it would be "generally conceded that these institutions of elementary learning are the best educational agents for all of the future citizens of our republic."[36]

But even Bennink often had difficulty envisioning such a prospect. Although he had introduced English instruction and more modern approaches in his school, the parents did not support him, and for several years, he was depressed about the "bleak, half-desolate field of Christian education." He believed, nevertheless, that God had called him to continue his work in Christian schools, even if he had to row "against certain wind and current." In 1904 he became principal of the Grandville Avenue Christian School in Grand Rapids, which had just completed an imposing eight-room structure. Here, as in many of the larger schools, conditions were starting to improve: Bennink's appointment as the first Christian school supervising principal a few years later enabled him to visit each classroom monthly and give leadership to a staff with little training and experience and even less grasp of what a Christian approach to education might entail.[37]

The Holland Christian School minutes show how Bennink gave such leadership when he was principal there from 1913 to 1920. Bennink, like other principals, prepared detailed course outlines for the various subject areas at each grade level. He required all teachers to hand in their plans and daily programs, which were discussed by the school board. Teachers who did not obtain a Michigan certificate were not re-appointed. Bennink provided the school with good textbooks and adequate reference works. He began an "opportunity room" for twenty-four mentally handicapped children, continued one of the first kindergartens in Christian schools, and started the first two high school grades. He arranged for an instructor to give his staff a course in Biblical history, pedagogy, and Reformed doctrines. Both he himself and invited speakers acquainted parents with the rationale and practice of Christian education.[38]

In the larger centres, the boards were also becoming more professional and knowledgeable about the operation of the schools. They often assigned two board members to visit the school on a monthly basis. At first, some teachers objected to such supervision; one stated quite openly that these matters "would surpass the comprehension of the committee." But boards continued to monitor the educational programs of the schools. In 1901, for example, the Baxter Street School board reported improved progress in first grade reading and instructed a small committee to develop a program of Biblical studies for all levels. A decade later the Holland board instructed its education committee to meet with the staff every three months to review the curriculum and make appropriate changes. The board also dealt with controversies about the choice of hymns and a presentation on sex education. One board passed written regulations that its principal was to compose a detailed course of study for all the grades and a daily program for all the rooms, with teachers' planbooks to be investigated by the principal. Other boards requested such courses of study to be discussed by the education committee and the board. Many boards were determined that proper curriculum planning took place and that they had a hand in it.[39]

Bennink also tried to improve teacher qualifications in the schools. The male teachers from the Netherlands had made teaching a career and obtained proper credentials, sometimes including degrees from U.S. universities. Few American-born men, on the other hand, took "upon their shoulders the great, the noble work of education." Other than the principals almost all teachers were women who often had "hardly outgrown their children's shoes" and lent incompetency and instability to the movement. Many taught with a third grade certificate, which one Calvin College instructor called "the shabbiest of all shabby titles to teach." In order that teachers would know how to apply Calvinistic principles in education, Bennink proposed that all Christian school teachers should be forced to take a "stiff examination" in Reformed doctrine, Biblical history, and Christian pedagogy. While some exams were set up, Bennink realized that this was but a start. What was needed was a Christian normal school with an attached model school. From 1918 to 1920 the Michigan Alliance of which Bennink was secretary backed an independent effort to operate a normal school, but lack of funds and small enrollments torpedoed the program.[40]

Throughout this period attempts to get the schools to cooperate in joint ventures often faltered. Already in 1892, Bennink had been involved in the first effort to organize the schools into a more united movement, becoming secretary of the first regional association, the Society for Christian Education on a Reformed Basis. Like the Dutch "Union," the association, consisting mainly of individuals interested in promoting Christian education, hoped to convince "citizens" of the necessity of association-controlled Christian schooling, to design an "after-examination" for teachers, to establish a Christian normal school, to provide "English textbooks in a Reformed spirit," and to give financial help to needy schools. But the association, not a federation of schools, was forced to give leadership by persuasion rather than by decision and never flourished. Its attempts to obtain tax refunds for those sending children to Christian schools were unsuccessful, and the corporation set up to underwrite the publication of Christian textbooks had to be dissolved. Interest dwindled, and in 1899 the association disbanded.[41]

Instead, the members decided to hold a meeting of school delegates twice a year. Using the Dutch model once again, a committee of five was appointed as **Schoolraad** [Advisory Council] and executive board. Bennink, a member of the Council, complained about the stubborn independence of the schools. True, the Advisory Council accomplished little, to a large extent because "resolutions passed at one [delegate] meeting were often rescinded at a following." However, the meetings provided a useful forum that caused boards to discuss teacher qualifications, the need for publishing English readers, and the development of a common program of instruction. These meetings prepared the ground for the establishment of more formal organizations of Christian schools, the four regional alliances. The first and largest of these was the Michigan Alliance of Christian Schools, organized in 1911, under whose auspices Bennink organized several two-day Christian Teachers' Institutes (likely attended by 75-125 teachers), wrote the first published **Course of Study** for Christian schools, and compiled the first directory of American Christian schools in 1918.[42]

Thus, between 1890 and 1920, Bennink and his Dutch-trained colleagues gave leadership that gradually strengthened the rapidly increasing number of schools, with respect to both their individual programs and mutual cooperation. Especially the larger schools were being run more professionally by both staffs and boards. The training of teachers, though still often inadequate, was improving. Most communities of any size had begun a school and the vociferous opposition of the 1890s had disappeared. The Dutch model of joint cooperation had led to regional alliances more suited for the American situation. When, in 1920, the National Union of Christian Schools was founded, indigenous leadership had matured to the point where it could carry forward the movement, and the organizational framework for joint action, also in the area of curriculum, was in place. As the next section will show, the schools were also becoming more Americanized in outlook and curriculum. A discussion of this transformation will give some indication as to whether the schools were able to—or even wanted to—implement a Kuyperian vision in the school. That, in turn, will lead to a discussion in the next chapter whether the schools had laid a sufficiently strong philosophic, pedagogic, and curricular foundation to be able to implement the lofty visions promulgated in their statements of aims and principles.

In 1916 Bennink could write: "We're winning! Thirty years ago this writer came to the United States and—found nothing. Nothing? No, nothing." But now, he continued, although there was still a lack of qualified personnel and not enough was known about practical pedagogy, the schools had become a viable movement in the Christian Reformed community.[43]

The Americanization of the Schools: Changing from Dutch to English

If religion is "a system of beliefs about the nature of the force(s) ultimately shaping a man's destiny, and the practices associated therewith, shared by the members of a group," then Harry S. Stout's argument that in America religion and ethnicity are inextricably intertwined and sometimes identical is a strong one. Such "ethno-religious faith," as Stout called it, "constitutes a basic, and often underestimated, force in American history." Stout identified three successive stages of development for ethno-religious faith: (1) the immigrant ethnic group being centred around an amalgam of ecclesiastical and national origins, (2) the immigrant unit integrating into a broad religious faith (e.g., white Protestantism), and (3) the broader grouping identifying as Americans, with such identification orienting itself around "The American Way of Life," i.e., around an optimistic faith in pragmatism, self-initiative, materialism, progress through American technology, and nationalism.[44]

Many Orthodox Calvinist Dutch-Americans have moved from Stout's first phase to the third without giving up their denominational

85

separatist stance. Christian Reformed Church members are proud of their Calvinist heritage and doctrines. Yet, at the same time, many have embraced "The American Way of Life." The move of the Christian schools towards English instruction paralleled the endorsement by many supporters of the white, middle class, American civil religion.[45] However, most Christian Reformed members did not fit Stout's second stage in that they maintained strict Calvinist doctrines and an emphasis on individual Christian faith.

Abraham Kuyper in the mid-1890s had already stimulated the Dutch settlers to move out of Stout's first stage. In his own Dutch weekly, also read in the U.S., he commented on a debate between Michigan state legislator G. J. Diekema and F. Kniphuizen. Diekema upheld the Christian character of the public school and argued that true patriotism could be taught only there. Kniphuizen replied that Michigan's laws made it impossible for public schools to be distinctively Christian, and that Americanization should not mean becoming an indistinguishable part of the mainstream of American society.[46] Kuyper reflected that the Dutch colonists must become Americans while maintaining and extending their Calvinistic influence on the life of the nation.[47] The foremost school leaders accepted this "melting pot" conception. The schools and their supporters were to Americanize while, with true American missionary zeal, transforming the American way of life: "God has given the Dutch to America . . . What for? That the Dutch might be the leaven and salt of a greater people."[48] American Calvinists were to fulfill their mission as Calvinists and as Americans in church, state and society. That being both a true American and a true Kuyperian might at times conflict was not considered, not even by Kuyper himself. America, with all its faults, was basically considered to be a Christian nation.

Principal Bennink, likewise calling for genuinely American Christian schools, held that the self-preservation of Dutch language and ethnicity would frustrate the unfolding of Calvinistic principles. In 1903 the Reverend J. Groen wrote that if the schools were to have a future as independent, Christian ones, then "the English language must be one of the most important subjects." But the "powerful" Dutch language was to keep alive "a certain pride of disposition and rightness in the expression of thought," and to promote true Dutch character. The Dutch language provided for a "natural development" of "old-Dutch simplicity, order, thrift and loyalty as well as the certitude of Reformed principles, institutions, and customs." The intertwining of religious faith, strength of character and a knowledge of Dutch caused the changeover from Dutch to English to be a lengthy and controversial one.[49]

INTO AN AMERICAN MOLD (1890-1920)

For a long time, Dutch was considered the superior language for teaching religious matters. The school in Kellogsville near Grand Rapids in the mid-1880s taught Biblical studies and reading in Dutch; most other subjects in English. When in 1892 the Baxter Street Christian School in Grand Rapids began an English school in the same building as its Dutch one, children were not accepted in the English school until they were nine years old in order to ensure proper religious tutelage. Ten years later the supporting church congregation almost unanimously accepted a plan whereby all children would receive instruction in English. However, the youngest room would continue to be in Dutch and a "floating teacher" would teach Dutch one day a week to the other rooms. Even so, the board gave permission to one parent to teach Dutch after school since he felt that the school's arrangements did not permit him to fulfill his religious obligations. A storm of criticism descended on a teacher who in 1911 publicly suggested the teaching of Dutch as a foreign language from grade 4 or 5 and up (rather than teaching religious studies in Dutch). Calvinistic beliefs, to be true to their heritage, were to be cloaked in the Dutch language.[50]

Nevertheless, the changeover, though slow, was inevitable. As time went on, fewer teachers were fluent in Dutch. The Baxter Street board in 1901 felt it necessary to tell its teachers that "it is demanded of them always to speak with appreciation of Dutch," and two board members were instructed to make up a "program of activities for Dutch for every room."[51] However, here, as elsewhere, the settlers became more acclimatized to the rapidly modernizing American society, with their children needing a good knowledge of English as more of them continued their education or entered business or the professions. Accordingly, the amount of Dutch instruction was gradually reduced and eventually discontinued. In 1915 the Advisory Council still overruled Bennink when he prepared a **Course of Study,** and compelled him to write the grades 1 and 2 outlines in Dutch.[52] Bennink did not hide his displeasure. In the published document he spoke of such Dutch instruction causing "interference" in the educational progress of the children, with the third grade students being "hopelessly short." Dutch, Bennink held, should be taught no more than once or twice a week to grades 6, 7, and 8, just enough for pupils to understand and speak it somewhat. In 1918 most schools still taught some Dutch, either part of the time or as a separate subject, and fifteen still taught the first few grades completely in Dutch.[53] Subsequently, however, as acculturation proceeded, its teaching declined and eventually disappeared.

The Americanization of the Schools:
Inculcating Patriotism

While most supporters favoured Americanization by the time World War I began, there was continued fear that the principles of the Calvinist faith would be eroded: "The calm, resolute, thoughtful Dutchman can be Reformed to the marrow of his bone; for that the American is too shifty, too superficial."[54] For some, however, Stout's third phase of enculturation was desired immediately. Already in 1901, a dedication speech at a new Christian school in Chicago challenged the audience to "hoist high the American flag over [the school] as a token of our belief that the Christian school can be, and indeed is, a truly American school."[55] Other voices called for English instruction not so much for extending Calvinistic influence as for the training of children as "enlightened American Citizens. . . . We don't want the Christian at the expense of the social."[56] Classroom prayers were to thank God "for the glorious country God has pleased to give us," and children must be taught "to love Old Glory." It became accepted as self-evident that Christians ought to be patriots, and that Christian schools were in harmony with American ideas.[57] Support for American nationalism steadily gained momentum.

At least one person recognized the inner contradiction between being "truly American" and giving wholehearted support for Calvinist Christian schools. Calvin College's J. G. Van den Bosch in 1907 realized that to many Americans the public school was "more sacred than home and church." Therefore, he predicted, even with the introduction of English, the schools would be viewed as "un-American and by that very token undesirable, perhaps even dangerous to the commonweal."[58] These words proved prophetic. In the 1910s, Christian schools were attacked "by those of our fellow-citizens who considered themselves Americans **par excellence**."[59] During World War I Christian school supporters were faced with a lurking fear of the immigrant. Newspapers accused Christian schools of being unpatriotic and condemned some Christian Reformed ministers for refusing to display the American flag during worship. Several states required instruction in English in all private schools. In Peoria, Iowa, both the Christian Reformed Church and the Christian school were burned towards the end of the war by a group of patriots, partly because they confused Dutch and **Deutsch**.[60] Soon after the war, several amendments were proposed to state constitutions to ban private schools. While defeated in Michigan and eventually ruled illegal by the U.S. Supreme Court, the referenda exacerbated the friction between public and private school supporters.[61]

Nevertheless, the people viewed attacks on the schools as attacks on their faith and gave increasing support to the schools even as the criticism mounted. Hadn't America been founded as a Christian nation and as such wouldn't Christian schools help maintain the U.S. as the superior nation of the world? After all, Christian schools taught children to "obey their government and promote its welfare . . . for God's sake. There is no surer foundation for true patriotism." Further, the schools were "as diligent in the active inculcation of patriotism and loyalty to country and good citizenship generally as are the public schools." The Calvinists' own leaders by this time called attempts to maintain Dutch unpatriotic and un-Calvinistic, and admonished the people to love America more than any other nation.[62] Christian schools were to be even more effective than public schools in inculcating American nationalism.

Curriculum materials for the schools also increasingly promoted loyalty to country. In his pre-World War I **First Lessons in Geography,** Bennink wrote: "I love my country very much . . . the best country of the whole earth . . . best of all the States, Michigan, my Michigan."[63] In the next volume the students were asked to answer "What is patriotism?" and "Why should we love our country?"[64] In 1915 Bennink re-emphasized his acceptance of American patriotism in the penmanship samples of his **Course of Study:**

> Our forefathers purchased liberty with their blood.
> Sail on, O Union, strong and great.
> Whatever makes men good Christians makes them good citizens.
> We join ourselves to no party that does not carry the Flag and
>   keep in step to the music of the Union.

Bennink hoped that these truths would sink "like a gem into the pupil's head and heart, never to be forgotten."

Such patriotism was also taught in history and civics:

> Our young Americans should receive a lofty idea of their great calling as future citizens of our beloved country. . . both for a perfect life on earth under the ideal conditions of our Constitutional provisions, and for entrance into the Kingdom of our Lord and Redeemer.[65]

Thus Bennink closely identified Christianity and American democracy. The authority of the government was granted by God, but in God's providence the American Constitution had established a perfect framework for the development of America as one nation under God. Therefore Christians should also participate fully in American commerce and economic progress. Significantly, Bennink held public school texts for history and civics courses to be "very acceptable."[66]

The only series of Christian school readers developed during this period, Gerhardus Bos' **Excelsior Readers**, also embraced the accelerating march of American patriotism. For example, the **Seventh Grade Reader** contained pieces on The Mayflower and the Pilgrims, Valley Forge, the occupation of Philadelphia by the British, the Gettysburg address, General Sheridan, as well as an expanded version of America: "O land beyond compare, thee I love best!" Henry Ward Beecher's **The American Flag** was printed in full: "How glorious has been its history! How divine its meaning! . . . Let us, then, twine each thread of the glorious tissues of our country's flag about our heartstrings." With an unbridled enthusiasm for the Promise that was the United States, Americanization was victorious, at least in these readers.[67]

But though by the early 1920s the schools had almost completely switched to English and promoted an uncritical loyalty to American patriotism, they were not yet "American" in some ways. In 1923, for example, a convention speaker said that the schools needed "to become" thoroughly American, with their work being conducted in the American spirit and with American methods.[68] Novelist David Cornel De Jong felt that the Christian school he attended in the 1920s aimed "to perpetuate our Dutch religious ways." The justification for Christian schools among most supporters, he claimed, was not to be a positive influence on American culture, but to guard young people against the worldly influence of non-Dutch, non-Calvinist Americans. Yet Dutch-Americans, according to De Jong, were "nearly hell-bent to become American in all material things."[69]

While De Jong may have overstated his case, his comments back Stout's main point. Though remaining Calvinistic in doctrine and morals, the Dutch Calvinists embraced American pragmatism and materialism in their everyday dealings. Adaptation rather than Christian mission became the main focus. Kuyper's antithesis still applied to personal morality but not to the political and economic arena, for America was "God's country." Kuyper's conception of societal pluralism was no longer considered adaptable to American society, except in the maintenance of association-controlled Christian schools. "Good citizenship" had become the American assimilationist brand. With most Dutch immigrants, Americanism had become as much of an ideal as Calvinism.

The Rationale for Christian Schools: Cultural Transformation or Isolation?

At the end of World War I, Christian school leaders argued that since the state must give equal rights to its citizens, "the position that the Bible should have a place in the public school is not tenable." Under the U.S. Constitution, only the Christian school could take into account the religious character of the child, base education on the Bible, and permeate instruction with the spirit of Christianity. Therefore, it was "our sacred duty and right to establish and maintain schools for Christian education" where children might be "fully equipped for the duties of life as Christian members of society and Christian citizens of our country."[70]   On this basis, a number of principles to guide Christian schools were formulated. The key one was the fourth:

IV. We believe that religion is at all times and everywhere an inseparable element of life and therefore of all true education. The service of God must dominate the whole of our life and must therefore form the controlling and unifying element of the education of our children.
- We hold the distinction between general and religious education to be false and contrary to the Word of God.
  - We believe that the arrangement by which a religionless education is provided for in the schools, supplemented by more or less religious instruction furnished by other agencies, does violence to the essential meaning of religion, is in direct conflict with the principles of sound pedagogy and must ever tend to an eradication of religion as a vital factor in life.[71]

What was emphasized, in other words, was that all of life, including education, was directed by religion.   Through Christian education, children should learn to see how God's hand influenced history, experience the unity of science and religion, and be prepared as Christians for a comprehensive task in state, society, and all other areas of life.

However, specific accusations against the public schools swayed parents more than positive principles for Christian education. Therefore the leaders also stressed that public education undermined Christian beliefs and based a superficial morality on the theory of evolution. An Advisory Council pamphlet held that the philosophical spirit of the public school waged war against the Spirit of Christ. The public school was based on "the secular humanistic standpoint," with a wide-ranging collection of "new fads" like sex hygiene, eugenics, and the Montessori method being introduced against the best interests of children. One teacher published a paper showing that in 1912 religious references in readers were found in fewer than two per cent of the selections. A boy being assigned a speech on evolution, the non-religious celebration of Christmas, the dropping of Christian hymns, the intermarriage of Dutch children with those of other ethnic backgrounds and faiths—these often were the down-to-earth reasons why parents opposed public education and enrolled children in Christian schools.[72]

By 1920, the leaders had convinced most constituents that Christian schools were not only desirable but also necessary. "This is our indictment against the public school," Bennink had thundered in convincing fashion, "it wholly ignores the fundamental need of the child in banishing the factor of religion from its domain."[73] More positively, the Calvinistic view that children needed to be prepared as Christians for the service of God and humanity in society, state and church had also found general acceptance, though often it was little more than a rallying cry. Many individual teachers made Christian faith an integral part of their instruction, and challenged their pupils to live Christian lives. But were they able to move beyond a personal morality and the inculcation of Calvinist doctrines? Did the education help to implement the broader Kuyperian vision of the transformation of culture through Calvinistic Christianity?

The discussions about the rationale for Christian education had done little more than lay down some general principles. Those principles gave little indication that community leaders had much of an idea, or even wanted to explore, how Christianity could interact, for example, with the arts or the sciences. At the local level, the Christian worldview presented to pupils tended to consist more of warning children against carnival attendance than in Christian scholarship transforming culture. Kuyper had been convinced that a Christian "world-and-life view" would affect all of life; the arts, the sciences, and also how these were to be taught in school. But how was this vision to be translated into classroom practice? By 1920, the question was seldom even asked. Kuyper's **Stone Lectures** about Calvinism as a life system were almost forgotten.

The move from Dutch to English during this time period had involved much more than a linguistic change. With their acceptance of English, many school supporters had also embraced the tenets of the American way of life. The Seceder background of personalistic piety and morality fitted well into this American framework. On the other hand, transforming culture along Kuyperian lines was a visionary dream not only difficult to define and to implement, but also one that would run counter to the faith in America as "the last, best hope of earth," as Abraham Lincoln had put it. Within the Christian Reformed community, there were still some such visionaries in 1920, as shown by the attempt to start a Calvinistic daily newspaper.[74] The next chapter will discuss whether such Kuyperians had any effect on the programs of the schools, and which other influences determined the curriculum.

NOTES

1. Included were B. J. Bennink, Gerhardus Bos, A. S. De Jong, L. Groeneveld, L. Hofstra, P. R. Holtman, H. Jacobsma, T. Joosten, M. C. Vander Meer, J. Van Tuinen, H. Venema, and J. Veltkamp. See Henry Beets, **De Christelijke Gereformeerde Kerk in Noord Amerika: Zestig Jaren van Strijd en Zegen** (Grand Rapids: Grand Rapids Printing Company, 1918), p. 419; and George Stob, "The Christian Reformed Church and Her Schools" (Th.D. dissertation, Princeton Theological Seminary, 1955), pp. 103-05.

2. Timothy L. Smith, "Immigrant Social Aspirations and American Education, 1880 - 1930," **American Quarterly** 21 (Fall, 1969): 523-43.

3. Sources for Table I: **Yearbooks** of the Christian Reformed Church; and Henry S. Lucas, **Netherlanders in America**, Appendix, Table I, p. 641. Christian school enrollments are estimates, since some school enrollments, when not given, were estimated from the number of teachers or from previous years' figures. The 1919-20 enrollment was interpolated from the 1918-19 and 1921-22 figures given in the Christian Schools **Yearbooks**. No figures were published for in-between years. For an explanation of the estimations in the last column, see footnote 8.

4. Herbert J. Brinks, **"Schrijf spoedig terug": letters from immigrants in America 1847 - 1920** (The Hague: Boekencentrum, 1978), p. 10.

5. J. Groen, **Onze lagere school** [Our elementary school] (Holland: H. Holkeboer, 1903), p. 13. For a description of modernization and its impact on Western nations, see Edward R. Tannenbaum, **1900: The Generation Before the Great War** (Garden City, N.Y.: Anchor Press/Doubleday, 1976).

6. **De Wachter**, Aug. 7, 1895 and Feb. 12, 1896; G. J. Diekema's speech in **Lichtstralen schijnende op onze schoolkwestie** [Light rays shining on our school question] (Grand Rapids: Vereeniging voor Christelijk Onderwijs op Gereformeerde Grondslag, n.d.,

circa 1895); and J. C. Lobbes, "Scholte's Footprints in Pella," unpublished paper, n.d., p. 7.

7. Christian Reformed Church **Acts of Synod** 1914, p. 30.

8. These figures are approximations. They are based on (1) the percentage of the total U.S. population between 5 and 20 years of age (declining from about 36 to 34 percent between 1890 and the 1920s); (2) the percentage of the U.S. population between 5 and 20 years old attending school (increasing from 55 to 65 percent between 1890 and 1920); (3) the assumption that these figures for the United States population are reasonably close to those of Christian Reformed Church members during this time frame.

9. The high schools were in Chicago (1918), Paterson, N.J. (1919), Hull, Iowa (1919), Holland (1920), and Grand Rapids (1920). See Arthur H. De Kruyter, "The Reformed Christian Day School Movement in North America" (M. Th. thesis, Princeton Theological Seminary, 1952), pp. 12-13; Stob, p. 262; and Henry Ryskamp, "The History of Calvin College and Seminary," unpublished manuscript, Chapter 5.

10. Only in the year of his death was Bennink's first name indicated as "Bernard." Likely his proper names were those of his father, Berend Jan, but he always signed his correspondence, even to close acquaintances, as "B. J. Bennink." Bennink had no surviving children, and his personal papers have never been found. See NUCS **Directory 1923-24**, p. 89; NUCS **Directory 1947**, pp. 52-54; H. Algra, **Het wonder van de 19e eeuw: van vrije kerken en kleine luyden** (Franeker: Wever, 2nd ed., 1966), pp. 247-48; biographical notes file for B. J. Bennink, Heritage Hall Archives; **The Banner,** Feb. 2, 1911, pp. 71 and 74; letters from B. J. Bennink to B. K. Kuiper from 1899 to 1906, contained in the B. K. Kuiper papers in Heritage Hall Archives; and **Christian Home and School,** April 1947, p. 53.

11. Timothy L. Smith, "Historic Waves of Religious Interest in America," in Richard D. Lamberty, ed., **Religion in American Society,** Volume 332 of The Annals of the American Academy of Political and Social Science [Philadelphia, 1960], pp. 15-16; Richard Hofstadter, **The Age of Reform** (New York: Alfred A. Knopf, 1955), esp. pp. 3-22.

12. J. Kuiper, **Geschiedenis van het Christelijk lager onderwijs in Nederland** (Amsterdam: H. A. Van Bottenburg, 1904), pp. 124-27; P. Oosterlee, **Geschiedenis van het Christelijk Onderwijs** (Haarlem: De Erven F. Bohn, 1929), pp. 206-07, 213; C. Gerretson, A. Goslinga, and J. L. Van Essen, **Groen Van Prinsterer: schriftelijke**

nalatenschap, vijfde deel; briefwisseling, vierde deel 1866-1876 [GSN V] (The Hague: Martinus Nijhoff, 1967), pp. 218-19; D. Langedijk, De geschiedenis van het protestants - Christelijk onderwijs (Delft: Van Keulen, 1953), pp. 169-72.

13. J. C. Rullman, Gedenkboek bij het vijftig-jarig bestaan van de Unie "Een School Met Den Bijbel" (Kampen: Kok, 1928), pp. 236-37. Today, the Union's annual collection is used to support Christian schools throughout the world, and in recent years CSI has received grants from it for its Biblical studies and science textbook writing projects.

14. Langedijk, pp. 287-90.

15. J. Kuiper, p. 167; H. Smitskamp et al., Honderd jaar Christelijk Nationaal Schoolonderwijs 1860-1960 [One hundred years of Christian National School Education 1860-1960] (Wageningen: H. Veenman, 1960), pp. 57-58; J. C. Rullman, p. 259; F. Kalsbeek, J. Lens, and J. B. Meijnen, Van Strijd en Zegen (Leiden: Eduard IJdo, 1904), pp. 491-92. The quote is from J. C. Rullman, p. 250.

16. Oosterlee, p. 290-91. Somewhat later, one article reprinted from a Dutch journal in De Calvinist of April 22, 1911 complained that Dutch Christian schools made little use even of those textbooks written specifically for Christian schools.

17. George Bos, "Obituary Sketch of Mr. B. J. Bennink," p. 53; H. Scheepstra and W. Walstra, Beknopte geschiedenis van de opvoeding en het onderwijs, vooral in Nederland, Derde herziene druk [Brief history of nurture and education, especially in the Netherlands, Third revised printing] (Groningen: J. B. Wolters, 1905), p. 72; F. Kalsbeek et al., p. 491; Langedijk, p. 295; Oosterlee, pp. 206-07, 214, 284; and Christian Home and School, Jan. 1942, p. 7.

18. For an English biography of Kuyper, see Frank Vanden Berg, Abraham Kuyper (St. Catharines, Ontario: Paideia Press, 1960, 1978). For a shorter biographical note, see pp. i-vii of Abraham Kuyper, Lectures on Calvinism [The 1898 "Stone Lectures"] (Grand Rapids: Eerdmans, 1931).

19. Abraham Kuyper, Pro Rege of het koningschap van Christus [Pro Rege or the kingship of Christ], in three volumes (Kampen: Kok, 1911). See, for example, Volume 2, p. 516. The initial quote by Kuyper is found in several of his writings. This translation is taken from W. Robert Godfrey, "Calvin and Calvinism in the Netherlands," in W. Stanford Reid, ed., John Calvin: His Influence in the Western World (Grand Rapids: Zondervan, 1982), p. 119.

20. Kuyper, Volume 3, pp. 182-83.
21. Godfrey, pp. 118-19; and James Donald Bratt, "Dutch Calvinism in Modern America: The History of a Conservative Subculture" (Ph.D. dissertation, Yale University, 1978), p. 37.
22. John J. Timmerman, **Promises to Keep** (Grand Rapids: Calvin College and Seminary and Eerdmans, 1975), pp. 20-21.
23. James Bratt described this point very well, though not with respect to school issues, both in his dissertation and in his essay "Dutch Calvinism in the United States in the 1920s: Americanization and Self-Definition" (Herman Ganzevoort and Mark Boekelman, **Dutch Immigration to North America** [Toronto: The Multicultural History Society of Ontario, 1983]), especially pp. 170-73. In an incisive analysis he showed how his three groupings (the Confessionalists, little influenced by Kuyper; and the two sides of the Kuyperians, the Antithetical and the Neo-Calvinists) dealt with controversies in the church and in the process defined what each meant by Americanization.
24. B. K. Kuiper already in 1903 in **The Proposed Calvinistic College in Grand Rapids** wrote that Christian schools, though independent, should hold themselves "bound to provide instruction which shall in every way come up to the standard of excellence required by the State" (Grand Rapids: Sevensma, 1903), p. 39.
25. Abraham Kuyper, **De schoolkwestie: V. De schoolwet voor de vierschaar van Europa** [The school issue: V. The school act before the tribunal of Europe], the last of a series of five pamphlets (Amsterdam: J. H. Kruijt, 1875), pp. 23-26.
26. Langedijk, p. 300; and **De Wachter**, July 17, 1895. Herbert T. Brinks in "The Origins of Christian Education in the Christian Reformed Church" (unpublished paper, 1982) documented that Kuyper advised Dutch-American Calvinists to start independent Christian schools, but that they should include persons of other than Dutch backgrounds (pp. 8-9).
27. Henry Beets, **The Christian Reformed Church in North America: Its History, Schools, Missions, Creed and Liturgy, Distinctive Principles and Practices, and its Church Government** (Grand Rapids: Eastern Avenue Book Store, 1923), p. 220-21. See also **The Banner**, Feb. 2, 1911, p. 73 and Postma, p. 94.
28. Louis Berkhof, "Our Principles; — Which Are They?", in **Six Lectures Delivered at the Michigan Christian Teachers' Institute** (Kalamazoo: Dalm Printing, 1914), p. 17; L. Berkhof and B. J. Bennink, **'n Tweetal lezingen** [Two lectures] (Grand Rapids: Michigan Alliance for Christian Education, 1917), p. 16; **Minutes of**

the Baxter Street Christian School, June 14, 1906 and July 17, 1906; **De Gereformeerde Amerikaan,** December 1907, p. 544; and **Sioux Center Nieuwsblad,** Nov. 10, 1915.

29. **De Wachter,** June 22, 1892; Donald Oppewal, p. 20. Richard Postma quoted a Mr. Van der Meer as saying in 1894 that "the shadow of the church is so great that not one ray of light can reach us" (NUCS **Directory 1923-24,** p. 93).

30. **De Wachter,** Feb. 23 and March 2, 1898.

31. **De Gereformeerde Amerikaan,** November 1898, p. 457; and Henry Zwaanstra, **Reformed Thought and Experience in a New World: A Study of the Christian Reformed Church and Its American Environment 1890-1918** (Kampen: J. H. Kok, 1973; Th.D. dissertation, Free University of Amsterdam), p. 35.

32. B. J. Bennink to B. K. Kuiper, October 20, 1898 (B. K. Kuiper papers, Heritage Hall).

33. Henry S. Lucas, **Netherlanders in America: Dutch Immigration to the United States and Canada, 1889-1959** (Ann Arbor: University of Michigan Press, 1955), p. 602.

34. Niebuhr's five categories included: (1) **Christ against culture,** in which Christ and Christian beliefs were seen as opposed to human achievements and the customs of society. In Canada, the Hutterites, for instance, have tried to shun Western culture in their separate colonies. Chapter 8 describes Christian school supporters who also favoured a "monastic" view of culture; (2) **The Christ of culture,** in which the life and teachings of Jesus were seen as the greatest human achievement of Western civilization, with the heritage of Christianity and Western civilization closely related, to be transmitted and conserved. Chapter 7 describes "liberal" Christian school leaders who came close to this position; (3) **Christ above culture,** a position that held that true culture was not possible unless, beyond all natural human achievement, Christ related men to a supernatural society and a new value centre. Thomas Aquinas as well as some of the "dualists" of Chapter 8 adhered to this view; (4) **Christ and culture in paradox,** whose proponents, like Martin Luther, believed that Christians throughout life were subject to the tension that accompanied obedience to secular and sacred authorities who do not agree, yet must both be obeyed. This position was not espoused in the Christian school movement; and (5) **Christ the transformer of culture,** in which Christ was seen as the converter of humans and their culture and society. John Calvin and the followers of Kuyper in the Christian school movement held this position

(H. Richard Niebuhr, **Christ and Culture** [New York: Harper and Row Torchbooks, 1951, 1956], pp. 39-44).

As will become clear in this book, Kuyper's followers, even today, often use the term "culture." The modern technical or anthropological meaning of "culture" in English was established by E. B. Tylor: "Culture . . . is that complex whole which includes knowledge, belief, art, law, morals, custom, and any other capabilities and habits acquired by man as a member of society" (A. L. Kroeber and Clyde Kluckhohn, **Culture: A Critical Review of Concepts and Definitions** [New York: Random House, Vintage Books, 1952], p. 81). A more modern definition in the Tylor tradition was the 1948 one by Herskovits: "Culture is essentially a construct that describes the total body of belief, behavior, knowledge, sanctions, values, and goals that mark the way of life of any people. . . . it compromises the things that people have, the things they do, and what they think" (Kroeber and Kluckhohn, p. 84). The "Kuyperians" have used a similar broad definition of culture; for them, it was a design and pattern of living expressive of definite ideals.

35. **Christian Home and School,** Jan. 1942, p. 7 and March 1947, p. 5; Baxter Street Christian School **Minutes,** Annual Report to Congregation, Dec. 16, 1901; J. C. Lobbes, "The Master Meditates: Memoirs of John Christian Lobbes," mimeographed manuscript in Heritage Hall Archives, n.d., p. 1; B. S. Sevensma to B. K. Kuiper, Feb. 2, 1898 and H. Triezenberg to B. K. Kuiper, Sept. 15, 1900 (B. K. Kuiper papers, Heritage Hall Archives); J. Groen, p. 14; and George Bos, "Memoirs of a Schoolmaster," unpublished manuscript in Heritage Hall Archives, n.d., p. 26. Of course, these conditions must be compared to public schools of that time, where rural schools buildings often were little better than sheds, with almost no equipment, and schools taught only the mere rudiments of the three R's. The quote is from B. J. Bennink, "Our Course of Study," in **Six Lectures Delivered at the Michigan Christian Teachers' Institute** (Kalamazoo, Mich.: Dalm, 1914), p. 77.

36. J. C. Lobbes, "The Master Meditates," p. 23; **Christian Home and School,** Jan. 1942, pp. 7-11; Commissioner of [Public] Schools in the [Grand Rapids] **Evening Press,** April 30, 1912; J. Groen, p. 15; and J. W. Brink, "Dutch Schools," reprinted from the [Grand Rapids] **Evening Press** in **Yearbook 1905** of the Christian Reformed Church, pp. 102-103.

37. B. J. Bennink to B. K. Kuyper, Aug. 29, 1899; Sept. 24, 1900;

March 10, 1901; Oct. 6, 1901; Feb. 8, 1902; and Oct. 30, 1904; **The Banner,** Feb. 2, 1911, p. 72; and **De Calvinist,** Aug. 5, 1911.

38. Holland Christian School Board **Minutes** from 1913 to 1917, and Berkhof and Bennink, **'n Tweetal lezingen,** p. 18. See also footnote 20, Chapter 5.

39. Baxter Christian School **Minutes,** Jan 31, 1889; Mar. 2, 1893; April 3, 1901; Oct. or Nov. 1901; Dec. 26, 1901; Franklin Street Christian School **Minutes,** Jan. 31, 1893 and June 27, 1899; Holland Christian School **Minutes,** Nov. 3, 1910; Feb. 2, May 5, Aug. 3 and 25, 1911; May 5, 1913; and **De Calvinist,** Jan. 13, 1911, p. 7.

40. **The Banner,** Feb. 2, 1911, pp. 72, 75; **De Calvinist,** April 8, 1911, p. 5; J. Broene, "The Qualifications Essential in a Christian Teacher," in **Six Lectures,** p. 36; B. J. Bennink, "What Is the Most Necessary Step for the Improvement of Our Christian Education?" in **Handwijzers: een vijftal referaten** [Signposts: five lectures] (Grand Rapids, Michigan: Eerdmans-Sevensma, n.d., lectures delivered on Nov. 16, 1911), pp. 3-4, 20; B. J. Bennink, in Berkhof and Bennink, **'n Tweetal lezingen,** pp. 20-31; and John A. Vander Ark, "Testimony: Origin and Development of Christian Education in the Midwest," unpublished manuscript, p. 20. Since 1900, Calvin College had also offered some education courses as part of its preparatory program, and around 1920 began to implement more extensive programs at the college level.

41. NUCS **Directory 1923-24,** p. 90; Constitution of the Society for Christian Education on a Reformed Basis (1895), available in Heritage Hall Archives; and **De Wachter,** June 22, July 13 and 27, 1892; Jan. 24 and July 4, 1894; and June 22, 1898.

42. For the circular to the schools calling for the establishment the Advisory Council, see **De Wachter,** July 5 and 12, 1899. See also B. J. Bennink to B. K. Kuiper, July 6, 1899; **The Banner,** Feb. 2, 1911; **Minutes** of the Baxter Street Christian School, April 2 and Nov. 3, 1903; and NUCS **Directory 1923-24,** pp. 100-01. The Holland Christian School minutes several times in 1914 mentioned Bennink organizing the first institute, resulting in the publication of **Six Lectures Delivered at the M.C.T.I.** The first teachers' organization was organized in 1894. However, few teachers attended. Through Bennink's efforts as president, the Michigan Teachers' Association was active for several years around 1910, but the organization disbanded in 1915. The difficulty was (and still is today) that the Christian school movement has not defined a meaningful role for teachers' associations beyond planning professional conferences, especially since regional and national

associations of Christian schools have always involved teachers and principals as well.

43. **De Calvinist,** April 1, 1916.

44. Harry S. Stout, "Ethnicity: The Vital Center of Religion in America," in **Ethnicity** 2 (June 1975) :204-24. Stout quoted Gerhard Lenski's definition of religion on p. 206.

45. For a discussion of the term "Civil Religion," see Martin E. Marty, **A Nation of Behavers** (Chicago: The University of Chicago Press, 1976). Marty showed that at least five overlapping and not always consistent notions contribute to the term: the actual values, ceremonies and loyalties common to Americans; the transcendent universal religion of the nation; religious nationalism; democratic faith; and Protestant civic piety. It has also been referred to as the religion of the American Way of Life, a mythology intolerant of behaviour and belief that does not fit the American mold. Marty argues that such a religion has manifested itself in behaviour based on a few unquestioned and usually unexamined beliefs about social reality. Such behaviour was also, by and large, adopted by Dutch Calvinism, and, with it, the underlying beliefs.

46. G. J. Diekema and F. Kniphuizen, **Lichtstralen schijnende op onze schoolkwestie** [Light rays shining on our school question] (Grand Rapids: Vereeniging voor Christelijk Onderwijs op Gereformeerde Grondslag, n.d., circa 1895).

47. Quoted in **De Wachter,** Nov. 4, 1896.

48. Semi-Centennial Committee of the Christian Reformed Church, **Gedenkboek der Christelijke Gereformeerde Kerk A.D. 1857-1907** [Memory book of the Christian Reformed Church A.D. 1857-1907] (Grand Rapids, 1907), p. 84.

49. **De Wachter** of Feb. 6, 1895, April 6, 1896, and April 28, 1897; J. Groen, pp. 6-7; and **De Calvinist,** June 3, 1911, p. 5.

50. John Van Tuinen to the Reverend J. W. Brinks, Oct. 1927 (B. K. Kuiper papers, Heritage Hall Archives); **Minutes** of the Baxter Street Christian School, March 22, April 26, and May 16, 1892; Jan. 9, 1901; April 3 and Dec. 17, 1902; and **De Calvinist,** May 27, 1911. There is some evidence that the more "American" teachers were not as Calvinistic in their views. For example, Mrs. Gertrude Brouwer, an early kindergarten teacher, in a 1910 speech to Christian school teachers, quoted Toronto's Inspector of Public Schools, James L. Hughes, that a kindergarten "preserves the child's originality and his tendency to transform his environment in harmony with his own plans." She added that play

is the "purest and most spiritual activity of man at this stage,"
and that structured kindergarten education leads the child to "a
pure and unsullied, conscious and free representation of the Divine
Unity." While Brouwer was fully aware of current educational
thought, her writings reflected little of Calvinistic views of sin
and grace, of God's providence and redemption. See **The Banner**,
Dec. 22 and 29, 1910. See also Baxter Street **Minutes**, Feb. 1,
1904.

51. **Minutes** of the Baxter Street Christian School, Feb. 8, 1901 and
Jan. 8, 1903.
52. This was also common in many public bilingual schools around 1900.
According to Olneck and Lazerson, the Germans were especially
successful in being allowed to use such an approach, "ensuring
ethnic continuity without socializing their children into separatist
enclaves" (Michael R. Olneck and Marvin Lazerson, "Education," in
Stephan Thernstrom, ed., **Harvard Encyclopedia of American Ethnic
Groups** (Cambridge, Mass.: Belknap Press of Harvard University
Press, 1980), p. 308.
53. B. J. Bennink, **Course of Study for the Elementary School for
Christian Instruction** (Kalamazoo, Mich.: Michigan Alliance of
Christian Schools, 1915), pp. 6, 33, 62; and **The Year-Book of
Schools for Christian Instruction 1917-18,** compiled and edited by
B. J. Bennink.
54. L. Berkhof, **Het Christelijk onderwijs en onze kerkelijke
toekomst** [Christian education and the future of our church]
(Holland: H. Holkeboer, 1905), p. 9.
55. **De Schoolbel**, Oct. 6, 1901, p. 3.
56. A pamphlet of the Englewood School for Civil and Biblical
Instruction quoted in **De Wachter**, Feb. 5, 1902.
57. **De Calvinist**, June 22, 1918, p. 3; and an article entitled "Primary
Schools for Christian Instruction Are in Harmony with American
Ideas," in the Aug. 3, 1918 issue.
58. J. G. Vanden Bosch, "The School and Christian Education,"
unpublished manuscript in personal papers, n.d. (circa 1907), pp. 2,
4, 9.
59. **Religion and Culture**, July 1921, p. 31.
60. James Donald Bratt, pp. 181-90. For a description of the impact
of patriotism on American society in general at this time, see R.
Freeman Butts, **Public Education in the United States** (New York:
Holt, Rinehart and Winston, 1978), pp. 183-85.
61. NUCS **Directory 1923-24**, p. 101; J. Van Hinte, **Nederlanders in
Amerika,** Tweede Deel (Groningen: P. Noordhoff, 1928), pp.

434-35. The U.S. Supreme Court in Pierce v. Society of Sisters 268 U.S. 535 (1925) rejected an Oregon statute which stated that all children must be educated by the state.

62. L. Berkhof, **Subjects and Outlines** (Grand Rapids, Michigan: Eerdmans - Sevensma, n.d., circa 1920), pp. 126-127; Zwaanstra, p. 318; and John De Jager in **Religion and Culture**, Nov. 1919, p. 33.

63. B. J. Bennink, **First Lessons in Geography for the Fourth Grade of Christian Schools** (Grand Rapids: Grandville Christian School Board, n.d. [either 1912 or 1913]), p. 28.

64. B. J. Bennink, **Lessons in Geography for the Fifth Grade of Christian Schools** (Grand Rapids: Grandville Christian School Board, n.d., circa 1913), p. 51.

65. Bennink, **Course of Study**, pp. 136-40; p. 40; and p. 80.

66. Bennink, **First Lessons in Geography**, p. 28; and Bennink, **Course of Study**, p. 79.

67. Gerhardus Bos, ed., **Seventh Grade Reader, Excelsior Readers for Christian Schools** (Grand Rapids, Mich.: Eerdmans-Sevensma, 1920), pp. 74 and 99, 79, 77, 83, and 41; and **Sixth Grade Reader** (1919), p. 313.

68. NUCS **Directory 1923-24**, p. 152.

69. David Cornel De Jong, **With a Dutch Accent: How a Hollander Became an American** (New York: Harper and Row, 1944), pp. 220-21.

70. L. Berkhof, **Subjects and Outlines**, pp. 120-123; L. Berkhof, **Het Christelijk onderwijs en onze kerkelijke toekomst**, pp. 5-6; L. Berkhof, **Christendom en leven** [Christianity and life] (Grand Rapids, Mich.: Eerdmans-Sevensma, 1912), pp. 23-24. A similar description is given in J. Groen, pp. 3-5.

71. "The Free Christian School: A Declaration of Principles," in G. W. Hylkema, **The Free Christian School** (Grand Rapids, Mich.: Eerdmans-Sevensma, 1918), p. 8.

72. L. Berkhof, **Het Christelijk onderwijs en onze kerkelijke toekomst**, p. 2; B. K. Kuiper, **The Proposed Calvinistic College**, p. 39; Hylkema, p. 22; J. W. Brink, **Welke is de school voor onze kinderen?** [Which is the school for our children?] (Holland, Mich.: Schoolraad and Holkeboer, 1904), p. 8; E. J. Tuuk, "The Public School, an Ideal and a Beacon," in **Six Lectures**, pp. 65-66, 70; Henry Van Zyl, "Sectarianism in Our Public Schools," **Religion and Culture**, December 1923, p. 105; George Bos, **Memoirs**, p. 26; J. Van Hinte, **Nederlanders in Amerika**, Tweede deel, p. 434.

73. **The Banner**, Feb. 2, 1911, pp. 71-75.

74. The Dutch Calvinists had launched a political study society in

1903, but plans for a political party foundered with the outbreak of World War I. Today, Dutch Calvinists in the U.S. are still active in the Association for Public Justice. A daily newspaper, **The American Daily Standard,** was briefly published in 1920-21. See John H. Bratt, "Dutch Calvinism in America," in W. Stanford Reid, ed., **John Calvin: His Influence in the Western World,** pp. 304-05. For detailed analyses of the various groupings within the Christian Reformed Church during the period under discussion, see the doctoral dissertations of James D. Bratt and Henry Zwaanstra. Both deal at some length with Kuyper's influence and its effects. I have restricted myself to his influence on the schools and their programs.

Mr. B. J. Bennink

Mr. M. Fakkema

B. J. Bennink, the **de facto** leader of the Calvinist Christian school movement between 1900 and 1920, and Mark Fakkema, General Secretary of the National Union of Christian Schools from 1926 to 1947.

5   The Search for Distinctiveness in an Era of Transition (1890-1920)

Recognizing the Issues

In 1890 the main curriculum concern of the Christian schools was that the Bible, the psalms and the three R's be taught adequately and, to a large extent, in Dutch. Soon, however, principals—especially the Dutch-trained ones—and school boards began to indicate an interest in more thorough curriculum planning. Gradually the importance of knowing Dutch decreased and of being perceived American increased, resulting in the schools feeling a greater need to define the uniqueness of their programs. But in new schools or ones with frequent staff changeovers, the pressures of day-to-day operation coupled with a lack of experience or expertise still meant that little thought was given to curriculum planning.[1] Still, by 1920, a substantial number of schools as well as the school movement as a whole had given some of thought to program planning and implementation.

The questions raised and issues discussed fell into three categories, with pedagogy being the first. A Christian approach to pedagogy was desired. The principals from the Netherlands had a thorough grounding in nineteenth century European educational thought, and kept abreast of Herman Bavinck's Dutch pedagogical writings within Kuyper's Calvinistic framework. Further, the progressive movement animated reflections about methodology (though this had more impact on Christian school writings in the early 1920s, as Chapter 6 will show). According to the articles written and speeches given, the two main pedagogical desiderata of the Christian schools at this time were the development of pupils' individual personalities, and "efficient" instruction. These concerns were discussed separately; no articles analyzed whether or how it was feasible to give instruction that accomplished both the one and the other. The former was more the concern of persons who had been educated in the Netherlands; the latter, of those with training at American colleges and universities.[2]

The second category of curriculum questions dealt with developing a suitable course of study. As Chapter 4 indicated, boards began to ask teachers to submit course plans for approval, sometimes instructing some board members to help draw them up. The Chicago Alliance of Christian Schools developed a course of study in 1911 in part to convince the Chicago Superintendent of Public Schools that Christian school graduates should be able to attend public high schools without special entrance examinations. That same year the Michigan Alliance of Christian Schools offered a $100 prize for the "best design of a course of study" that would "create a much needed, and diligently sought for uniformity in the teaching of our schools." Of the four attempts to write one, the Advisory Council chose B. J. Bennink's manuscript, published in 1915. It presented a "working plan of the school, a series of acts in teaching, orderly arranged, so as to prescribe the subject matter taught, and the time for each subject or part of each subject allotted." These efforts were animated by the desire to develop distinctiveness and to match or surpass public school standards.[3]

Finally, questions were raised with increasing frequency about the appropriateness of readers and textbooks in the schools. Minutes from 1890 to 1920 show that boards knew that the curriculum was determined to a large extent by the choice of textbooks. Therefore, they often discussed the purchase of new books and examined sample copies. Almost the first decision of the Franklin Street Christian School board after its election in May 1892 was to visit the school to examine the textbooks "in the presence of the schoolmaster." During the next few years, it repeatedly evaluated books for Biblical studies, reading, arithmetic, history, and nature study. On the whole, the textbook content chosen differed little from that in public schools. Sometimes parents suggested books they deemed suitable, but, more often, they complained about some of the texts being used, especially English readers. To help the boards, the Society of Christian Education on a Reformed Basis already in 1895 appointed a committee to evaluate textbooks.[4]

School leaders recognized that such evaluations would not resolve the "textbook problem," as it came to be called. The Reverend Klaas Kuiper, president of the Society, wrote, also in 1895:

> With thankfulness we note that an anonymous writer, discussing the readers in our schools, comes to the conclusion, "You have no Christianity." This admission is valuable. It must echo through all of America among our people, so that our people may know about the textbooks that are used in our schools: "No Christianity." New textbooks must come.[5]

Soon a consensus had developed that distinctive Christian textbooks were essential and, by 1903, most local boards indicated they were willing to put aside funds for worthwhile writing projects such as English readers. Because of "sharp criticism and petty jealousies," however, plans were scuttled the following year. Yet leaders continued to point to the "crying need" for Christian textbooks in reading, history, geography, and physiology. In 1917 one author re-emphasized that textbooks could not be "neutral." Skipping objectionable parts in public school texts did not solve the problem; a total worldview determined the spirit of the texts. If the schools did not soon obtain textbooks to fit their character, he concluded, many supporters would begin to say, with some justice, "We might as well do away with our schools."[6]

But the movement had produced few writers and no arrangements to edit and publish manuscripts. Further, pointing to the existing need was done more easily than agreeing on alternative content and approaches. As a result, only a few textbooks were published during this period: A. Bremer's primer for teaching the Dutch language, B. J. Bennink's geography manuals for grades 4 and 5, and Gerhardus Bos' **Excelsior Readers** for grades 4 to 7.[7]

This chapter, then, first discusses the pedagogical framework for the curriculum and the scope of its content. It also considers the extent to which both Kuyper's thinking and the contemporary American education scene influenced the programs of the schools, and analyzes how reading books written specifically for Christian school children defined the community's ethos and lifestyle. What characterized the school movement during the period were, first, the movement toward Americanization (described in the previous chapter), and, secondly, a search for distinctiveness and educational quality.

The Pedagogical Framework for the Curriculum

In early schools, good pedagogy meant keeping tight control, at times by means of a "rod of wood." Nevertheless, schools soon realized that teachers needed to be proficient in more than administering the rod, and that intimidation and total silence did not necessarily lead to good learning. To help its teachers develop suitable pedagogical methods, one board purchased methodology books for its teachers. Many boards began to release their teachers to attend educational conferences. Articles on pedagogy appeared in print. By the end of World War I, Bennink, for one, believed that a unique approach to pedagogy was more basic to a Christian school than a distinctive curriculum.[8]

However, while most Christian school educators agreed on a few pedagogical points of departure, no uniform approach, or even a consistent attempt to develop one, existed. Dr. Herman Bavinck's Dutch **Paedagogische beginselen** [Pedagogical principles] was strongly recommended to all teachers soon after its initial publication in 1904.[9] Ten years later a speaker who later became president of Calvin College reproachfully asked at a teachers' institute how many teachers had actually read it thoroughly—and then himself, significantly, referred to and used a number of standard psychology and methodology books in his lecture, but not Bavinck.[10]

Like several other leaders, this speaker had a vague, unspecified notion that a teacher who radiated a sound Christian character and had a thorough grasp of Calvinistic principles would somehow make methodology "Christian." Such a teacher would be able "to teach history, geography, and so forth, **in the light of** Reformed Doctrine." Unfortunately, he left it at that, giving his listeners no insights how to accomplish this. Consequently, for practical methodology, teachers were given little concrete, uniform direction. A few, mainly at the primary grades, looked to Pestalozzi. Those trained in American normal schools applied what they learned there. Likely the many teachers with almost no training used the methodology of the classrooms they had attended or observed to guide themselves.[11]

Nevertheless, the leaders did agree on a few generally accepted pedagogical presuppositions. The first was the importance of the development of the individuality of the child. Christian freedom should not lead to obstinate individualism nor to a "socialistic" leveling of individual personality, wrote D. Veltman in 1912. Since the Bible itself fostered personality differences, teachers should treat their pupils as distinct subjects rather than as uniform objects. Veltman was worried that graded classes, daily drill, the "legion" of incompetent teachers, and the large classes would prevent the nurture of well-developed individual personalities.[12] For such nurture, said another speaker, "all of education must be permeated with true moral principles"; "deadening" homilies would do little to nurture children.[13]

Some available Dutch publications gave concrete suggestions for developing such individuality. For example, one author explained, while penmanship instruction should teach the general requirements of beauty and clarity, children ought also to be encouraged to show and develop their own personality in and through their handwriting.[14] Albeit leaders like Bennink agreed with the overall concern and were aware of such suggestions, they did not incorporate them in their writings. Neither, like Bavinck, did they attempt to develop a pedagogical theory based on a Biblical view of the person. Agreement on broad principles did not lead to general acceptance of specific ways to implement them.

Like Christian school educators before them, leaders were united in condemning Rousseau's educational ideals. During this period they related such ideals to the current "reform pedagogy" which had led to "a wild jungle of folly, prejudice, and bungling," with children doing whatever they desired. Instead, a main feature of Christian schools was to be a "wholesome conservatism" in curricular structure, choice of content, and pedagogy. Acceptable sourcebooks were the nineteenth century **Theory and Practice of Teaching** by David P. Page and **Lectures on Teaching** by J. G. Fitch. These valued the role of parents in education, affirmed that teachers were doing "their Heavenly Father's business," and stressed that teachers must be tactful and sympathetic.[15]

Yet at least one aspect of the progressivism of the age did influence the schools, viz., the push for "efficiency." For instance, J. G. Van den Bosch, a Calvin College English instructor who also taught some education courses for its preparatory department, promoted both curricular conservatism and a reform conception of pedagogical efficiency. He held that Christian faith would enhance man's natural energy and that therefore the efficiency of Christian schools could and should transcend that of other schools.[16] In 1918 Mark Fakkema, later General Secretary of the NUCS, similarly wrote several articles "to seek to improve our school efficiency." Reflecting Bobbitt's thinking, he said that Christian schools must have "a proper and well-defined purpose or end in mind" and then "employ the best means to attain that desired end".[17] Van den Bosch and Fakkema, like many Christian school educators after them, accepted that Christian school methodology ought to be an efficient version of what had traditionally been done in public schools.

In the 1890s teachers often assumed that knowledge and attitudes were to be developed mainly through factual recall of basic concepts. Sometimes the whole school would participate in daily rote arithmetic and phonics drill.[18] Factual recall had an important place, especially at the grades 3, 4 and 5 levels (after children were considered to have outgrown Pestalozzi's methods and before they were thought to be able to make inferences and apply knowledge). A case in point were B. J. Bennink's grades 4 and 5 geography manuals. These were, except for Bremer's Dutch primer, the first textbooks written specifically for American Christian schools. Their main thrust was memorization of basic concepts. Each lesson was concluded with a list of factual questions whose answers could be found directly in the text. Only at the higher level were a few special lessons inserted with more open-ended questions, including comprehension and value ones: "How can sterile soil be made fertile?", "Life on earth is sometimes called a 'journey through a desert.' Why?" A 1906 language test similarly indicated that terminology and grammar knowledge were stressed at the expense of effective language use.[19]

Except for questions where Christian values might be applied, only the occasional educator moved beyond the advocacy of mental recall. Principal Henry Van Zyl, later to become education professor at Calvin College, instructed his teachers to ensure that "all pupils always understood why they do a certain act this way or that way." He indirectly took issue with Bennink: geography was much more than learning facts and was to show, for instance, the interdependence of people commercially and industrially.[20] More typical, however, were the June 1917 grade 8 graduation examinations set by the Michigan Alliance of Christian Schools. Here factual recall was paramount, complemented here and there with questions requiring higher level thinking. In geography and Biblical studies most questions were ones like "Name and locate ten large islands." In history a question asking students to identify ten given dates in American history was balanced with "the American people recognize and reward their great men. Explain and illustrate this statement." Straightforward grammar and language usage questions predominated the English exam, although the pupils also wrote a composition.[21] Memorization of facts and concepts comprised a large portion of learning in the schools.

Nevertheless, leaders did agree that Pestalozzi's conception of **Anschauung** [sense-impression] was one that should be applied in some subject areas and at certain levels, in part because Pestalozzi was considered an intellectual heir of Comenius, and the latter had "worked untiringly, unselfishly, and devotionally for the advancement of education along Christian lines."[22] While the application of Froebel's guided and progressive play activities in kindergarten were recommended occasionally, of all nineteenth century educational thinkers only Pestalozzi received frequent mention. Bennink based his nature study and some of the arithmetic work on object lessons. He also structured learning from the concrete to the abstract; in grade 4, for instance, he moved from classroom and living room maps to an overview of the continents. A speaker to the Michigan Christian Teachers' Association similarly told teachers to use objects and images to convey thoughts and values [i.e., Pestalozzi's sense knowledge before thought knowledge] in kindergarten and the primary grades. Van Zyl also had his teachers use concrete models, pictures, maps, and, in arithmetic, geometric solids, geoboards, and "iron ring" counters. Although Dutch-trained principals had been acquainted with Herbart, he was not mentioned in

Christian school writings before 1920, and specific instances of his influence appeared only after that date.[23]

Throughout the period 1890-1920, Christian school writings promoted tactful, empathetic dealings with children so that their personal development would not be stifled. But while a unique Christian pedagogy was said to be desired, much of the learning used the traditional memorization/recitation system. Neither the ideas of Calvinist educator Bavinck nor of pedagogues like Herbart were consistently expounded or applied, although Pestalozzi's methods were given some limited applications. Except for the unspecified concept of "efficiency," progressivism made little impact. As the next chapter will show, its influence was felt mainly in the early 1920s when the number of teachers trained at American normal schools and colleges became significant.

The Scope of the Curriculum

In the 1890s the day of the ungraded Kalamazoo Christian School started with the singing of Dutch psalms and hymns, followed by the vivid telling of Bible stories, a strength of Dutch-trained teachers. Arithmetic and reading followed. Students used a standard public school reader for whatever level they were at. The afternoon included drill in U.S. history and geography. Twice a week many visitors would be attracted to the concluding story telling from Dutch history, pirate lore, or **Uncle Tom's Cabin**. Before 1900 other Christian schools had even more limited programs, consisting of only Biblical studies and the three R's. The addition of subjects such as geography, history, civics and physiology depended on the whims of individual teachers. Certainly music, art and physical education were considered of minor importance.[24]

Despite slight diversifications during the next twenty-odd years, the schools continued to exhibit a fairly narrow curriculum scope. While the three R's and Biblical studies were prominent, a consensus did develop that geography and history were worthwhile, at least at two or three grade levels. The process of Americanization resulted in the subject of civics being mentioned more often, to help students "become worthy citizens" and recognize that "all authority comes from God." In addition to Biblical studies, the program sometimes consisted of the "usual subjects" of the public school because the school participated in public school exams. In 1906, for instance, Christian school graduates in Kalamazoo were examined by the county in arithmetic, grammar, history, geography, civics, spelling and orthography, literature, physiology and penmanship. Significantly, when the Michigan Christian schools set their own examinations a decade later, the subjects were almost identical: only some composition questions replaced literature, and Biblical studies was added. With the pressure of such examinations, and the importance attached to Biblical studies and, at least before World War I, to Dutch, the fine arts continued to be neglected.[25]

The belief prevailed that the influence of John Dewey and others had broadened the scope of the curriculum too much, and that this had led to superficiality in school learning. Charles McMurry was quoted favourably: "There are more studies than children can learn well."[26] Bennink reflected the view of the NEA Committee on Economy of Time in Education that nonessentials should be eliminated when he wrote in 1914 that "simplicity and thoroughness are essential to right education." The public school curriculum, he held, was too crowded and congested for good learning; quality rather than quantity was important.[27] Similarly, J. G. Van den Bosch was proud of the fact that in the "ordinary subjects" like the three R's, geography and American history, Christian school graduates compared favorably "with those of our splendidly equipped public schools." That Christian schools spent little time on "such luxuries as music, drawings, and nature study" was wholesome, for they did little to train the mental faculties.[28]

Bennink embodied these notions in his 1915 **Course of Study.** In the primary grades, the only subject besides Bible Study and the three R's was nature study; in grades 4 and 5, geography. Dutch, singing, geography, history, and civics were recommended in one or two of grades 6, 7, and 8. In grade 8 geography was dropped to make room for physiology and general science. For drawing and music there was no time in the curriculum, and, besides, Bennink felt, the average teacher lacked the ability to teach them. Bennink also left out "fads" like manual training, physical culture, domestic science, and art construction.[29]

Another principal lauded Bennink's document since it was "based on Calvinistic principles and surpasses other [public school] courses of study in simplicity and thoroughness."[30] Nevertheless, he felt Bennink had reduced the course offerings a little too much: history and nature study, for example, were better taught each year. He did not object to the exclusion of the fine or manual arts, however. While other authors pointed out that the introduction of manual training would stimulate an efficient industrial economy, no evidence suggests that any school taught this subject or was influenced by the agricultural education movement, except that Calvin College's high school department offered a senior level agriculture elective. Schools were to teach the basic academic subjects and not follow the "progressive" proliferation of subjects.

The scope of subject content was to be limited, as well. A quote by Charles McMurry on the cover of Bennink's fourth grade geography manual highlighted his main motive for writing it: "One of the chief advantages of a wisely ordered course of study is the economy of determining the **simple leading aims** which should control the teacher's work."[31] Bennink deliberately restricted his grade 4 manual to basic facts of the natural features, resources, and societal institutions of the students' own municipality and state.

Bennink's **Course of Study** outlines similarly focused on "essentials":

> The study of geography has been overdone. The textbooks contain such an abundance of material which is an impossibility to cram into children's heads, and the result is that finally the pupils of our American schools do know very little more than nothing after having studied it several years (sic).[32]

In history, only the rudiments and the basic dates were to be stressed. In Biblical studies, students were not to be filled with "undigestible dogmas and theological problems" but with the straightforward teachings of Christ. Students learned to write by practicing, and grammar, of little value in itself, should be delayed until the higher grades. The classic novels, too difficult for the first eight grades, would reduce or eliminate enjoyment of reading. In arithmetic, the quality of work could be improved by eliminating "non-essentials" such as "impractical and impossible problems" and difficult parts of percentage. The fine arts were limited to some singing and note reading to enhance church worship, and to "some spare moments on a rainy day" for "drawing for amusement."[33]

Other principals agreed with Bennink's overall intent even if not with some of the details. Too much time was spent on things that were too difficult and unimportant, Mark Fakkema agreed in 1917. One principal wrote that Bennink could have simplified some subjects even more (e.g., by dropping grammar altogether in the first eight grades). The programs of the schools reflected such views. Often the scope of the curriculum was narrower still than what Bennink suggested. For example, one teacher complained that the recommended subject of physiology was "sadly neglected in our Christian schools." Even principals like Van Zyl who viewed the curriculum somewhat more broadly relegated the teaching of art to the last period on Friday afternoon, as if it was a pleasant but unimportant diversion. Schools were determined to stick to "the essentials," and to teach those well.[34]

Clearly, the curriculum was divided into separate subject compartments, by grade levels. This held even for the various language arts components:

> During the reading period pupils should read: don't connect a language lesson with it; abstain from asking so many questions about what has been read, that everything is taught but reading.[35]

Teach one thing at a time, Bennink said; that's the way to keep things simple and straightforward for the students. The Christian schools rejected Bavinck's conception of the curriculum as an "organic unity" in which all the components were interconnected.[36] Curriculum integration was not even considered as a possible alternative.

But although the scope of both the choice of subjects and of their content was to be restricted, the standards of achievement for what was taught were to be kept high. The Baxter Christian School already in 1901 administered examinations that determined the promotion of students from one semester to the next. The examination questions were first approved by the board. When the Kalamazoo school first participated in public school examinations, principal George Bos was proud that "although more than half of the [public school] youngsters failed our whole class passed." The problems in arithmetic and a grammar test he gave his students in 1906 also showed that he maintained high standards. The Michigan Alliance tried to ensure that the standards of its school leaving examinations were similar or higher than those in public schools.[37]

Like many other educators of his time, Bennink saw grade eight as the culmination of education for the vast majority of students. Most, he believed, did not have the ability to continue academic studies. However, as in public education, more and more students did go on to secondary education. In 1916, Calvin College's high school department matched public school standards by requiring students to take three courses in English, two in mathematics and Latin, and one in Biblical studies, history and physics. They could take electives in history, languages, sciences, mathematics, and a half course in agriculture. English consisted of "standard" classics such as Silas Marner, Macbeth, and Browning and Tennyson's poetry. Ryskamp added that "if there was any philosophy back of this [curriculum] planning it did not readily become explicit." The program was based on that for college-bound public school students, with the addition of Biblical studies.[38]

Simplicity and thoroughness—those key words of Bos summed up the approach taken in constructing programs of study for Christian schools. While McMurry was invoked to give "simplicity" proper legitimacy, Christian school educators gave the term their own definition. McMurry's 1906 **Course of Study in the Eight Grades** included much of the "complex" content that Bennink had criticized and had excised from his own course of study.[39] Christian educators certainly did not see eye to eye with McMurry on curriculum issues. What they desired was a narrowly circumscribed program that was based on "Calvinistic principles." The next section will examine the extent to which Calvinistic conceptions affected the programs.

A Dual Kingship: Christ and Public Education

Chapter 4 showed how Abraham Kuyper's conception of "sphere sovereignty" caused the control of Christian schools to move from the churches to separate societies. Such associations, Kuyper held, were directly accountable to God and were to implement a program that taught pupils to see and experience that Christ is King of every "square inch" of the "total expanse of human life." Kuyper left it to others to explicate how the instruction and curriculum of Christian schools could accomplish this. Some Dutch educational leaders took the view that the curriculum content would differ little, but that the teacher's overall stance was all-important. In science, for example, teachers would impress on students that nature displayed God's handiwork and thus inculcate them with a sense of proper wonder and awe. In history they would show the work and leading of God. Through music and art they would teach students to recognize that God's grace gave beauty of song and line and colour. Other authors agreed with this approach but added that the choice of content would also be affected. Geography, for instance, must show the relationship between God's providence and everyday labour by discussing how Calvinists had tried to implement their world-and-life view in practice.[40]

These Dutch authors reasoned from their basic beliefs and assumptions to infer conclusions about Christian school practices. Non-Christians, they held, because of common grace, would reach some of the same conclusions. However, the Kuyperian framework always was their starting point and this, they believed, would lead to distinctively Christian schools. Further, if Christians were serious about the Kingship of Christ, then the schools must show the relevance of such Kingship for all of society and culture. Several North American clergy wrote booklets about Christian education that also used

115

this Kuyperian framework. The Reverend John Groen in 1903 gave some basic aims for various subjects (e.g., arithmetic should develop the mental capacity to be involved in commerce and enable pupils to act honestly with their neighbours). The Reverend G. W. Hylkema in 1918 wrote that Christian schools should make the child see that "all truth is in reality God's truth" and that "here lies the great antithesis between purely secular and Christian education." He did not develop the implications for the curriculum, however, other than to say that history and nature study were to reveal the handiwork of God.[41]

Key American Christian school educators of the period usually did not use such starting points in their reasoning about curriculum. For example, Calvin College's J. G. Van den Bosch knew Kuyper and Bavinck's writings well, but his pragmatism contrasted sharply with the attempts of Kuyper's followers to reason from pivotal beliefs. For instance, he argued that some Christian school graduates would have to go to vocational schools since such schools were efficient and produced results, but that establishing Christian vocational schools would be "fraught with danger" because of its expense. Moreover, the perils for students in public vocational schools were "not nearly so great and subtle as in cultural [i.e., academically-oriented] schools."[42] The "Kingship of Christ," in other words, did not extend to vocations. If not too costly, Christian schools were worthwhile for protecting children from the contamination of non-Christians. But Van den Bosch had little sense of Christian schools leading to cultural transformation.

The first textbook published for American Christian schools, **Simple Reading Instruction for Families and Schools,** also had a limited vision of the "Kingship of Christ." This Dutch language primer was intended for Christian schools as well as for children unable to receive Dutch instruction in a school setting. It taught all the basic Dutch phonic patterns, using many concrete memory aids. However, even though the author hoped that the book would aid "the spread of the knowledge of truth and the expansion of His Kingdom,"[43] the content was not explicitly "Christian." The author accomplished his aim indirectly: a knowledge of Dutch reading would make it possible for students to read sound Calvinistic religious works. He did not consider that the content of the primer might also contribute to the students' understanding of what a Christian life entailed.

Even Bennink did not accept Kuyper's view that Christian faith affected all scholarship. Rather, he classified subjects into "principal" and "neutral" ones. Convictions and principles counted only in subjects such as reading, geography, history, civics, physiology, and science. The "neutral" subjects were arithmetic, grammar, spelling, writing,

116

theory of music, and drawing. Therefore subjects like drawing and music might just as well be left to better equipped and financed American city schools.[44] Even in a "principal" subject like geography, the concepts taught could be the main ones of standard textbooks, with some "value" statements and questions added in which Calvinistic beliefs would come into play. The "Kingship of Christ," for Bennink, applied to selected subjects only, and within those subjects it played a limited role.

Organizationally, Bennink had caught Kuyper's vision and promoted, for example, association-controlled Christian schools. Religiously and philosophically, however, he thought within a narrower Seceder framework. His **Course of Study** emphasized personal morality and piety but contained almost no references to the Christian's calling to be actively engaged in society. Its recommended church history outline included Seceder leader Hendrik De Cock but pointedly left out any mention of Abraham Kuyper.[45] Bennink had lost his earlier enthusiasm for Kuyper. Yet likely the Seceder strain in his thinking, in conjunction with his dynamism and integrity, made him acceptable as the **de facto** leader of Christian schools in the 1910s. A book reviewer said that one of his booklets for children was "so good that it should be sold out in a few weeks."[46] The supporting community seemed to agree, even though, as becomes clear in the next section, Bennink's writings confined the "Kingship of Christ" to the "spheres" of personal faith and morality.

Nevertheless, a number of principals were known for instilling their students with an awareness that Christianity was to affect every phase of human endeavour. The first question on a spelling test of Dutch-trained A. S. De Jong asked: "What is a Christian? Define briefly." A civics quiz asked, "Who instituted government? Why?", while one in physiology queried, "Who made the human body? How did he make it? Is it yet in the original condition as it came from the Maker's hand? If so, or if not, explain." One former student recounted giving a presentation on the providence of God in his eighth grade history class in 1913. He received a low mark on a composition for referring to a church service in a slighting manner.[47] Principal Henry Van Zyl impressed on his teachers that "in each lesson we let the Bible speak." His basic aim in geography was to show "that God is the source and fountain of all that pertains to the existence of this earth and the fullness thereof as well as the maintenance of the same." In history the fundamental theme was that "God rules all," and that "He uses persons and nations to accomplish His eternal counsels in His way." This was done by emphasizing "cause and effect, characteristics of certain periods, struggle for principles." U.S. history was to be taught within the context of its European roots, and current events in terms of their historical connections.[48]

One observer concluded that pupils in Christian schools were taught "Bible truths in connection with all their lessons throughout the day."[49] However, in practice this applied more to principals like De Jong and Van Zyl than to the many young and poorly trained teachers. A number of the latter resisted Dutch, and with the scarcity of qualified teachers, boards were happy to find teachers who just had a reasonably good general knowledge, were orthodox in their religious beliefs, and led an exemplary life.[50] Few had given a Christian approach to education any serious thought. Also, many teachers believed the "fallacy," as Gerhardus Bos called it, that Christian education was public education to which prayer and Biblical instruction had been added. He complained that schools adapted public school programs and methodology:

> Subjects of instruction that are superfluous must be taught in order to mimic the public school. Subjects that are especially needed are sometimes scrapped from the timetable and the curriculum. . . . A good curriculum needs to be made practical and useful and having value for life.[51]

However, in order to gain legitimacy for the schools, public school practices rather than Kuyperian principles were often used for direction. For instance, graded classes were often introduced to enable Christian schools to measure up to public school standards. Most methods and textbooks were ones used in public schools. Reviews of such textbooks frequently recommended them for accuracy and interest, without critiquing their underlying philosophy. One of the first accomplishments of the Chicago Alliance of Christian Schools was to show that its schools were as "complete" as public schools so that their graduates could enter public high schools without taking entrance examinations. The Michigan Alliance 1917 grade 8 graduation examinations contained, besides the Biblical studies component, only one question that could not have appeared on its public school counterpart; viz., the question in civics, "Who is the Originator of all government? Explain." Bennink in 1914 said that often "the ideal of our schools was to follow the public schools as closely as we could."[52]

Not all Christian educators were pleased with this state of affairs. A New Jersey group was concerned that American Christian schools did not understand and apply the implications of Kuyper's thinking, and therefore in 1918 published a translation of a Dutch book on Christian instruction. It advocated, for example, that history should show how humans had worked out or failed to work out God's purposes for civilization. Science was to teach children that God was the source of all scientific laws and that therefore they should be thankful for how science and technology could develop God's world. Since all of life was subject to the Kingship of Christ, education was to be broad in scope, including subjects like art and economics. The children were to learn through concrete activities that tailors and shoemakers, astronomers and economists all were called to serve God in their activities and work.[53]

However, judging from American writings for Christian schools and the curriculum materials that were used and developed, this type of thinking had little influence on American Christian schools in the 1910s. In theory, Christ was King over all aspects of the school's program. In practice, the immigrants' Seceder background, the process of Americanization, and the limited training of the teachers usually restricted such Kingship to the teaching of religion and morality. More often than not, existing public school practices determined the nature and scope of the curriculum. Christian school loyalties were divided between Christ and public education.

Defining an Ethic and Lifestyle Through Children's Reading Books

What pupils were given to read indicated how the community believed children should think and act. This was especially true for books that were written specifically for Christian school students. An analysis of such reading materials shows that inculcating a personal morality based on a rigid moral code was viewed as a foremost task of the Christian school. Individual piety was far more important than an all-embracing Calvinistic "life-system" that was, in Kuyper's words, "able to fit itself to the needs of every stage of human development, in every department of life"[54]—or more important even than Calvinist doctrines. This section discusses the reading materials that were used to promote the ethos of the schools' community.

Between 1890 and 1920, imported Dutch Christian school readers were available and used in the schools. However, finding acceptable English readers was more difficult. The Franklin Street Christian School in 1895 used **Sanders' School Readers.** Like most nineteenth century readers, these promoted the commonly accepted virtues of kindness, obedience (especially to God and parents), honesty, modesty, moderation, and hard work. The Protestantism presented in these readers, however, was too liberal for many Christian school supporters. While God was shown as the source and fountain of every blessing, the name Jesus Christ was avoided and in the third Reader the only Bible passage consisted of texts from Proverbs likely chosen not to offend non-Christians. Doing good rather than faith was shown to be the way to win God's favour. One anonymous author in **De Wachter** attacked the use of these readers since they were of the "Groningen" direction. He concluded that true Christian faith could not be found either in these or in the McGuffey readers. Finding alternatives, however, proved difficult for boards.[55]

In 1895 the Society for Christian Education on a Reformed Basis offered $100 for the best manuscript it received for English readers. Since there was little reaction, B. J. Bennink started to write a series himself, working with then-university student B. K. Kuiper as editor. Bennink put his whole being into this work, consulting public school superintendents about the latest developments in readers and using current readers to check at what level specific words should be introduced. He wanted the work to be "a product of American brains," suitable for American children. Because he felt his English to be deficient, he turned to B. K. Kuiper for aid with American idiom. But although the committee evaluating the manuscripts said that the "spirit and direction" were good, it rejected their publication because of the language and grammar. However, Bennink himself wrote B. K. Kuiper that this was an excuse: most likely, he said, the real difficulty lay with the content. Indeed, one person had criticized a part of Bennink's work for "finding the name of our Saviour" only once. Bennink had emulated the approach and conversational tone of Dutch **Réveil** author De Liefde, believing that teachers could "add salt [i.e., religious and moral principles] to the meal" where appropriate. He had tried to incorporate a general Christian view of life into common topics such as rain and sunshine. His critics wanted a more explicitly "religious" document.[56]

Over the next few years, Bennink wrote three children's booklets that his critics could certainly not have faulted for a lack of religious emphasis. They dealt with the insurmountable cleavage between believers and unbelievers (i.e., Kuyper's antithesis), and the self-destruction children could cause by falling into the temptations of sin. While this was balanced by the happiness one could find in conversion, the resulting Christian life was narrowly defined in terms of leading a life of prayer and worship, avoiding immorality and materialism, and proselytizing for Christ. Like nineteenth century public school readers, Bennink stressed obedience to parents and acceptance of one's lot. His sole English booklet was unrealistic in its portrayal of the life of Christians. When the heroine was unable to attend a Christian school, she became ill because "the sunshine of God's Word" was absent in the public school. While children could not be perfect, they should always **try** to do the right thing. His chapters contained and often ended with a religious or moral lesson.[57]

What was missing in Bennink's books was how children and families could live Christian lives of joy in their everyday activities, serving God in "every sphere of life," as Kuyper had put it, in the way many readers for Dutch schools had captured it around that time. Bennink's tendency towards a personalistic piety as embodying the essence of Christian living was also evident from his other writings. One used source material from a "Midnight Mission" association to give a strident and emotional warning to young people to stay away from ice cream parlours and dance halls so that they would not become one of the 60 000 "white slave" prostitutes that were purported to die in the U.S. every year. Sample penmanship lines in his **Course of Study** included many moral aphorisms stressing obedience to parents, duty before pleasure, and the virtue of hard work. Students were to be inculcated with the knowledge that the earth was "God's handiwork, the mighty fulfillment of His infinitely wise plan." For Bennink that implied, above all, that students must learn to obey God, parents, teachers and the government, as well as, when adults, helping to operate Christian schools and institutions for the sick and insane.[58]

Bennink and other leaders continued to be distressed that no suitable Christian readers were available. Many schools used the Lutheran **Standard American Readers** (the "Concordia Readers") in the 1910s. However, these "failed to give complete satisfaction probably because they were inferior to the better class of public school Readers in every respect save insofar as they provided religious sentiment."[59] Bennink also recommended Hesba Stretton's **Jessica's First Prayer** and **Mary Jones and Her Bible** as books suitable to be used as readers, although G. Bos later criticized them for their poor language.[60] Therefore, the schools welcomed the first Christian school readers, Gerhardus Bos' grades 4 to 7 **Excelsior Readers for Christian Schools**, published in 1919 and 1920. Their main intent was to make students responsible for their conduct and its results. Most lessons were "permeated with thought and ideas" to teach pupils to "trust in God and do the right."[61]

What were the "lessons" to be learned from these readers? First, diligence and hard work would pay off in the long run ("Honest little Peter Grey,/Keeps at work the livelong day./ . . . He is climbing up his

121

way/On life's ladder day by day"). Proper behaviour included the virtues espoused in most Victorian readers: modesty, politeness, kindness to the disadvantaged and to animals, honesty, thankfulness, and, above all, obedience to parents, elders, and God. Some selections conjure up chimerical paragons like the boy who faithfully kept a book of thanks listing all good things people had done to him and then read it regularly to make himself more contented. Since Bos was trained in a Dutch Christian Normal School, his inclusion of passages that reflected the "Groningen" Enlightenment direction, a major cause of dissatisfaction with Dutch public schools in the 1830s and 1840s, was surprising. A poem about the faithfulness of a dog to his master, for instance, concluded that humble, gentle and loving conduct would result in a "divine" life—a far cry from the Calvinist emphasis on salvation through grace rather than virtue.[62]

Bible selections pointed out God's faithfulness but more often presented moral maxims ("A good tree bringeth not forth corrupt fruit"). Descriptive selections were artificially strained to drive home a point. The lesson from "Autumn" taught that "Grass withereth, the flower fadeth: but the word of our God shall stand forever." A description of downhill sledding demonstrated how easy it was to coast downhill morally. While trust in God would lead to material wealth, children must nevertheless accept their lot in life. As Longfellow's poem from which the series' title was taken showed, so long as pupils continued to struggle, the hardship of this present life would soon be transformed into the glories of the hereafter.[63]

Two other types of selections should be noted. First, some science content was included, always with a fitting moral or religious application. Being able to retrieve a penknife with a magnet taught that "knowledge is power. Gather it now. . . . The fear of the Lord is the beginning of wisdom." A description of growing coffee plants ended with "the trees of God are full of life." If pupils didn't like their climate in March, they were to remember that "God knows what is best." Science became important for the morals it taught.[64]

Most of Bos' selections were taken from nineteenth century public school readers. This was possible because Bos and many of his colleagues had their roots in the personalistic piety of the Secession which closely paralleled the Methodist brand found in nineteenth century public education—despite Calvinist fears of the "superficiality" of the latter. Kuyper's Calvinistic "world-and-life view" had little effect on the content, as becomes especially clear in a comparison with some Dutch Christian school readers written around this time. One grade six volume of a popular Dutch series described everyday, realistic situations that drew children into the stories. Morals came into play naturally as part of a lifestyle, without comment. Father bought flowers to cheer Mother, but he was careful to check their price and condition. Surprises planned for Mother's birthday showed the joy of doing things together as a family. The reader mentioned, almost in passing, that a hymn of thankfulness followed the singing of "Happy Birthday." The children delighted in telling Mother a ghost story, and Mother used the opportunity to ask how you could overcome being afraid.[65]

In the **Excelsior** readers, a study of the coffee plant studiously avoided any reference to the growers and reapers and their conditions ("it is commonly gathered. . . it is then dried"). In contrast, the Dutch reader dealt with the human element and pointed out the unfortunate health hazards associated with cocoa and chocolate manufacture. Life was not exclusively rural and idyllic, but city life was described to discover the marvels of technology as well as some of the problems it had caused. A water main break was used to show both the fun it gave children and how water was distributed in cities. Religious references about God's providence and His omnipotence arose unobtrusively. Being a Christian did not mean following a set of moral rules which, when strictly kept, led to a divine reward. Rather, a Christian life consisted of a complete lifestyle that promoted love for God and neighbour, and used God's creation and the technology humans developed to bring about truth, justice, and wholesome conditions throughout society.[66]

These readers were available to Bos when he compiled his own. Had he understood and accepted what Dutch authors believed to be implications of Kuyper's thinking, Bos' readers would have included different types of selections. Likely Bos consciously rejected the approach of these Dutch readers, believing that they did not sufficiently emphasize explicit morals and religious truths that were to guide conduct. This was also indicated by the reviews of the Bos readers, which were almost unanimous in their praise ("breathing a Christian spirit"; "suitable as to contents"; "permeated with a good religious spirit"; "the stories are very interesting and teach a splendid moral"; "by it all is fostered the reverent piety and holy fear of the Lord God"[67]). Only Calvin College's professor of Dutch language and literature—one of the few of its faculty members who appreciated later Dutch Calvinistic philosophical developments—sounded some reservations. The Christianity of the readers, he wrote, was restricted too much to personal salvation and morality and did not give a Christian cosmological view of society and culture.[68]

Except for the first volume, sales of the readers were slow: "though not without merit [they] failed of general adoption as basic readers," because of their format and the "trifle too much" moralizing. George Bos, Gerhardus' brother, later wrote that "they were not considered up to date because they missed illustrations," a general criticism of the reviewers. On the whole, though, reviewers found "very little to criticize." The **Christian School Magazine** published a positive review in 1924 to indicate that "the Board of the Union of Christian Schools recommend (**sic**) these readers to all our schools." In other words, even though the appearance and the excessive sermonizing were criticized, the leaders of the movement agreed with the basic thrust and philosophy of the series.[69] Kuyper's emphasis on a sweeping Calvinistic worldview had been reduced to the inculcation of church doctrines and moral teachings that could be added to suitable secular curriculum content. Dutch Calvinists had become conservative Americans.

Molding Young Minds and Hearts in Accordance with Divine Commands

One of Bennink's final acts as pivotal Christian school leader from 1890 to 1920 was the compilation of the first **Yearbook of Schools for Christian Instruction 1918-19.** His many "fillers" revealed that his focus had shifted from developing distinctively Christian curriculum materials to developing and instilling in teachers a uniquely Christian theory of pedagogy. Giving children "the right view of life" could come only from teachers with "a warm interest of soul for soul," ones who empathized with their pupils.[70] He firmly believed that "the teacher must breathe into each lesson-body a living soul." In his 1929 retirement speech he sadly noted that the schools had "failed miserably in the development and construction of a distinctive system of pedagogy."[71]

Yet, paradoxically, Bennink did not try to develop or adapt or implement the views of the one Calvinist who had written extensively about a Christian approach to pedagogy, Herman Bavinck. When Bennink quoted Bavinck, he did so not for his educational conceptions, but for saying at one time that "now that victory over the world is impossible, secession is necessary." Bennink added:

> Christians must be seceders as soon as the development and growth of their christian life is endangered by coming too much in contact with the world. This is true of their children also, and therefore we do not allow them to go to the school of the world.

124

SEARCH FOR DISTINCTIVENESS (1890-1920)

The constitution of all christian life is contained in these three short words, spoken to Abraham, the first seceder: **"Get thee out."** That means also me, and you, and all the christian teachers.[72]

Bennink, an avid reader of Kuyper, was aware of the educational publications of Kuyper's followers. He was therefore deliberate in emphasizing his Seceder roots and, concomitantly, setting aside Kuyper's vision of "Christ the transformer of culture" and taking a position closer to what Niebuhr labeled as "Christ against culture." He failed to develop the broad cultural vision of the later Kuyper. The torch of leadership that Bennink passed on to "our young American leaders"[73] around 1920 was one that was fuelled by Calvinist doctrines and Seceder devoutness and morality.

In the end, Bennink and his colleagues failed to forge a foundation that would have enabled the schools to move along a distinctive path on the network of educational roads. True, Biblical studies was taught as a subject and personal religious and moral virtues were expounded. The scope of the curriculum was restricted to what were considered essentials, and those were taught well. Further, the schools presented God as the ultimate source of natural laws and of the authority and insight that made it possible for America to be a great nation. But the pedagogy and the content in most subjects differed little from that in the more traditional public schools. Bennink himself in his **Course of Study** labeled many subjects as "neutral" ones, leading some of Bennink's colleagues to complain about the movement's "narrowness of life view."[74] But the movement as a whole did not seriously study the Dutch writers that had begun to develop some curricular implications of Kuyper's "world-and-life view."

By 1920 Dutch immigration to the U.S. had slowed to a trickle. The process of Americanization with its adoption of the basic tenets of the American way of life also meant that there was less interaction with and acceptance of Calvinist thought in the Netherlands. As the post-World War II Dutch emigration to Canada later revealed, Christian schools in the Netherlands and in the U.S. were on diverging paths. Kuyper's ideas had not found roots in the curriculum planning of Christian elementary schools, nor in Calvin College's preparatory department. When young American leaders began to take on the mantle of leadership at the founding of the National Union of Christian Schools in 1920, the schools had gained fairly general acceptance among Christian Reformed members and had improved their educational quality. However, there was no clear vision about the educational philosophy and the direction of the curriculum.

Conditions had made the formulation of such a philosophy and direction difficult to achieve since most church and school leaders had their roots in the Secession, not in the Kuyperian movement. The conservative immigrant subculture they headed lacked cultural astuteness. For them, education was important mainly for economic advancement and for the inculcation of traditional Calvinist doctrines and values. The Americanization process had progressed far enough that many Christian school supporters no longer wanted to apply Calvinist thinking in the Netherlands directly to American situations even where that might have been applicable. Moreover, the group had not brought along thinkers who could give well-defined philosophical and pedagogical direction; leadership in the schools had to come from men who worked long hours in the classroom or in the church. Perhaps the surprising thing was that even when parents no longer saw much need for Dutch language instruction, their conviction about the need for Christian schooling was so strong that the schools not only survived but became creditable institutions of learning.

At the end of his life in 1947, Bennink was justifiably hailed for his "whole-hearted devotion and efficient service," for "raising the educational standard of the schools," and for "pleading unceasingly for greater religious distinctiveness in the Christian school curriculum."[75] Bennink had devoted his whole life, as he so aptly put it himself, to molding "young minds and hearts in accordance with Divine commands."[76] But his view of these Divine commands was a religion that had relevance mainly for personal piety and morality. As such, it might improve the lives of individual Christians in society but it would not change the direction of society itself, as Kuyper had set out to do. The move away from Kuyperian Calvinism towards conservative Americanism—a process to which Bennink contributed—some years later was to lead to a decade of defensive reassessment of the role and future of the schools.

NOTES

1.   For instance, when E. R. Post was appointed the first principal of the Baldwin Christian School in Wisconsin in 1918, his preparation for teaching was limited to a course in the history of education taken as part of Calvin's preparatory program. When he arrived in Baldwin, he just ordered some textbooks from available publisher's catalogues, sight unseen. In Biblical studies, he taught

all eight grades directly from the Bible. For the other subjects, he followed the textbooks he had ordered. There were few instructions beyond the requirement that he should teach Dutch a half day per week. (Interview with E. R. Post, Grand Rapids, Michigan, April 20, 1983.)

2. To a certain extent this echoed the two strains that developed in American progressive education. Representative of the former was D. Veltman (e.g., **De Gereformeerde Amerikaan**, June 1912, p. 267); of the latter, Calvin College's J. G. Van den Bosch (e.g., **Six Lectures Delivered at the Michigan Christian Teachers' Institute** [Kalamazoo, Michigan: Dalm, 1914], pp. 53-56).

3. **The Banner**, Feb. 2, 1911, p. 73; Holland Christian School **Minutes**, Jan. 17, 1912, Art. 6; B. J. Bennink, "Our Course of Study," in **Six Lectures**, pp. 75-76.

4. Franklin Christian School **Minutes**, 1892-96; Baxter Street Christian School **Minutes**, 1901-12; **De Wachter**, May 29, 1985. Even Bennink in his **Course of Study for the Elementary School for Christian Instruction** (Kalamazoo, Mich.: Alliance of Christian Schools for Michigan, 1915) wrote that "any one of the leading [history] textbooks is acceptable" (p. 72).

5. **De Wachter**, Nov. 6, 1895.

6. Baxter Street Christian School **Minutes**, Nov. 3, 1903; George Bos, "Memoirs of a Schoolmaster," unpublished manuscript, no date, p. 46; **De Schoolbel**, June 24, 1909, p. 2; **De Calvinist**, March 3 and 10, June 2 and 9, 1917; L. Berkhof, "Is the Continued Existence of Our Schools Justified?" in **'n Tweetal lezingen** [Two lectures] (Grand Rapids, Michigan: Alliance of Christian Schools, 1917), pp. 13, 16.

7. A. Bremer, **Eenvoudig leesonderwijs voor huisgezin en school** [Simple reading instruction for family and school] (Grand Rapids, Mich.: A. Bremer, 1910; illustrated by B. J. Bennink); B. J. Bennink, **First Lessons in Geography for the Fourth Grade of Christian Schools** and **Lessons in Geography for the Fifth Grade of Christian Schools** (Grand Rapids, Mich.: Grandville Avenue Christian School Board, n.d., circa 1912); Gerhardus Bos, **Excelsior Readers for Christian Schools** (Grand Rapids: Eerdmans-Sevensma): **Fourth Grade Reader** (1920), **Fifth Grade Reader** (1919), **Sixth Grade Reader** (1919), and **Seventh Grade Reader** (1920).

8. **Christian School Magazine**, Dec. 1928, pp. 609-10; **De Schoolbel**, June 24, 1909; Baxter Street School **Minutes**, Dec. 2, 1903; and Bennink's "fillers" in the **Yearbook of Schools for Christian**

Instruction 1918-19.

9. K. Schoolland, **Peadagogische** (sic) **Beginselen, door Dr. H. Bavinck** [Pedagogical Principles, by Dr. H. Bavinck], **De Gereformeerde Amerikaan,** March 1905, pp. 97-102. This essay review appeared only five months after the October, 1904 date shown by Bavinck in his introduction to the book.

10. J. Broene, "The Qualifications Essential in a Christian Teacher," in **Six Lectures,** pp. 23-39.

11. Ibid., pp. 34-35; De Calvinist, Dec. 9, 1911, p. 8. Also see footnote 50 in Chapter 4.

12. D. Veltman, "Het Christelijk onderwijs tegenover het socialistisch streven" [Christian education versus socialistic tendencies], in **De Gereformeerde Amerikaan,** June 1912. See especially p. 267.

13. De Gereformeerde Amerikaan, April 1904, pp. 162-75.

14. J. C. de Moor, **Waarom Gereformeerd schoolonderwijs?** [Why Reformed school education?] (Kampen: J. H. Kok, 1906), pp. 20-23.

15. **De Calvinist,** Dec. 12, 1914; J. Broene, "Rousseau and Reform Pedagogy," in **Handwijzers: een vijftal referaten** [Signposts: five lectures] (Grand Rapids: Eerdmans-Sevensma, 1911), p. 33; J. G. Vanden Bosch, "Our Schools - What They Are and What They Should Be," in **Six Lectures,** p. 46; David P. Page, **Theory and Practice of Teaching: or, The Motives and Methods of Good School-Keeping** (New York: A. S. Barnes, 1854). Page is referred to by L. Berkhof in **Christendom en leven** [Christianity and life] (Eerdmans-Sevensma, 1912), p. 33, and in the list of books recommended for reference by teachers in Bennink's **Course of Study.** J. G. Fitch's **Lectures on Teaching** (New York: Macmillan, 1881) was used by J. Broene in "The Qualifications Essential in a Christian Teacher" and also appeared in Bennink's list. The quote is from Page, p. 346.

16. J. G. Van den Bosch, "Our Schools - What They Are and What They Should Be," in **Six Lectures,** p. 53. For a description of moves toward efficiency in public education during this time, see, for example, R. Freeman Butts, **Public Education in the United States: From Revolution to Reform** (New York: Holt, Rinehart and Winston, 1978), pp. 190-192.

17. **The Christian Journal,** Nov. 9, 1918, p. 3.

18. Gernant, pp. 609-10. Joseph M. Rice complained similarly of many public schools "crowding into the memory of the child a certain number of cut-and-dried facts," and decried their mechanical pedagogy and the fact that they did "nothing beyond securing

certain **memoriter results**" (Joseph M. Rice, "Our Public School System: A Summary," **The Forum** 15 [June 1893]: 507-09).

19. Bennink, **First Lessons in Geography**, p. 28; Bennink, **Lessons in Geography**, p. 15; and George Bos, "Do Our Children Learn Enough?" **Christian Home and School**, Oct. 1957, p. 11-12.
20. Course outlines prepared by Van Zyl between 1913 and 1922 for the Hull, Iowa, Christian School (Henry Van Zyl personal papers, Heritage Hall Archives), pp. 35, 48.
21. De Calvinist, August 4 and 11, 1917.
22. Ibid., March 4, 1911.
23. Bennink, **Course of Study**, pp. 11-15, 31; Bennink, **First Lessons in Geography**, p. 19; De Calvinist, Dec. 9, 1911, p. 8; and Van Zyl course outlines, pp. 33, 48. At least in the literature, both Pestalozzi and Herbart seemed to have a greater impact on public schools than on Christian ones.
24. De Calvinist, Aug. 26, 1911; **Christian School Magazine**, Dec. 1928, pp. 609-10; **Christian Home and School**, March 1947, p. 5; and **Christian Home and School**, Oct. 1957, pp. 11-12.
25. Baxter Street Christian School **Minutes**, Feb. 1901, Art. 15; Holland Christian School **Minutes**, Nov. 3, 1910 and Feb. 2, 1911; J. Groen, **Onze lagere school** (Holland, Mich.: Holkeboer, 1903), p. 6; Baxter Street Christian School **Minutes**, Annual Report, Dec. 26, 1901; and **Christian Home and School**, Oct. 1957, pp. 11-12.
26. **Handwijzers, een vijftal referaten** (Grand Rapids, Mich.: Eerdmans-Sevensma, n.d. [circa 1912]), p. 13.
27. Bennink, **Course of Study**, p. 5; **Six Lectures**, pp. 81-84.
28. **Six Lectures**, p. 45-48.
29. Bennink, **Course of Study**, p. 5-6, 10.
30. G. Bos in **De Calvinist**, April 28, 1917, p. 6.
31. Bennink, **First Lessons in Geography**, front cover.
32. Bennink, **Course of Study**, p. 42.
33. Ibid., pp. 44, 56-58, 69; **De Calvinist**, Sept. 2, 1911, p. 5 and Feb. 20, 1915, p. 5.
34. **De Calvinist**, Feb. 3, 1911, p. 6; April 14, 1917, p. 5; April 28, 1917, p. 6; and May 5, 1917, p. 6; Van Zyl course outlines, p. 38.
35. Bennink, **Course of Study**, p. 39.
36. Bavinck had written, "Religion, history, geography, language, arithmetic, drawing all touch each other during every moment; they support, carry, benefit each other. That is why it is contrary to the character of the elementary school to separate the various subjects too much" (H. Bavinck, **Paedagogische Beginselen** [Kampen: Kok, 1904], p. 110).

37. Baxter Street Christian School **Minutes,** Feb. 6 and June 5, 1901; George Bos, "Memoirs," p. 33; **Christian Home and School,** Oct. 1957, pp. 11-12; and **De Calvinist,** Aug. 4 and 11, 1917.
38. Christian Reformed Church, **Yearbook 1916,** pp. 91-93; B. S. Sevensma to B. K. Kuiper, April 25, 1898 and June 22, 1899; J. G. Van den Bosch to B. K. Kuiper, Nov. 20, 1902; Henry Ryskamp, "The History of Calvin College and Seminary" (unpublished manuscript, Ryskamp personal papers), Chapter V, n.p.
39. See Charles McMurry, **Course of Study in the Eight Grades** (New York: Macmillan, 1906).
40. J. Woltjer, "De opvoeding door de school" [Education by the school], in A. Anema et al., **Christendom en opvoeding** [Christianity and education] (Baarn: Hollandia, n.d.), pp. 105-06, 117; De Moor, pp. 22-23.
41. Groen, p. 5; G. W. Hylkema, **The Free Christian School** (Grand Rapids: Eerdmans-Sevensma, 1918), p. 28.
42. J. G. Van den Bosch, "Vocational Education," in **Handwijzers: een vijftal referaten,** pp. 58-70. The quotes are taken from pp. 67 and 69-70 of this publication and from **Six Lectures,** p. 51.
43. Bremer, p. 4.
44. **Six Lectures,** p. 89.
45. Bennink, **Course of Study,** p. 118.
46. A review of Bennink's **Twee vaders gezocht en gevonden** [Two fathers sought and found] in **De Gereformeerde Amerikaan,** Nov. 1901, p. 528.
47. "A Tribute to Mr. A. S. De Jong by a Former Student," **Christian Home and School,** April 1947, pp. 5-6.
48. Van Zyl course outlines, pp. 46-47, 50-51.
49. Jacob Vander Zee, **The Hollanders of Iowa** (Iowa City: State Historical Society of Iowa, 1912), p. 270.
50. In Holland, Michigan, for instance, the board felt it could not rehire one teacher who was "a visitor of the skating rink," and another who questioned the doctrine of the resurrection (Holland Christian School **Minutes,** April 27, 1911).
51. **De Schoolbel,** June 24, 1909, pp. 1-2.
52. George Stob, "The Christian Reformed Church and Her Schools" (Th.D. dissertation, Princeton Theological Seminary, 1955), pp. 126-27; Baxter Street Christian School **Minutes,** Dec. 13, 1912; Holland Christian School **Minutes,** Aug. 3, 1911; reviews in **De Calvinist** in the 1910s (e.g., March 24, 1917, p. 5); **Christian Home and School,** April 1954, p. 117; **The Banner,** Feb. 2, 1911, p. 73; **De Calvinist,** Aug. 11, 1917; and **Six Lectures,** p. 80. Although

criticizing this attitude, Bennink at the same time wrote that for history "any one of the leading textbooks is acceptable" (**Course of Study**, p. 72).

53. A. G. D. Gerritsen, **Christian Instruction**, trans., P. Stam Jr. (New Jersey: Eastern Schoolboards and E.C.T.A., 1918), esp. pp. 7, 9-13.

54. Kuyper wanted Calvinism "to furnish human society with a different method of existence, and to populate the world of the human heart with different ideals and conceptions." See Abraham Kuyper, **Lectures on Calvinism** (Grand Rapids, Michigan: Eerdmans, 1931), pp. 15, 17, 190-91. The quote is from p. 171.

55. Franklin Street Christian School **Minutes**, Mar. 22, April 26 and Aug. 27, 1895; Dec. 21, 1898; Bennink's **Course of Study**, pp. 27-28; **De Wachter**, Oct. 30, 1895; Charles W. Sanders, **The School Reader, Third Book** (New York and Chicago: Ivison, Blakeman and Taylor, 1860). Interestingly, I found no reports of the McGuffey Readers being used in Christian schools.

56. **De Wachter**, July 10, 1895; B. J. Bennink to B. K. Kuiper, June 1, 1895; Aug. 24, Sept. 26, Dec. 3, and Dec. 26, 1898; Feb. 15, April 19, May 25, and July 6, 1899; and May 19, 1900. Unfortunately, I was unable to find a copy of Bennink's manuscripts or other specific references to them. His own sketchy references indicated that he tried to write enjoyable, engaging Christian readers. His own later children's books and Bos' readers published twenty years later were much more didactic than his stated intent for these readers.

57. B. J. Bennink, **Carried in His Bosom** (no publisher or date), p. 6.

58. B. J. Bennink, **In de onderwereld of, de vloek der blanke slavernij** [In the underworld or, the curse of white slavery] (Grand Rapids, Michigan: H. H. D. Langereis, 1913); **Course of Study**, pp. 127-30; Bennink, **Lessons in Geography**, pp. 5-11; Bennink, **First Lessons in Geography**, pp. 28-32.

59. William J. Van Melle, "The Textbook Problem," in NUCS **Yearbook 1922**, p. 101. These readers are often referred to as the **Concordia Readers,** being published by the Concordia Publishing Company.

60. Bennink, **Course of Study**, pp. 57, 66; **De Calvinist**, April 28, 1917, p. 6.

61. **Seventh Grade Reader**, preface; **Fifth Grade Reader**, pp. 182-83.

62. See, for example, **Fourth Grade Reader**, pp. 194-95; **Fifth Grade Reader**, pp. 79-81; and the selections "Of Dress" (grade 6; modesty), "What It is to Be Polite" (7), "On Respect for the Aged, and on Politeness" (7), "Be Not Overcome of Evil, but Overcome

Evil with Good" (5), "Our Pet Squirrel" (4--"Be Kind to harmless animals"), "Two Market Boys" and "The Young Witness" (5; honesty); "A Book of thanks" (4). The quote is from the **Fifth Grade Reader,** pp. 136-37.

63. **Fifth Grade Reader,** pp. 12-13, 79-81, 166, 180-82; **Sixth Grade Reader,** p. 6-9, 106-07, 112-15, 149-51.

64. **Fifth Grade Reader,** pp. 81-82, 22-24; **Seventh Grade Reader,** pp. 31-33.

65. H. Wagenvoort, In ruimer kring I [In a broader circle I] (Groningen, J. B. Wolters, 1913), pp. 5-17.

66. **Fifth Grade Reader,** p. 23; **In ruimer kring III,** p. 94 and selections throughout; **In ruimer kring I,** pp. 24ff. American public school readers early in the twentieth century, while no longer as explicitly moralistic as the **Excelsior** ones, also ignored the social, economic and political change of the age. Instead, they presented unrealistic, idyllic portrayals of family and rural life. See Ruth Miller Elson, **Guardians of Tradition: American Schoolbooks of the Nineteenth Century** (Lincoln: University of Nebraska Press, 1964).

67. **De Wachter,** April 9 and Sept. 3, 1919; **The Banner,** Sept. 25, and April 10, 1919; **The Christian Journal,** March 29, 1919; and **Christian School Magazine,** May 1924, pp. 673-74.

68. John J. Timmerman, **Promises to Keep** (Grand Rapids: Calvin College and Eerdmans, 1975), p. 58; **The Christian Journal,** Aug. 30, 1919.

69. George Bos, "Memoirs," p. 46; **The Christian Journal,** March 29, 1919; **Christian School Magazine,** May 1924, pp. 673-74; **Christian Home and School,** June 1954, p. 18.

70. **Yearbook of Schools for Christian Instruction 1918-19,** compiled by B. J. Bennink, pp. 13-14, 28, 35, 84. Bennink put this into practice in his own classroom in an outstanding way, according to a former student (interview with John De Bie, Aug. 5, 1983).

71 Bennink, **Course of Study,** p. 172; **De Wachter,** June 26, 1929, pp. 407-08.

72. **Six Lectures,** p. 83.

73. **The Banner,** Feb. 2, 1911, p. 71.

74. **De Calvinist,** June 9, 1917.

75. **Christian Home and School,** April 1947, in a piece entitled "Congratulations to Mr. and Mrs. Bernard J. Bennink."

76. Bennink, **Course of Study,** p. 94.

First class of the Eastern Christian High School, 1919-20, in Paterson, New Jersey. The teacher at the far right rear is Gerhardus Bos.

6   A Bulwark against the Force of Modernism (1920-1945)

Preserving the Heritage

Christian school supporters greeted the founding of the National Union of Christian Schools [NUCS] in Chicago in 1920 with optimism. Principal Andrew Blystra expressed this confidence clearly albeit tritely:

> There is a great future, providing the movement is led in the right direction and is guided by a policy that, free from all narrow-mindedness, holds high the standard of our principles and reveals a vision of the future.[1]

Blystra's "narrow-mindedness" referred to those schools that, fearing a loss of local control, were unwilling to act in concert, and to those reluctant to adapt to their American context.   However, he believed the NUCS could overcome such self-centeredness by improving and supervising the programs of its member schools and by providing support materials.   American-trained Mark Fakkema, principal of the Chicago Christian High School since its establishment in the 1918, became full-time General Secretary of the NUCS in 1926 to promote Christian education and to encourage the writing of Christian learning materials.

Not surprisingly, however, the "vision of the future" was a fragmented one, and often it harkened back to the past.   Social isolationism and particularism characterized the many schools refusing to submit to central educational leadership.   Many, especially in Michigan, even declined to join the NUCS in its early years.   NUCS' supervisory role was scuttled in 1923 when its schools defeated the board's recommendation to appoint a superintendent.   The NUCS soon decided to concentrate on public relations rather than on potentially obtrusive educational leadership.[2]   The intent of such promotion activities was to espouse and defend traditional Calvinism.   This, leaders felt, would help schools to be the "front-line trench in fortifying our youth against the 'isms' of the day."   Such "isms" were especially modernism, evolutionism, and socialism and communism.[3]   Between the two world wars, a fortress mentality guided the schools.

A BULWARK AGAINST MODERNISM (1920-1945)

There were fears that the bulwark of Christian education was crumbling. In American society, the fragmentation of the progressive synthesis had led to discord over what true religion entailed, and, consequently, "a great concern for preservation of the truth in particular religions." While the Christian Reformed Church had to a large extent remained isolated from the now-fragmented "progressive synthesis," it showed the general anxiety of conservative Christians that doctrinal and moral truth needed shoring up. Such anxiety took place within the context of widespread apprehensions of doom and fear of a chronic deterioration of civilization.[4] Within this context H. J. Kuiper, editor of **The Banner** and foremost Christian Reformed spokesperson of the period, in 1929 saw ominous signs of the decline of Christian education. Principal A. S. De Jong warned that the schools suffered from anemia because of a lack of progress in the application of Calvinistic principles. Reflecting the world-wide sense of decadence, he added in 1936 that "our schools are doomed, **unless** we repent of our laxity, our cold-hearted indifference, our worldly-mindedness."[5] Decreasing enrollments amplified these concerns, with the schools growing little between 1921 and 1929, and not regaining their 1929 peak until 1941.[6] The portion of Christian Reformed children attending the schools dropped from more than half in 1918 to 46 percent in 1938.[7]

Several factors brought about this slump. First, parents were divided and sometimes unsure why they sent their children to the schools. Some believed the schools provided a good "atmosphere." Others feared the teaching of false doctrines and evolution in the public schools. Still others just followed their preacher.[8] One result of Americanization was that Kuyper's vision of Dutch Calvinism's potential unique contribution to American culture seemed less attainable and, to many, less relevant. The rationale for the existence of the schools had become less secure.

Connected with this was the fact that most of the schools' programs, materials, and methods had failed to become distinctive. Relatively little curriculum development and "much unthinking adoption and application of ideas" of contemporary education took place in the late 1920s.[9] The distinctive features of the schools' programs were Biblical studies courses and the teaching of strict moral standards, rather than a unique approach to pedagogy or curriculum. The schools' distinctiveness, argued Vancouver's Reverend John De Jong in Lynden, Washington in 1941, was that teachers and students avoided worldly amusements and were imbued with a sense of holiness.[10]

Three other causes of the dispiritedness were not unique but especially pertinent to Christian schools. First, in 1922 more than half of the teachers had no training beyond high school. Even by the mid-1940s, many teachers took only a few summer courses and one month of practice teaching beyond high school. Poor salaries caused rapid turnover. The many teachers who did not intend to make teaching a lifetime career often were lethargic about professional upgrading, and about developing insight into what a Christian program of instruction should entail. In 1944 fewer than one quarter of new teachers had taken their training at a Calvinistic college. It was, in all, "extremely difficult for teachers to give **Christian** instruction."[11]

Further, scarcity of suitable materials and a lack of support staff exacerbated the dichotomy between theory and practice. Some teachers were "thoroughly Reformed in their life and world view, and sound in their educational thought but far removed from it in practice."[12] The **Christian School Magazine** itself in April 1929 failed to recognize the connection between theory and practice, stating it would deal with theory but leave methodology to secular journals. The link between Calvinistic principles and classroom practice was often a tenuous one.

Finally, the depression that burst the bubble of American prosperity also caused a psychological depression—as well as putting a virtual stop to new immigration from the Netherlands. Enthusiasm waned for a cause that required a great deal of effort and funds. Some parents no longer had any discretionary income that could be used for Christian education. Several schools were forced to close. Enrollment declined by seven percent from its 1929 peak. However, where Christian schools continued to exist, the majority of church members still believed that Christian education was one of the obligations of child rearing. Their leaders had continued to rally them: "Our strength lies in the conviction that we are on God's side." The schools were to protect children from "godless" moral, social, and economic values that dominated America and its schools. Public schools had become "a menace to the spiritual and physical welfare of the younger generation."[13]

Thus while there were concerns about the present and future state of the schools, the church and school leaders viewed them as necessary defenses against the inroads of secularism. Thus pedagogical and curricular thinking between 1920 and the end of World War II emphasized that the schools were to be a "bulwark against the mighty tide of worldliness" in the decaying American culture.[14]

A BULWARK AGAINST MODERNISM (1920-1945)

Defending the Calvinist Faith

The strength of this bulwark, the schools believed, depended especially on the effectiveness of the Biblical studies programme. Calvinists considered the Bible to be the basic guide for their religious, moral, social, and economic life. In the Christian school, the study of the Bible was to show how God ruled the world, how He provided a way of salvation through Jesus Christ, and that He had established norms for ethical, political, social, and vocational activity. Therefore, the NUCS and its member schools took Biblical studies to be the core and most important subject of the curriculum. As such, it was scheduled for the first period each morning.[15]

The fundamental principles of the Bible were to permeate all branches of instruction. Biblical studies, the foundation of the curriculum, was to form an "organic unity" with the other subjects so that together they would explicate and infuse a Christian worldview. Yet typical was one author who, while emphasizing that the Bible promoted the use of music for singing God's praises, nevertheless did not indicate how Biblical studies could give guidelines for the music curriculum or insights about music. In fact, the main Bible studies textbooks did not even mention the Biblical book of Psalms or other passages dealing with music. The infrequent examples given of "organic unity" remained at a theoretical level, so general and vague they had little if any impact on the curriculum. Neither course outlines nor other curriculum materials showed how Biblical studies, either alone or in conjunction with other subjects, could develop a comprehensive worldview. Nor did they show how religious principles were "the foundation of all other learning." Yet the conviction remained strong that Biblical studies should be such a core subject.[16]

Leaders agreed that the church rather than the school should teach church doctrines directly. The school's task was to instill knowledge and insight, not to evangelize. Biblical studies would focus on "sacred history," which would give "a bird's eye view of the Bible." Thus a 1926 questionnaire sent to principals assumed that Biblical studies would consist of chronological accounts of Biblical history. The aims for Biblical studies, especially for the grades 1-6 levels, were stated accordingly:

Grade 1-4: To acquaint the pupil with Bible stories.
Grade 6: To have the student see the historical continuity of Bible content. The Bible stories . . . are now arranged and fixed in the minds of the pupils in their chronological order.

Not until grade eight did these aims mention "furnishing our pupils with the rudimentary framework of our view of life"—without any indications of how this was to be done. Specific aims concerning the study or analysis of the relationship of the Bible to other subject areas were lacking.[17]

Of course, even at the grades 1-4 levels, the actual aims did include more than acquainting pupils with Bible stories. Bible stories were used to point to God's providence, His grace, His care. They taught "general truths," such as "it is possible to be learned and civilized without being regenerated." A Bible lesson sometimes emphasized "the application of its truth to the practical phases of life." For example, Peter's denial of Christ led to a discussion of leadership. This lesson concluded that Christians, though sinful, could nevertheless contribute to making America "take a leading part among the nations of the world." More commonly, Bible stories were used to illustrate virtues such as obedience and thankfulness. Virtue was a demand of God, whether or not it resulted in immediate reward. A definite even if unstated aim of Biblical studies was to imbue the students with Christian piety.[18]

Most Biblical studies publications tried to attain such aims by emphasizing knowledge of facts and concepts found within the covers of the Bible.[19] For example, the main Biblical studies series of the period, the NUCS **Bible Study Manuals** series, published in five parts between 1935 and 1940, was a chronological, factual study of the historical books of the Bible.[20] A typical lesson asked students to read a Bible passage and answer a number of factual questions. The only question requiring some thought beyond recall was the last optional one which asked students to suggest a suitable title for the lesson. Each lesson concluded with word study and memory work. Some included completion exercises (filling in blanks) or map study. Except for a brief introductory section, the teachers' manual consisted of the answers to the questions. The emphasis on verbal information considered most worthy of study resulted in an arid intellectual formalism in the series and, indeed, in the atmosphere of many schools using the series. The learning of isolated facts and propositions did little to reflect the Biblical concept of knowledge which signifies a unification of intellect, feeling, and action. Students had no opportunity for personal response, and the only items of personal relevance were admonitions, for example, to trust God and be honest (unlike Jacob), or to be courageous in the face of evil (like Joseph). Although such injunctions were briefly stated as "truths" in the introductions, no provision for discussion and analysis was made.[21] The series looked at Biblical studies as an isolated academic subject, thereby discouraging carry-over into other subjects and into school and home life. The series' structure reflected the prevalent view that the school's task, in contrast with that of the church and the home, was primarily academic. Also, the series conformed with the predominant receptable view of learning held by the schools.

Schools usually taught "church history" as an integral part of the Biblical studies program in the upper levels of elementary schools. The first textbook published by the NUCS was B. J. Bennink's popular 1925 **Sketches from Church History.** Its theme was that neglect of prayer and apostasy had been the downfall of the Christian church throughout the ages. This course was to instill "spiritual patriotism, inspiring us to withstand the foes of God's people, and to be true and faithful crusaders under the Banner of the Cross." Bennink did not hesitate to point out the shortcomings of such "foes" as the Catholics and, especially, the "Modernists." However, other than encouraging mission activity, he said little about what it meant to be "part of the great work which the Lord has assigned to His people on earth."[22]

Thus, Biblical studies was to expand cognitive knowledge of Biblical and church history, in the hope that this would increase children's understanding and application of Biblical "truths" and Calvinistic moral standards. In this way, the purity of the faith and the orthodoxy of the church would be maintained. According to intents stated in general articles, Biblical studies was to undergird the whole curriculum. In practice, however, both the early-morning time slot allotted to it and the way it was taught divorced the subject from the rest of the curriculum. It did not serve as a functional "core." Even when history teachers, for instance, used Biblical passages, they usually did so without reference to anything taught in Biblical studies. Moreover, since the subject focused almost exclusively on the facts of Biblical and church history, it could and did not serve to enthuse students "for the principles and ideals of Christian culture."[23] Indeed, only an occasional theologian with Dutch Kuyperian roots still spoke in such terms.

Upholding Puritan Morality and Warding Off "Modernism"

The Christian Reformed Church expected Christian schools "to keep the morals of their pupils on a high plane." H. J. Kuiper revised a Bible text slightly but significantly to read "true piety, the fear of God, is the beginning of wisdom."[24] Teachers were to model such godliness by avoiding "flippant conversation, worldly dress, furtive powder-puff exercises, questionable amusements" as well as "laziness and sluggishness." They were to warn especially against theatre attendance, dancing, and card playing, the three "worldly amusements" condemned by the Christian Reformed Church. The NUCS itself wrote that "today the secularized public school system has become a powerful agency in our country making for godless morals and Christless lives."[25]

Such views influenced the curriculum. One teacher exhorted her colleagues to counteract expressions in English like "Fate had decreed," since God rather than fate decreed everything in life.[26] Tests asked students to write compositions on topics such as "Overcome evil with good" and explain why copying was wrong. Pupils also had to do some moral reasoning:

> A certain man needs money badly. He goes to a person asking for a loan. That man is willing to do it at 8% interest. Is it right or wrong? Why?[27]

In history, the evil effects of personal and national sinfulness were emphasized. A basic principle of history was that "nations who seek God will receive His blessing and that those who forget Him will be destroyed." The corruption of the Grant administration in the U.S. thus became an important historical topic. The struggle between managements and unions early in the twentieth century was used to teach that selfishness characterized all social classes. In short, the curriculum was to uphold "the best principles of the Puritan New Englanders."[28]

Applying Calvinistic principles to the curriculum meant teaching morals. Principal G. Van Wesep outlined a model citizenship course consisting almost exclusively of teaching a different virtue each month, such as perseverance or uprightness of conduct. Gerhardus Bos applied "Christian principles in mathematics" by discussing usury, counterfeiting, overcharging, underpaying laborers, and irresponsible investment. For Bos and many of his colleagues, a Christian approach in a subject area meant the inclusion of problems or situations from which moral lessons could be drawn.[29]

Meanwhile, throughout the 1920s and particularly in the aftermath of the Scopes trial, the Christian Reformed Church had struck out at any evidence of "Modernism," i.e., at what it considered the false teaching and corrupting influence of liberal Protestant thought. With respect to education, modernists were held to be responsible for a whole array of evils: moral laxity, promotion of evolutionism, overemphasis of insignificant topics such as recreation in the curriculum, and perversion of the aims of education. Above all, modernism led to "worldliness." Communities watched teachers carefully to see whether they condoned such influences, or whether, "because of a lack of well-defined objectives," they used public school materials affected by modernism. Some of the clergy also became concerned that the lay leadership of the schools might not maintain orthodoxy. H. J. Kuiper regularly wrote that even though schools were independent entities, the Christian Reformed church should supervise the religious aspect of the school, settle doctrinal disputes, and question prospective teachers about their beliefs and lifestyles. If the Calvinistic heritage was to be safeguarded, the defenses had to be fortified.[30]

These issues came to a head in the Chicago Christian High School in the mid-1930s. When its staff was accused of worldliness in 1930, it published a defense that took a swipe at the church's narrow views of worldliness. The worldliness inherent in materialism, ruthless competition, social order evils, and war as a policy of national aggrandizement, the staff wrote, was "more destructive of the Christian life than the worldliness of play." That conclusion did not sit well with the clergy, nor with one of the school's teachers who accused her own colleagues of replacing Calvinistic principles with a social religion.[31] But the lay leadership of the school was also interested in the social implications of Christianity. It appointed its teacher of Biblical studies, Dr. Frederick H. Wezeman, to be principal. Wezeman was popular with the board, parents and students, but was viewed with suspicion by some of the clergy who believed him to lean towards theological liberalism.

By 1935, Wezeman had developed fifteen detailed Biblical courses, with voluminous mimeographed notes for his students. One Chicago clergyman, examining these notes and finding a number of instances of "modernism," published a book detailing how the school had become a "channel" for the heresies of Modernism. The school board published a lengthy retort, accusing the minister of engaging in an unjustifiable witchhunt. Because Wezeman was also a minister in the Christian Reformed Church, the controversy was brought to the church's annual synod in 1937 where Wezeman was forced to make a humiliating confession of guilt and repentance by repudiating, as he put it, the few erroneous statements in his courses.[32]

Although doctrinal purity was the focus of the dispute, there were a number of curricular implications. First, who was to control the curriculum, especially the Biblical studies component? A church synod committee consisting of clergy and seminary professors stated that "we should jealously guard our precious heritage by a careful supervision of all Bible teachings in . . . our schools for Christian instruction."[33] But school boards felt that they were responsible. The Wezeman case did not resolve this issue. Some ministers did not easily let go of the reins. In most communities major disputes were avoided only because the clergy molded the views of the supporting communities. Those views, in turn, shaped most of the curriculum decisions made by the boards of the schools.

A second curriculum issue that arose was the claim of some leaders by the mid-1930s that modernism and progressive education had the same anti-Christian roots. The Chicago board had written that Wezeman had made Bible instruction "consistent with the more progressive methods employed in other departments."[34] Wezeman presented the social context of Bible books, attributed Martin Luther's actions in part to his psychological make-up, and had students use original source documents rather than their Calvinist interpretations. Also, he made frequent use of the project method in studying Bible books. All this was criticized by the clergy. They could tolerate methodological progressivism almost as little as theological liberalism. But here the clergy did not get its way, at least in Chicago. Although Wezeman revised his manuals for doctrinal soundness, his basic approach and methodology were left intact and continued to be taught to his students.[35] Perhaps as a result of this, despite his manifest abilities and participation in subsequent curriculum debates, Wezeman was never directly involved in NUCS curriculum work. Pedagogically, as we shall see, Wezeman's approach remained an exception. The schools continued to be conservative educational institutions, fearful to sail into uncharted curricular and pedagogical waters and careful to remain within the currents of orthodox Calvinist doctrine and morality.

Pedagogical Forays:
1. Using the Shield of Bavinck

The scholars quoted most often in Christian education writings between the World Wars were the Dutch theologian and pedagogue Herman Bavinck and America's John Dewey—the former usually positively; the latter, negatively. This section will consider Bavinck's influence; the next, that of progressive education. Two books published in America in 1928 and 1935 summarized and discussed Bavinck's thought for teachers and teachers-in-training. These were based on his major educational work, **Paedagogische beginselen** [Pedagogical principles]. Bavinck, like his confrere Abraham Kuyper, held that Christian values and norms should guide all activity, from the simplest handicraft to the study of philosophy. This principle also provided the foundation for his fundamental aim of Christian education: to develop the whole human personality through true piety, sound knowledge, and genuine culture.[36]

Bavinck called Comenius, Rousseau and Pestalozzi "prophets" of education since they developed educational methodology on the basis of their ideals and philosophy. Although interested in defining a Christian counterpart, he recognized that through "common grace" all educational thinkers had developed some valid pedagogical methods. Such methods, he held, should be screened to ensure they fitted the pre-determined philosophical framework. Then a "scientific pedagogy" was needed that used empirical investigations to determine which of those methods were effective. Herbart, Bavinck added, was the first to lead pedagogy into such scientific, experimental channels.[37]

Bavinck enunciated educational ideals congruent with a Biblical view of the person and his relation with God and society. Concurrently he searched for suitable methods from diverse educational "prophets" as well as pedagogical "scientists." In line with Pestalozzi's **Anschauung** [sense-impression], Bavinck recognized the place of object and visual education and manual activities. However, Bavinck also believed God had revealed Himself especially through language. Moreover, his empirical observations made it clear to him that language explained, directed investigations, opened new worlds, and interpreted thought. Therefore, he concluded, auditory perception and language understanding and expression were of foremost importance in education, even though learning based on other perceptions should also have a place. Further, knowledge had both inherent and instrumental value, and therefore neither life practice, nor pupil interest, nor immediate utility could separately or collectively determine the choice of subject matter.[38]

Bavinck adapted many pedagogical methods on the basis of his conception of the Biblical view of the person as a responsible image bearer of God. He construed Herbart's conception of molding the individual to include the conscious self-activity of the individual. Since teachers' personalities were not to be structured by any specific pedagogical schemas, he did not advise the strict use of Herbart's five steps. In the classroom, teachers were to awaken interest; recitations based on memory only were dull and useless. Even though some indoctrination was inevitable in any school situation, coercive imposition of a system of thought was inconsistent with individual freedom. Young people were to be encouraged to evaluate family, social and religious beliefs and practices.[39]

Many of Bavinck's recommended procedures could be found in America's Christian schools. His emphasis on language was reflected in the importance attached to Bible and history story telling, discussion, recounting, making notes, and composition work. The popular 1928 NUCS publication of Heyns and Roelofs, **Christian Interpretation of American History,** followed Bavinck, for instance, in suggesting diverse methods to suit the particular age of the child, the nature of the class and school and the personality of the teacher. For the recitation method it proposed ways of meaningful student involvement such as outlining notes and drawing out the main points. It demonstrated how teachers could use the problem and project methods, contests, and structured group work, and gave **Anschauung** its due with the analysis of artifacts such as models, pictures, and original documents or their facsimiles. The authors also reiterated Bavinck's view that history enlarged the students' vision and understanding mainly through words and language. Bavinck's conception of the "organic unity" of the disciplines was used in a section on the correlation between history and geography, reading, literature, and government.[40]

Bavinck was quoted frequently in articles about education. The importance of maintaining a proper balance between the individuality of children and their membership in society, and of the primacy of the teacher's personality in the classroom represent some of Bavinck's recurring themes. His emphasis on piety and authority appealed to Christian school supporters, while his eclecticism made almost everyone feel comfortable with some of his pedagogic recommendations.[41]

Yet the eclectic nature of his work also made Bavinck's influence appear greater than it was. First, some of his ideas had always been accepted in Christian schools. Instances of this were his insistence that religious and ethical education should form the core of the curriculum, and that lecture and recitation, if used properly, were valid modes of teaching and learning. Secondly, many of his suggestions were based on nineteenth century educational thought that would have been adopted by the schools in any case, such as the frequently recommended use of models, maps and pictures that enabled students to learn by seeing and touching as well as hearing. Third, Bavinck could be called upon to defend almost any pedagogic mode. Heyns and Roelofs' suggested use of the problem and project methods, for example, based on progressive thought, could also be defended on the basis of Bavinck's notion of conscious self-activity. Yet some methods that Bavinck frowned upon, such as variations of the Herbartian five steps, were nevertheless popular.[42]

In fact, Bavinck's approach was brandished as a shield to defend prevailing or favoured methods, not to develop comprehensive pedagogical theory or practice. His suggestions that could have changed the mode or content of learning significantly, such as his suggestions that pupils be given opportunity to grow educationally in "proper social mediums" outside of school, had little impact. The same was true for his view that authority be used to lead children to more responsibility and freedom.[43] A subject like mathematics remained more important in the curriculum than history even though Bavinck suggested the reverse since "the spirit is nobler than matter; the person is more significant than nature."[44] Authors discussed Bavinck's conception of the "organic unity" of the curriculum in terms of relating and integrating subject disciplines, but failed to indicate how this could be accomplished. Van Zyl's class notes for the basic teaching methodology course taught at Calvin College around 1940 indicated that little attention was paid to Bavinck. Cornelius Jaarsma, one of the few persons who showed in-depth appreciation of Bavinck's ideas and tried to apply them, made little headway and made a conscious decision to teach at a state college rather than at Calvin College.[45] By and large, Bavinck served as a source of convenient quotes to defend the status quo. Christian school methodology and curriculum content continued to parallel closely that of the non-progressive American public school.

Pedagogical Forays: 2. Fending Off the Phantom Attacks of Progressivism

Between the World Wars, Christian school leaders failed to develop thorough and incisive critiques of progressive education that could have been used to advance Christian educational thinking and practice. Leaders, skeptical of Dewey's scientific method approach to ethics and his secular social gospel sense, blinded themselves to the fact that some of Dewey's notions were not unrelated to Bavinck's desire that teachers awaken interest in their pupils and that learning was to be socially relevant. This was true in Dewey's case in the call for a change in education from passive and inert recipiency to more active, expressive, and self-directing learning through the scientific solving of problems germane to the interests of the pupils. But the Christian schools gave little attention to progressivism until, late in the 1930s, criticism of it started to mount in the American press.

One of the first articles by a Christian school leader, typical of most that followed, appeared in 1937. The author, a principal, neglected Dewey's argument that moral principles and training were inherent in community life and in education. Rather, he focused solely on Dewey's claim that no moral ideals and standards existed except those experienced through scientific or empirical verification in a social context, i.e., that truth was functional rather than absolute, implying that neither Dewey nor his followers like Kilpatrick could accept unchanging religious truths. By extrapolating this statement, the author, without giving any evidence, concluded that pragmatism and its related progressive education thinking was responsible for America's apostasy and the breakdown of the influence of the Christian church. The next year theologian Louis Berkhof, in a similar vein, wrote that no distinctions existed between Darwinian evolutionism, progressivism, and behaviourism in that all ruled out God and religion.[46] Such statements by Calvinists were understandable reactions to Dewey's signing of the 1933 Humanist Manifesto, which stated that modern science made "unacceptable any supernatural or cosmic guarantees of human values."[47] However, the narrow focus of the criticism precluded Christian schools from standing back and gauging the education taking place in their own classrooms in terms of some of Dewey's legitimate insights into the nature of education.

One author did propose in the **Calvin Forum** that progressive education might not be all bad. He criticized the Christian schools for emphasizing the acquisition of information, stating that this led to "unintegrated and barren Christian living." Students needed inquiry to develop "free or open minds that can live in a free society." However, his article only served to intensify the attack. "Dewey's method and his philosophy cannot be separated," wrote one respondent, "The consistent 'democratic' or inductive method also appears to do violence to the Biblical conception of man in his fallen state." Several months later five solicited reactions were published. Most reflected NUCS' Mark Fakkema's view that Dewey's ideals were "anti-Christian."[48]

Indeed, the most acid and distorted condemnation of progressivism came from Fakkema's pen. He had visited four California "progressive" schools, where, he claimed, education could be compared to the activities in a zoo. Kindergarten children, he asserted, were sitting on the floor like small animals "on a lower wrung (sic) of the evolutionary ladder." No training of the mind nor any moral discipline occurred "lest the teacher poison the evolutionary mind." Learning was incidental to the self-chosen activities. As the logical outcome of evolutionism, progressive education was retrogressive and caused illiteracy and juvenile delinquency.[49] Fakkema's conclusions were actually his **a priori** assumptions which governed the interpretation of his observations. Moreover, like Albert Lynd a decade later, Fakkema confused illustration with proof, and assumed that modern school practices were bad because they were based on Dewey's philosophy of pragmatism, which in turn was purportedly based on evolutionism.[50] Fakkema should have been aware of the distinction between philosophy and the science of pedagogy which Bavinck, for one, had clearly described. Fakkema's caricature of progressive education was nevertheless distributed in pamphlet form to all teachers and board members.

Such condemnations, however, did not mean that progressive education had not influenced the schools. In 1923, an article sanctioned by the NUCS board enjoined teachers to profit from "the progressive tendencies in our American public and Roman Catholic schools."[51] Teachers also wrote about their attempts to introduce self-activity and project approaches. Mark Fakkema himself introduced a column in which the contributor, influenced by Kilpatrick's **The Project Method**, described how the project could be used as a purposeful activity which is the "end point of a problem," developing "initiative, leadership, and independence in solving problems." A number of articles indicated that the project method was not only used but also accepted even by traditional principals as long as it did not supplant "regular work." Also, articles in the 1920s proposed curriculum development based on Franklin Bobbitt's method of "activity analysis" or scientific investigation of humans in their social settings. In order to help schools to set curriculum priorities and plan learning activities in line with the psychological needs of children, this model, almost identical to that of the Twenty-Sixth N.S.S.E. **Yearbook** (and used in at least one subsequent Christian school language course outline), consisted of a large number of specific skill-based objectives: "To enlarge the vocabulary by consciously adding to it useful new words encountered in every line of work." Scientific curriculum development had found at least some disciples among Christian school leaders.[52]

Indeed, a significant number of the effects of progressive education on the curriculum mentioned by Lawrence Cremin also came about in Christian schools. Because of the schools' small size, lack of funds, and the conservatism of Christian school supporters, these effects often occurred more slowly. Examples include the reorganization of the schools to contain separate junior high schools; a gradual introduction of industrial arts, home economics, and physical education courses; more attractive textbooks; more supplementary devices like flash cards and workbooks; and, of course, the use of projects and activities to supplement (though not to supplant) more traditional procedures.[53]

From the early 1930s on, however, both the depression and the religious milieu led to a more conservative climate. Discussion of methodology decreased, and gradually anything that could be considered "progressive" became anathema. Traditional approaches were once again

148

hailed. One principal said, "Instead of 'continued change and becoming,' the Christian school teaches constancy . . . instead of individual experimentation, the Christian school indoctrinates her pupils, teaching them systematically the eternal verities." Teachers similarly chose traditional lecture and discussion approaches.[54] Progressivism was equated with the heresies of modernism, evolutionism, and ethical relativism. The 1920s intrusions of a few characteristics of progressive education, nevertheless, had helped the schools provide a more balanced methodology. Progressivism had certainly not made threatening or debilitating inroads into the Christian school movement.

Yet especially in the early 1940s the marching orders were clear: the defenses had to be shored up or the traditional stability of the schools might be undermined. Fending off these phantom attacks of progressivism did not greatly affect the schools; they were already safe within the fold of conservatism. Rather, the forays against progressivism helped the leaders rally their supporters against the perceived weaknesses of the public schools—and, by implication, behind the bulwark of Christian education.

The Gordian Knot of the Christian School Curriculum

B. J. Bennink's 1915 **Course of Study** failed to forge a consensus regarding "Christian" curriculum. In 1923 the Chicago Alliance of Christian Schools tried once again to do so:

> How must we apply our principles—this is the Gordian knot which must be untied by all those who follow worthily the calling of the Christian teacher.

Its document held that the knot could be cut only if those principles were thought of as "attitudes of heart and mind which must be caught by the pupils." An intellectual or mechanical teaching of religious and moral maxims would have little effect on students; rather, teachers should radiate attitudes such as reverence toward God.[55] Andrew Blystra, likely one of the authors of this document, illustrated this in two articles. In one, he narrated how a teacher could model "warmth of love" and an acceptance of faith in God while conducting an oral language lesson. In another, he argued that teachers who love "God's truth" in the beauty and symmetry of figures will in turn inspire their pupils to love and adore God.[56]

However, Christian school leaders were not convinced that the Gordian knot had been cut. One wrote that not all Christian principles could be "lived out" in attitudes in the school and that, in any case, the distinction between teaching by precept and through attitude was a "false antithesis."[57] Indeed, which attitudes were involved or how they could be transferred from teacher to student by means of the curriculum was not made clear. The Chicago Alliance failed to develop any further its view of what made a curriculum Christian.

Subsequent curriculum articles and materials disclosed three other distinct (though not always mutually exclusive) notions of how the knot of Christian curriculum ought to be cut. The most common, often implicit one, was that Christian principles and moral truths could be added to a secular curriculum. Mark Fakkema said that in addition to what public school teachers did, Christian school teachers should also acquaint pupils with Calvinistic principles. Thus an art outline listed standard skills and activities, with the introduction asking teachers to remind pupils that God's designs in His creation were perfect and that His laws governed beauty, unity, balance and rhythm.[58] Although the Chicago Alliance document had criticized such an approach as adding a little Christian "salt" to secular "food," it was the easiest and most common way to "Christianize" the curriculum.

Another view, that the interpretation of subject matter made the curriculum Christian and that all facts needed to be interpreted "Christianly," was worked out in most detail in history.[59] The interpretation of history began with the assumption that America, founded on Protestant and democratic principles, was singularly able to promote and perpetuate true liberty and justice. Thus, first of all, any events considered favorable to America's development were interpreted as part of God's plan; any deleterious happenings were the result of human sin. God's will decreed that the Thirteen Colonies became "one nation that was to be an example to the world of civic and religious freedom." God used the Iroquois to help keep America English and Protestant. Washington was God's gift to America, and he "was signally aided by the blindness which Providence seemed to have inflicted on the enemy." Conversely, the Civil War was God's retribution for the offense of slavery. Secondly, the progress of civilization was a blessing that reflected the progressive unfolding of God's world plan. Thus scientific and technological inventions were "God's gracious method of lightening the curse of sin and making life more pleasant and agreeable," even though an invention like the automobile might also be used for evil purposes such as aiding crime.[60]

Not that there was agreement about the interpretation of all historical "facts." Two authors had encouraged the NUCS to develop a history manual because American history books did not interpret the

Mexican War to have been caused by an illegitimate desire for territorial expansion. Yet the subsequently published NUCS manual concluded that "America was amply justified in making war." Another author, in writing about the futility and bestiality of war, asked whether "we have not been indulging overmuch in a spread-eagle and superficial cant when called upon to treat matters of national interest." However, the NUCS manual defended the "brave fighting" of the English before the Revolution, and of the Americans during and after the Revolution. The defense of "Manifest Destiny" was an overriding theme in the interpretation of history. It influenced not only how facts were interpreted but also which ones were included. For instance, the treatment of the native people at the hands of the whites would have detracted from showing that America had always striven for true liberty and justice, and was excluded from the NUCS manuals.[61]

A final view of how a Christian curriculum should be constructed embraced all the previous ones. A Biblical worldview was to give the spiritual basis and the philosophical equipment to develop "a God-centered system of thought which unites all instruction in its one ultimate purpose, namely, the glory of God." This notion was strong on generalities, e.g., "the Biblical view of life should constitute the golden thread running through the entire teaching process," but devoid of practical suggestions. A Grand Rapids Christian High School statement of objectives stated that the whole curriculum was to be "guided primarily by the light of Scripture." Yet its six individual and three social objectives included only one that could not have been found in a public school counterpart, viz., the "spiritual" one: "A fostering of Christian faith and life, and of all the Christian virtues." In practice, the all-encompassing worldview conception of Christian curriculum was very limited in its application.[62]

Two of these four Christian curriculum views remained undeveloped: the one in which students absorbed proper attitudes from their teachers, and the one which embodied a comprehensive worldview. The other views which aimed at injecting religious precepts into secular material and at interpreting factual material Christianly were more commonly applied, perhaps because the basic public school curriculum could then be used with minor modifications. John De Boer was on solid ground when he wrote in 1929 that "we have been copying also the curriculum practices of the public schools, adding perhaps a few details to lend a religious air to the instruction." Almost all textbooks used at this time were standard public school ones. Course outlines and textbooks prescribed by some of the states were accepted without question, as were curriculum accreditation requirements. Schools took pride in the fact that graduates did well on state and standardized tests. Little was done "to organize courses specifically designed for Christian schools."[63]

Decisions to fall in line with public education sometimes were made deliberately. Principal Blystra stated that since the movement was small, "ours is rather the privilege to follow, consciously, in the wake of larger tendencies." This gave the schools the opportunity to scrutinize trends closely before accepting them. True enough, articles about methods of teaching reading, spelling, and composition; about the introduction of health programs; about the use of standardized tests, objective test questions, and the normal curve in evaluation all reflected the current trends in contemporary educational literature. None showed serious attempts to develop approaches deliberately based on "Christian principles." The common view was that "what our present society . . . considers necessary to be taught in the schools, we also must teach our children."[64]

Except for the addition of Biblical studies, the schools' subject organization therefore also followed that of the traditional American public schools. When grades 9 and 10 were started in Edgerton, Minnesota in 1939, for instance, Biblical studies and English were taught each year. The grade 9 program also included algebra, geography, and general science; grade 10 included geometry, biology, and world history. However, no provision was made in the standard five-period day for physical education, the fine arts, or industrial arts or home economics. The introduction of the latter subjects lagged for a number of reasons. Not a few parents and teachers believed "handwork" was second-rate and should not replace "mindwork." Colleges, including Calvin College, gave credit only for academic subjects. The cost of introducing some of these subjects could be prohibitive. While commercial courses were introduced in Grand Rapids when its high school was founded in 1920, industrial education was not introduced until eight years later when a public school made its facilities available. Music gradually became more common, but drama remained controversial for many years because of the condemnation of the theatre by the Christian Reformed Church and the paucity of "suitable" plays. Yet on the whole, except for a slower introduction of electives, curriculum organization and practices paralleled those of public schools.[65]

Clearly, the Gordian knot of Christian curriculum—how Calvinistic principles were to result in the implementation of a uniquely Christian curriculum—had not yet been "untied." Hence, concerns about the lack of distinctiveness of the curriculum and about the worthwhileness of

152

Christian schools increased. If the Calvinist faith affected all areas of life, why wasn't that apparent in the curriculum? By the 1940s, Bavinck was felt to be outdated, but no other Christian theory of education was available. The organization and content of the curriculum as well as instructional methodology imitated that of the public sector. Besides Biblical studies, the only subjects prone to Christian interpretations were history and geography. Already in 1929 John De Boer had called for a "widespread program of curriculum investigation in curriculum-problems facing our schools," suggesting a method to do this involving both NUCS and Calvin College educators.[66] However, as will become clear, dissatisfaction with the continued lack of curricular distinctiveness did not lead to tangible action until 1943.

Writing Geography Materials: Contentions
Within the Bulwark

Christian school educators agreed that their curriculum materials should reflect "Christian principles." However, there the agreement ended. Projects that liberally sprinkled Bible texts or moral rules throughout factual material, or that gave "Christian" interpretations of historical or geographical facts received legitimate criticism for often being simplistic or superficial. But the critics were unable to provide acceptable alternatives, and few curriculum efforts between the wars received general endorsement. Some projects died after a lengthy period of unsuccessful incubation while others, published by the NUCS, did not sell well. Many project discussions were surreptitious, perhaps not to hurt the feelings of those involved. Consequently, the issues remained unclear and productive dialogue about curriculum development for Christian schools was stifled.

Efforts to provide geography materials for the schools provide a case in point. In 1922 George Bos wrote a fifth grade geography book, apparently using B. J. Bennink's earlier manuals as a model. The NUCS textbook committee examined the manuscript but recommended against its publication, citing prohibitive costs. Other causes, however, lurked in the background. The committee did not think that Bos' presentation of basic facts in its intended small, soft-cover format was American enough. With shaky logic but clear intent, it reasoned that America's egalitarian educational system required large, colourful books, not small handbooks. The latter suited European schools that "fit pupils for their destined place in society." The Christian schools were to be part of the American "system," which, instead of "skill and drill," now aimed at such progressive notions as "self-realization, initiative and originality."

153

A textbook needed to be an elaborate source book for a "happy combination" of the memory-recall and problem-project methods. Rather than a manual which served only the memory-recall method, schools should use standard public school texts and develop teachers' guides "prepared by our men."[67]

The NUCS board told Bos only that publishing a geography book would be too expensive. Undaunted, in 1923 Bos himself went ahead and published 750 copies of his **Practical Geography for Christian Schools,** most of which sold quickly.[68] The NUCS board was in an awkward position. The organization had been established three years earlier partly to make curriculum material available. Now before it had published anything, an individual had printed and distributed a book, turned down by the NUCS, for which there was some demand. The board decided to investigate the Bos textbook once more. A few months later it recommended the text as a supplementary one and expressed a willingness to "take over and edit the next edition."[69]

This decision was taken despite a new textbook committee report condemning the book for

> interspersing the instruction . . . with Biblical references, religious truths, and Christian principles to such an extent that the application of Christian principles is rendered strongly intellectual in character and mechanical in performance. It is evident that the author believes that constant reference to Bible truths, frequent quoting of Scripture texts will have a hallowing effect upon the teaching.[70]

Such criticism was valid. Bos applied figurative Bible texts to concrete geographical phenomena. He used one text, for instance, to "prove" that the earth was a sphere moving through space. Tacked-on morals distracted from major geographical concepts, e.g., the Klondike gold rush was described in terms of the Biblical text, "But what shall it profit a man, if he shall gain the whole world, and lose his own soul?"[71] Moreover, geographical facts and their religious "truths" were to be accepted and memorized in rather fragmented fashion. The choice of geographical facts had been determined by standard public school geography texts. Bos did not see any need for dealing with the impact of physical features on culture, or how it might be possible for Christians to make contributions to the development of culture and society.

The Christian school movement would have been well served if the NUCS board had used discussions about these shortcomings as a launching pad for developing a theoretical basis for curriculum work.

But the board was not open about the textbook committee's misgivings, and consequently even at the end of Bos' life he still believed that the main shortcoming of his book was its lack of coloured maps and beautiful illustrations. The board affirmed this belief by asking Bos and his brother to write another geography book, with the textbook committee to edit their work.[72]

The board at the same time overruled the textbook committee's recommendation that Iowa's C. Aué be asked to write the NUCS geography publication. With that, the board rejected Aué's emphasis on cultural geography. Aué in his geography articles had written about the "cruelty and wickedness" displayed in black-white relations; the unholy alliances between Christian missions and commercial enterprises; and the need to distribute God's gifts of food, clothing, and resources equitably. He wanted to develop geography courses around cultural themes such as how humans have provided for shelter and food, in order for pupils to understand both that God was the "Giver of all good and perfect gifts" and that they could "learn from other nations."[73]

By failing to give reasons for deciding not to publish the Bos book, yet using him as a writer and rejecting Aué's cultural approach, the board during the next ten years did not seem to know what it wanted philosophically, pedagogically, or curricularly. Bos first worked on a new textbook and then on a teachers' manual, under the auspices of the NUCS textbook committee. Its publication was constantly said to be pending shortly—and always was unavoidably delayed. Bos withdrew from the project in 1929, and although a number of other authors worked on the project, enthusiasm waned. Frustrated with the lack of progress, the Michigan Alliance of Christian Schools developed its own course of study in geography in 1934.[74]

The NUCS geography project, and a history guide developed at about the same time, ran aground to a large extent because the board was unwilling to set out a clear direction and failed to capitalize on opportunities to stimulate curriculum thought. A contributing factor was the reluctance of Christian school educators—including members of the textbook committee and the board—to support projects that did not have their total and complete approval.[75] No climate of open discussion was created that might have helped the NUCS to begin to develop well-grounded curriculum approaches. By its actions surrounding geography curriculum work, the board tightened rather than loosened the Gordian knot of Christian curriculum development.

Sensing the Problems Within the Bulwark

Enrollment in the Christian schools slipped only slightly (by about seven percent) during the depression of the 1930s. Most parents continued to believe that Christian schools were not just a luxury but a necessity for their children. However, by this time the efforts of Kuyper-influenced leaders to make the schools institutions promoting cultural transformation, never understood by most supporters, had been forgotten. The rationale for Christian schools for most parents was isolation from secular society. Complaints of Grand Rapids Christian High School parents, for example, focused on profanity and evolutionism in the textbooks. More and more, parents also wanted the schools to stress academic excellence so that graduates could make their mark in American society. A strong parental lobby to update Grand Rapids' system of teaching bookkeeping resulted directly from a concern that the school would be as good as or surpass public school standards. Christian school distinctiveness for most parents meant maintaining strict morals, orthodox religious instruction, and a good academic curriculum without frills.[76]

The schools helped to cast their pupils into the mold of the Christian Reformed subculture. In a protected environment, they were taught to be orthodox and obedient members of the church and patriotic citizens of America. Moreover, they learned that to be the one implied the other. America was founded on Christian ideals, and any problems America faced were the result of not living up to those ideals. Therefore, parents accepted the traditional public school curriculum, unlike their forefathers in the Netherlands one hundred years earlier. At the same time, they approved materials such as Heyns and Roelofs' **Christian Interpretation of American History,** which emphasized more than public textbooks could the providence of God and the necessity of an exacting Protestant morality—and did so within the framework of the American dream.

Mark Fakkema's leadership as NUCS general secretary from 1926 to 1947 had not helped the schools advance their curricular thinking. Although he travelled far and wide to meld the individual schools into one movement and to start new schools, eventually his leadership foundered on contradictions. He promoted distinct Calvinistic education, but his increasingly reactionary views led him to establish close contact with fundamentalists (especially Baptists) by the mid-1940s. He knew Kuyper's vision of Calvinism as a dynamic cultural force, but set it aside for emotional sorties against evolutionism and progressivism. Although he had defended society control rather than church control of the schools, in 1947 he left the NUCS to work for an association with many church-based schools. On the one hand he said that all activities in life must "spell homage to God, our King," and therefore was critical of the direction and content of the public school curriculum, yet on the other hand he felt that the Christian school curriculum could be the same as that of the public school as long as the "spirit" of Christianity was added. In a 1946 pamphlet, Fakkema quoted five reasons for Christian schooling, all negative or defensive: deterioration of home life; inability of churches to keep young people as members; moral breakdown in society; inefficiency of learning in public schools; and the rising threat of Catholicism and atheism. For Fakkema and most Christian school supporters, the schools were to be bulwarks guarding against the disintegration rife in society and its public schools.[77]

Not everyone shared Fakkema's defensive attitude, however. For example, two NUCS nature study readers in the later 1930s tried to instill appreciation for a positive Christian lifestyle by portraying children who took pleasure in being active in and exploring "God's great outdoors." In an easy and engaging style, author Marion Schoolland wrote honestly about children's feelings and emotions, openly discussing people's shortcomings and how to cope with them. The readers contained numerous suggestions for activities and projects, and were attractively designed. Despite favourable reviews, however, they did not sell well. One likely reason was that their use necessitated some integration of science and reading. Also, Schoolland presented a joyful Christian way of life, giving explicit religious or moral truths only sporadically. Most schools were not ready to accept Schoolland's approach.[78]

By the end of World War II, the schools had failed to work consistently within a definite pedagogical framework such as that of Bavinck, or to develop their own theory of instruction. They favoured conservative public school approaches to methodology and curriculum. They feared progressive education, more for philosophical than educational reasons. The diverse existing views of a Christian curriculum were seldom delineated clearly. General slogans abounded; their translation into classroom practice seldom occurred. Little agreement about the value of specific curriculum projects existed. Even the NUCS Biblical studies series, written to defend the Calvinist faith, came under increasing attack for being too intellectual and not providing a core for the curriculum.

B. J. Bennink's words to the 1931 meeting of the Michigan Alliance still rang true in 1945: "Our cause as a whole has not made enough progress . . . . As schools we must be willing to give up our individuality, to become part of a better whole."[79] Even Mark

A BULWARK AGAINST MODERNISM (1920-1945)

Fakkema started to see that not all problems could be attributed to progressivism and modernism; some had arisen from within. He believed that such problems could be overcome if the NUCS would emphasize public relations work. This would arouse all supporters to become involved so that "with God's blessing [we may] regain in time whatever territory has been lost and may aid growing school communities to make even greater progress."[80]

However, the NUCS board realized that such promotion, while possibly extending the bulwark of Christian education, would not put it on a solid foundation. Wranglings ensued between the board and Fakkema about the nature of his role in the organization. Criticism of Fakkema's educational and curriculum leadership increased. The board re-established an education committee to develop educational principles and policies, so that the NUCS could "exert more influence upon its schools and upon its teachers." This committee set about in 1943 to publish a course of study "based on a Christian philosophy of education," and to develop Christian textbooks.[81] Various persons became involved in drawing up a philosophy of Christian education to direct future work. The movement finally realized that Christian education needed to be shored up from within if it was to remain a viable educational alternative. A new phase in the development of Christian education was about to begin.

NOTES

1. Speech by principal Andrew Blystra just before the founding of the NUCS in 1920. Andrew Blystra personal papers, Heritage Hall Archives.

2. Henry Kuiper, "The National Union Begins to Function," **Christian Home and School,** June 1954, pp. 16-19. Of the eight parts of Fakkema's job description, six included the infinitive "to promote," and the other two were "to gain membership" and "to solicit funds."

3. NUCS **Convention Papers 1938,** p. 21. Also see the many quotes in Louis Y. Van Dyke, "Above Circumstances and Conditions: Convention Addresses of the NUCS, 1935-1945," in James A. De Jong and Louis Y. Van Dyke, eds., **Building the House: Essays on Christian Education** (Sioux Center, Iowa: Dordt College Press, 1981), pp. 7-25.

4. Timothy L. Smith, "Historic Waves of Religious Interest in America," in Richard D. Lamberty, ed., **Religion in American**

Society, Volume 332 of The Annals of the American Academy of Political and Social Science (Philadelphia, 1960), p. 17; J. Huizinga, In the Shadow of To-Morrow, trans. by J. H. Huizinga (London: William Heinemann, 1936), especially pp. 1-5.

5. The Banner, Sept. 6, 1929, p. 596; Christian School Magazine, Feb. 1929, p. 637; and NUCS Convention Papers 1936, p. 2.

6. Enrollment figures in NUCS Yearbooks and Annuals:

1921	12 127	1929	14 022	1937	13 747	1945	18 448
1923	12 582	1931	13 710	1937	13 668	1947	21 503
1925	13 243	1933	13 000	1947	14 320	1948	22 570
1927	13 508	1935	13 360	1947	15 629	1949	23 970

The decline from the 1929 enrollment peak was slightly but not significantly greater than for public and other private schools. Once enrollment had bottomed out, Christian school enrollment increased much more quickly than either public or private enrollment, even with little or no immigration. Between 1939 and 1949, for instance, public school enrollment declined 1.3%; private school enrollment increased 29.5%; while Christian school growth was 75.4%.

7. NUCS Convention Papers 1938, pp. 20-21; Christian Reformed Church Acts of Synod 1943, pp. 73-74. It reached fifty percent once more in 1943.

8. The Banner, Sept. 6, 1929, p. 596; NUCS Convention Papers 1938, p. 41; Religion and Culture, Nov. 1921, p. 85.

9. The Banner, Sept. 6, 1929, pp. 596-97. In 1927 the Chicago Alliance submitted a proposal to the NUCS Annual Meeting that steps be taken to restore the schools' distinctive character (NUCS Eighth Annual Meeting, Aug. 31-Sept. 1, 1927).

10. Christian Home and School, Nov. 1941, p. 6.

11. NUCS Yearbook 1922, p. 86; Albert J. Boersma, In the School of the Master (Sioux Center, 1971), p. 68; NUCS Convention Papers 1938, pp. 39-40; The Banner, Sept. 6, 1929, p. 596; Christian Home and School, Jan. 1936, p. 5; NUCS Yearbook 1935-36, p. 3; NUCS Annual 1944, p. 48; and The Witness, Jan. 1925, p. 29.

12. NUCS Convention Papers 1938, p. 38.

13. NUCS Yearbook 1945, p. 108. Christian Home and School, April 1938, p. 7; Faithful Workers in the House of God, 1938 NUCS promotion pamphlet, p. 5; and Religion and Culture, Nov. 1924, p. 84.

14. The Banner, Sept. 15, 1933, pp. 741 and 747. While the relationship of the Christian Reformed Church to American fundamentalism has always been ambivalent, its attitude towards

American culture during this period was shaped both by its pietistic tradition and by the manifestations of fundamentalism in American society between the two world wars. The Scopes trial had symbolized the clash of nineteenth century conservative Christian American culture with what fundamentalists labelled "modernism." Such modernism in a narrow sense referred to the application of scientific and social methods in applying religious principles to the needs of living persons. More loosely, fundamentalists used it to describe modern culture and intellect, believed to be increasingly decadent. Within conservative Christian churches, vehement attacks on such modernism occurred in efforts to maintain their own social and ideological identity. See George M. Marsden, **Fundamentalism and American Culture** (Oxford: Oxford University Press, 1980) and Richard Hofstadter, **Anti-Intellectualism in American Life** (New York: Knopf, 1963). Many Dutch Calvinists did not consider themselves Fundamentalists since, unlike the latter, they put a great deal of emphasis on God's sovereignty and the Christian's responsibility to serve God in all areas of life. Yet their Seceder piety made them join forces with the Fundamentalists in opposing "modernism" and "worldliness." See Joseph H. Hall, "The Controversy over Fundamentalism in the Christian Reformed Church 1915-1966" (Th.D. dissertation, Concordia Seminary, St. Louis, 1974).

15. "Summary of Replies to Sacred History Questionnaire," **Christian School Magazine**, Nov. 1926, p. 261.

16. Nick Yff, pp. 73, 77, 81; NUCS mimeographed report, "The Union Bible Course Now Available" (circa 1934); L. J. Flokstra, "The Christian Day School's Share in Giving Biblical Instruction," in NUCS **Convention Papers 1925**, pp. 80-81; and Henry Beets, **The Christian Reformed Church in North America: Its History, Schools, Mission, Creed and Liturgy, Distinctive Principles and Practices, and Its Church Government** (Grand Rapids: Eastern Avenue Book Store, 1923), pp. 221-23. For more than twenty years, **Banner** editor H. J. Kuiper spoke of applying Biblical principles to all courses--without giving any concrete illustrations of what he meant. See **The Banner** of Aug. 16, 1929 and Nov. 11, 1949, for example.

17. **The Banner**, Sept. 5, 1930 and Nov. 11, 1949; L. Berkhof, "The Teaching of Sacred History in Our Schools," mimeographed speech, n.d., p. 1; L. J. Flokstra, p. 18; "Summary of Replies to Sacred History Questionnaire," p. 261; **Christian School Magazine**, March 1927, pp. 325-26.

18. Christian School Magazine, Nov. 1922, p. 143; Sept. 1924, p. 724; Jan. 1925, pp. 848-51; Jan. 1927, p. 291; NUCS Convention Papers 1925, p. 81; Christian Home and School, Jan. 1938, p. 4; Teachers of the East, Teacher's Guide for Bible Study (Pre-Publication Edition for Grades One to Four, 1936), pp. 23 and 26.

19. See, for example, C. R. Jaarsma, R. H. Postma and J. Tuls, Outline of Sacred History for Christian Instruction (Grand Rapids, Michigan: Van Noord, 1920), which was full of questions such as "In what language was the Old Testament written?," and "Which of the Ten Commandments refers to the Sabbath?" (pp. 10, 13).

20. A. Blystra et al., Bible Study Pupil's Manuals (Chicago: NUCS), Part I (1935), Part II (1936), Part III (1935), Part IV (1937) and Part V (1940), with one teachers' guide for the whole series.

21. Bible Study Manual Part I, pp. 34, 35, 39. One publication took a somewhat different approach: W. Heyns' Outlines and Notes on Bible History, Old Testament, Second Edition (Grand Rapids: Van Noord, 1921). Without denying that the Bible had a dogmatic and moral side, Heyns looked at it primarily as the description of how God acted to redeem His people and the creation, and how people responded in faith (or lack of it). This is referred to in Reformed circles as the historical-redemptive approach. Heyns' approach gained little favour compared with the more directly moralistic and exemplary materials. With few curriculum materials available, it placed only seventh in the frequency of popularity in the 1926 questionnaire to the principals.

22. B. J. Bennink, Sketches from Church History (Grand Rapids, Michigan: Eerdmans for the NUCS, 1925). A second edition, revised by A. S. De Jong, was published by the NUCS itself in 1936 under the title The Church in the World. The quotes are from pp. 10, 11 and 181 of the 1925 edition. A. S. De Jong in the 1936 edition inserted several paragraphs on "the sway of God's rule" extending to the "spheres of family, state, commerce, industry, science, and art," but gave no specific examples (The Church in the World, p. 13). One other church history book published during this period, D. H. Kromminga's A History of the Christian Church for High Schools (Grand Rapids, Michigan: Eerdmans, 1945), was too difficult and was not used a great deal.

23. G. W. Hylkema, "The Aim of Christian Education," NUCS Yearbook 1929-30, p. 103.

24. The Banner, Sept. 5, 1930, p. 788. H. J. Kuiper stated the latter this in a speech summarized in the Nov. 1922 issue of Christian School Magazine and reprinted in full in the Feb. and March

1923 issues of **The Witness.**

25. **The Witness,** March 1923, p. 60; **Christian School Magazine,** Nov. 1922, p. 151; **The Banner,** Sept. 5, 1930, p. 788; and NUCS, **Faithful Workers in the House of God** (1938), p. 5.

26. Effie J. Zwier, "The Teaching of English," **Christian School Magazine,** March 1923, pp. 264-65.

27. **Christian School Magazine,** March 1931, p. 934.

28. Garrett Heyns and Garritt E. Roelofs, **Christian Interpretation of American History** (Chicago: NUCS, 1928), pp. 12, 92, 146-48. For a description of those Puritan principles, see Richard Reinitz, ed., **Tensions in American Puritanism** (New York: John Wiley, 1970). The Puritans' strain of piety (p. 1), was characterized, among other things, by total responsibility for one's behaviour; a pursuit of one's calling based in diligent labour; duty and obedience, especially to God; a sense of mission and "chosenness"; the pursuit of truth, righteousness, justice, and mercy; and self-examination. Bernard Bailyn in **Education in the Formation of American Society** (New York: Random House, 1960) has shown how the New England Puritans applied these principles to the education of their children.

29. NUCS **Convention Papers 1926,** p. 69; **Christian Home and School,** Feb. 1939, p. 7.

30. **The Banner,** Sept. 5, 1930, p. 588; Sept. 7, 1934, p. 744; Jan. 15, 1937, p. 52; April 25, 1947, pp. 516-17, 537; May 2, 1947, pp. 548, 569.

31. **Christian School Magazine,** Nov. 1930, pp. 933-34; March 1931, pp. 926-30.

32. Herman Kuiper, **The Chicago Situation: A Word of Warning to the Churches** (Chicago: Calvin Press, 1935); The Chicago Christian High School Board, **The Truth About the Chicago Situation** (Chicago: Christian High School Press, 1936); James Donald Bratt, "Dutch Calvinism in Modern America: The History of a Conservative Subculture" (Ph.D. dissertation, Yale University, 1978), p. 287; Christian Reformed Church **Acts of Synod 1937,** p. 115.

33. Christian Reformed Church **Acts of Synod 1936,** p. 139.

34. **The Truth About the Chicago Situation,** p. 8.

35. Ibid., pp. 83-87, 125-27. The most frequently attacked manual was Wezeman's "Project Studies in the Book of Amos." A comparison of the revised version available in Heritage Hall Archives with the criticisms made over a number of years by various ministers and committees indicates that Wezeman revised only the specific

paragraphs that were attacked for doctrinal unsoundness.

36. Herman Bavinck, **Paedagogische beginselen** (Kampen: Kok, 1904), pp. 52-53; J. Brederveld, **Christian Education: A Summary and Critical Discussion of Bavinck's Pedagogical Principles,** translated by two members of the faculty of Calvin College (Grand Rapids, Michigan: Smitter, 1928), pp. 34-35, 63-65; and Cornelius Jaarsma, **The Educational Philosophy of Herman Bavinck: A Textbook in Education** (Grand Rapids: Eerdmans, 1935), pp. 135-36, 224-25. Bavinck did not define what he meant by "sound knowledge" and "genuine culture."

37. Brederveld, pp. 21-24, 31-32.

38. Ibid., pp. 97-101; Jaarsma, pp. 218-19; Bavinck, pp. 115-17, 144-45.

39. Jaarsma, pp. 215, 220-22.

40. Heyns and Roelofs, pp. 15-50.

41. See, for example, NUCS Yearbook 1929-30, p. 118, and **Christian School Magazine,** April 1928, p. 507.

42. Teachers of the East, pp. 9-10; **Christian School Magazine,** Nov. 1922, p. 138; March 1923, pp. 299-303; April 1923, pp. 324-28; Jan. 1927, front page; **Christian Home and School,** Jan. 1938, p. 4.

43. Jaarsma, pp. 222-23, 226-27.

44. Bavinck, p. 111.

45. NUCS **Convention Papers 1932,** p. 49; **Christian School Magazine,** Oct. 1926, p. 249; Henry Van Zyl, class notes for **Principles of Teaching in Elementary School,** circa 1940; **Christian Home and School,** Nov. 1943, p. 5.

46. George J. Van Wesep, "Pragmatistic and Christian Education," **Calvin Forum,** June 1937, pp. 247-48. Louis Berkhof, "Dualism in Education," **Calvin Forum,** Feb. 1938, p. 149ff.

47. The 1933 Humanist Manifesto as reprinted in Rockne McCarthy et al., **Society, State and Schools** (Grand Rapids: Eerdmans, 1981), p. 117 (the fifth thesis).

48. Cornelius Bontekoe, **Calvin Forum,** Feb. 1942, p. 138; N. J. Monsma, **Calvin Forum,** May 1942, pp. 215-16; and **Calvin Forum,** Oct. 1942, pp. 35-40.

49. **Christian Home and School,** Aug. 1944, pp. 6-8.

50. Sidney Hook made these points about Albert Lynd's **Quackery in the Public Schools** (Boston: Little, Brown and Co., 1953) in his essay, "Modern Education and its Critics," in Israel Scheffler, **Philosophy and Education** (Boston: Allyn and Bacon, 1958), pp. 275-80.

51. "The Domestication of Our Schools," **Christian School Magazine,** Nov. 1923, p. 453. Within the Catholic schools, in contrast to

the conservative Christian schools, "calls for more progressive pedagogy and curriculum abounded" between the World Wars. See Marvin Lazerson, "Understanding American Catholic Educational History," **History of Education Quarterly** 17 (Fall 1977): 313. Catholicism included a much broader spectrum of social backgrounds and views than Calvinism. Also, it was not affected as directly by the threat of "modernism" as were conservative Protestant groups. Moreover, it was less hesitant to copy public school trends in "secular" subjects than those Calvinists who held that the curriculum should be unique in all subjects.

52. **Christian School Magazine**, April 1922, pp. 31-35; Sept. 1922, p. 88; March 1924, p. 612; Oct. 1924, pp. 760-61; NUCS **Convention Papers 1926**, pp. 59-61. Writers were aware of Bobbitt's book **The Curriculum** (e.g. **Christian School Magazine**, May 1923, p. 369). In 1922 the term "objective" was first introduced in a scientific sense (**Christian School Magazine**, Dec. 1922, p. 176). The language course of study was John A. Van Bruggen's in his personal papers in Heritage Hall Archives. Van Bruggen had taken courses with Chicago's Ralph Tyler around 1940, and the latter's influence was evident.

53. For Cremin's summary, see **The Transformation of the School**, pp. 305-08.

54. **Christian School Magazine**, March 1928, pp. 489-91; May 1928, pp. 522-23; and April 1931, pp. 1031-32; NUCS **Yearbook 1933-34**, p. 80; Van Wesep, p. 248. See also, for example, C. Aué and H. C. Verhulst's **A Practical Guide for the Christian Instruction of United States History** (Sioux Center, Iowa: Roelofs Brothers, n.d., circa 1932) which emphasized factual knowledge of dates, persons, and events.

55. The Alliance of Christian Schools of Chicago and Vicinity, "Introduction to Course of Study for the Christian Elementary School" (mimeographed, 1923), pp. 3, 7, 12, 14.

56. **Christian School Magazine**, March 1929, pp. 659-60; and Nov. 1924, pp. 784-800.

57. Written as marginal notes in the copy of the Alliance's "Introduction" in John A. Van Brugghen's personal papers in Heritage Hall Archives.

58. **The Christian Journal**, Jan. 4, 1919; **Christian Home and School**, March 1939, p. 9.

59. See, for example, W. H. Jellema, "What Ought We to Mean by Distinctive Christian Teaching?", **Christian School Magazine**, Feb. and April 1924; Dorr Kuizema, "The Problem of Teaching the

Principle," **Christian School Magazine,** Sept. 1926. Schools have taught history for at least four reasons: acculturation; the understanding of social problems to lead to enlightened citizenship; an analysis of history, enabling one to manage it; and the development of critical thinking. Christian school educators taught history to acculturate, i.e., to expose students to the essential meanings, values, and attitudes of Western culture and, especially, a Christian subset of that culture. Thus Heyns and Roelofs' manual attempted to explain, to trace events to their causes, and to understand the forces behind historical movements so that students would understand that the "essence" of history lay in the battle between the forces of good and evil (pp. 7-8). Important topics therefore included "a correct view of the origin of our nation" (p. 11) and the maintenance of a "national morality" (p. 12). In geography Aué balanced such acculturation with an emphasis on understanding social problems and helping students to use and apply geographical concepts and principles. There was almost no emphasis on developing critical thinking and reasoning.

60. **Christian School Magazine,** Dec. 1922, pp. 177-80; Jan. 1923, pp. 211-14; Feb. 1925, pp. 880-83; P. Hoekstra, "American Ideals and Christian Education," in NUCS **Convention Papers 1926,** pp. 72ff.; NUCS **Annual 1937-38,** pp. 44-47; **Christian Home and School,** Dec. 1945, pp. 7-8; Heyns and Roelofs, pp. 90, 120, 123; and C. Aué, "United States History for Christian Schools," mimeographed class notes, n.d., pp. 5-7, 15-16.

61. **Christian School Magazine,** Jan. 1923, p. 210 and June 1924, pp. 698-99; Heyns and Roelofs, p. 126; **Christian School Magazine,** Oct. 1926, pp. 242-43. Native people were dismissed with lines such as "By 1890 the last frontier was closed, all the Indians had been subdued and enclosed in reservations, and the people began more intensive occupation of lands already in their possession" (Heyns and Roelofs, p. 152). "The people," of course, referred to the whites. Slavery had been "the great blight of our national life" for which the nation was "severely punished" (p. 127), but the Civil War transformed the South of "slavery and secession" into the New South of "Union and freedom" (p. 144). The possibility of Blacks still being treated poorly after the Civil War was not considered.

To its credit, the NUCS did not take on the publication of a text by Albert Hyma [**World History—A Christian Interpretation** (Grand Rapids, Michigan: Eerdmans, 1942)], although Hyma was a college text author for at least two large publishers.

Typical was Hyma's dismissal of Rousseau and his ideas: "He was an unfaithful husband, a neglected parent, a vicious, deceitful character, and a false prophet in general" (p. 289). As Hyma's correspondence shows, he slanted his writings to suit what his audience wanted to hear, whether that audience was a secular, a NUCS, or a fundamentalist one. Hyma's relationship with the NUCS was always an uneasy one, and the NUCS did not publish any of his materials.

62. **Christian School Magazine**, March 1926, pp. 162-64; Dec. 1923, pp. 484-93; NUCS **Yearbook 1925-26**, p. 151; and Grand Rapids Christian High School, "A Brief Statement of the Ideals and Objectives of Christian Secondary Education" (n.d., likely developed soon after the start of the school in 1920).

63. **Christian School Magazine**, Feb. 1923, p. 250; June 1923, p. 405; Oct. 1929, p. 738; NUCS **Minutes**, May 24, 1928, Art. 8; Grand Rapids Christian High School, **The Emblem**, Jan. 1930, p. 4; John A. Vander Ark, "Testimony: Origin and Development of Christian Education in the Midwest," transcript of tape in Dordt College archives, 1977, p. 12; interview with E. R. Post, April 20, 1983; Albert J. Boersma, **In the School of the Master** (Sioux Center, privately published autobiography, 1971), p. 64; A. J. Boersma personal communication, Sept. 7, 1983.

64. Andrew Blystra, speech given to teachers circa 1930, in his personal papers, Heritage Hall Archives; Dorr Kuizema, "Principles of School Organization," **Christian School Magazine**, Nov. 1927, p. 425.

65. J. C. Lobbes, "The Master Meditates: Reflections on 46 Years of Teaching," mimeographed manuscript, no date (circa 1959), p. 43; **Christian School Magazine**, Sept. 1922, pp. 71-73; Oct. 1924, p. 769; March 1930, p. 811; and December 1930, pp. 956-57; NUCS Annual 1929-30, p. 131.

66. **Christian School Magazine**, Oct. 1929, p. 738.

67. Report of the NUCS Textbook Committee to the NUCS Board of Directors, "For the Solution of Text Book Problem," mimeographed report, 1924, pp. 1-2; NUCS Textbook Committee, "Text Books and the Writing of Manuals for Our Teachers," mimeographed report, 1922, pp. 1-2; NUCS Board of Directors **Minutes** Dec. 1, 1922, and March 2, 1923; George Bos, "Memoirs of a Schoolmaster," p. 45.

68. [George Bos], **Practical Geography for Christian Schools, First Book** (privately published, 1923); George Bos, "Memoirs of a Schoolmaster," p. 45.

69. NUCS Board of Directors **Minutes**, Feb. 22, 1924.

70. Handwritten report of the textbook committee to board; n.d. (probably Feb. 19, 1924 and dealt with at the board meeting of Feb. 22, 1924).
71. George Bos, **Practical Geography,** pp. 8, 90.
72. George Bos, "Memoirs of a Schoolmaster," pp. 45-46; NUCS Board of Directors **Minutes** Feb. 22, 1924.
73. C. Aué, "The Teaching of Geography," **Christian School Magazine,** Jan. 1925, pp. 859-60; typed report "Geography for Christian Schools" (n.d.), pp. 1, 5, and 6; and "A Final Systematic Review in Geography," mimeographed manuscript, n.d.
74. NUCS Board of Directors **Minutes,** Aug. 26, 1926; Aug. 31, 1928; June 12, 1929; June 27, 1930; June 26, 1931; NUCS Executive Committee Minutes June 3, 1927; June 8, 1928; and June 12, 1929; Textbook Committee **Report,** June 27, 1930; Michigan Alliance of Christian Schools **Minutes,** Nov. 6, 1934.
75. C. Aué and H. L. Verhulst, **A Practical Guide for the Christian Instruction of United States History** (Sioux Center, Iowa: Roelofs Brothers, n.d., circa 1932); NUCS Board of Directors **Minutes,** June 28, 1935. The Feb. 19, 1924 report of the textbook committee stated: "The committee has taken the position that no texts shall be recommended unless it can do so without qualifications and apologies."
76. Interview with E. R. Post, April 20, 1983; **Christian School Magazine,** Oct. 1929, p. 737; **Christian Home and School,** Sept. 1945, p. 5.
77. **The Banner,** Aug 29, 1929, pp. 584-87; Sept. 6, 1929, pp. 600, 612; **Christian Home and School,** March 1936, p. 7; and Nov. 1939, pp. 14-15; NUCS **Annual 1922,** pp. 6-7; NUCS **Annual 1923-24,** p. 4; Mark Fakkema, **New Christian Schools . . . On the Pacific Coast: A Return to God's Word in Education** (Chicago: NUCS pamphlet, 1946).
78. Marion Schoolland, **God's Great Outdoors Series Four** (Chicago: NUCS, 1939) and **God's Great Outdoors Series Five** (Chicago, NUCS, 1938). For some of the reviews, see **Christian Home and School,** Sept. 1938, pp. 9-10, and **The Banner,** June 1, 1939, p. 506.
79. Michigan Alliance of Christian School **Minutes,** Dec. 15, 1931.
80. Mark Fakkema's report to the NUCS Annual Meeting, Aug. 13, 1940.
81. **Minutes** of the NUCS Board of Directors Aug. 27, 1941; Aug. 28, 1941; Nov. 19, 1941; Dec. 26, 1941; April 25, 1942; Dec. 30, 1942; and March 9, 1943 letter from NUCS board to C. Zylstra; Biblical

A BULWARK AGAINST MODERNISM (1920-1945)

Studies Committee **Report** to NUCS Board of Directors, June 9, 1942.

Built in 1892, the Christian Reformed Theological
School was sold for $20 000 in 1920 to become
the Grand Rapids Christian High School.

7 Quests for Purpose: Divergent Curriculum Orientations (1945-1977)

"Marching On"

In 1947, exactly one hundred years after the first Dutch settlers arrived in Michigan, Richard Postma, National Union of Christian Schools president, announced that the NUCS would launch more serious and intensive "educational development" efforts. In an article entitled "Marching On!," he called for a distinctive Christian school philosophy, objectives, methodology and curriculum policies through "daring experimentation and bold pioneering."[1]

Postma's announcement came at an opportune time. Enrollment in NUCS schools expanded rapidly from 16 974 pupils in 1944 to 59 535 in 1965 (from 25 to 9 244 in Canada during the same period). By 1960, more than seventy percent of North American Christian Reformed families with access to Christian schools sent their children to them.[2] Further, in the U.S. Christian school interest had increased among other denominations. American teachers had become more qualified and were also better informed about the current American educational scene.[3]

The new educational thrust began in 1943 when the NUCS board, acting on complaints of schools that the organization was giving little educational leadership, appointed an education committee. NUCS Executive Secretary Mark Fakkema recognized that the movement needed a course of study and more Christian textbooks based on a Christian philosophy of education. He himself, however, spent most of his time promoting Christian schools among, for example, Baptists belonging to the National Association of Evangelicals. In 1947 the NUCS Board appointed John A. Van Bruggen as Educational Director and put him in charge of the overall NUCS program, replacing Mark Fakkema.

Van Bruggen's appointment signalled two decisive policy directions for the NUCS. First, a prime goal became to give schools educational

help.   Secondly, the NUCS decided to "maintain its own distinctive
character," i.e., to limit its clientele to persons of Reformed and
closely related persuasions.[4]   As a result of these policy directions and
his demotion, Fakkema resigned, becoming director of the newly-formed
and more broadly-based National Association of Christian Schools
(NACS).   Although the NUCS paid Fakkema's salary for one more year,
it rejected his dream of the NACS becoming an umbrella organization
for all North American Christian Schools.[5]

Meanwhile, Van Bruggen immediately initiated conferences and in-
service training sessions to consider a Christian philosophy of education,
a "Christian approach" to the teaching of individual subjects, and the
development of Christian textbooks.[6]   The same year, the NUCS
published a **Course of Study for Christian Elementary Schools.**   During
the remainder of Van Bruggen's six-year tenure, the NUCS published a
church history textbook, a music hymnal, and a physical education
manual.   It also developed an ancient and medieval history textbook and
planned a junior high school literature series.   Further, Van Bruggen
helped to set up a foundation to raise funds for curriculum
development.[7]   However, his attempts to co-publish textbooks with
groups such as the Lutheran schools failed.

Van Bruggen, like Van der Brugghen in the 1840s and Bennink in
the 1890s, felt strongly about the need for Christian textbooks.
"Giving a teacher a man-centered textbook to build a God-centered
approach," he said, "is like asking a mason to build a wall with a
pick-axe."   NUCS-developed textbooks would help schools retain their
identity and imbue children with "the Calvinistic interpretation of life."
Van Bruggen was disheartened that the textbook program faltered once
he left the NUCS in 1953 to teach at Calvin College.[8]   In 1957
Seattle's Albert E. Greene said that "the advances now in progress are
thrilling" but five years later a school in his area called the NUCS
textbook program "disappointingly thin."[9]   Van Bruggen's strong thrust
had dissolved with the leadership change and the movement's failure to
find a consensus about theoretical direction and its curriculum
orientation.

When appointed, Van Bruggen immediately involved supporters in
developing a "definite, clear and applicable" theory of Christian
education.   Several initial documents had already been drafted by the
NUCS Educational Committee.   Calvin College president H. Schultze
prepared a fifteen-page statement for the 1947 **Course of Study.**   Even
Schultze himself recognized, however, that its generality prevented it
from affecting curriculum development efforts:

> We must come to a clear conception of the basic thinking back of
> our Christian school movement before we shall be adequately

172

prepared, for instance, to take upon ourselves the tremendous assignment of the preparation of textbooks.[10]

Two years later a thesis by Arthur De Kruyter set forth a "statement of philosophy" and its implications, but the schools and its leaders gave it little heed, likely due to its religious generalities and its uncritical acceptance of public school practices. A "clear-cut, well-defined Christian philosophy of education" was still lacking.[11]

Indeed, the attempts to develop such a theory underscored the deep seated differences of views within the movement. In 1953 the NUCS published a booklet containing two unrelated essays.[12] The first, a modification of the 1947 **Course of Study** statement, tried to reconcile different views, but its five pages were too vague to help program planning. Cornelius Jaarsma, author of the second paper, leaned towards a personal relevance curriculum orientation, i.e., for him, the curriculum needed to provide personally enriching and meaningful experiences for the child (see Table II for a description of the four orientations referred to in this chapter). Christian school educators, however, failed to use his paper to formulate educational policies. Jaarsma himself complained that none of the available statements had become a "living conviction finding expression in meaningful concepts that guide one in his educational theory and practice." Likely this could be attributed to a "lack of underlying agreement in the system as to what is involved in making [the Calvinistic] school distinctive."[13] One influential group, for example, favoured an academic orientation; that is, they held that the curriculum should focus on the great products of human rational thought as exemplified by the traditional subject disciplines. Yet this group had not submitted a statement for inclusion in the NUCS booklet.

However, school practitioners continued to call for a more generally acceptable guiding statement at NUCS annual meetings. As a result, in 1966 Nicholas Wolterstorff, a philosophy professor at Calvin College, sketched the outlines of a new approach in an address entitled, **Curriculum: By What Standard?** Subsequently, Calvin College education professor Henry Beversluis tried to forge a consensus about the basis of NUCS curriculum work by writing **A Christian Philosophy of Education** (1971). This book provided the starting point for the NUCS curriculum manual **Principles to Practice** (1973), which, in turn, set the stage for a scientific curriculum framework. In the late 1960s and 1970s NUCS curriculum developers often applied this framework with a cognitive processes orientation, in which transferable inquiry skills rather than content were the focus of the curriculum.[14]

CURRICULUM ORIENTATIONS (1945-1977)

TABLE 2

SUMMARY OF CURRICULUM ORIENTATIONS

CHARACTERISTICS	ACADEMIC ORIENTATION	PROCESS ORIENTATION	PERSONAL RELEVANCE ORIENTATION	SOCIAL RELEVANCE ORIENTATION
Basic aims	mainly subject matter concepts, generalizations, procedures, interpretations, explanations	cognitive processes most likely to transfer to other situations; methods of moral reasoning and decision making	development of the whole person, especially religiously and/or morally, socially, communicatively, emotionally.	development of knowledge about and analysis of social and cultural phenomena and conflicts.
Content	traditional subject matter disciplines; content chosen to exemplify best human's rationality and the structure of a discipline; little integration	problems that exercise intellectual facilities; choice of particular content relatively unimportant	depends on interest of pupils; multi-disciplinary investigations included	multi-disciplinary societal phenomena and problems, with substantial integration of subject matter disciplines.
Learning strategies	use the method of gaining knowledge in the disciplines; pupil motivated through value of content as well as interesting teaching techniques	students are given personal opportunities to conceptualize, analyze, evaluate make choices, etc.	interest of pupils in starting points; varied and personalized activity including both individual and group work	cognitive strategies balanced with methods of value clarification, moral reasoning etc. Traditional receptor learning supplemented with discussions, projects.
Role of teacher	inculcator of systematic knowledge	problem and question generator	facilitator who stimulates and guides	escort and guide
Evaluation procedures	reproducing and applying knowledge int its various disciplines	test items, assess the levels of process achievement reached	related to personalized activities; subjective emphasis	applying knowledge and values and testing insight into social situations and dilemmas
Relation of education and society	social problems are assumed to be able to be understood and solved in terms of a knowledge of the traditional disciplines	developing students' critical process abilities will enable him to function in society	emphasis on "microsociety" in classroom which allows children to develop social relationships, usually in a non-competitive setting	a range of views from students being prepared to adapt to the present cultural milieu to totally reconstructing it.
Curriculum structure	linear, technological model possible	technological model desireable to ensure all major processes are learned systematically	rejection of technological model; planning is flexible, depends on concrete situation.	technological possible but not likely because of the complex nature of cultural problems.
Examples (General/Christian school)	Hutchins/Jellema	Bloom/Triezenberg	Holt/Jaarsma	Freire/Van Dyk (Kuyperians)

174

This chapter discusses the various curriculum orientations in the Christian school movement after World War II, using categories similar to those defined by Eisner and Vallance (see Table II).[15] None of the positions described fits precisely into one of the four categories, and proponents of certain orientations sometimes also shifted their views as time went on. Yet the views of the spokesmen described here all lean strongly towards one of the four categories, with modifications to suit Calvinistic beliefs. The chapter first deals with the two opposing orientations of the 1940s and 1950s, viz., the academic and personal relevance orientations. It considers how Wolterstorff later emphasized a social relevance orientation which involved pupils with current social issues. It shows how Beversluis tried to synthesize the foregoing, with the NUCS curriculum department formally adopting the Beversluis document. However, the chapter concludes, the NUCS in actuality accepted a process orientation, while also conceiving of curriculum planning as a technical undertaking that closely related means to pre-specified ends. Finally, Canadians, fresh from the Netherlands, in Kuyperian fashion tried to weld the social and personal relevance orientations into a unified approach, and began to develop some of their own materials and approaches.

The focus of this chapter, then, is on theoretical curriculum thought. Chapter 8 will discuss how specific curriculum issues arose and were dealt with by the movement, and how the different orientations as well as other factors affected development in some specific instances. Chapter 9 concludes the discussion of the post-World War II age with an analysis of local examples, particularly in British Columbia.

Developing "Freedom of Mind" Through an Academic Curriculum Orientation

The academic curriculum orientation conceives of curriculum as the body of disciplines to be "covered" by pupils but it includes a spectrum of views. Perennialists like Robert M. Hutchins and Mortimer Adler wanted schools to teach "perennially contemporary" values of Western civilization's cultural heritage, while essentialists like Arthur Bestor and Canada's Hilda Neatby emphasized an intellectual, basic education taught in a traditional manner.[16] Sometimes an academic orientation has led to a sterile "banking" or receptacle mode of learning, with pupils receiving, memorizing, categorizing, and repeating information in traditional subjects disciplines. But other adherents have attempted to mold the full person through content that was believed best to exemplify human culture, taught to cultivate the pupil's rationality.

During the late 1940s and 1950s, several eloquent Christian school leaders, accepting Hutchins' and Bestor's criticism of the progressive tendencies of American education, popularized this orientation, though tempered to reflect a Calvinist worldview. Calvin College English professor Henry Zylstra, for instance, stood solidly in the Reformed tradition:

> Christianity versus culture: no, it is the fundamentalist heresy. Culture alone: indeed not, it is the liberal heresy. Christianity through culture: the religious in man governing, shaping, determining the scientific, artistic, social in him, precisely; it is the Reformed truth.[17]

For Zylstra the implication of this statement, however, was that Christian education was to be a "liberal" one. In a 1950 principals' convention speech he lauded "traditional education" since it would lead to human freedom, "the thing that gives a culture its large importance, it being only mind that can make culture." Modern education failed to do justice to the rational intellect. Schools were to offer a liberal education based on the ideas of Plato and Aristotle, Augustine and Calvin, Bacon and Milton, Matthew Arnold and Jacques Maritain to ensure that learning led to "the idea of the freedom of the mind of man."[18]

What did this imply for education? Knowledge was more important than ability, and subject content of greater significance than methodology. Furthermore, the "funded wisdom" of the ages, embodied in the humanities, ought to be emphasized. The three R's and foreign languages gave access to Greek, Roman, German, and French thought and wisdom. Zylstra vigorously attacked pupil-centered education which, he believed, substituted "a personal world of self for an objective world of reality" and avoided "concentration on essentials." A strong traditional liberal emphasis would make education "Christian":

> Presumably there is no such thing as a Christian semicolon, or a Calvinistic participle. But there is such a thing as a Christian view of life. According to this view, God is rational, his world is a **universe**, and the mind of man is capable of order. It may be that a Deist could say as much. We should say no less. We have therefore a job to do.[19]

Zylstra's colleague, philosopher W. Harry Jellema, similarly told Christian school principals in 1949 that all students needed a liberal curriculum consisting of classical literature, history and Latin. In the late 1950s Jellema, then a board member for the Grand Rapids Christian High School, proposed that almost all students take a liberal program, "the shortest road for bringing the pupil to the height . . . of past human insight into the nature of the real and good, and into the meaning of Christianity." Students must take a minimum of thirty-five credit hours of English (out of 160 credit hours required over four years for high school graduation), forty hours of foreign languages (Latin and either German or French), twenty-eight hours of history and social science, but only a maximum of ten hours altogether of mathematics and natural science. English stressed disciplined, logical study of topics such as rhetoric, mythology, and literary criticism; the one fine arts course, Greek and Gothic architecture and history of painting. Weak students would, instead of Latin, study the Greek and Latin classics in translation "to recapture the classic mind, especially as compared with the Christian." For them, a study of medieval and modern culture replaced modern languages. Even students in Jellema's proposed commercial, industrial and domestic streams were to spend two-thirds of their time and effort on liberal education.[20]

For Jellema, Christian education consisted of disciplined learning about the cultural products of Western civilization. Because of God's gift of common grace, such cultural phenomena, he held, could often be accepted as Christian ones. Jellema had thus moved close to the position of Christian rationalists who believe that the best in civilization harmonizes with Christian belief, and, implicitly, distanced himself from the view of Christ as the transformer of humans and their culture. Moreover, the church and the home and not the school were to confront the student directly with the necessity of faith and personal commitment. With Kuyper's conception of the antithesis between Christian and non-Christian thought pushed into the background, some Christian school supporters mistrusted this stance as too accepting of "worldly" culture. They feared that it might lead to an eventual secularization of the schools.[21]

Despite such suspicions, this academic approach affected a number of Christian school leaders in the 1950s. Calvin College education professor Lambert J. Flokstra also contributed to this. The "field of education," he claimed, was marked by "a lack of proper appreciation of humanistic and classical tradition, a raising of the scientific method to the level of a dogma, an undue concern with social adjustment and personality development, an increasing emphasis on vocationalism."[22] Such trends, he believed, had infiltrated the Christian school system and must be stopped. One principal similarly echoed Bestor that the "traditional curriculum" was suitable both for "the man with the Ph.D. degree as well as the man with the hoe, for none of us has come anywhere near exhausting its riches." He wanted literature, language and history rather than typing and salesmanship taught in the Christian schools.[23]

The two textbooks prepared during John Van Bruggen's time as NUCS director dealt, significantly, with important aspects of the cultural heritage of the United States: **The Church in History** and **The Story of the Old World**.[24] Both showed the "cultural storehouse" emphasis favoured by the academic orientation. The books transmitted, the authors believed, the leading time-tested ideas of mankind. Student questions emphasized the development and influence of cultural ideals: How did Greek culture affect the spread of the Gospel by the early church? What was the culture of Greece? What evidences did this period [thirteenth century] show of the revival of culture?[25] The author of **The Story of the Old World** wrote he had presented "the gist and genius from each period of civilization" while reminding pupils that God directed the destinies of nations.[26] Schools should familiarize students with the roots of Western civilization, emphasizing throughout the development of the Christian church and a Christian interpretation of history.

Thus Jellema, Zylstra and Flokstra, aided by spokesmen like Hutchins and Bestor as well as the conservative milieu of the Christian school movement, had some influence during the 1950s on NUCS curriculum efforts and attitudes. Yet, as the next chapter illustrates, that influence was tempered by the reality of schools having to provide teachable programs for an ever-increasing percentage of students finishing high school. Jellema and Zylstra and their followers, however, never wavered from their view that schooling was to be directed primarily at the cultivation of students' intellects.

Developing a "Love for God's Grace"
Through a Personal Relevance
Orientation

The most thoughtful and prolific opponent of the academic position was Cornelius Jaarsma. His doctoral dissertation at New York University had dealt with the educational work of Herman Bavinck, but he had also worked for some years in "first hand study of the educational frontiers of America."[27] After being Dean of Instruction at Slippery Rock State College in Pennsylvania and education professor at Wheaton College in Illinois, Jaarsma became head of Calvin College's secondary education program in 1947. There, he quickly took issue with an intellectualist approach to education:

> [Dr. Hutchins] practically ignores the total human personality and forgets that education is as much emotional and as much social as intellectual . . . . One of the emphases in Christian education is the education of the whole personality.[28]

For Jaarsma, school learning was much more than the acquisition of knowledge through intellectual discipline. Just as the Bible presented knowledge of God not with ready-made concepts but with "life known in the midst of living it," learning should take into account the "whole-person-in-action." Intellectual traditionalism, Jaarsma held, was "far removed from life in its educative process." Subject matter served not as an end in itself but as a medium to provide opportunities in guiding the child's personal development and "self-fulfillment as a religious being."[29]

Although critical of the progressives' ultimate aim, Jaarsma accepted progressive education notions more than most Christian school educators, and held that "learning and living belong together." The scientific study of the educative process would help education meet the needs of individual children. Schools must function "in a democratic social order" since it was "most conducive to the promotion of the God-given rights of man."[30]

Jaarsma agreed with the progressives that "we often live our way into our thinking." However, he believed that the progressives neglected the existence of ultimate and binding norms for human life. Such norms also meant that "we must think our way into our living." For Jaarsma, as for many progressives, personalities were developed "by active participation in the on-going process of a socially guided activity." Children's "spontaneous, natural interest" should be the starting point for learning. Since interest in learning activities was not always immediate, sometimes coercion might be necessary. However, this was to take its cue from the dignity of the child and take into account that all significant knowing ended in interest.[31]

For Jaarsma, the relationship of the individual to God was of paramount importance. Therefore the foundation of such educational values as "justice, vocation and health" was piety or spirituality. The learning of facts, truths and values was to call forth a personal commitment to what the learner held to be true, authentic, and reliable. Teaching about culture focused on the child's personal relationship to God rather than on Abraham Kuyper's Christian development of culture as an organism. For a study of the Eskimo, the important issues became, "How are they living without Christ? What is being done to bring the Christ? What is our obligation who know the Christ to them who know him not?" The Christian school curriculum must "undergird the daily conversion of the child" through self-understanding developed by student exploration and expression.[32]

Within this context teachers were to develop an understanding of a common core of subject matter that related to the student's life outside of school and had "genuine educational significance." Thus Jaarsma suggested "areas of coherence" or "areas of living" such as the language arts, social studies, the natural sciences and mathematics, and the arts. Skills were to be mastered in connection with the development of these broad areas, and teachers should be assigned "to facilitate correlation and integration of areas." Subject matter as well as teaching methods were to be chosen for their contribution to the growth of personality:

> When we are studying or working in the area of arithmetic in the fifth grade, we are conscious of a **God-related** motivation, seek true ideas and good workmanship in knowledges [sic] and skills, and practice helpfulness to, and cooperation with our peers.

Jaarsma's orientation to curriculum, then, was a modified "personal relevance" one. Through the encouragement of self-understanding, self-acceptance and self-discipline pupils would learn to assume the responsibilities of life. The curriculum should provide a total experience that led to personal development and growth. Yet, as a Calvinist, Jaarsma, differing from those promoting a pure personal relevance orientation in public education, insisted that teachers go beyond stimulating and guiding students. They should make certain learning tasks compulsory because of their potential future interest and relevance. Above all, teachers should structure all learning activities so that students would come face to face with God's claim on their lives.[33]

George Stob in his 1955 doctoral thesis claimed that Jaarsma's school of thought, "because it fits so well with much of the prevailing evangelical spirit of American Christianity, as well with the pietism of the Christian Reformed Church," prevailed in practice.[34] True, Jaarsma did have some influence, as evidenced by the Christian Reformed Church's 1955 statement on the **Principles of Education** and his prominent role at several NUCS Conventions.[35] Stob, however, lacked perspective because of his closeness to the scene, basing his conclusion more on schools' devotional exercises than on curriculum content. He neglected that Jaarsma faced stiff opposition, particularly from his

Calvin College colleagues. Some suspected Jaarsma of fundamentalist tendencies with his emphasis on personal commitment and his narrow view of the Christian's role in culture.[36] His writings must have appeared too child-centred with Mark Fakkema's condemnations of all progressive educational practices having received wide distribution just a few years earlier. Jaarsma himself believed that academic traditionalism dominated the Christian schools.[37]

Jaarsma did help principals and boards reject extreme academic essentialist positions and did influence some individual teachers. Generally, however, the Christians schools did not give him a thoughtful hearing. Except for a junior high school literature series,[38] the NUCS curriculum materials during this time would have been difficult to use with Jaarsma's approach to education. His statement of philosophy published by the NUCS in 1953 was seldom quoted or used and quickly forgotten. In the Seceder tradition, schools embraced an emphasis on "daily, lively, vital faith" but at the same time rejected the "fads and fashions" of Jaarsma, preferring "basic skills."[39] Christian schools were not ready to consider carefully Bavinck's Calvinistic approach to education, especially when it involved choosing some methods that the progressive movement had also promoted. Progressive notions made little direct impact on the Christian schools.

Attempting to Forge Consensus Through Eclecticism

In 1966 Calvin College philosopher Nicholas Wolterstorff set out a framework for curriculum development in a brief, seminal pamphlet, **Curriculum: By What Standard?** Wolterstorff developed the view that neither an academic nor a progressive curriculum orientation by itself would lead to a satisfactory Christian school program. Like Jaarsma, he argued that the schools must educate for "the full life of man" and must do far more than cultivate rational and intellectual capacities. For example, physical education and art should also occupy a significant place in the curriculum. But Wolterstorff, much more than Jaarsma, called for an emphasis on contemporary Christian analyses of the "ultimate loyalties and fundamental perspectives" underlying the works of humans and the institutions of society. Students' awareness both of Christian traditions and of contemporary Christian thought and activity assumed importance. However, as individuals, students must be given room to develop and prize their uniqueness rather than suffer "under the tyranny of social conformity."[40]

Wolterstorff made clear that he stood squarely in the Kuyper tradition. Christians should neither withdraw from society nor accommodate themselves to it. Rather, Christian schools should equip students "to live the Christian life in contemporary society." The curriculum should encompass the whole realm of human culture so that, upon graduation, students could "actively contribute to the formation of a Christian culture," i.e., to a design of living expressive of Christian ideals. Like George Counts, Wolterstorff spoke of the schools as instruments for social change. Unlike Counts, however, he held that Christian faith was the starting point for such cultural transformation. The Christian community must build a Christian culture, with different members being able to specialize "in the performance of different aspects of this whole task." Therefore social studies courses, for instance, must place "a good deal of emphasis on the Christian approach to contemporary social issues" such as the racial problem and a Christian view of work and the welfare state. Instead of providing pat answers to such problems, "we must encourage [students] to think matters through" and stress creativity, whether that be in discussions, problem solving, using art media, or devising experiments. Schools must get students "to think and speak and act for themselves, as Christians." A Christian social relevance orientation had a prominent place in Wolterstorff's view of the curriculum.[41]

Though short on specifics, Wolterstorff's ideas struck a responsive chord, with a number of leaders once more calling the NUCS to develop a comprehensive statement of philosophy.[42] The NUCS Education Committee committed itself to producing such a statement. It once again tried to balance Kuyper's conceptions of antithesis and common grace: "We recognize as indispensable the two-pronged emphasis toward maturation: the pursuit of godliness and the involvement in culture . . . . The Christian life, hopefully, has both elements."[43] The resulting 1971 publication of N. Henry Beversluis' **Christian Philosphy of Education,** more a compilation of curriculum theories than a comprehensive philosophy of education, was intended to guide NUCS curriculum development and practices in the schools.

Beversluis, however, failed to give concrete form to Wolterstorff's intent to emphasize Calvinistic social relevance in the curriculum. Rather, he developed a position that, in eclectic fashion, chose those aspects of the Jellema, Jaarsma and Wolterstorff positions acceptable to most Christian school educators. He hoped that in this way the schools would go "beyond taking sides" by adopting the best of various approaches. Like Jellema, Beversluis held that the Christian school must "prominently emphasize as one of its major concerns the intellectual life of young Christians." The experientialists were right in eliciting personal responses from the learner and in promoting "interest, activity, participation, discovery, and freedom." A balance needed to be struck "between regard for experience and readiness of learners and regard for the inherent structures of the subjects studied." Beversluis also incorporated Wolterstorff's view that the Christian school was to prepare students for building a Christian culture, although he shifted the emphasis from cultural formation to "cultural obedience" and excised Wolterstorff's references to analyses of contemporary social issues.[44]

To forge a consensus of these diverse views, Beversluis developed a three-dimensional taxonomy of learning goals: the intellectual, moral, and creative dimensions. The intellectual dimension (Bloom's cognitive domain), included "comprehension, memory, divergence, discovery, judging, evaluation." Its intent was to relate Jellema's classical knowledge with Wolterstorff's broader contemporary concerns, using traditional subject content. Beversluis' second dimension, moral growth, paralleled Bloom's affective domain and dealt with attitudes, values, discriminations, and choices. Learning in this dimension would guide students to a deeper commitment "to the true and the good," helping them make Christian moral decisions that would lead to Jaarsma's commitment and piety. Finally, Wolterstorff's notion of creativity became the third dimension of learning that gave "focus and substance and expression to a young person's intellectual and moral growth." By encouraging spontaneity and originality throughout the curriculum, the creative dimension could foster self-acceptance and provide a way for students to respond to God and his world.[45]

While the emphasis on creativity was a welcome one for schools that had traditionally shunned free expression of ideas and abilities, Beversluis' taxonomy fell short in several respects.[46] For one, even though Beversluis himself emphasized that all three dimensions were to be carried on at once during any learning activity, later NUCS curriculum development often artificially separated objectives, and hence learning activities, into the three dimensions. Yet the three categories were neither distinct nor comprehensive. Spontaneity and originality in the creative dimensions, for instance, could be defined only in terms of knowledge and ability objectives. Inducting young people into the complexity of moral choice might be the prime component of moral growth, as Beversluis claimed; however, he neglected that all moral issues involved important cognitive concepts. For both the creative and the moral dimensions, Beversluis tried to describe the type of response he would like to elicit from students, response that involved the intellectual dimension as well as two not mentioned by Beversluis: skills and dispositions. Cognitive and motor skills involving ordered and coordinated actions that must be practiced (e.g., logical, handwriting,

CURRICULUM ORIENTATIONS (1945-1977)

and typing skills) had no place in Beversluis' schema. Nor did Beversluis recognize that dispositions, which encompassed much more than the moral attitudes and behaviour, also formed a legitimate and essential domain of educational objectives.[47]

Despite the shortcomings of the taxonomy, Beversluis developed a position in which all Christian school educators could find something to their liking. Yet none would be completely satisfied. For the intellectualists there was too much emphasis on "response"; for followers of Jaarsma, not enough on the development of the whole personality of the child; for Kuyperians, an over-emphasis on individual moral choice and not enough on Christians attempting to transform society. Yet Beversluis' eclecticism meant that his position did not become a focus of controversy. Instead, it provided a basis for the NUCS publication that was to guide its curriculum work, **Principles to Practice.**[48]

Developing a Curriculum Orientation
Within the National Union of
Christian Schools

The discussions culminating in Beversluis' book were accompanied by moves to carry out NUCS curriculum work more systematically and coherently. Already in 1959 the NUCS issued ten criteria for the publication of curriculum materials, including one dealing with their "philosophic impact." The organization had also encouraged teachers to prepare units for publication using a format closely related to the Tyler rationale: objectives; learning experiences and activities; suggestions for approaches, integration, and materials; and evaluation. However, without a support staff, only a few of these voluntary units materialized. Progress on other projects was also frustrated by the lack of staff. Not until late in 1964 did the NUCS decide to develop a well-organized plan to implement a complete educational program. Soon, curriculum consultants were appointed in language arts (1965), the social sciences (1966), and science. In 1968 Dr. Henry Triezenberg, who was just completing a Ph.D. in science education at the University of Wisconsin, was appointed science consultant and director of the curriculum department.[49] Despite limited financial and human resources, Triezenberg initiated a wide spectrum of new curriculum initiatives during the next decade.

Increased systematization accompanied this burgeoning level of activity. John A. Vander Ark, NUCS Executive Director from 1953-77, reported in 1966 that "our Christian school system has reached new levels of sophistication. . . .we are presently in a period of tremendous change of both curriculum content and method." To meet the curriculum needs of the schools various subject committees were appointed. In 1968 Henry Triezenberg developed a paper, "Organizing the NUCS Curriculum Effort," later slightly modified to become the NUCS Curriculum Department Operational Policy. This document detailed three phases of development, four phases of dissemination, and five phases of testing and research, each with sub-points such as "grade-placement listing of clear, concise, specific, and testable objectives." Bloom's taxonomy and its implied scientific approach became the guiding framework for curriculum development. For example, curriculum objectives were to be

> written in such a clear, concise and specific way that test items can be written to measure pupil achievement in both knowing and understanding, cf., **The Taxonomy of Educational Objectives** (Bloom). Objectives related to attitudes should also be written in a testable manner.[50]

Implied in this approach was a view of curriculum as a means-ends, systematized technical undertaking. The NUCS began to prize technically sophisticated sequential models of curriculum development and efficient management processes. "Objective" questionnaires with computed means and ranks determined curriculum priorities.[51] Annual curriculum reports reviewed specific developments and plans in great detail but, in typical technological fashion, dealt little with the overall direction of curriculum work nor with the philosophy or meaning of its content and approach.

Influenced by the general curriculum development trends of the times, the NUCS curriculum department, in the Bobbitt-Charters tradition, approached curriculum in terms of functional efficiency. Learning was defined in terms of particular competencies; knowledge, in terms of identifiable, discrete entities; evaluation, in terms of test items that assessed specific behavioural ends. Questions such as "What implications does a Biblical view of knowledge have for the contours of the curriculum, the choice of subject matter, and methodology?" were answered only within a pre-determined scientific framework. Certainly the curriculum department strove for distinctively Christian approaches. However, with a paucity of Christian foundational analysis and increasing pressure to publish new materials rapidly, the department uncritically used the common curriculum development model prevalent in North America, without clearly understanding the philosophical implications of this model for the materials it produced.[52]

The NUCS curriculum department redirected Beversluis' three curricular dimensions to adapt them to a process orientation. Growth

185

in knowledge now meant "identifying observations, concepts, and generalizations." The emphasis was placd on specific cognitive processes that were enhanced through activities requiring their use. Students were to learn Gagné's verbal chains through recall activities, concepts through classification, and higher order rules through analysis, synthesis, application and interpretation.[53]

Similarly, the creative dimension of learning stressed the execution of verbal, social and physical performances like tying a shoelace or communicating "novel responses." The moral dimension became the "decisional" one, focusing on the ability to choose rightly, in moral as well as aesthetic, legal, and logical situations. While Christian education involved "interaction between internal, subjective, unmeasurable aspects and external, objective measurable aspects," the emphasis in curriculum was to be on measurable behavioural objectives and learned capabilities. Attitudes, for instance, were to be measured in terms of a student choosing "a course of action toward some person, object, or event" (e.g., opting to share lab equipment with others).[54]

By emphasizing such individual "personal decisions" extraneous to the subject matter, the department moved away from a social relevance orientation. Its "social responsibility" goals (e.g., the student contributes to classroom atmosphere and operation, helps others and is willing to be helped), while worthwhile in themselves, contributed little to Wolterstorff's vision of building a Christian culture with students becoming dissenters and reformers of societal phenomena and structures. The NUCS wanted students to learn "to put their faith to work in all areas of life," but its goal statements indicated that this referred to living a personal moral life within the existing (and acceptable) social and academic milieux and structures.[55]

Henry Triezenberg's work in science illustrated such curriculum thinking. Realizing that the science programs in most NUCS schools were sorely lacking and that action needed to be taken before the NUCS could develop its own science materials, Triezenberg set out to promote the elementary Science Curriculum Improvement Study (SCIS) and the junior high Intermediate Science Curriculum Study (ISCS) materials that used laboratory settings where students would perform and learn the diverse process skills of science. These programs, he believed, would stimulate students to observe and analyze the order of God's creation, and also confront them with situations where they had to make personal value choices. Triezenberg was so successful in conducting in-service training sessions and in writing materials for the ISCS program that by 1974 most students in American NUCS junior high schools used the ISCS program.[56]

186

CURRICULUM ORIENTATIONS (1945-1977)

Triezenberg could promote programs like SCIS and ISCS because he believed that values were extrinsic to content:

> A serendipitous result of the Christian school ISCS trial is the ease with which attitudes and values can be taught in an ISCS classroom. . . . The value of personal integrity and honesty in reporting data is more easily taught in an individualized and sequential curriculum.[57]

ISCS did not develop a Christian perspective any more or less than other programs but could well be used "to indirectly teach Christian attitudes and Christian principles of social interaction." Triezenberg measured whether the curriculum had taught values like human dignity and social responsibility through items such as "helping someone who has spilled equipment" and "working more quietly so other students can work." A full page on "process themes" overshadowed five lines of "conceptual schemes" in his goals of a Christian science education. This statement also included seven personal values "developed in the process of science," such as "delight (Excitement of science) in investigating [God's] world."[58]

Triezenberg's work stimulated science teaching in NUCS schools and helped to move science teachers beyond an intellectual lecture/discussion approach. Many teachers became involved in pilot projects, in-service activities, and test item and, later, unit development. Many classrooms where students had done little more than reading about science turned into beehives of hands-on science investigations. The science units written under Triezenberg's leadersip around 1977 were brimful of motivational student activities. Triezenberg also deliberately and carefully used learning activities to teach personal Christian moral values. Like Van der Brugghen in the 1830s, he saw that this could not be accomplished by means of moralizing homilies. Rather, he structured the classroom so that students were given opportunities to make frequent moral decisions.

Under Triezenberg's leadership, however, the NUCS curriculum department did not seem to realize that neither choice of subject matter nor techniques in curriculum making themselves are value-free. Its use of specific and measurable behavioural objectives meant that social justice tended to be interpreted exclusively in terms of a personalistic morality. Content was chosen more because it was a good vehicle for teaching cognitive processes than for giving students a sense of the function and relevance of a subject like science for society. As the next section shows, that made the direction of much of NUCS' curriculum work during the 1970s unacceptable to many Kuyperians, especially those in Canada.

Canadian Curriculum Voices

In the mid-sixties, the children of the Dutch immigrants to Canada who had started the first Christian schools in Canada in the 1940s and 1950s began to discuss the direction of their curriculum. Many of them had been influenced after 1955 by Calvin College's Kuyperian philosopher, H. Evan Runner, and, consequently, by the philosophical thought of Dr. Herman Dooyeweerd. The latter's four-volume **New Critique of Theoretical Thought** is still the landmark of a Calvinistic, Kuyperian approach to philosophy.[59] In the Netherlands, however, little curriculum thinking for Calvinistic schools had taken place since the death of Herman Bavinck in 1921. Therefore, Canadian Christian school leaders could look to the Netherlands for philosophical and religious direction but not for specific curricular guidelines.

The leaders agreed that the schools must provide pupils with the tools that would bring about culture change in harmony with Calvinistic Christian values. In 1965 Editor Albert Witvoet of the Canadian **Christian School Herald** wrote:

> We believe that God gave man a cultural mandate. . . . Our organizational life, therefore, must also be moulded in a Christian way. This, Christian education must teach and practise or else it has no business calling itself by such a lofty name.[60]

Other leaders added that chapel services did not make a school Christian, but, rather, a curriculum oriented to Jesus Christ as King of the entire cosmos. Labour and industry, economics and communication, art and literature—all needed reformation. A beginning needed to be made, impossible as the task might seem. Christian schools were to help students "shape a new culture in response to the norms of [God's] Word" [i.e., the Bible].[61]

Within this context Ray Klapwyk, in his mid-twenties and soon to be principal of the Hamilton Christian School, in 1965 called for a unique Christian curriculum. He accused teachers of not basing their teaching on a Christian philosophy of education nor on corresponding, definitive aims. Essentially, then, schools taught the Ontario public school curriculum. Rhetorically, he asked, "What reason remains for our schools to stay in operation if we have nothing distinctive to offer?" Like Bennink early in the century, Klapwyk expressed disappointment that little had been done to develop a Christian curriculum. Schools, he asserted two year later, must study "the scientific, philosophical, ethical, aesthetic, political standards and conceptions of cultures and civilizations; noting, in contrast, the mind of Christ." In a theme that

188

was to recur often, Klapwyk held that Christian schools were to analyze ideals of both Western and non-Western cultures from a Christian viewpoint. The grades 5-8 social studies curriculum, for instance, must study the structure of human society, including cultural differentiation; development of the family, church, state, school, industry, and labour organizations; the Christian view of office and authority in each sector; and "the principle of sphere sovereignty applied." The Christian school curriculum must establish and develop a Christian view of human beings, their environment, and their task in life. That task was "to be culturally active" in obedience to God in church, state and society.[62]

The person who was most influential among teachers in advancing such views was Canadian Arnold De Graaff. De Graaff, trained at the Free University of Amsterdam, was a psychology professor at Trinity Christian College in Chicago in the late 1960s, moving to Toronto's Institute for Christian Studies in 1970.[63] Leading many curriculum writing workshops in Ontario in the early 1970s and co-authoring an integrated curriculum for the primary level called **Joy in Learning,** De Graaff tried to balance personal and social relevance orientations, albeit, as time went on, he swung more to the personal relevance side.[64] He held that teachers were to prepare children for "unfolding and developing" the world for the benefit of all people," with the Bible providing a guiding vision of life. Schools must not brainwash children, however subtly, into accepting such a Biblical truth. Teaching and learning activities must respect and enhance children's selfhood and integrity. **Joy in Learning** tried to accomplish this through a large number of multi-disciplinary, open-ended learning activities arranged by themes.[65]

During the 1970s, most Canadian curriculum articles and projects reflected and extended De Graaff's thinking. Michael Welton, for instance, hired in the summer of 1971 as a curriculum researcher for Arnold De Graaff, denounced one standard social studies textbook as proclaiming "a false gospel of self-and-communal fulfillment" that reduced "the cosmic theatre of God to a supermarket." He concluded that

> It is up to Christians who take the creation seriously to show, along with other oppressed peoples, that the way out of the present crisis in the school room of the democratic mansion is through a critique of the very foundations of the entire educational enterprise.[66]

The 1972 book **To Prod the "Slumbering Giant"**, published in Toronto, attempted such a critique.[67] Its chapters on the Christian school curriculum and on the place of the Christian school in society once again emphasized the Christian's role in society and culture. John Van Dyk, a Canadian teaching at the Calvinistic Dordt College in Iowa, wrote:

> From the earliest grades our children must be taught to understand that to be a Christian is not just to be an American citizen like any other American with some church going and personal witnessing attached; but rather. . .they must be Christians who understand what their corporate task is as agents of the reconciliation of Jesus Christ, and how to go about that task in an apostate, God-ignoring, and hell-bound civilization.[68]

Natural science, for instance, was to be understood as "cultural activity, as an obedient or disobedient response to the will of the Lord" and not as "so many independent and unrelated bodies of abstract facts." Similarly, the humanities must not just "instill a set of values and a sense of morality" but lead to an understanding of "the nature of art and language and all other fields so that these dimensions of God's world, too, can be reclaimed for Jesus Christ."[69]

The strong language of **To Prod the "Slumbering Giant"** added fuel to the curriculum fires that kept some Canadian Christian school communities in turmoil in the late sixties and early seventies. Klapwyk was one of those who felt the book was too harsh in its assessment of the states of both public and Christian education but yet was influenced by it. Together with three other principals, he published an extensive paper on Christian education based on the curriculum chapters of the book. This was submitted to the Niagara Regional Office of the Ontario Ministry of Education with the claim that "the vision and the aspirations described in this paper are representative of the Ontario Christian school movement as a whole."[70]

Among the fundamental objectives of the Christian school the paper included giving students an understanding of the unity, coherence and interdependence of the created world; helping them to be a reforming influence in society; and developing, with the supporting community, "a Christian culture and lifestyle as directed by God's Word." The grades 7 to 10 curriculum, based on a model in **To Prod the "Slumbering Giant"**, included a core with topics such as social issues, communication in society, the impact of technology on culture, and the place of the fine arts in society. To unify the curriculum, the mandatory courses related directly to this core. A social studies example showed how the student could learn that "the dominant values [of a culture] shape human life, integrating the various physical and historical factors of past and present." Skills must be "practiced in a meaningful setting" since the foremost goal was that students develop "a more articulate, knowledgeable awareness of a Christian VISION for the practice of Man's Task."[71]

In the same vein, Henry Aay, then a lecturer at Wilfrid Laurier University, set out a framework for the geography curriculum of Christian schools which emphasized social relevance. His basic questions for the study of geography were "how have societies, in the context of culture, adapted themselves to and transformed their environmental setting, and how must man respond to the norm to love and take care of the earth?" The interaction of the natural ecosystem with human cultural activity provided the model for geographic study. Geography needed to prepare students "to take up a political calling to involve themselves in environmental issues in their local community." Aay's application of a Kuyperian vision of education had concrete results: since that time, the Ontario Alliance of Christian Schools has published a number of extensive units using both Aay's model and his expertise.[72]

Canadians, however, did not all agree with such a social relevance orientation for the Christian school curriculum. Already in 1967 and 1968 some indicated that they could not understand why the writings of Klapwyk and De Graaff were necessary. They felt the work done by "our parent organization, the National Union of Christian Schools" was very suitable for Canadian schools and charges of "a lack of a Christian curriculum" disturbed them.[73]

The Canadian Kuyperians did not remain united, either, with two distinct emphases developing. Persons like Van Dyk and Aay, without denying the importance of helping children develop their own personality, put their emphasis on preparing children to become Christian critics and reformers of society (a social relevance orientation). Followers of De Graaff, in contrast, more and more favoured a laissez-faire setting in the school where children's interests had a great deal of bearing on the curriculum and the learning activities (a personal relevance orientation). Most Christian school supporters, however, wanted a more structured curriculum and classroom setting than De Graaff—after all, as Calvinists they believed children to be sinful from birth and therefore in need of disciplined instruction. As a result, De Graaff gradually lost his influence with the schools after the mid-1970s, but, as the next chapter shows, not before his leadership had resulted in a number of curriculum publications. The Kuyperians, in the meantime, continued to fill the key leadership positions in Canadian curriculum efforts.

CURRICULUM ORIENTATIONS (1945-1977)

A Quest for Purpose

In contrast with the 1920s and 1930s, the post-World War II age saw a great deal of emphasis on curriculum development by the NUCS. Canadian schools, once they had become somewhat stable, also showed much concern for a unique, Christian curriculum. Leaders everywhere agreed that Christian schools, if they were to be worthwhile institutions, needed a curriculum that was more distinctive than one that just added a Biblical studies course to a public school program. Yet little agreement about the orientation of such a curriculum existed.

However, unlike the inter-war period, the movement did not become introspective and defensive. Rather, despite internal disagreements, it actively developed curriculum guides and textbooks. The schools renewed the discussions that had been held early in the century about the purpose of Christian education and its implementation. In the United States, except for Jaarsma's use of Dutch Calvinist sources, this now took place completely within the American context. In Canada, with its recent immigration, the discussions tried to apply Dutch theoretical ideas to the Canadian scene with the same zeal that Bennink demonstrated at the turn of the century.

Donald Oppewal presented curriculum views in the Christian schools as a "bi-polar tension" between intellectual Calvinism (i.e., an academic orientation) and a Calvinism that emphasized personal piety and personal relevance.[74] Peter De Boer recently claimed that a synthesis of these two positions had been reached in the writings of Wolterstorff, Beversluis, and, more recently, the publication of **Shaping School Curriculum: A Biblical View**.[75] However, the actual situation was more complex. In 1977, all of Eisner's orientations were still represented, with a narrow version of the academic orientation being present more strongly in the classroom than in the literature.

Jellema and Jaarsma and their supporters confronted each other in the 1950s. Should an academic or a personal relevance orientation characterize the Christian curriculum? Wolterstorff refused to become involved in this dualism and instead chose a social relevance position. Beversluis' attempts at an eclectic consensus found little direct opposition--but was redirected by the NUCS curriculum department's process-directed reinterpretation of Beversluis' intellectual, moral and creative taxonomic categories. After 1965 Canadian writers also entered the fray. Like Wolterstorff, they considered themselves Kuyperians. However, soon they manifested two different emphases, viz., personal and social relevance.

Beversluis' attempt to forge a consensus had been a noble though not very successful one. Perhaps some truth existed in all these orientations, but Beversluis had not analyzed various views well enough to present a coherent, unified, all-encompassing view. On many occasions the various groups had little dialogue and even less appreciation for each other. One of the difficulties was the use of language. When Beversluis and Triezenberg used a term like "social justice," they meant something quite different from Wolterstorff or the Canadian Kuyperians. Sometimes seeming agreement broke down with the realization that vast differences still needed to be bridged. Some Canadians wrote and acted as if the NUCS had never developed any curriculum positions or materials worth considering. Concomitantly, the Americans did not understand that the new brash immigrants were unwilling to accept the American way of life and that Canadians with their more recent European philosophical and religious background looked askance at what they perceived as the superficial, pragmatic American society.

What complicated matters even more was that the NUCS adaptation of Beversluis' taxonomy was neither comprehensive nor logically consistent. This meant that curriculum writers using its framework interpreted it to suit their own purposes. NUCS social studies publications, for instance, balanced an intellectual approach with a social relevance one, implicitly recognizing that a concept like justice could not be taught just through the cognitive processes defined for the three taxonomic dimensions nor in terms of narrowly focused behavioural objectives.[76] One reviewer criticized the NUCS taxonomy because it lacked preciseness and comprehensiveness and it tended to fragment learning, but then added that

> the chapters on music and physical education are the most admirable examples of breakthrough [i.e., through the taxonomy], leaving behind the restrictions of the intellectual, decisional, creative taxonomy and giving full rein to the diversity of learnings that ought to characterize our learning centers.

Only those who favoured a technological process orientation or those who felt free enough to bend it to suit their own ends used the taxonomy extensively.

Despite the differences in curriculum orientations, the widespread discussions renewed the vigour of educational planning. The discussions and, even more so, the curriculum development and implementation projects created enthusiasm for attempts to provide a distinctly Christian program. True, Postma's 1947 call for "daring experimentation and bold pioneering" was usually evident only in programs like ISCS that were also accepted in public schools. Yet unlike the defensive stance

193

they had taken in the 1930s, the schools now supported a strong quest for purpose, stimulated by the self-reflection of the mid-1940s, the American curriculum debates of the 1950s and 1960s, and the renewed Kuyperian influence through post-World War II emigration to Canada.

Both in the 1950s and in the 1970s various curriculum projects established that Christian education consisted of more than a fearful escapism. Curriculum development received more attention, and the various orientations tried, with varying degrees of success, to wed a Christian view of life with current educational approaches. At least the schools had reached a consensus that building the house of Christian curriculum was more profitable than fearfully defending it. However, the differences in curricular directions still prevented united development efforts.

NOTES

1. Richard Postma, "Marching On!," **Christian Home and School,** July-Aug., 1947, p. 5.
2. Results of a survey reported in NUCS **Annual 1960-61.**
3. Cornelius Jaarsma in the Jan. 1957 issue of **Torch and Trumpet** reported that "more than half of the teaching personnel have four years or more of post-high school education," with thirteen percent of the teachers having a master's degree (p. 19).
4. Resolution 7, Annual Christian School Convention, Aug. 1946.
5. The reasons for the disagreements between Mark Fakkema and the NUCS Board have been described, for instance, by Arthur De Kruyter in "The Reformed Christian Day School Movement in North America" (M.Th. thesis, Princeton Theological Seminary, 1952), pp. 21ff. See also the interview with John A. Van Bruggen by Dr. J. Herbert Brinks, Heritage Hall, Dec. 1972 and letters by Mark Fakkema to the NUCS Board of Directors (June 24, 1947) and to historian A. Hyma (Jan. 8, 1951, in Hyma's personal papers, Heritage Hall Archives). Fakkema did suggest joint curriculum ventures, but the NUCS stated that "we must insist on keeping our education distinctive and completely Reformed" (NUCS Report to the Christian Reformed Church Synod, **1950 Acts of Synod,** p. 413). Even today, little contact and no cooperative curriculum planning exists between the Association of Christian Schools International (ACSI), which includes most schools of the now-defunct NACS, and NUCS/CSI.

6. John A. Van Bruggen to the NUCS Board, Mar. 11, 1947.

7. For a description of the start of the foundation, see **Christian Home and School**, Dec. 1949, p. 13. In 1950 the foundation contributed $20 000 to NUCS curriculum development efforts. By the 1982-83 budget year this annual grant had increased to $125 000, with the 1975-established Canadian counterpart contributing another $46 000.

8. NUCS **Minutes**, July 20, 1951, Art. 20; **Christian Home and School**, July-Aug. 1947, p. 7; and Van Bruggen interview with J. Herbert Brinks, Dec. 1972. Van Bruggen correctly pointed out that besides the publication of Biblical studies textbooks and teachers' manuals, little was done that had not been started during his years at the NUCS. This changed only when Henry Triezenberg and Gordon Oosterman began their curriculum work in the late 1960s.

9. Albert E. Greene, Jr., NUCS **Annual 1957**, p. 157; report about overture from Seattle's Watson Groen Christian School at NUCS Board of Directors meeting, March 8, 1962.

10. NUCS **Annual 1947**, p. 84; **Christian Home and School**, July-Aug. 1947, p. 6; NUCS Educational Committee **Minutes**, May 9, 1947; documents in Van Bruggen's personal papers in the Heritage Hall Archives; NUCS, **Course of Study for Christian Schools** (Chicago, 1947); and Henry Schultze, "Desperately Needed--A Philosophy of Education," **Calvin Forum**, June-July 1950, p. 239. Schultze's conclusion was shared by Edwin H. Rian in **Christianity and American Education** (San Antonio: The Naylor Co., 1949), p. 207.

11. Arthur H. De Kruyter, "The Reformed Christian Day School Movement in North America." Examples included "Intellectually, he must think as God thinks" (p. 67), and, "Generally speaking, the methodology which is found in Christian schools is a cross-section of the general methods of education" (p. 75).

12. John L. De Beer and Cornelius Jaarsma, **Toward a Philosophy of Christian Education** (Grand Rapids: NUCS, 1953).

13. Donald Oppewal, **The Roots of the Calvinistic Day School Movement** (Grand Rapids: Calvin College Monograph Series, 1963), p. 37-38; Cornelius Jaarsma, **Torch and Trumpet**, Jan. 1957, p. 16.

14. Nicholas Wolterstorff, **Curriculum: By What Standard?** (Grand Rapids: NUCS, 1966); N. Henry Beversluis, **Christian Philosophy of Education** (Grand Rapids: NUCS, 1971); Henry J. Triezenberg et al., **Principles to Practice** (Grand Rapids: NUCS, 1973).

15. Table II shows my adaptation of Eisner and Vallance's curriculum orientations. The latter are described, for example, in Elliot W.

Eisner, **The Educational Imagination** (New York: Macmillan, 1979), pp. 50-73. I do not consider "curriculum as technology" a separate orientation, but a development approach that can be used in several of the other orientations, as the chart shows.

16. Glenys G. Unruh and Adolph Unruh, **Curriculum Development: Problems, Processes, and Progress** (Berkeley, Ca.: McCutchan, 1984), pp. 99 and 104. This orientation has also been referred to as academic rationalism, liberal and/or humanistic education, intellectualism, intellectual traditionalism, and the discipline approach. The word "discipline" had a dual meaning. For example, Bestor held that the curriculum entailed disciplined study in five disciplines, i.e., "discipline" referred both to traditional subject areas and to training the faculties of the mind. For a description of these views, see Robert Maynard Hutchins, **The Conflicts in Education in a Democratic Society** (New York: Harper, 1953); Mortimer J. Adler, **The Paideia Proposal: An Educational Manifesto** (New York: Macmillan, 1982); Arthur Bestor, **Educational Wastelands** (Urbana: University of Illinois, 1953); and Hilda Neatby, **So Little for the Mind** (Toronto: Clarke Irwin, 1953).

17. Henry Zylstra, **Testament of Vision** (Grand Rapids: Eerdmans, 1958, 1961 paperback edition), p. 99.

18. Hutchins' intellectualism was discussed at the 1949 Christian School Principals' Conference (**Proceedings**, pp. 25-26). Henry Zylstra quoted him to back Zylstra's arguments for traditional liberal education (**Testament of Vision**, p. 85). Most of Zylstra's quotes used here were either first given in speeches to Christian school conventions. The quotes in this paragraph are from pp. 82 and 83.

19. Zylstra, pp. 117. See also pp. 86-89, 114.

20. **Proceedings**, Conference for Christian High School Principals, Calvin College, June 27-29, 1949, pp. 23-24; W. Harry Jellema, "Statement of Academic Needs, Grand Rapids Christian High," n.d., pp. 4, 5, 7-8, 11, and 12.

21. George Stob in the conclusion of his 1955 doctoral dissertation said that the Jellema group at the time was "held either suspect because it stands too close to worldly culture or else too far removed from what is conceived to be the specific purpose of the Christian school ("The Christian Reformed Church and Her Schools" [Th.D. dissertation, Princeton Theological Seminary, 1955], p. 430).

22. Lambert J. Flokstra, **Christian Education—Tradition or Conviction?** (Grand Rapids: Calvin College, 1958), p. 19.

23. C[ornelius] B[ontekoe], "Of—Do We Want the Traditional?", **Christian Home and School**, Nov. 1951, p. 17.
24. B. K. Kuiper, **The Church in History** (Grand Rapids: NUCS and Eerdmans, 1951); John De Bie, **The Story of the Old World** (Grand Rapids: NUCS, 1954).
25. B. K. Kuiper, pp. 6, 132.
26. John De Bie, speech on "The Problems of Writing a Christian Textbook," July 28, 1950.
27. **Christian Home and School**, Nov. 1943, p. 5.
28. Conference for Christian High School Principals, **Proceedings**, Calvin College, June 27-29, 1949, p. 25.
29. Cornelius Jaarsma, "Content or the What of Education," in Donald Oppewal, ed., "Bi-Polar Tensions in Christian Education" (Calvin College Educ. 304 Syllabus, 1971), pp. 6, 9; Conference for Christian High School Principals, **Proceedings**, Calvin College, June 27-29, 1949, p. 16; Aug. 6, 7, 1951, pp. 70, 74; Cornelius Jaarsma, ed., **Fundamentals in Christian Education** (Grand Rapids: Eerdmans, 1953), pp. 234-35.
30. **Christian Home and School**, Jan. 1944, p. 11; Feb. 1944, p. 7; and Cornelius Jaarsma, unpublished lecture on "A Christian Philosophy of Education," part of a series of four lectures in Jaarsma's personal papers, Heritage Hall Archives (n.d.), p. 26.
31. **Christian Home and School**, Jan. 1944, pp. 9, 11; Feb. 1944, p. 6; and Jaarsma, lecture on "A Christian Philosophy of Education," pp. 24-25.
32. **Christian Home and School**, Jan. 1944, p. 8; Jaarsma, "Content or the What of Education," p. 10; Jaarsma, **Fundamentals in Christian Education**, pp. 18-20, 237-39; and Jaarsma, "The School and Our Present Society," transcript of speech, n.d., p. 5 (Heritage Hall Archives). Later in his life Jaarsma sought more of a balance of this personal relevance orientation with a cultural relevance one. In a 1965 article on the teaching of French, for example, he emphasized the importance of putting the study of French language in the context of French history and culture, mainly for personal development and self-fulfillment, but also "to get a French view of American life and culture" (**Christian Educators Journal**, Fall 1965, pp. 28-32).
33. **Calvin Forum**, Dec. 1955, p. 57; Conference **Proceedings**, Aug. 6, 7, 1951, p. 72; Jaarsma, "A Brief Overview," pp. 19-20; and Jaarsma, "Content or the What of Education," p. 7. The quote is from **Calvin Forum**, Dec. 1955, p. 57.
34. George Stob, p. 430.

35. Christian Reformed Church 1955 Synod, **Principles of Christian Education** (Grand Rapids: NUCS, 1955). One of the themes was that "education is the nurture or bringing up of the whole man, and comprises all of life. . . . The human intellect cannot be parceled out for instruction independently of the emotional life or the life of the body" (p. 9).

36. Peter P. De Boer, **Shifts in Curriculum Theory for Christian Education** (Grand Rapids: A Calvin College Monograph, 1983), pp. 16.

37. Conference **Proceedings**, Aug. 6, 7, 1951, p. 74.

38. Alice Fenenga, Gertrude Haan, and Beth Merizon, eds., **The Pilot Series in Literature** (Grand Rapids: NUCS): **Book 1** (1957), **Book 2** (1959), and **Book 3** (1964). The editors chose content on the basis of "spiritual significance, general significance, and interest appeal." The editors' stress on creating interest and relating the literature to the students reflected more of a personal relevance than an academic emphasis. Of course, how a teacher would use the books would affect the actual orientation in the classroom much more than the content of the anthologies.

39. Albert T. Boersma, **In the School of the Master**, pp. 71-72.

40. Nicholas P. Wolterstorff, **Curriculum: By What Standard?**, pp. 9-16. Wolterstorff has contributed substantially to the analysis of educational issues in the Christian school movement. The gradual shift in his views is a reminder that although a person's thinking may lean to certain curriculum orientations, only seldom does a person fit precisely into one category; views evolve and develop and straddle specific "pigeon holes." Wolterstorff headed a Calvin College Curriculum Study Committee that in 1970 published **Christian Liberal Arts Education**. This report rejected both a "pragmatist" and a "classicist" view of the college curriculum, opting instead for "an extensive and intensive engagement in the disciplines" in order "to prepare a wide range of young people for living the Christian life in contemporary society;" i.e., he welded the academic and social relevance orientations. At a CSI convention in the late 1970s Wolterstorff, only partly tongue-in-cheek, suggested that home economics should be the core course in the curriculum. Here he explicitly rejected the academic orientation and put more emphasis on a personal relevance one. This was further developed in his conception of "tendency learning" in **Educating for Responsible Action** (Grand Rapids: CSI and Eerdmans, 1980). His **Until Justice and Peace Embrace** (Grand Rapids: Eerdmans, 1983) implies that such

tendency learning should prepare students for Christian social commitment and action.

41. Ibid., pp. 11-16. Wolterstorff, like most followers of Kuyper, used the word "culture" in a comprehensive sense, viz., as the total body of belief, knowledge, sanctions, values, and goals that described a design and pattern of living. See also George S. Counts, **Dare the Schools Build a New Social Order?** (New York: John Day, 1932).

42. For example, Seattle's Albert E. Greene wrote an article, "Wanted: A Christian Philosophy of Education," in the October 1966 issue of the **Christian Educators Journal,** and British Columbia's Syrt Wolters made similar entreaties to the NUCS (NUCS Executive Committee **Minutes,** Oct. 11, 1967, Art. 2.3).

43. From a report on the importance of a statement of Christian philosophy discussed by the Education Committee on Feb. 4, 1967.

44. Beversluis, pp. 22-24, 36, 37, 44, and 51. Almost half of chapter 2, as Beversluis acknowledged, was based on Wolterstorff's **Curriculum: By What Standard?** But Beversluis deleted references to contemporary social issues found, for example, on pages 11 and 16 of Wolterstorff's pamphlet.

45. Ibid., pp. 39-41, 52-59. For descriptions of Bloom's taxonomy, see Benjamin S. Bloom, ed., **Taxonomy of Educational Objectives, Handbook I: Cognitive Domain** (New York: David McKay, 1956), and David R. Krathwohl, ed., **Taxonomy of Educational Objectives, Handbook II: The Affective Domain** (New York: David McKay, 1964). Bloom's taxonomy of educational objectives, probably the best known classification of learning goals, divided such goals into three domains perceived to be independent: the cognitive, affective, and psychomotor.   Within each domain the taxonomy tried to delineate a hierarchy of capabilities.

46. The 1947 NUCS **Course of Studies** had also divided some objectives into three categories: intellectual, moral, and volitional, where the volitional was similar to what philosophers have described as tendency or dispositional learning (pp.   323-24).   Wolterstorff's **Educating for Responsible Action** (Grand Rapids: Eerdmans and CSI, 1980) rejected Bloom's, Beversluis', and the modified NUCS taxonomies in favour of one paralleling the standard philosophical categorization of types of knowledge ("knowledge-that"/knowledge; "knowledge-how"/ability; dispositions/tendency learning).   Ironically, Wolterstorff came to this conclusion while writing a book for the NUCS that was to describe the "decisional" (i.e., Beversluis' moral) dimension.

47. Beversluis did not fall victim to Kohlberg's inclination to assign more importance to the justification of moral choices than to actual moral action. Indeed, Beversluis said that the curriculum must induct young persons "into the complexity and variety of moral obligations, choices, ambiguities, tensions, allegiances, and behaviors that human life presents to all observant persons" (Beversluis, p. 55). Yet his failure to distinguish clearly between strategies to develop abilities to make moral choices on the one hand and to develop appropriate dispositions on the other resulted in suggestions that seemed contradictory. The curriculum must teach students to analyze "moral tensions and ambiguities" in terms of attitudes, values, justification, and actions. However, they must also learn that "they must make [vexing] choices at times with the help of rules and codes, but more often with the help of only a sensitive conscience" (Beversluis, pp. 56-57). Except for the fact that Beversluis emphasized to teachers the necessity for confronting students with moral issues about which they had to make responsible but yet often difficult choices, Beversluis gave little concrete help to teachers in his domain of "moral growth."

48. Henry Triezenberg et al., **Principles to Practice.** There have been two other analyses of curriculum theory in Christian schools, both looking at the theory from a more philosophical viewpoint than I have. Peter De Boer's 1983 **Shifts in Curricular Theory for Christian Education** and Tony Vander Ende's 1980 unpublished paper, "Conflicting Conceptions of Truth and Implications for Christian Curriculum" each dealt with curriculum at both the school and the college levels; neither included a discussion of the actual orientation of the curriculum work of the NUCS. De Boer, like myself, concluded that Beversluis tried to achieve a "blending," although he was more optimistic about the success of such an eclectic approach than I am. Vander Ende found that Beversluis' concern for content and methods of inquiry made him retain an academic orientation (p. 25). While Beversluis did lean more towards such an orientation than to any other, he borrowed liberally from the other orientations as well.

49. NUCS **Annual 1959-60,** p. 115; NUCS Education Committee **Minutes,** Nov. 11, 1961 and April 26, 1966; NUCS Board of Directors' **Minutes,** Aug. 12, 13, 1963, Art. 17; and Feb. 20, 21, 1964, Art. 23; NUCS Executive Committee **Minutes,** Dec. 29, 1964, Art. 2 and Feb. 7, 1968, Art. 19; NUCS **Directory 1965-66,** p. 152.

50. NUCS Director's message to Board, Feb. 17, 18, 1966; NUCS

Executive Committee **Minutes,** Nov. 10, 1965, Art. 3; NUCS Policy Paper "Organizing the NUCS Curriculum Effort"; later, in revised form, "NUCS Curriculum Department Operational Policy." The quotes are taken from the Oct. 30, 1969 version, pp. 2-4.

51. NUCS Curriculum Administrator's Annual Report, June 30, 1972; NUCS **Directory 1974-75,** p. 207. See also the July 1972 and the Aug. 1974 self-evaluation reports, as well as the Curriculum Department Report to the NUCS Executive Committee, Sept. 25, 1973.

52. For a critique of such an approach, see Herbert M. Kliebard, "The Rise of Scientific Curriculum Making and Its Aftermath," in **Curriculum Theory Network** 5(1975): 27-38.

53. **Principles to Practice,** p. 2; NUCS Curriculum Department **Annual Report,** Spring 1974, p. C-30.

54. **Principles to Practice,** p. 2; NUCS Curriculum Department **Annual Report,** Spring 1974, p. C-31.

55. **Principles to Practice,** p. 3; Henry J. Triezenberg and Donald Oppewal, **Goals for Christian Education: Priorities and Needs, PACE Module #2** (Grand Rapids: NUCS, 1977).

56. **Principles to Practice,** page S-5; **Christian Home and School,** Mar. 1969, pp. 18-19. Triezenberg spent time on leave to write for the ISCS project in Tallahassee, Florida.

57. **Christian Educators Journal,** May 1970, p. 6.

58. Henry J. Triezenberg, **Science and Personal Values** (Grand Rapids: NUCS, n.d., circa 1973), pp. 28, 33-34, 72. One of the reasons Triezenberg recommended the ISCS materials, for example, was that "processes of science include a degree of unity with processes of other disciplines" (p. 27).

59. Herman Dooyeweerd, **A New Critique of Theoretical Thought,** 4 vols. (Amsterdam: H. J. Paris; Philadelphia: Presbyterian and Reformed, 1953-1958).

60. Albert Witvoet, "The Christian School And Its Cultural Task," **Christian School Herald,** June-July 1965, p. 13. As before, "culture" was used in a very general sense to describe the design and pattern of living of the society in which the immigrants found themselves. "Cultural mandate" referred to God's requirement that all aspects of society be developed in harmony with Christian principles.

61. John Van Dyk, "The Enemy Within: Secularism in Christian Education," **Torch and Trumpet,** Oct. 1969, pp. 13-14; and Gordon Spykman, "What Makes Education Christian?" in NUCS **Directory 1971-72,** p. 235. See also John Vriend, "No Neutral Ground: Why

I'm Committed to Christian Education," in John Vriend et al., **To Prod the "Slumbering Giant": Crisis, Commitment, and Christian Education** (Toronto: Wedge, 1972), p. 12.

62. **Christian Home and School,** Jan. 1965, pp. 4, 5; Mar. 1967, pp. 6, 7-8; April 1967, p. 7, and May/June 1969, p. 6.

63. The Institute for Christian Studies had opened in 1967. Although soon located next to the University of Toronto campus, an association of members operated it independently. Today, the Institute has a government charter to offer a Master of Philosophical Foundations degree, and offers doctoral programs in cooperation with the Calvinistic Free University in Amsterdam, the Netherlands.

64. Compare, for example, Arnold De Graaff, "The Need for a Christian Curriculum," **Christian School Herald,** March 1968, with his later **Joy in Learning.**

65. Arnold H. De Graaff and Jean Olthuis, **Joy in Learning** (Toronto: Joy in Learning Curriculum Development Centre, 1973), esp. pp. 5, 7, 9, 10, 12.

66. Michael R. Welton, "Crisis in the Classroom," **Vanguard,** Sept. 1971, pp. 21-22.

67. John Vriend et al., **To Prod the "Slumbering Giant": Crisis, Commitment, and Christian Education.** All seven authors were Canadians, although two of them taught at Dordt College in Sioux Center, Iowa.

68. John Van Dyk, "Building a Curriculum with the Kingdom Vision," in **To Prod the "Slumbering Giant",** pp. 103-104. Van Dyk gave this essay as a lecture in a number of American and Canadian communities. Elsewhere in the essay he carefully used the adjective phrase "North American " rather than the "American" in this quote.

69. Ibid., pp. 105-106.

70. **Christian Home and School,** March 1974, p. 6; and W. H. Hultink, R. Klapwyk, J. Stronks, and J. Vriend, "Christian Education in Ontario--1973," mimeographed paper (Hamilton, 1973), p. i. The Ministry did not react to the report.

71. W. H. Hultink et al., pp. 12-13, 37, 43-44.

72. Henry Aay, "Geography: Calling and Curriculum," **Christian Educators Journal,** Nov. 1976, pp. 16-19; Jan. 1977, pp. 11-14. The most recent units using Aay's model are William Hordyk et al., **Man and the Coniferous Forest** and **Man and the Temperate Grassland** (Hamilton: Ontario Alliance of Christian Schools, 1983).

73. See, for example, the report by John De Boer, chairman of the

Ontario Alliance of Christian Schools Education Committee, **Christian School Herald,** March 1968, p. 7, and Albert Hengstman, "Christian Education in the Year of the Lord 1967," **Church and Nation,** Jan. 20, 1968.

74. Donald Oppewal, "Bi-Polar Tensions in Christian Education."

75. Geraldine J. Steensma and Harro W. Van Brummelen, eds., **Shaping School Curriculum: A Biblical View** (Terra Haute, Indiana: Signal, 1977). Peter De Boer's analysis is found in his **Shifts in Curricular Theory for Christian Education** (especially p. 32).

76. See, for example, Gordon Oosterman, William C. Hendricks, and Leroy D. Stegink, "Social Studies: Challenges to Understand Man," in **Principles to Practice,** p. SS-5; and Gordon Oosterman, ed., **Geneva to Geelong** (Grand Rapids: NUCS, 1974).

77. Norman De Jong, **Christian Educators Journal,** Nov. 1974, p. 16.

This 1923 photograph shows the first (1911) Christian
school building in Lynden, Washington.

8 Dealing with Curriculum Issues: Some Examples (1945-1977)

Influences on the Curriculum

Christian School supporters have been quick to agree with general statements concerning the basic aims of the Christian school:

> The school as a complement to the home and the church will be an instrument of leading children into a full life that is truly restored with God, and has the right relationship with God's world.[1]

However, while such generalities served as rallying points, they also camouflaged the differences that existed about the meaning, and, even more, about the implementation of such statements. Such differences usually arose from specific issues at a school or from questions arising during the implementation of curriculum projects: Should industrial arts be introduced? Is the **Catcher in the Rye** a novel that should (dis)grace the Christian school classroom? Why isn't Mary being told the Bible stories in the traditional chronological way? Is our school up-to-date in its science program?

How Christian school communities addressed and resolved such issues can be explained only in part by the diversity of existing curriculum orientations. The social, political and economic temper of the times, for instance, affected Christian school planning and implementation as it did public schools. Parents believed that for social and economic advancement their children should stay in school longer and employers began to expect higher educational qualifications. The trend toward universality of high school education meant that schools were forced to offer an increasing diversity of programs and courses.[2] Also, the aftermath of Sputnik did not leave the Christian schools untouched, with "new math" and new science approaches being accepted without criticism as being "consistent with our goals."[3] As in public education, the importance attached to education and increasing prosperity reduced pupil-teacher ratios significantly in the post-World

205

War II period, allowing for more flexible teaching techniques as well as a greater variety of options.[4]

Secondly, the personal characteristics of individuals involved with the schools influenced curriculum. The lack of forceful curriculum leadership within the NUCS after John Van Bruggen left in 1953 meant that the organization took few new initiatives for more than a decade. Also, the stable, conservative Dutch Calvinists often simplistically and unconsciously identified the traditional as Christian and the modern as secular.

Thirdly, the Christian school movement, as one principal wrote in 1951, was part of the contemporary American educational scene, and affected by it.[5] In a 1956 study of the Grand Rapids Christian Schools, Michael T. Ruiter wrote:

> Christian teachers are subject to at least two effects of reform and change in the public schools of the United States. One is the adoption of theories and practices which oppose the Biblical view of man and the world. The other effect is a reaction to the new "progressive" education which causes the teacher to return to the old traditional methods of teaching, some of which are questionable. Both of these conditions exist in the Grand Rapids Christian Schools.[6]

This situation typified many of the schools during the 1950s and 1960s. Public education trends set the tone in curriculum. Little was done to design courses specifically for Christian schools, except in Biblical Studies. The social studies textbooks recommended in the 1947 NUCS **Course of Study** were standard public school ones. The Michigan schools endorsed the state's requirement for a course on government which used **Time** and **U.S. News and World Report** to "take up daily problems of democracy." A NUCS Annual Meeting assumed that Christian schools accepted public school subject requirements and their suggested allotted times without question.[7]

In Ontario, the Christian schools were also affected by the general educational environment. At the grades 11 and 12 levels (no schools offered grade 13 in the 1960s and early 1970s) the schools met many Ministry of Education organizational and curriculum requirements in order to be accredited. For example, the high schools adopted the four- and five-year streaming of 1960s "Robarts plan" for high school reorganization. Because of their small size, the arts and science streams prevailed, with the four-year arts and science program becoming a catchall for students not able to cope with a university entrance program.[8] The Canadian Kuyperians developed a Christian counterpart to Ontario's Man in Society course and taught it to all students, not just to those in the four-year stream as the Ontario Ministry of Education originally intended.[9]   Schools viewed the Hall-Dennis report, **Living and Learning,** with suspicion because of its "humanistic" (i.e., child-centred rather than God-centred) thrust.   Nevertheless, Christian high schools adopted the credit system introduced in Ontario in the wake of the Hall-Dennis report, although most schools, both for philosophical reasons and because of size limitations, continued to require a substantial core of compulsory subjects.[10] Progressive notions found in the Hall-Dennis report such as student discovery, exploration and inquiry, a more integrated curriculum, flexible group instruction, field experiences, abandoning letter and percentage grades—all these found proponents also among Christian school teachers in the early 1970s, albeit among a minority.[11]   The conservative nature of most teachers and parents tempered the climate of reform fueled by the Hall-Dennis report in a period of social unrest.   The retrenchment caused by Ontario's return to pedagogical conservatism later in the 1970s was therefore not very severe for Christian schools.

The intersection of public and Christian school concerns was largely unavoidable.   Unlike the Amish, Christian school supporters, in Calvinistic fashion, had remained in the mainstream of society. In their efforts to influence society, they could not help but be directed by the currents of general educational thought and practice.   Also, a quest for quality education often overshadowed the desire for uniqueness.   To prove such excellence, both to themselves and to the outside educational community, external standards developed for public education were used.   A significant number of teachers held that subject matter should be consistent with the best in public education. Many curriculum articles did not even consider the desirability of alternative Christian approaches.[12]

One further major curriculum issue led to major disagreements in the late 1960s, especially within a number of Ontario communities and between the Ontario Christian school movement and the NUCS.   While parents and leaders agreed that the schools must educate children to become responsible followers of Jesus Christ, they supported three distinct (though not totally independent) emphases of how this was to be accomplished.[13]   The first emphasis was that since contemporary secular society had a deleterious influence on children, the Christian school must, in the first place, isolate children from that society. This "monastic" view fitted Richard H. Niebuhr's "Christ against culture" categorization.[14]   While no curriculum projects sustained this view, many Christian school parents and teachers did.   The teaching of a novel such as John Steinbeck's **To a God Unknown** was anathema because it contained an uncritical description of an illicit sex scene. The NUCS board turned down its literature committee's recommendation that high quality stories, in spite of some profanity, be included in an anthology. The board did not want to offend those who held a monastic view of the Christian school. For this group, to prepare children for living an obedient, Godly life did not mean cultural engagement. Rather, potentially evil societal influences were to be banned from the child's environment as much as possible.[15]

A second emphasis, the dualistic one, had also been common in the 1920s and 1930s. This view held that the Christian school was to teach Christian faith and standards of conduct besides "neutral" subject matter. Children would improve the quality of life through individual, Christian moral contributions to society. In Niebuhr's model this view would be closest to the "Christ above culture" stance that has also characterized many Roman Catholic Christians. A school could teach **To a God Unknown** as long as it emphasized the illicit nature of sexual relations outside of marriage. Christian faith was to be brought to bear only on "spiritual and moral needs," on the "inner life."[16] Many though not all supporters of this view saw little necessity for unique Christian curriculum materials other than for Biblical studies and closely related courses.

The third view, an integrationist one, held that the school should prepare the child "to build a totally new way of life in Christ" in which he was trained "to do everything, including his politics and business, in an integrally Christian manner." Christ transformed culture, and Christian faith integrated the whole curriculum. Even the teaching of Latin must "press Christ's claim upon men and society."[17] **To a God Unknown** would lead to an analysis of Steinbeck's naturalistic views of life and a concomitant deepened understanding of a Christian stance. For the integrationists, ideology influenced the selection of content, its interpretation and its uses. Therefore, a distinctive Christian curriculum was necessary in all subject areas. At the same time, as the last chapter showed, some Canadian integrationists favoured personal relevance much more than others, and those emphasizing social relevance disagreed about the extent to which schools should prepare children to build a new, Christian social order.

Kuyperian integrationists believed that the NUCS favoured a dualistic view of Christian education. They based this, for example, on this NUCS-approved curriculum criterion:

CURRICULUM ISSUES (1945-1977)

The curriculum must be. . . . designed to impart knowledges and skills normally set by current curriculum standards and to teach moral and spiritual values for living a life in Christ.[18]

The Kuyperians objected to "knowledges and skills" being chosen primarily on the basis of "current curriculum standards," and to the Christian life being limited to "moral and spiritual values." They criticized the NUCS-promoted "neutral" ISCS program augmented with some personal moral values. Curriculum content should be chosen, they held, to help children become Christians who could address social issues and promote Christian justice and freedom.

The Canadian integrationists (who formed by far the strongest corps for this emphasis) complicated the issue by concurrently wanting to forge a Canadian identity for their Christian schools. They chided the NUCS for not taking into account the aspirations of its expanding Canadian sector. Canadians based such criticism, for instance, on the fact that it took twenty-five years to convince the American majority that the NUCS needed a name change to reflect its international scope.[19]

Various influences, then, shaped the Christian school curriculum from 1945 to 1977: the social, economic, and political context; the psychological characteristics of leaders and supporters; contemporary educational thinking in the public sector; the conflict between the monastic, dualist, and integrationist views of how the Christian school should accomplish its basic aim; Canadian nationalism; and the curriculum orientations among leaders and teachers. This chapter shows how different subsets of these influences provide an explanatory framework for five different curriculum situations in the post-World War II period: the resolution of the "liberal" vs. the "practical" debate; the march of curriculum thinking within the NUCS organization; curriculum controversies in Ontario; and, finally, approaches and writings in two representative subject areas: Biblical studies and science.

The Liberal vs. the Practical and the Traditional vs. the Modern

The clash between the academic and personal relevance orientations in the Christian schools led to a debate in the 1950s about the balance between "practical" and "liberal" courses in the curriculum. To what extent should industrial arts and other vocationally oriented subjects be taught in the curriculum, if at all? Those holding an academic orientation were opposed to giving them a prominent place.

209

CURRICULUM ISSUES (1945-1977)

A Christian school could utilize the traditional subjects, the "broad areas of cultural activity," with much greater impact than "so-called practical, vocational subjects," also for future vocations. Narrow vocational training would make individuals economic machines and narrow technocrats. One writer recommended that even in commercial programs students should not take more than one commercial course per semester. Another wrote that only a full academic program would truly develop the mind and "lead the way back to sound learning and genuine piety."[20]

The "practical" proponents argued, on the other hand, that education should nurture the whole person and therefore balance the liberal and the practical. Skilled craftsmen had God's approval as much as professional persons. Schools should allow students to develop their potential through basic exploratory practical training.[21] The defense for home economics harkened back to that in public education fifty years earlier:

> The Latin declensions may be forgotten, the history notes left gathering dust, but the man and woman who can contribute to the Christian home so that all who live there will feel they are a harmonious unit, blessed by God and responsible to Him, will remain a tribute to their Lord and Maker.[22]

Gradually, the inclusion of some practical courses became accepted. Calvin College's Cornelius Jaarsma, who favoured a personal relevance orientation, was a key figure at the 1956 NUCS Annual Convention that resolved that schools should add more practical electives to their programs. Five years later, leaders criticized James Bryant Conant's recommendations for comprehensive high schools with a large assortment of vocational courses. But, by then, they agreed that basic shop and home economics courses were beneficial. After 1961, discussions about the appropriateness of "practical" courses ceased. Instead, the focus had shifted to the problem of inadequate training in the applied arts, and on the preparation of curriculum guides. A 1970 NUCS publication argued that Christian schools must teach industrial arts so that students would understand the dignity of labour and would begin to deal with the "great question" facing society: How can we effectively convert technological growth into cultural and spiritual growth?[23] Canadians, with their more recent Kuyperian background, never questioned that practical subjects could contribute to the education of the whole child, even for college preparatory students. They introduced industrial arts courses as the schools became established financially. By the 1960s, both in the U.S. and Canada, the expediency of offering practical courses was no longer debated.[24]

CURRICULUM ISSUES (1945-1977)

What had caused the demise of the academic opposition to practical courses? Theoretical discussions about curriculum orientations had less impact than three other contextual factors: the increasing universality of high school education, the improved economic status of parents that enabled schools to offer a few industrial courses, and high school accreditation requirements. Accreditation became important for U.S. college entrance after World War II. Therefore, Christian high school principals in the late 1940s agreed on a uniform system of requirements identical to those of the U.S. North Central Accreditation Association. Standard academic subjects were accordingly supplemented with practical electives chosen from drafting, industrial arts, home economics, commercial subjects, and physical education. Within three or four years almost all Christian high schools had accepted these requirements and had become accredited. The Holland, Michigan, Christian High School, on the other hand, "refused to water down its curriculum with certain vocational and life-adjustment courses," therefore losing North Central accreditation in 1958.[25]

But Holland was an exception. A survey of eighteen U.S. Christian high schools in 1955-56 showed that more than half taught enough practical courses to offer general and commercial streams as well a college preparatory one.[26] The general courses, intended for students not bound for college nor office jobs, consisted of a selection of college preparatory courses plus some practical electives. The two schools offering an official industrial arts stream limited industrial arts to "general shop" and/or woodworking courses. Financial constraints prevented the acquisition of proper facilities and equipment for other industrial arts courses. Yet schools did not want to lose students to public schools with vocational programs that parents deemed more suitable for teenagers unable or unwilling to cope with a strictly academic program. At the same time, some parents insisted that their children, even when weak academically, remain in Christian high schools. These elements combined to convince almost all U.S. Christian high schools to broaden the scope of their practical course offerings but to include only a few select industrial arts courses.

Contrasting views on classroom methodology also caused the main actors in the academic vs. personal relevance debate to collide. In 1948, Cornelius Jaarsma condemned the "formal, coercive regimentation" of the Christian schools. W. Harry Jellema, his intellectualist opponent, replied that the schools were right in insisting on "good classwork, efficiently done," rather than doing "unit projects, and that kind of business." Most backed Jellema not because they understood his aim to train the rational mind through a study of the best Western thought, but because they implicitly identified traditionalism to be a Christian characteristic. John A. Vander Ark, NUCS Executive Director from 1953 to 1977, lauded the schools for maintaining "a steady curriculum of conventional subjects for basic education" and refusing to "dabble in untried theories." One author used William C. Bagley's 1955 reflections on Canada's superior "traditional" education to defend the formal traditional approaches of Christian schools. The "Christian" emphasis on duty, discipline, memorization and respect for tradition was contrasted with "secular" tendencies to let students follow their natural impulses and learn by doing.[27]

A few educators did want to break away from traditional approaches. The NUCS 1947 **Course of Study** presented the curriculum in terms of daily information packages, but also recommended differentiated history assignments such as reports, making collections, art work, construction of historical models, class trips, and interviews and investigations. On the whole, however, Jaarsma's suggestions for teaching the basic three R's skills in a more open and integrated way appear to have had little impact, at least until the late 1960s. Then, perhaps for the first time since the early 1920s, some teachers began once again to consider more creative and open techniques. For instance, a 1963 survey had indicated that reading instruction in Christian schools followed conservative lines, using a consistently traditional phonetic approach with workbooks. However, around 1970 some articles began to appear that promoted personalized reading programs in Christian schools.[28]

In the early 1970s, as in public schools, controversies of the "open" versus the "closed" classroom arose. Calvin College's Peter De Boer argued that the needs of the child required a classroom that was an informal community and a workshop for learning. Canada's Arnold De Graaff published an extensive integrated curriculum for such a setting. John Borst, typical of the opposition, held that the "secret of learning lies in repetition, not in an endless line of 'relevant' experiences which pupils may find enjoyable for the moment." Open education, he continued, led to confusion and was based on the wrong notion of "the natural goodness of man." In another article he criticized the emphasis on experiments in science, social problems in geography, and experience in Biblical studies. Instead, he favoured a systematic, factual inculcation of traditional subject matter that was a truncated variant of an academic curriculum orientation. Views of both the "open" and the "closed" proponents depended more on cultural background and psychological propensities than on philosophical or religious views. Although both De Boer and Borst began from a Biblical

212

view of the person, each used only those aspects that fit their own inclinations, arriving at opposite conclusions.[29]

After 1960, then, the traditionalism of the schools came under increasing attack. The mood for change in the 1960s revealed itself in educational innovation, also in the Christian schools. By 1970 some teachers were implementing more "progressive" learning activities. The NUCS publication **Principles to Practice** advocated that cognitive processes be taught through "personalized" student inquiry. Change had become acceptable at least to some segments of the movement.[30]

Thus four influences shaped the liberal vs. practical and the traditional vs. the modern debates: social, political and economic trends such as the **Zeitgeist** of the 1960s; current public education trends such as the increased emphasis on science programs in the early 1960s; the conservative inclinations of Christian school supporters; and the conflict between the academic and personal relevance orientations. By the mid-1970s the schools had become more open to new curriculum directions, but generally still moved cautiously.

The 1953-1966 Curriculum Interlude in the National Union of Christian Schools

John Van Bruggen's departure from the NUCS in 1953 created a curriculum leadership vacuum not filled for more than ten years. The director's statement to the NUCS board in 1954 that nothing new had been initiated typified the next decade.[31] The NUCS developed few curriculum publications except those commenced by John Van Bruggen, ones submitted voluntarily by individuals, and ones in Biblical studies. World history and health textbook discussions led nowhere despite the availability of authors.[32] A 1957 questionnaire indicated strong support among the schools for the development of a Christian basal reading program. The NUCS education committee, however, believed that "in view of the tremendous problems involved in this project, we should proceed with caution," and several years later, mainly for economic reasons, abandoned further planning. For the committee, readers with a Christian worldview might be desirable, but were not essential. The lack of new initiatives resulted in criticism in the late 1950s that the NUCS had a limited educational program. The NUCS board itself several times indicated its displeasure with the lack of progress made by education committee and staff, and reiterated that it was committed to prepare "Christian instructional materials in all areas of the curriculum."[33]

For its part, the education committee not only faced limited resources but also wanted uniquely Christian materials acceptable to a large segment of the schools. It did not want to retreat to a monastic view of the Christian school, and expressed its disappointment with one proposal for being "distinctive only in the omission of objectionable projects." Yet many constituents were satisfied with a program that in subjects other than Biblical studies used non-Christian materials—as long as these did not promote obviously offensive points of view. Accordingly, during 1957-58 almost ninety percent of the NUCS publications sold consisted of Biblical studies, church history, and religious music publications.[34]

A 1956 NUCS Annual Meeting resolution indicated that also before Canadian influence within the NUCS became prominent, a number of supporters did embrace an integrationist view:

> Be it resolved that our several Christian schools exact every means at their disposal to increase student awareness of the responsibility of the Christian to enter into, permeate, and direct every sphere of cultural activity, thereby to give witness to the Lordship of Christ among his fellow men.[35]

However, the dualistic view predominated in curriculum publications: one's Christian duty was to lead a moral life in an American society whose structure and direction could be accepted uncritically.

The contents of a civics textbook published by the NUCS in 1966, **Under God,** displayed such dualism. The theme of the text was summed up as follows:

> God has made us in America stewards of the choice gift of a representative form of government. We are guardians of this gift. If you want a republic to continue to be the best form of government for our land, keep and urge others to keep, the pledge of loyalty, faithfulness, and obedience to our nation. Do your share as a citizen to see that our nation provides liberty and justice under God.[36]

The author assumed without question that the American Declaration of Independence and Constitution harmonized with Christian beliefs, and that the institutions of American government such as the defense and prison systems served a Christian conception of justice. America, more than any other nation, enabled its citizens to exercise "their God-given, inalienable rights to life, liberty, and the pursuit of happiness." Liberty equalled freedom under the law, and justice meant equal treatment before the law. The book failed to analyze, however, how laws and structures themselves could establish justice or injustice, or what a Christian conception of justice might entail. Good Christian citizens did not become dissenters and reformers, but were to accept without question the basic tenets of American government and its semi-religious ceremonies such as pledging allegiance to the flag. Good citizenship required voting and running for office intelligently, preventing crime, working hard, and being courteous and courageous. Individual Christian morality was all that was needed to "christianize" America. With the references to "under God" and the passages with Biblical references deleted, the book's themes were markedly similar to other patriotic civics textbooks in print. A dualistic view of the school, and of the Christian's role in society, prevailed.[37]

Lack of consistent progress on projects rather than philosophical direction caused the NUCS board to fill the curriculum leadership gap after 1965 by appointing several curriculum consultants, with Henry Triezenberg taking many new initiatives as head of the curriculum department. The basic view of the Christian school continued to be one, however, in which moral ("decisional") learning was added to "objective" content. This led, as the next section shows, to contentions with the new generation of educational leaders in Canada whose ideal was to reform both education and society within a Kuyperian framework.

Stirrings in and around Ontario
1967-1977

Clashes about curriculum matters occurred not only between the NUCS and part of its Canadian contingent, but equally within the Ontario Alliance of Christian Schools and a number of its school committees. One such school was the Toronto District Christian High School whose board policy stated that the English curriculum should contain "a responsible, critical evaluation of modern literature." However, a major confrontation resulted when vice-principal Bert Witvoet decided to teach **The Catcher in the Rye** in 1967-68:

> To the extent that an author artistically reveals God's world, his work is valuable for the study of literature. To the extent that an author reveals the worldly spirit of his age he is valuable for the study of an age. . . . Our students must realize that in the study of literature they deal with life. Only then can they meaningfully prepare for a life of service to God. . . . There is no safety in protectionism.[38]

Despite its policy, the board decided that, because of complaints, Witvoet could not teach the novel in 1968-69. A number of new board

215

members, supported and led by two American pastors of Christian Reformed congregations in the Toronto area, not satisfied with this decision, continued to voice their objections to Witvoet's teaching, calling for his dismissal.[39] The board compromised by demoting Witvoet from vice-principal to classroom teacher.

But opposition to Witvoet and his followers continued. In the spring of 1969, the board discussed whether to cancel Witvoet's popular grade 12 "Christian Life" course, which formed the genesis of the Kuyperian **Man in Society** course now taught by almost all Canadian Christian high schools. It also dismissed the education committee chairman, an instructor at Toronto's Institute of Christian Studies [ICS][40] who supported Witvoet. The staff signed conditional contracts, stipulating the need for mutual discussions regarding educational policy changes. Although a group of ten clergymen intervened on behalf of the staff, the board declared the teaching positions vacant. It wanted to rehire only those teachers who would not question the board's policy decisions. Consequently, all teachers left the school en masse at the end of the school year.[41]

The conflict between the monastic and the integrationist views formed the heart of the dispute. The board indicated it wanted "to carry on the tradition of the 'narrow way.'" It favoured a traditional receptacle approach to learning that would inculcate Calvinist beliefs and morality. The staff, on the other hand, believed that

> students must be prepared to stand responsibly in this world with a witness to the gospel that reaches out to the mind of the twentieth century man, and that exposes the student to the spirits of this world in a biblically responsible way. In no way does the staff wish to be part of a traditionalistic and protectionistic trend.[42]

The teachers' social reconstructionist's stance led to an emphasis of open-ended analyses of societal structures and phenomena. But board members objected, for instance, to Witvoet taking his class to a theatre to analyze a movie.[43] In the end, cooperation became impossible.

Conflicting views also arose at the provincial level. Since Canadian integrationists had made little headway in influencing the direction of NUCS curriculum work,[44] Toronto's ICS, and particularly its psychology professor Arnold De Graaff, decided to become involved in curriculum development. Starting in 1970 the ICS organized a number of summer curriculum writing workshops. To the dismay of the NUCS, the Ontario Alliance of Christian Schools, a NUCS district, decided by a 17-15 vote to enter into a sponsorship of these workshops with the

ICS.[45]   Not only were the summer workshops popular among Christian
school teachers, but four years later the ICS established the Joy in
Learning Curriculum Development Centre [CDC] to facilitate Canadian
Christian school curriculum publications. While the Centre assured the
NUCS it was not a "Canadian counterpart to NUCS,"[46] nevertheless
many Canadians viewed it as an alternate source of curriculum
materials.

The NUCS was far from pleased with these developments.   Its
board executive committee became concerned that part of the
curriculum funds traditionally donated to the NUCS would now be
diverted to ICS efforts. Further, the NUCS warned, "no one must be
deluded into thinking that no difference in direction of curriculum
construction exists."   The Ontario Alliance was a district of the NUCS,
and therefore, the NUCS held, was bound to implement NUCS policy
rather than going its own way in curriculum planning.   Thus the NUCS
opposed joint efforts by the Alliance and the ICS unless resulting
materials were "evaluated by and distribution rights given to the NUCS."
In an effort to ensure that its voice was heard clearly in Ontario, the
NUCS appointed part-time curriculum consultants in the province whose
sole task was to promote NUCS curriculum materials.[47]

After a 1972 meeting with Ontario Alliance and ICS
representatives, the NUCS board stated that "broad agreements were
reached" after months of "adverse criticism of NUCS Bible and
literature materials."[48]   But Canadian curriculum efforts continued to
be acceptable to the NUCS only if they would fit into the pre-
determined NUCS mold:

> H. Triezenberg is preparing a paper which will show specifically
> how people working in Ontario can contribute to and receive from
> NUCS curriculum effort.[49]

In actual fact, the "broad agreement" meant little.   In 1974, the NUCS
once again complained about "the alarming news" that its part-time
social studies consultant in Ontario planned a curriculum writing
conference without the NUCS structuring and approving the project:

> Our understanding is specifically that the consultants will not
> offer independent curriculum materials development services, but
> that District 10 [i.e., the Ontario Alliance] will continue to rely
> on the NUCS for this.[50]

Friction also increased between the Alliance and the NUCS about
the Alliance's right to provide services to its Ontario schools as it saw
fit.   In 1977, Jack Fennema, an American who had been Executive

217

Director of the Ontario Alliance for two years and had been caught in the eye of the storm, called for more diversity of curriculum work within the Christian school movement. The NUCS, he charged, wanted to impose its own program on Canadian schools, not wanting to make room for the Canadian integrationist influence:

> [Canadians] know who they are theologically and philosophically, to a great extent, because they know from where they have come. They are interested in thinking through what it means to be a Reformed [i.e., Calvinistic] Christian within the 20th and 21st century Canada. They are very concerned over what impact they are making on Canadian society and culture. The curriculum and instruction within the Canadian Christian school reflect this.[51]

The two major, intertwined Canadian curriculum concerns about cooperation with NUCS were the implementation of an integrationist emphasis and the establishment of a Canadian identity within the NUCS. The board of the largest Christian school system in Ontario in 1977 stated its misgivings in a submission to the NUCS Executive Director:

> One of the main concerns is the need for development of Christian curriculum materials that reflect our Reformed, Kuiperian [sic] view of education. These materials have to fit our schools and therefore need the direct involvement of our leaders and teachers. . . .
> Our schools need a Canadian and Ontario identity. We are a maturing school system that is ready to direct its own affairs. Our boards, teachers, and committees can identify with the Ontario Alliance or with a Canadian school movement but not very well with a Grand Rapids office directed and staffed by Americans . . . . NUCS curriculum department does not seem to understand our way of thinking or our needs.[52]

While few wanted to secede from the NUCS, many Canadian leaders wanted more flexibility within the organization so that the Canadian sector would have more responsibility for its own affairs.

The foregoing curriculum disputes came to expression especially among Ontario's Christian schools, although they were not limited to them. The British Columbia schools, forming a separate Canadian district of the NUCS since 1962, offered curriculum workshops and courses in the late 1960s. The first one, taught by ICS supporters, emphasized the "ground motive of education" and the "foundations" of a social studies curriculum. The NUCS refused to become involved in these workshops, and also turned down B.C.'s request to publish ICS-developed materials under NUCS auspices as a service to Canadian Christian schools. As a result, a group of seven key B.C. Christian schools leaders in 1976 sent a letter to all B.C. school boards stating that the "the NUCS has not been particularly responsive to specific interests of Canadian Christian schools." One member of the group also wrote the NUCS that its curriculum work was "not highly thought of" in B.C. The issues had spread to the westernmost region of Canada.[53]

However, the curriculum issues that divided communities and caused friction between the NUCS and Canada often were not clearly understood. Many leaders and supporters assumed there were two opposing camps, while in actuality a range of unanalyzed views existed. B. C. principal Gerald Bonekamp saw all curriculum issues in terms of his own traditional, monastic stance versus the ICS-supported personal and social relevance orientation. He accused the ICS of promoting a "political gospel preached merely for the sake of society rather than the saving of a soul."[54] Seeing this as the sole issue, he failed to recognize that Triezenberg's dualistic process orientation was equally at loggerheads with his own. What complicated the picture was that those favouring a traditional receptable approach to learning could--and did-- prefer either the monastic, the dualistic, or the integrationist emphasis. In turn, those holding an integrationist view of the school could--and did--lean to either the academic, the personal relevance or the social relevance curriculum orientation. The issues were clouded further by the search for a unique Canadian identity by many Canadians, and by the unwillingness of the NUCS to consider any curriculum framework but its own. The next sections show how such diverse positions influenced curriculum development in Biblical studies and science.

Biblical Studies in the Curriculum

Since for the NUCS Biblical studies formed the core of the curriculum, development of such study materials consumed a considerable part of its curriculum resources. Until the late 1960s, these materials served primarily to teach factual Bible knowledge. Then, a reaction set in against using "sterile, scholastic, Reformed theologies" that did not seem to affect the lives of children. Programs were called for that would help the student "take up his religious calling in life."[55] Students' personal response became as important as memorizing Bible facts.

The Biblical studies component of the 1947 NUCS **Course of Study** was based on the 1930s NUCS **Bible Manuals**. Although the **Course of Study** suggested additional activities such as studying the

Bible directly and allowing time for discussions, criticism mounted that the program lent itself mainly to a narrow factual approach.[56] Therefore, in 1958 the NUCS appointed a committee of Michigan principals to develop a grade 1-6 Biblical studies teacher's manual that became the basis for new student books, the first of which were published in 1958.[57]

However, the approach still differed little from the Biblical studies program published twenty years earlier. The grades 4-6 books, for example, consisted of a chronological, factual survey of events in the Bible. Each lesson began with a short introduction, included some word study and memory work, and asked a number of recall questions. In spite of a few more varied learning activities, the shortcomings of the earlier books had not been overcome. The approach was factual and repetitive, far removed from the everyday life of students.[58] Biblical studies still did not serve, as the NUCS intended, as the integrating core of the curriculum.

In response to increasing criticism the NUCS set out in 1966 to plan a new Biblical studies program, **Revelation-Response**.[59] It intended to promote the pupil's "ability to extend and apply basic concepts of the Bible to his whole developing Christian life" through "wise decision-making and consequent involvement in problem-solving."[60] The program was precisely planned and systematically executed, with curriculum writing teams using Bloom and Gagné's work to define and categorize specific objectives and learning activities in the intellectual, decisional and creative "dimensions" of learning. For example, the intellectual dimension included objectives and activities involving memory, conceptualization, differentiation, application, and higher order transfer. The writers also incorporated Ausubel's advance organizers and his suggestions for guided discovery learning. Further, they identified "human performances" and "external evidence" to evaluate "measurable" learning, and wrote appropriate "resource pools of [test] items matched with objectives."[61]

Throughout, the program stressed processes more than content or understanding:

Included in the **intellectual** dimension are, first of all, the **skills** of interpretation. These skills involve analyzing the immediate covenant community and the general contexts of [Bible] passages, viewing the passages in the light of Christ, and making applications.[62]

The decisional dimension activities gave specific guidelines and exercises for engaging in personal decision making, while the creative dimension provided opportunities "to make unique, authentic response to God."[63] A typical activity in the intellectual dimension asked grade 4 pupils to recall, on the basis of stories that the class had acted out, what prophets did. They then developed the context by analyzing and describing what life would be like in a boarding school for "prophets-in-training." A "decisional" activity required pupils to decide on "a project of service" since "our class has learned that we must be servants also." The creative dimension received its due with activities such as "Write a poem on being a follower of Christ."[64] It was acting, analyzing, writing, deciding, creating, and responding, rather than the acquisition of a knowledge of Biblical facts and events that the authors considered of foremost importance.

However, the authenticity of student response was often undermined by a behavioural approach as can be seen from the two objectives for a grade 4 lesson on creation:

1. The students will comprehend God's greatness as Creator by seeing the bulletin board stripped of all its nature pictures.
2. Each student will write a thank you prayer for one item in God's creation which he is personally glad exists.[65]

The program then suggested that the children should pray these thank you prayers aloud in a group. Thus children were encouraged to execute teacher-approved responses which, in the behavioural tradition, easily became forced and manipulative:

List ways that God can use you right now as a sixth grader as His instrument in sharing the Gospel.
From the list you just made write **one** suggestion that you will promise to **do** before the end of the semester. Then pray about it, committing yourself to God's will in this deed.[66]

From the vantage point of the Bobbit/Tyler tradition, the curriculum was a good one. It was well-organized; it took into account the needs of the child and contemporary life; it was attractively designed; it directly related ends and means; and it supplied a wealth of teaching suggestions. However, the application of a scientific curriculum development model also reduced the grand sweep of Biblical revelation to narrowly defined behavioural objectives, with resulting fragmentation of knowledge. Even the way the objectives were stated ("The students will be able to . . .") implied a mechanistic conception of human beings. The designers failed to see that authentic response best comes about through open-ended expressive outcomes, not by specifying performances beforehand.

221

Questions about the framework of this program soon arose. One of the project's theological consultants found that his views of how the Bible should be taught were transformed beyond recognition by the scientific process orientation.[67] Those favouring a traditional academic approach opposed the program because of its lack of historical sequence, its emphasis on student response rather than recall and understanding, and the use of what were considered frivolous pedagogical devices such as cartoons. Many continued to use the 1958—or even the 1930s—curriculum materials.[68]

The most vigorous opposition to **Revelation-Response**, however, came from Canadian educators led by Arnold De Graaff, whose European philosophical tradition made them suspicious of the scientific approach to curriculum development. Unhappy that they had been prevented from giving meaningful input, they felt that the new program did not enable pupils to function as free, responsible human subjects. The task of the school, De Graaff said, was to enable students to take up their calling in society with deepened understanding of the Christian worldview. Rather than being a source of discrete moral lessons, the Bible gave a general faith direction and perspective for life. Therefore structured but open-ended learning activities must emphasize the central thrust of the various Bible books and the Bible as a whole.[69]

De Graaff's summer workshops in the early 1970s developed a number of classroom units for Biblical studies.[70] Eventually, these led to the publication of a manual such as **Of Kings and Prophets**. A typical section of this guide gave 20-50 pages of cultural, historical, and religious background information clarifying the theme of a Bible book or of a cluster of chapters, followed by a collection of student activities including dramatizations, group projects, building models, and writing "new reports." The teacher focused on questions such as "How do the first twelve chapters of I Kings show that Israel was very much a part of the cultural patterns of the ancient Near East?"[71] Self-actualizing activities that balanced a personal and a social relevance orientation were to help children gain an understanding of what the Bible said about their role in society as Christians. This approach contrasted sharply with the original **Revelation-Response** publications, where the focus of the learning activities was on processes or skills that would lead to specific and pre-determined personal religious and moral responses.[72]

Americans within the NUCS Christian schools put more emphasis on the role of the individual Christian; Canadians, on communal action within society. This came to expression particularly in the two grade 12 Biblical studies courses developed, respectively, in the U.S. and

Canada. Traditionally, the U.S. grade 12 course taught theological doctrines. However, such a course satisfied neither the NUCS nor its Canadian schools: it was too church-centred and encouraged largely recall and comprehension. In 1975, to replace this course, the NUCS published a series of six **Biblical Perspectives** booklets that emphasized personal morality. For instance, one booklet asked students to apply "Christian principles" to making personal decisions about smoking and about their plans after high school. Another emphasized the importance of breaking through personal alienation and individual ethnocentrism. Cultural concerns that moved beyond individual decisions were limited in both booklets to the last two pages.[73]

Throughout the 1970s, Canadian Christian high school teachers worked on developing an alternate course that dealt with the implications of Biblical norms and directives for society and culture. Groups of teachers came together during summers to write units on the community, the self, friendship, courtship and marriage, government and justice, education, work and the job, and communication. These were eventually gathered and rewritten as **Man in Society: A Study in Hope.**[74] One reviewer described the course as a Christian alternative to MACOS (Man: A Course of Study)[75] and continued:

> The course has two strong interrelated and overlapping dimensions: sociological and religious (not necessarily in that order). Although the authors have not described specific objectives their general objective is . . . to shape, alter, and transform secular society into a more adequately defined Christian model.[76]

By analyzing aspects of Canadian society in the Kuyper tradition, students, on the basis of an understanding of Biblical conceptions of terms such as love and justice, envisioned the need to transform their lives and their societal environment according to Biblical principles.[77]

Yet despite these distinct tracks, American and Canadian educators were moving somewhat closer by 1977. Both the NUCS curriculum department and the Canadian Kuyperians had consciously rejected traditionalism and an academic curriculum orientation. Both stressed active student involvement in learning, though with different intents and degrees of structure. While the original **Revelation-Response** components were based on specific performance goals in well-defined categories, the NUCS in 1976 implicitly admitted the shortcomings of its scientific process approach with the publication of a grade 4-6 revision that softened the more blatant behaviouristic features. Also, its 1975 **Biblical Perspective** series had not been developed using a scientific and tightly systematized process. The latter books still downplayed but did not completely neglect social relevance, while the Canadian **Man in Society** also included units focusing on persons as individuals and their relationship with family members and friends.[78]

In short, Biblical studies curriculum writers moved beyond a traditional, factual-recall approach during the 1960s and 1970s, although in many classrooms such an approach lingered. About the time that Schwab called the general curriculum field "moribund,"[79] Christian schools recognized that also some of their curriculum approaches needed modification. Leaders no longer favoured a narrow academic orientation to Biblical studies, but opted for a process orientation (in the U.S.), or a mixed personal and social relevance one (in Canada). The U.S.-Canada difference was accentuated, as became especially clear in the **Man in Society** textbook, by Canadians wishing to express their national identity in and through the curriculum. By 1977, the more conservative climate of the times plus the acclimatization of Dutch Canadians to their North American setting were beginning to temper the utopian reconstructionism of the Kuyperians of the early decade. At the same time, many American supporters began to recognize the shortcomings of an exclusive process approach, especially one that manifested behavioural tendencies. Discussion and cooperation between the two sides was gradually becoming possible. In the late 1970s, all three Canadian NUCS districts considered the appointment of curriculum coordinators who were to be catalysts in developing and implementing distinctive Christian curriculum approaches and materials. In that respect, at least, Canadian Christian schools were more convinced of the importance of such work than their American counterparts.

Science in the Curriculum

A major aim of science in Christian schools was to make clear that God the Creator directed and controlled the universe, making use of scientific laws He embedded in physical reality. The scientific method, useful as it might be, must not be taken as the only reliable way of obtaining truth and knowledge. The Bible was "the point of departure and final authority" for a Christian, and a Christian worldview would determine one's approach to science. At the same time, scientific conclusions must be solidly grounded in scientific evidence and reasoning, and the Bible was not a source of scientific conclusions.[80]

Agreements about such basic presuppositions, however, did not prevent Christian schools from giving short shrift to science education.

CURRICULUM ISSUES (1945-1977)

A 1949 survey showed that fewer than one third of the elementary schools taught science in all eight grades, and that existing programs were limited in scope. Only one out of six had proper equipment, and none reported students doing experiments individually. Twenty years later, the situation had improved little: "The science education program in most elementary schools is in a truly lamentable state."[81] The Sputnik "crisis" did have an impact on the secondary science curriculum. After 1958, a flood of articles appeared that accepted, with little if any analysis or criticism, new public school science programs. Teachers lauded programs such as the Biological Sciences Curriculum Study (BSCS) since they shifted the emphasis "from knowing the facts to knowing **how** the facts were and are being found out." The NUCS curriculum department's push for schools to implement the Intermediate Science Curriculum Study (ISCS) was readily accepted, particularly since as a doer of science the student would develop "skills and tools of science that he takes with him into other areas of life beyond the classroom"--an assumption that, ironically enough, was not backed by empirical evidence. Objections to the new programs were not philosophical but pragmatic. For instance, some courses were considered too difficult or not practical enough for students not going on in science. Most American Christian schools, however, quickly accepted the new programs.[82]

Most science educators in the 1950s and 1960s had a dualistic view of the role of the Christian school. The key differences between NUCS and public school curriculum guides lay not in content or approach, but in tacked-on references to God's greatness, the insertion of one or two Bible passages, and the discussion of a religious or moral application at the unit's conclusion. A unit on sound, for example, included the objective "to help pupils see how they can use sound for God's glory." This was met at the end of the unit by teachers calling to mind the privilege pupils had to make and use sounds to God's glory.[83] Teachers considered the ISCS program "a valid vehicle" since they could use it to "encourage such values as honesty, respect, courtesy, stewardship and consideration for the opinions of others," and to discuss concerns "about the ultimate use to which science should be put."[84]

Opposition to this approach came, once again, mainly from Canadian educators. They criticized the new science programs for creating "little scientists" rather than emphasizing the historical development of science, its cultural setting and social consequences, and its relation to other kinds of studies.[85] Half a dozen teachers gathered in British Columbia in the summer of 1971 to develop grades 6-10

225

science outlines that would help Christians "reform creation out of the grip of sin and build up the City of God on the foundation of Christ." The learning of science started with everyday phenomena from which scientific aspects were abstracted in order to define concepts and discover theories and laws. Then such theoretic knowledge was re-integrated into the students' direct life experience. Thus the grade 6 units on animals, plants, states of matter, and solutions and mixtures all used the context of a forest community to provide a relevant setting for the scientific concepts. In grade 8 an extensive unit on technology sketched its historical development, considered how human beings have given technical form to a local industry, and investigated how economic and political factors influenced the application of technology.[86] Informal investigations, research projects and classroom discussions balanced laboratory activities. However, the group, lacking continuous leadership and financial resources, wrote neither classroom units nor student materials and consequently influenced only the attitudes and practices of some individual teachers.

In the mid-1970s several publications illustrated the contrast between NUCS' process approach and De Graaff's attempt to balance personal and social relevance orientations. In 1976 NUCS published the first trial editions of an extensive series of grade 3-6 science units. In **Interpret the Sky**, a unit about weather, experiments such as reading and recording temperatures and precipitation, determining the effects of heat and pressure on air, and measuring wind strength, wind chill, and relative humidity dominated. The learning processes embedded in such experiments, the authors hoped, would transfer to other situations and thus prepare children for life. The unit dealt with the relevance of weather itself for the child or for society in only one sentence: "It determines whether you wear a warm jacket or a bathing suit, whether you play inside or outside, or whether you sweat or shiver." The "Christian" aspect of the unit consisted of several references to God's power and providence, a couple of activities involving praising God, and, at the end, some Bible text references dealing with weather--plus the fact that students were "reading God's world" as they performed their investigations.[87]

The Canadian publication **Joy in Learning**, co-authored by De Graaff, had a different, social relevance theme for physical science:

> The children need to be led to discover and experience how all of creation works together to make the earth a good place to live for man, that man has the responsibility to unfold the earth rightly and that by selfishness, greed and carelessness he can spoil the creation and disrupt life.

The section on weather reflected the authors' concern about the impact of weather on everyday life:

> Weather affects plants and animals, and plays an important part in many human activities. It can be a destructive force in transportation, communication, farming, etc. Man cannot control the weather, but weather forecasting helps people to plan ahead and to take precautions.

The section asked children to observe and record the weather in a less structured, more open-ended way than the NUCS unit, leaving more initiative to teachers and pupils. Unlike the NUCS units, all investigations were coupled with questions such as "How does weather affect plants? animals? people? traffic? farmers? airplanes? communication?" and "Why is it important to know from what direction the wind is blowing?" Also, the section integrated scientific investigations with activities such as creative writing, creative movement exercises, making displays and murals, and "enjoying and using" poems about the weather. The unit contained no explicit religious references. Its approach was a "Christian" one, the authors believed, because the integrationist emphasis of the manual taught a comprehensive, responsible Christian way of life. Both the choice of activities and the type of questions asked intended to call children "to follow God's good order for life. . . , unfolding and developing [God's] creation for the benefit of all people."[88]

These two publications typified the contrasting approaches of the NUCS curriculum department and Toronto's Curriculum Development Centre. Both held that while God was the creator and sustainer of the universe, modern science had to be taken seriously as a field of investigation. The NUCS adopted a process orientation, adding some religious references and teaching personal moral virtues as students went about their investigations. **Joy in Learning,** on the other hand, tried to choose both content and methodology on the basis of a Christian view of life. Viewing the child as a subject who must take on a responsible task in society, it tried to balance the personal and social relevance orientations to the curriculum.

The availability of these materials, of course, did not guarantee their use. Indeed, the evidence indicates that neither approach was used consistently by more than a minority of teachers. The NUCS units did not form a complete program, and, because they were not interdependent, teachers often used only one or two to supplement their standard public school textbooks. **Joy in Learning** served more as a sourcebook for learning activities to be inserted into existing science and social studies programs than as a comprehensive program. Moreover, at the elementary level, the science program continued to be a stepchild for at least two reasons. First, many elementary teachers had little background in science and felt uncomfortable with teaching especially physical science topics. Secondly, preparing science activities and experiments was time-consuming. Nevertheless, although public school textbooks continued to dominate the science programs, both the NUCS units and **Joy in Learning** did influence teachers to adopt a more activity-oriented approach in science.

The Basics in Christian Education

Since the end of World War II, Christian schools have, to a large extent, moved with the ebb and flow of general North American curriculum trends. Except for Biblical studies, accreditation requirements and economic conditions often determined course offerings. Schools usually chose course content on the basis of public school textbooks, courses and, at the grade 12 level, examinations. Canadian grade 12 students wrote provincial examinations when and where available, while in the U.S. students bound for college wrote the Scholastic Aptitude or American College Tests examinations. As in the public sector, the strong moves for a classical liberal education gradually receded after the 1950s, even though many classrooms continued to be traditional in content and structure. Only two Toronto-area Christian elementary schools consistently implemented an "open" approach.[89] American schools quickly embraced the post-Sputnik laboratory-oriented science programs. Almost all schools just as quickly loaded the "new math" aboard its curriculum and gradually, like public schools, jettisoned it. The Christian school curriculum in both the U.S. and Canada headed with the prevailing winds.

Curricularly, the Christian schools drifted rudderless from the mid-1950s to the mid-1960s. Then, proponents of each of the monastic, dualistic, and integrationist views of the Christian school tried to steer the ship in all three directions at once, with the rough seas of rapid curriculum change in the public sector making the situation even more stormy. Some integrationists even launched a lifeboat with the Canadian flag hoisted high in the form of the Curriculum Development Centre. They refused to follow a dualist course, especially if it were powered by a technological process engine.

However, by 1977 the storm had spent its force somewhat. Both the lifeboat and the main ship wanted to steer into integrationist waters—even if the lifeboat continued to be suspicious of the main ship's tendency to wander off in a dualist direction. Cautious communication began again in 1978, with the NUCS and its Canadian districts establishing a Canadian Curriculum Council to advise NUCS regarding Canadian concerns. The first act of the Council was to indicate that within integrationist waters different curriculum orientations were possible and that curriculum projects should receive backing if they seemed valid in terms of their own orientation.[90]

In the 1970s NUCS Biblical studies and science curriculum development displayed the behaviourist process orientation more than other subject areas. The document guiding language arts curriculum development, for instance, promoted a critical understanding of contemporary society that would enable pupils to relate a Christian religious vision to "the human and worldly realities of life."[91] Canadians objected to NUCS literature anthologies and language arts guides during the 1960s and 1970s more for their lack of Canadian content and suggestions for discussion than for the type of literature chosen.[92] Similarly in social studies, NUCS consultant Gordon Oosterman re-interpreted NUCS' "decisional learning" to give it an integrationist and social relevance thrust. He wanted to bring Biblical conceptions of justice and stewardship to bear on studies of cultures and current societal problems. In a book called **The People: Three Indian Tribes of the Southwest,** Oosterman wrote:

> From their fellow Americans, especially those who are Christians, the Cherokees deserve more understanding and respect. . . . For many years they have been treated badly. It's long past time for the Cherokees, as one of the remaining American Indian tribes of the Southwest, to be blessed with greater justice, prosperity, and love from their fellow man.[93]

Oosterman also helped Canadians implement such a perspective in Canadian social studies. For example, the 1977 publication **A Difficult Journey** stressed that Canada, as a nation committed to justice, should give native people and Métis a place of honour in society, enabling them to share fully in the nation's opportunities.[94] Thus, in these areas, Canadians and Americans were not as far apart as in Biblical studies and science. Viewpoints did not split purely along national lines; the positions of key personnel also had significant influence.

At the root of many curriculum discussions was a recurrent question: What were the basics in Christian education? Just after World War II, one principal reiterated Bennink's view of the 1910s that a Christian school be characterized by simplicity and thoroughness. He said, for example, that teachers should teach Montreal and its

229

significance as a seaport rather than drill into children the names of twenty Canadian ports. Similarly, D. H. Walters in 1950 called for a "Back to the Basics" education that dispensed with "non-essentials" and "time-consuming experiments" as well as with athletics and extra-curricular activities.[95] Over the years, however, the scope of the curriculum did broaden. By the 1970s schools assumed music, art, and physical education as necessities that were part of the basics.

But even in the mid-1970s disagreements about the basics still reflected conflicting conceptions of the aims of the Christian school. Triezenberg took the basics to be what was tested on the Iowa Test of Basic Skills, viz., fundamental reading, spelling, language usage, research, map reading and arithmetic capabilities. For him, the basics were identical for all schools: "It's what a child does with his basic skills that is really important."[96]

Wolterstorff and De Graaff approached "basics" from a different point of view altogether. The school, Wolterstorff said, must help the Christian community be a revolutionary vanguard, ushering in a new order. Basic to Christian education, therefore, was the teaching of alternative perspectives and theories that would "equip its children to make their own unique contribution to the cause of God's people in the world."[97] For De Graaff, the teaching of the "basic skills" was meaningful only if it took place within an integrated and personally-involving curriculum developed around a Christian vision of life. True basics were knowledge and abilities that would help children become witnesses and servants of such a vision in opposition to a Western culture "dedicated to the values of economic progress."[98]

But were the schools ready for such a vision? Wolterstorff himself had doubts:

> [The school] must communicate **alternative** perspectives, perspectives faithful to the biblical vision of reality and on God's purpose for the church in the world. Yet when one scrutinizes Christian schools, all too often one does not find such alternative perspectives. Rather, one finds secular perspectives to which are attached piecemeal supplements and correctives.[99]

Calvin College's historian George M. Marsden reiterated that Christian schools ought to enable students to "change the culture and the community for Christ." However, all too often students experienced their schools as "conservative embodiments of all the values of the status quo."[100]

Even though De Graaff, Wolterstorff and Marsden wanted the schools to stimulate Christian social reform, they needed to take into account the age-old reality that schools reflect, to a large extent, the character of their supporting community.[101] That community, as the next chapter will show also for Canada, was not one that easily bred reformers and dissenters. Rather, it usually consisted of conservative, orthodox Calvinists who accepted the American way of life. Schools by their nature tend to be conserving institutions. Therefore the vision of De Graaff, Wolterstorff and Marsden was severely tempered in practice even where it was not completely neglected or opposed. In the mid-1970s, many leaders, like Kuyper and Bavinck around the turn of the century, once again shared an integrationist vision of the basic aims of Christian education and of how such aims should be accomplished. However, whether such a vision could be consistently implemented in the Christian school curriculum remained to be demonstrated.

NOTES

1. Jennie Visser, "How Character Is Developed in the Christian School," in A. Witvoet, ed., **Learning Under the Lamp of God** (Hamilton, Ont.: Christian School Herald, 1965), p. 15.

2. This affected Canada later than the U.S. First, the general Canadian retention rate between grades 9 and 11 was still climbing rapidly in the 1960s. Secondly, many Dutch immigrant children in the 1950s and early 1960s for economic reasons entered the work force as soon as they could leave school, a trend that changed rapidly in the mid- and late-1960s.

3. **Christian Educators Journal,** June 1965, p. 12ff; April 1965, pp. 14-15, 32.

4. The pupil-teacher ratios for all CSI schools declined from 31.8:1 to 23.6:1 between 1945-46 and 1971-72. This was remarkably close, for example, to the corresponding Ontario public school figures of 29.9:1 and 23.6:1. The ratio in Canadian CSI schools was appreciably higher than that for U.S. CSI schools in the mid-fifties (35.1:1 at the Canadian peak in 1955-56; 27.6:1 in the U.S.), but by the late 1970s the difference was only about one additional pupil per teacher in Canada.

5. **Christian Home and School,** Oct. 1951, p. 12.

6. Michael T. Ruiter, **How Well Are the Grand Rapids Christian Schools Doing Their Job?** (Grand Rapids: Central Council of Christian School Boards, 1956), n.p.

7. NUCS, **Course of Study for Christian Schools** (Chicago, 1947),

pp. 213-14, 226-27; notice to Holland's high school English teachers on Oct. 28, 1958, listing all the English textbooks in use in their school; **Proceedings** of the Conference for Christian High School Principals, June 27-29, 1949, "Report of the Social Sciences Committee," p. 152; NUCS **Annual Meeting,** Aug. 15-17, 1950, Art. 80; Albert Hengstman, "Report on Visits to the Ontario Christian Schools, Nov. 13-Dec. 18, 1961" (NUCS **Minutes** files).

8. Robert Stamp called the Robarts plan a "temporary triumph of vocationalism." This was true for public but not for the newly-established Christian schools, which had almost no facilities or funds for such programs (Robert M. Stamp, **The Schools of Ontario 1876-1976** [Toronto: University of Toronto, 1982], pp. 204-206).

9. In May, 1984, this Christian school course made headlines in Alberta because on one page it described religions such as Islam and Buddhism as "false transcendent religions." The government's Committee on Tolerance and Understanding used this solitary quote as a basis for recommending the incorporation of private schools into the public school system, with closer supervision of the schools' curriculum. The committee neglected, as one reporter put it, the "mitigating appeals for tolerance of other religions" made elsewhere in the course, as well as the fact that the Edmonton Christian High School, for one, made service work among homeless teens, unwed mothers, and the incarcerated an integral part of the program ("The Call for a Private School Takeover," **Alberta Report,** May 21, 1984, pp. 22-25, 52).

10. The Report of the Provincial Committee on Aims and Objectives in the Schools of Ontario, **Living and Learning** (Toronto: Newton Publishing, 1968).

11. See, for example, **Christian Educators Journal,** Spring 1962, pp. 4-6 (the ungraded school); April-May 1967, pp. 10-12 (grades and evaluation); May 1969, pp. 22-23, Nov. 1970, pp. 29-31, and Sept. 1973, pp. 30-31 (discovery method, math labs, individualization).

12. An editorial in **Christian Home and School,** Dec. 1953, emphasized the Christian school's special role to pursue and cultivate excellence (pp. 14-15). Already in 1952 most schools administered standardized tests to evaluate standards of education (NUCS Education Committee **Minutes,** April 18, 1952). See also **Christian Educators Journal,** June 1965, p. 14 (mathematics); Nov. 1965, pp. 28-31 (geography); Jan. 1970, pp. 22-24 (social studies); **Christian School Herald,** Dec. 1963, p. 5 (history); **Christian Home and School,** Oct. 1968, p. 15 (music); NUCS Curriculum Department **Report,** Sept. 28, 1972 (uncritical acceptance of SCIS

and ISCS).

13. These emphases were described, for example, by John A. Olthuis, "Towards Implementing a View of Christian Education," in John Vriend et al., **To Prod "The Slumbering Giant"** (Toronto: Wedge, 1972), pp. 147-48. He called them the hothouse, the sprinkling, and the Kingdom views respectively. A similar distinction was made in 1957 by Donald Oppewal who described three common attitudes: (a) a Christian school needed a Christian atmosphere but most of the curriculum did not need to be distinctive; (b) the public school curriculum had to be infused with Christian assertions at strategic points; and (c) the curriculum needed to be distinctive. The latter, according to Oppewal, was oft-mentioned but rarely pressed to a practical conclusion (Donald Oppewal, "Toward a Distinctive Curriculum for Christian Education," **Reformed Journal**, Sept. 1957, pp. 21-22).

14. For a brief description of Niebuhr's categorization, see footnote 34, Chapter 4.

15. Literature anthology revision committee report, Nov. 10, 1972, Art. 3; Executive Committee **Minutes**, Nov. 15-16, 1972, Art. 19; Albert J. Boersma, **In the School of the Master** (Sioux Center, 1971), p. 72. **To A God Unknown** was one of those involved in the controversies in the Toronto District Christian High School in the late 1960s described later in this chapter. The various factions involved expressed the views related in this section.

16. Milo Okkema, "Christian Education and American Culture," **Christian Home and School**, Oct. 1962, p. 15; Jan. 1963, p. 19.

17. Olthuis, pp. 147-48; **Christian School Herald**, May-June, 1963, pp. 7-8.

18. No. 4 of "General Standards for NUCS member Schools," adopted by NUCS Executive Committee, May 7, 1969.

19. A name change was requested regularly by the Canadian sector starting as far back as the 1955 NUCS Annual Meeting, where "Canadians suggest a name change to International Union of Christian Schools or Union of Christian Schools in America" (**Minutes**, Art. 13). The name change to "Christian Schools International" was approved in August 1978.

20. Henry Zylstra, **Testament of Vision** (Grand Rapids: Eerdmans, 1958, 1961 paperback edition), p. 100; **Proceedings** of the Conference for Christian High School Principals, June 27-29, 1949, p. 10; C[ornelius] B[ontekoe], **Christian Home and School**, June 1951, pp. 18-19; Jan. 1952, pp. 16-17; April 1952, pp. 12-13; Milo Okkema, "The Place of the Commercial Department in the

Christian High School," unpublished paper, 1953, pp. 34-35; and Hero Bratt, **Christian Home and School,** Nov. 1956, pp. 18-19.

21. **Christian Home and School,** Feb. 1955, pp. 11-12; March 1955, pp. 13, 19; and Jan. 1957, p. 13.

22. Beatrice Ligtenberg, "In Defense of Home Economics," **Christian Home and School,** Jan. 1957, pp. 12-13.

23. NUCS Principals' Conference, Aug. 14-16, 1961. pp. 3, 4, 19; NUCS **Directory 1963-64,** p. 155; and NUCS Semi-Annual Report for Board of Directors, Feb. 1967, p. 9. Gerald Laverman, **Industrial Arts in the Christian School,** (Grand Rapids: NUCS, 1970), pp. 15, 17-18; James Bryant Conant described his views in **The American High School Today** (New York: McGraw-Hill, 1959).

24. Because of financial constraints only a few shop programs were available in Canadian Christian High Schools by the mid-1970s. However, by 1983 five of the six schools in B. C. with senior secondary grades had an industrial arts facility. The other school offered an extensive work experience program. Generally, as in the U.S., Canadian Christian schools have favoured courses teaching general life skills rather than specific vocational ones.

25. NUCS, **A Uniform System of Credits for Christian High Schools** (Grand Rapids, 1950). See also **Proceedings,** June 27-29, 1949, pp. 53, 75-111 (esp. 75, 79-80); NUCS Education Director Report and Board Contractum **Minutes,** Oct. 19, 1948; memorandum by James P. Hoekema et al., to Committee on Christian High School Credits, May 16, 1949; transcript of John A. Van Bruggen interview by Herbert J. Brinks, Heritage Hall Archives, pp. 12-13; Raymond J. Geerdes, **Torch and Trumpet,** Sept. 1958, p. 15. In the wake of the U.S.S.R. Sputnik, the national press jumped to Holland's defense. Articles in the press included ones in **National Review, Saturday Evening Post, Life,** and **The Chicago Tribune.**

26. Bert P. Bos, superintendent of the Holland Schools for Christian Education, compiled the survey in December 1955 and January 1956 (Holland Christian Schools files, Heritage Hall Archives).

27. **Proceedings** of the Conference for Christian High School Principals, June 18-21, 1948, p. 123; John A. Vander Ark, **22 Landmark Years** (Grand Rapids: Baker Book House, 1983), p. 22; Henry J. Kuiper, "The Elements of Our Curriculum," **Christian Home and School,** Oct. 1956, p. 10, quoting William C. Bagley in **The Education Digest** of May 1955; E. Van Halsema, "The Practical Realization of Fundamental Educational Aims," outline of speech to Principals' Conference, n.d. (likely in early 1950s); **Christian Home and School,** Oct. 1951, pp. 12-13.

28. NUCS, Course of Study (1947), pp. 221, 227; Torch and Trumpet, Jan. 1957, p. 7; John A. Van Bruggen, "Survey of Reading Instruction in the Christian Schools 1963," mimeographed report compiled with the help of nine students (Van Bruggen personal papers, Heritage Hall), pp. 69-71; Christian Home and School, March 1972, pp. 12-15; and Christian Educators Journal, Sept. 1973, pp. 22-24.

29. Peter P. De Boer, "A Case for Informal Education in Christian Schools," Christian Educators Journal, Nov. 1974, pp. 24-30; Arnold De Graaff and Jean Olthuis, eds., Joy in Learning: An Integrated Approach to the Elementary School (Toronto: Joy in Learning Curriculum Development Centre, 1973); Christian Home and School, Oct. 1973, pp. 24-26; and Oct. 1975, pp. 6-8.

30. See, for example, Daniel R. Vander Ark, "Experimenting with the Humanities at Holland Christian," Christian Home and School, Sept. 1974, pp. 8-10; and Henry J. Triezenberg et al., Principles to Practice (Grand Rapids: NUCS, 1973), pp. S-7, S-12, S-13.

31. Director's Report to the NUCS board, Feb. 4 and 5, 1954. His subsequent reports (e.g., Feb. 9-10, 1956) were characterized by a great deal of detail and positive administrative initiatives, but no long-range educational aims or plans for the organization.

32. A junior high literature series published in the late 1950s had been initiated during Van Bruggen's tenure. Art publications by Rose Van Dyken and Edgar Boevé were developed through their individual initiatives. See also Education Committee Minutes, Dec. 9, 1955, Art. 14; March 10, 1956, Art. 9(c).

33. Christian Home and School, Dec. 1957, p. 7; NUCS Education Committee Minutes, Jan. 10, 1956; July 14, 1956; May 14, 1960; NUCS Directory 1961-62, pp. 125-26; and NUCS Board Minutes, Feb. 12-13, 1959; and Aug. 10, 11 and 14, 1959.

34. NUCS Board Minutes, Oct. 11, 1957 and Dec. 6, 1958; NUCS Education Committee Minutes, April 4, 1956; NUCS Directory 1958-1959, p. 108.

35. NUCS Annual Meeting Minutes, Aug. 8-10, 1956.

36. William C. Hendricks, Under God: A Government Textbook (Grand Rapids: NUCS, 1966), p. 17. Quotes are taken from the 1981 edition, updated slightly from the original.

37. Ibid., pp. 10, 36-38, 51-52, 66, 159, 169, 180-84, 196, 204, 236-40. The book's sole criticism of American government was that some government officials had not always been fair or honest. The American NUCS community generally accepted the views of Under God; the NUCS 1962 Annual Meeting decided to send

complimentary copies to members of the U.S. Supreme Court, the House of Representatives, and the Senate. Gordon Oosterman's 1971 teachers' manual did take a more careful look both at the American economic system (p. 140) and at Christian political alternatives (p. 131). For a secular counterpart to **Under God**, see, for instance, William H. Hartley and William S. Vincent, **American Civics** (New York: Harcourt, Brace and World, 1967). Its patriotism and religious tone paralleled that of **Under God**, although with few explicit references to a Deity: "to secure the blessings of liberty" (p. 146), and "our faith in America" (p. 253).

38. Albert Witvoet, "Notes on **Catcher in the Rye**," mimeographed, 2 pp., 1968.
39. Albert Witvoet, "My Answer to the Charges," mimeographed (1968), p. 4.
40. The Institute for Christian Studies was founded in 1967 in Toronto by the Association for the Advancement of Christian Scholarship [AACS], formerly known as the Association for Reformed Scientific Studies. This book uses today's "ICS" designation.
41. Toronto District Christian High School Association, "Letter to all members," May 15, 1969; The Staff of the Toronto District Christian High School, letter to all parents and supporters, May 21, 1969. I was a member of the teaching staff of the school at the time.
42. Staff letter, May 21, 1969, pp. 1, 3.
43. Witvoet, "My Answer to the Charges," p. 3. See also the letter of P. Speelman to the NUCS Executive committee in which he accuses Kuyperians like Witvoet of being influenced by Marcuse and wanting to give "new meaning" to the traditional views of such things as "literature, leisure time, film, sex, morals" (May 20, 1970).
44. The NUCS **Directory 1962-63**, p. 163, for instance, reprints a resolution passed at the Annual Meeting complaining about the American nature of NUCS publications.
45. NUCS, "Summary of Discussions on Ontario Summer School," May 13, 1970, p. 1; Curriculum Department **Report** to NUCS Board of Directors, Feb. 15, 1975, p. C-2. Mimeographed publications for Biblical studies, social studies, science, and mathematics resulted from jointly-sponsored workshops in this and subsequent summers.
46. Curriculum Department **Report** to NUCS Board of Directors, Feb. 15, 1975, p. C-2.
47. NUCS Executive Committee **Minutes**, March 12 and 13, 1970; Nov. 15-16, 1972; March 21, 1973; NUCS, Summary of Discussions on

Ontario Summer School, May 13, 1970, p. 2; NUCS Administrative Staff Minutes, March 31, 1970, June 13, 1972 and March 12, 1973; John A. Vander Ark's report to NUCS Board of Directors, March 1971, p. 4.

48. Report of the meeting of OACS and NUCS representatives, Dec. 17, 1971, and OACS Special Newsletter, Jan. 1972; NUCS Board of Directors, Agenda, March 16, 17, 1972, Art. 6(c).

49. NUCS Executive Committee Minutes, May 8-9, 1972.

50. H. Triezenberg to Gary Endhoven, Ontario Alliance of Christian Schools Secretary, May 22, 1974.

51. Jack Fennema, "Distinctives of the Canadian Schools," mimeographed summary of a presentation at the 1977 NUCS Annual Meeting, pp. 1-2. See also summary of proceedings of the OACS/NUCS meeting in Windsor, May 26, 1977, Art. XX, p. 4.

52. The Association for Christian Education of St. Catharines, "Concerns and Proposals Made to Dr. M. Ruiter," mimeographed brief, Oct. 18, 1977, pp. 1-2, 4.

53. NUCS Board of Directors Agenda, Aug. 12, 13, 15, 1968 (Report by John Vanderhoek); NUCS Executive Committee Minutes, Feb. 7, 1968; Jan. 21, 1969; NUCS Board of Directors Minutes, Aug. 2, 1971; NUCS Administrative Staff Minutes, April 3, 1972; letter from F. De Vries et al. to Christian school boards in British Columbia, Aug. 20, 1976; NUCS Administrative Staff meeting Minutes, Apr. 3, 1972, Art. 6, reporting on a letter by Adrian Peetoom.

54. Gerald Bonekamp, "Authority—Behind the Classroom Door," in Harry Van Dyken et al., Viewpoint: Five Essays on Christian Education (Reformed Fellowship of Canada, 1974), p. 26.

55. Arnold De Graaff, "The Nature and Aim of Christian Education in Biblical Studies," in Dennis Hoekstra and Arnold De Graaff, Contrasting Christian Approaches to Teaching Religion and Biblical Studies (Grand Rapids: Calvin College, 1973), p. 49.

56. Sidney Dykstra, "Bible Study in the Christian School," Christian Home and School, May 1961, p. 4; H. Triezenberg to H. Van Brummelen, Feb. 19, 1981, based in part on information supplied by John A. Vander Ark.

57. This program, referred to as the Bible Historical Study Series, consisted of Bible Curriculum Guide, K-3 (1958); Martha and Jessie Mae Bruinooge, My Bible Guide 4, 5, and 6 (1960, 1961, and 1962); Edward Bossenbroek, Old Testament Studies (in three parts, 1958, 1959, and 1960); Francis Breisch, The Ministry of Christ (in three parts, 1961, 1962, 1963); and Francis Breisch, The Kingdom

of God (1958).

58. Sheri Haan, "A Curriculum Design," **Christian Educators Journal,** March 1970, pp. 29-31. Haan criticized Biblical studies teaching for having "over-used expository teaching and learning" (p. 31).

59. NUCS, **Revelation-Response Series,** consisting of seven modules at the primary grades (1974), three student books for grades 4-6 (1971 with a revised edition in 1976); two student books for grades 7 and 8 and four books for grade 9 (1974 with a revision of the grades 7 and 8 books in 1982). All grades 4-9 materials include teacher's manuals and, except for grade 9, test item books.

60. NUCS **Directory 1968-69,** p. 198; NUCS Annual Meeting **Minutes,** Aug. 14, 1969, Resolution 9-69. Little overt attention was given to developing critical thinking skills, with terms such as "decision-making" and "problem-solving" being defined ambiguously if at all.

61. Louis Vos, Henry Triezenberg, and Judy Bandstra, **Revelation-Response: Its Distinctive Approach** (Grand Rapids: NUCS, 1977), pp. 29-39; Marian Nienhuis, Edgar Bosch, and Louis Vos, **Test Items for Grade Four Revelation-Response: A Resource Pool of Items Matched with Objectives** (Grand Rapids: NUCS, 1975), p. xix. Nienhuis wrote test items related to each objective, Bosch edited the test items and objectives for their technical quality, while Vos edited them for their validity (p. ii).

62. Triezenberg et al., **Principles to Practice,** p. B-1.

63. Ibid., p. B-2.

64. **Revelation-Response** student workbook, grade 4 (1971), pp. 46, 98-99.

65. Quoted from the Grade 4 **Revelation-Response Teacher's Manual** (1971) by Dennis Hoekstra, writer of the original rationale for **Revelation-Response,** in Dennis Hoekstra and Arnold H. De Graaff, **Contrasting Christian Approaches to Teaching Religion and Biblical Studies,** p. 31.

66. **Revelation-Response** student workbook, grade 6 (1971), pp. 95-96.

67. Personal conversations with Gordon Spykman of Calvin College in 1979 and 1982.

68. Memorandum from Henry Triezenberg re: article submitted by Dr. J. M. Frame about **Revelation-Response** program, Nov. 6, 1972; letter from Langley, B. C., Christian School Society, April 1, 1974 and reply by H. Triezenberg, May 23, 1974 (CSI archives, Grand Rapids); Bernard E. Brune, "'Revelation-Reponse' in Bible Teaching," **The Outlook,** May 1975, pp. 20-22. Sales figures for

1975-77 show that 43% of student books sold for grades 4-6 were **Revelation-Response** (1971 and 1976 editions), 52% were **My Bible Guide,** and 5% were still the 1935 **Bible Manuals.** In other words, almost sixty percent of grades 4-6 students were still using programs that emphasized receptacle learning.

69. Chris Bosch, **"Revelation-Response,** Some Questions and Observations," unpublished paper, Edmonton, 1975; NUCS Executive Committee **Minutes,** Nov. 6, 1969 and Dec. 17, 1969; NUCS Administrative Staff **Minutes,** Nov. 19, 1969; Hoekstra and De Graaff, pp. 38, 49-50.

70. The earliest units were the 1970 mimeographed units published by the Institute of Christian Studies in Toronto for grade 4 (Parts I and II), and units on specific Bible books for high school (Deuteronomy, Luke, Acts, and Revelation). In 1977 Toronto's Joy in Learning Curriculum Development Centre also published Don Sinnema, **Reclaiming the Land: A Study of the Book of Joshua.**

71. Harry Fernhout, **Of Kings and Prophets: A Study of the Book of Kings** (Toronto: Joy in Learning Curriculum Development Centre, 1979), pp. 14-90 (esp. p. 85). Although published in final form only in 1979, this publication had been written a number of years before, partly in reaction to the approach of the **Revelation-Response** program.

72. The revised 1976 editions of the grades 4-6 materials were less behaviouristic than the first ones, and the revised grades 7 and 8 books (1982) showed much less evidence of a scientific approach. The NUCS community did discuss both Simon's values clarification processes and Kohlberg's stages of moral reasoning. However, neither was applied directly in Biblical studies programs, including the grade 12 "ethics" course described in the next paragraph. This was par*ly because values clarification was believed to lead to ethical relativism, while Kohlberg's approach would lead only to moral reasoning, not to actual Biblically-based moral decisions. Triezenberg, for one, believed that his decisional learning avoided "the subversive teaching of situational values" (**Christian Home and School,** Dec. 1975, p. 25). Nevertheless, a literature anthology guide published by NUCS did use values clarification (**Christian Educators Journal,** Jan. 1977, pp. 18-19).

73. Lewis Vander Meer, Arnold Snoeyink, and Sandy Vander Zicht, **Biblical Perspectives Series** (Grand Rapids: NUCS, 1975): **Decision Making,** pp. 22, 35, 43, 62-64; **The Christian in the World,** pp. 17-20, 46-47.

74. Ary De Moor et al., **Man in Society: A Study in Hope** (Grand

Rapids: CSI, 1980). Preliminary versions of this course were used throughout the 1970s in various parts of Canada. Eight authors were listed; ten other persons were acknowledged as contributing to the project. All but one, CSI social studies consultant Gordon Oosterman, were Canadian Christian high school teachers.

75. Jerome S. Bruner et al., **Man : A Course of Study** (Cambridge, Mass.: Educational Development Center, 1970). **Man in Society** focused more specifically on sociological concerns than MACOS did.

76. **Christian Educators Journal**, Feb.-March 1983, pp. 28-29.

77. Based on personal conversations with the two main authors of the final edition, Ary De Moor and Gordon Oosterman. Ironically, because of Canadian pressure, the NUCS published the final version of this project, though not without objections to the project's social relevance emphasis by NUCS personnel other than Oosterman.

78. Some Canadian schools like the Edmonton Christian High School taught Biblical Perspectives in grade 10 and **Man in Society** in grade 12 in the late 1970s, arguing that the social relevance emphasis should gradually increase as students became older.

79. Joseph J. Schwab, **The Practical: A Language for Curriculum** (Washington: National Education Association, 1970), p. 1.

80. **NUCS Course of Study** (1947), pp. 287-88; **Christian Educators Journal**, Winter 1965, pp. 15-16; Nov. 1970, p. 27; **Proceedings: Conference for Christian High School Principals**, Calvin College, June 27-29, 1949, p. 67. Christian school leaders, while firmly believing in creation, often looked askance at strict "scientific creationist" positions, and have held that evolutionism should be fully discussed in class, even if criticized from a Christian framework (**Christian Educators Journal**, Jan. 1968, pp. 20-21 and March 1976, pp. 19-20; Nicholas P. Wolterstorff, **School and Curriculum** [Grand Rapids: NUCS, 1969], pp. 21-24). The first major creationist biology textbook published in 1970 received two negative and one positive review (**Christian Educators Journal**, April 1972, pp. 23-28). There was a fear of the philosophy of evolutionism on the one hand but of unscientific arguments and misleading claims of "scientific creationism" on the other. While scientific investigation was based on the trustworthiness of God and His laws, conclusions must result only from sound empirical and rational evidence.

81. **Proceedings**, June 27-29, 1949, pp. 63-65; **Christian Home and School**, Dec. 1959, p. 3; and Vernon J. Ehlers, report to the NUCS

Executive Committee, May 19, 1969.

82. Christian Educators Journal, Fall 1964, pp. 13-15; Winter, 1965, pp. 13-16; April-May, 1967, pp. 20-21; May 1969, p. 21; and Jan. 1971, pp. 24-25.

83. NUCS Science Committee, Manual for Teaching Science, Grades 5 and 6 (Grand Rapids: NUCS, 1957), pp. 28-32. For similar examples see the other units in the manual. Also see Christian Educators Journal, May 1968, p. 15.

84. Christian Educators Journal, May 1969, p. 20; Gerald Bakker, "On Placing Limits on Christian Education," in Russel Maatman and Gerald Bakker, Contrasting Christian Approaches to Teaching the Sciences (Grand Rapids: Calvin College, 1971), pp. 17, 18.

85. Robert E. Vander Vennen, "Christian Perspective for Science Teaching," Christian Home and School, July-August 1966, pp. 7-8. Vander Vennen, Dean of Chicago's Trinity Christian College in Chicago at this time, later became executive director of the association operating Toronto's ICS. This type of approach was expanded in the Curriculum Workshop in Natural Science, "Natural Science Outlines, Grades 6-10" (Richmond, B.C.: Christian Educators Summer School, 1971); and Bruce De Boer and Herman Proper, "High School Science Curriculum" (St. Catharines and London, Ont., 1972).

86. "Natural Science Outlines, Grades 6-10," pp. 2-48.

87. Yvonne Van Ee and Henry J. Triezenberg, Interpret the Sky (Grand Rapids: NUCS, 1976).

88. Joy in Learning, pp. 42, 220, 227, 222-229, 5.

89. The Immanuel Christian School in Scarborough, Ontario, and the Central Christian School in Toronto.

90. Canadian Curriculum Council Minutes, Nov. 30 and Dec. 1, 1978, Art. 2C ("The Curriculum Framework Discussion," p. 4).

91. Henry J. Baron, Donald Oppewal, and Eugene C. Hage, "Man in Communication: Language Arts," in Triezenberg et al., Principles to Practice, p. LA-1.

92. Adrian Peetoom in a "Critique of Rationale for Thematic Units," Christian Educators Journal, April 1972, pp. 21-23, did not dispute anthology selections, but quarreled with the "still prevailing dualism" of the NUCS thematic teacher guides. These, he felt, accepted "some sort of neutrality of material . . . to which Christian teachers then add their particular faith commitment" (p. 23). The John Knox Christian School in Burnaby, B. C. in the mid-1970s contentedly used one NUCS literature anthology, but on each copy pasted a Canadian flag on top of the cover's Statue of

Liberty.

93. **Christian Home and School**, April 1976, p. 21; Gordon Oosterman, **The People: Three Indian Tribes of the Southwest** (Grand Rapids: NUCS and Eerdmans, 1973), p. 46.

94. Chris Bosch et al., **A Difficult Journey: Blackfoot, Cree and Métis on the Western Plains** (Grand Rapids: NUCS, 1977, trial ed.), especially pp. 82-83.

95. **Christian Home and School**, Dec. 1949, p. 15; NUCS Annual 1950, p. 115.

96. **Christian Home and School**, March 1973, pp. 14-15.

97. **Christian Educators Journal**, March-April 1978, pp. 6, 18-20, 30.

98. Ibid., March-April 1978, pp. 7, 23-25.

99. Ibid., March-April 1978, p. 30.

100. **Christian Home and School**, Feb. 1970, pp. 5-6.

101. Sociological studies in the United States have shown that Catholic schools have had little impact on attitudes or behaviour (Joseph H. Fichter, **Parochial School: A Sociological Study** [Notre Dame, Indiana: University of Notre Dame Press, 1958]; Peter Rossi and Andrew Greeley, **Education of Catholic Americans** [Chicago: Aldine, 1966]). The only reasonably extensive survey involving American Christian school students showed that both Catholic and Christian school students had a more positive perception of the police than public school ones. However, when factors such as church attendance and occupational level of parents were controlled the differences became statistically insignificant (Donald Bouma, **Kids and Cops** [Grand Rapids: Eerdmans, 1969], p. 81-85).

Top to bottom: the first Calvinist Christian schools in
Ontario (Holland Marsh, founded in 1943; building
constructed in 1947); Alberta (Lacombe, 1945);
and British Columbia (Vancouver, building constructed two years after 1949 founding).

9 Features of the Schools at the Local Level (1945-1977)

Practices in Local Schools

In education, a large gulf exists between curriculum rhetoric and actual classroom practice. A teacher's interpretation as well as the local context puts a stamp on the way curriculum materials are used. A teacher must cope with her background, interests and abilities, and the characteristics of her particular class. Traditional approaches may be easier and safer than breaking new ground. Boards may pay lip service to an official curriculum document but in actuality have a different agenda for the classrooms under their supervision.

In an effort to bridge the gap between what was said and what was actually done in NUCS classrooms, this chapter focuses on practices in local schools. Chapter 7 discussed curriculum orientations of Christian education leaders. Chapter 8 demonstrated how the Christian school movement addressed some key educational issues and how it developed classrooms resources. This chapter looks at influences on and characteristics of several local Christian schools: the Vancouver Christian [Elementary] School, the first British Columbia NUCS school, established in 1949; Fraser Valley Christian High School, established in 1964, for which Vancouver was one of the original feeder schools; Abbotsford, a rural school established in 1953; and Lynden, Washington, whose two schools, established in 1910 as the first Christian schools west of Iowa, still function today in a small town close to the Canadian-U.S. border.

Two of the three B.C. schools were started by post-World War II Dutch immigrants; the other, Vancouver, soon after its founding also depended on them for most of its enrollment and leadership. Therefore, this chapter first summarizes post-World War II Dutch immigration to Canada and the corresponding growth of Canadian NUCS schools. This context clarifies some curricular features as well as certain differences between the Canadian schools and those in Lynden, Washington.

Post-World War II Dutch Calvinist Immigrants
and Their Thinking

The small number of pre-World War II Dutch Canadians rapidly assimilated into Canadian society. Traces of the 29 000 Dutch immigrants entering Canada between 1901 and 1945 faded quickly.[1] In 1931 only 33% of Dutch immigrants still used their mother tongue, compared with 58% of the German, 70-76% of the Scandinavian, and more than 85% of all other ethnic groups.[2] The only identifiable Dutch Canadian group were the 2 000 members of thirteen small Christian Reformed Churches spread from Vancouver to Southern Ontario. But the church had not been founded just to preserve Dutch language and customs. For example, during the 1930s, only a few years after its founding, the Vancouver Christian Reformed Church already broadcast its church services in English on CJOR in an attempt to evangelize and broaden its ethnic base.[3]

A large new wave of 130 000 Dutch immigrants entering Canada from 1948 to 1957 quickly outweighed that small band of largely English-speaking Calvinists. Eighty percent of the 44 000 new immigrants who were Orthodox Calvinists joined the Christian Reformed denomination,[4] and soon established Christian schools. In 1948, only two Christian schools existed (in Holland Marsh, Ontario and Lacombe, Alberta) with an enrollment of 129 students. This grew to twenty-three schools with 2 764 students in 1958; to fifty schools with 7 184 students in 1963; and to ninety-one schools with an enrollment of 14 342 in 1977.[5]

A number of reasons caused this post-war emigration and the disproportionate percentage of Orthodox Calvinists among them. The Netherlands had been devastated by the war and prospects looked bleak. Strife in Indonesia and its 1949 loss as a colony hindered economic and social recovery. Indonesian expatriates added to the internal population explosion. To solve these major problems, the government continued much of the state control of the German occupation. The Orthodox Calvinists lacked the dynamic leadership of the pre-war years and socialists overshadowed their influence in Dutch society. Further, they feared the secularization of Dutch society and the threat of future wars in Europe. Encouraged by both the Dutch and Canadian governments, many left for Canada "to begin again, to build up a new life that could be good, secure, safe and clearly responsive to God's law for life in all its aspects."[6]

Once again, religious beliefs and practices more than language and social customs identified these Orthodox Dutch Calvinists as a distinct subgroup in Canadian society. The new immigrants wanted to speak

246

LOCAL SCHOOLS (1945-1977)

English and accept Canadian social mores as quickly as possible. One new post-war church paper, **Church and Nation,** contained Dutch and English articles, but its bilingual masthead appeared in English and French. In 1959, only a few years after the largest Dutch immigration influx, the Vancouver Christian School refused to distribute a new Canadian Christian school magazine, **The Christian School Herald,** because it contained some Dutch articles.[7]   Yet the faith of the Orthodox Calvinists was so strong that they established and have maintained many institutional expressions of their religious beliefs.

Although behaviourally the Dutch Orthodox Calvinists assimilated quickly into Canadian society, their religious identity made them function as a distinct ethnic group. For example, the churches and their related organizations gave members a self-identity and provided the focus for primary social relationships. Also, structurally the Dutch Calvinists continued Abraham Kuyper's model of distinct, Calvinist organizations. Besides churches and schools, they also founded a Christian Labour Association, Citizens for Public Justice, Christian Farmers Federations in Ontario and Alberta, and organizations to provide personal and family counselling, housing for senior citizens as well as the mentally handicapped, and post-secondary educational institutions. While such institutions provided a sense of belonging and common purpose, the immigrants also set out to "make an impact upon Canadian life and culture" by attempting to involve other Christians in their ventures.[8]

In some communities friction developed between the established church members and the new post-World War II immigrants about starting Christian schools. The old-timers viewed with suspicion the newcomers' liberal attitudes towards smoking and drinking, as well as their rashness. Many established ministers (almost all Americans) wanted the immigrants to fund the churches adequately before Christian schools were begun, particularly since in some congregations the membership "increased 100% in number, while the collection increased about 5%." Besides, the old-timers felt that the public schools, particularly in the rural areas, were still reasonably Christian. The new immigrants, who had participated in the Kuyperian movement in the Netherlands, were disappointed with the old-timers' narrow moral focus and their lack of progress in setting up Christian schools and other Christian institutions. Post-war clergymen from the Netherlands put less emphasis on personal conversion and more on the significance of Christian faith for all dimensions of culture. They often asserted that Christian schools should proceed posthaste, both to benefit the children and to establish the notion that Christian institutions must be founded in all spheres of life.[9]

LOCAL SCHOOLS (1945-1977)

The more thoughtful new immigrants propounded the same two-fold theme of their early twentieth-century U.S. predecessors. First, Dutch Calvinists were to "partake in the cultural development of a nation that doesn't have enough people to undertake this big and grand task." Therefore, they must learn English and acculturate quickly. Secondly, while Canada was "kind to each church," it must still "learn **completely** that God is King over all things (and must be recognized and served as such)".[10] This called for distinctive Christian schools. Since Canada was a pluralistic nation, government schools should avoid religious exercises and religious content altogether but support parents in operating non-public schools. God could be at the centre of all of life only in Christian schools.[11]

Having taken their government-financed Christian schools for granted in the Netherlands, many Calvinistic Dutch immigrants were not clear about their reasons for seeking to establish Christian schools in their new land. While many parents agreed with the old-timer clergymen's emphasis on protectionism from secular influences, the leaders of the new immigrants looked beyond this and wanted the schools to enable children to serve God by taking an active part in community and national affairs in a Christian way.[12] This was to be accomplished through a unique curriculum:

> The Christian school must keep its goals clearly before itself. It must determine its program content completely independently on the basis of such goals. . . . It may not let itself be dictated to by an outside conception of knowledge. The pupils of Christian schools may not become "island inhabitants," but they must be able to stand in the full human life and, if possible, begin to take on leading positions. But bringing pupils to such possibilities must happen with complete preservation of the unique character of our schools.[13]

Such writings, and related Sunday sermons, convinced most immigrants that Christian schools were necessary. Even the unconvinced felt pressured to comply with what the community as a whole believed to be an expression of obedience to God.

The First Canadian Christian Schools

The first attempt to start a Canadian Dutch Calvinist school took place in Neerlandia, Alberta in 1918. Unable to amass the necessary funds, the thirty dirt-poor homesteader families instead advertised for a Christian teacher for their district school.[14] When in 1945 an

248

LOCAL SCHOOLS (1945-1977)

Edmonton minister reported the establishment of the first Alberta "free" [i.e., non-public] Christian school in Lacombe, he implied that Neerlandia's school was not "free" since it had to cope with "the problems which are bound to arise when one aims to give Christian instruction in a public school." This set off a vigorous debate. The Lacombe school faced the same curriculum restrictions that Neerlandia did, said one defender of Neerlandia's arrangement, since both public and private schools were required to follow the same curriculum. Lacombe, he continued, had "nothing but a Public School in a Reformed [i.e., Calvinistic] jacket." A second writer added that only the ownership of the building differed, for both schools had Christian teachers and used essentially the same curriculum materials.[15]

However, unlike in nineteenth century America, the debate was largely theoretical. Only two Canadian communities existed where a Dutch concentration enabled the immigrants to control the local public school.[16] Nevertheless, the debaters on both sides had made some valid points. For instance, the curriculum of early Christian schools like Lacombe did consist of little more than the government-prescribed curriculum, taught in a traditional way, to which Biblical studies had been added. On the other hand, the Christian character of instruction was likely more secure in the long run in a non-public school. Certainly public education could never cater to specific Calvinist beliefs. Schools like Lacombe, supporters said, were free to work towards a distinctly Christian curriculum, whereas Neerlandia was bound by law to the government-prescribed curriculum. Since the new immigrants settled in heterogeneous communities, the Neerlandia option was not open to them. Except for Neerlandia, all locations with a sizable Calvinist population eventually started a Christian school.

Lacombe, one of two Canadian Christian schools begun by pre-World War II immigrants, taught eight grades in a one-room building erected on the Christian Reformed Church property. The curriculum followed the provincial one, although the teacher omitted "any teaching not in accordance with our conviction." She used the last half hour of the day to teach Biblical studies, and once a week studied missionary stories. In 1949 two more schools began in Edmonton and Vancouver, the first in a church basement with twenty-three pupils and the latter in a converted house with eleven pupils. One of the first principals of the Vancouver school reported that at the start the school lacked a library, a projector, science equipment, and sufficient supplies. However, "both teachers and students seemed to understand this situation and worked hard, concentrating on the three R's." Poor as conditions might be, students received a thorough training in the fundamentals.[17]

249

LOCAL SCHOOLS (1945-1977)

The first Canadian school in Holland Marsh, Ontario, predated the Lacombe Christian school by two years. The original Dutch Calvinist settlers of this vegetable-growing community had started a public school in the 1930s, but when they lost control due to a broadening population base, they started a Christian school in a church room in 1943. Although Ontario requirements did not specify adherence to the public school curriculum, its program likely differed little from that in Lacombe.[18]

Once the trickle of immigration became a stream, schools grew rapidly. The immigrants did not want the schools to be perceived as isolationistic and ethnic. They named some schools after John Knox explicitly to counteract the Dutch impression. But the schools were identifiable by Dutch idiom and accent, by the Dutch mannerisms of teachers and students, and by European rather than North American methodology (especially more lecture and recitation). Despite this, NUCS observers from the U. S. commended the quality of teaching in the 1950s, although one added that the "Christian aspect of teaching was not always realized."[19]

In any case, supporters pressed on, eventually adding high schools. By 1967 the five Canadian Christian high schools included the Fraser Valley Christian High School in Surrey, B. C.[20] Continuing programs of teacher summer courses, emphasizing analyses of the theoretical foundations of Christian education and of a Christian approach to content in subjects such as social studies and science, began in Ontario in 1957 and in B. C. in 1968. A plaque unveiled at the Toronto District Christian High School in 1965 made clear the intent of all these activities: "Unless you serve God with singleness of heart and mind, this school will be a place of darkness."[21] The remainder of this chapter will focus on how local schools tried to fulfill such intent.

Characteristics of Some Local Schools

The first Christian school in British Columbia, Vancouver Christian School, was a venture of both Christian Reformed and Presbyterian parents. Of the original eleven pupils in 1949, three had Anglo-Saxon surnames; the others, Dutch. Within three years, the school had grown to one hundred students in eight grades.[22] This influx was due almost entirely to new Dutch immigrants; not until the early 1970s did Vancouver achieve its original intent of being truly interdenominational.

At first, money was scarce, facilities were substandard, and teachers had little time to consider a distinctive curriculum. However, the school gradually improved. The Lynden Christian School

250

superintendent indicated in a 1960 inspection report that the curriculum for basic subjects was well taught. In the late 1950s and late 1960s the principals emphasized the importance of upgrading teacher qualifications, textbooks, equipment, library acquisitions, and facilities. At least some students were impressed with their teachers' attempts to show "the leading hand of the Lord in their classes, and not just in the facts":

> We learn about how God made the earth and all the beautiful things in it . . . . We are taught in Health how wonderful our bodies are made, and in Social Studies how great the world we live in is. In Science we learn about how beautiful are the plants, animals and insects. We are taught many things, but most of all, we learn about God.[23]

The second NUCS school in B.C., the Abbotsford Christian school, was begun in the local Christian Reformed Church in 1953. Most early teachers were inexperienced, some with training only in the Netherlands. They had no time to reflect on program planning, focusing, rather, on basic facts and skills. Teachers emphasized memorization of "bare facts," but did little discussion or project work. They stressed grammar rather than creative writing, and limited fine arts, by and large, to the singing of hymns and a little drawing. As late as 1969, a NUCS inspector told the school that it needed to "work more towards developing creativity of students and more pupil participation." Nevertheless, teacher qualifications, academic standards, students' work habits, and teacher-student relationships all gradually improved during the school's first twenty years of existence.[24]

One feature of British Columbia's Christian schools in the 1950s and 1960s was a strong emphasis on maintaining standards. In November of the year the school opened, the Vancouver parents asked "what progress there was made to bring our curriculum up to the public school standard," with the board replying that "this was being taken care of." Two months later the secretary reported that the board had requested a Department of Education inspector to visit the school "to check if our educational curriculum is to the standard required."[25] Like other Christian schools, the school had been started for religious rather than social or economic reasons. Nevertheless, parents did not want their children's progress to be impeded because of their schooling. The school certainly should not hinder upward social mobility even if this was not the basic reason for its establishment.

The half-dozen Dutch-trained principals in B.C. around 1960, only gradually becoming aware of their new North American educational context, believed they upheld standards through pupils "gaining knowledge," i.e., through students memorizing, recalling and reciting basic information in Biblical studies, language, arithmetic, history, and geography. Like Bennink early in the century, these men disliked the voluminous North American textbooks. Simple outlines of basic facts and a straightforward phonetic approach to reading would help students advance quickly.[26]

With the growing interest in standardized tests in education in general, principals who had attained some knowledge of the public education scene in B.C. began to administer some of these standardized tests. In 1960 Vancouver Christian School's principal indicated to the parents that twenty percent of the pupils had performed below their grade on grade 3-7 achievement tests. This, he added, was "caused mainly by children who came from Holland less than one year ago and by several others who came from other schools." However, he boasted, more than sixty percent performed "above the required grade level in one or more subjects."[27] Such concern about achievement test results stemmed to a certain extent from the board members' and teachers' desire to convince themselves, their parents, and their communities of their academic equality with public schools. After all, many parents had emigrated in order to advance themselves and their children economically. While they considered education to be only one of many factors that could help such progress (most immigrant children at this time did not finish high school because of the many job opportunities), Christian schools must be academically on at least an equal footing with public ones.

Not until the 1970s did some schools begin to question the narrow focus on the basics as tested by achievement tests. In 1973 Vancouver's principal Frank De Vries squared off with Langley's principal Gerald Bonekamp about the teaching of basics. De Vries, influenced both by the general momentum for neo-progressive change and by his Kuyperian roots, emphasized the importance of an integrated curriculum. A study of water, he said, should involve looking into "boating laws, ecology, baptism, art, transportation, hydro-electricity, the feel of water, the beauty of water, etc.," so that children would "see the **whole** picture instead of an unrelated part of one." The basics would be taught as an integral part of such thematic topics. Pedagogically, De Vries called for more openness:

> With such freedom, of course, children tend to become much more open in their responses. This will tend to make us uncomfortable. But their responses would be honest ones with which we can work. The problem seems not how much freedom pupils can handle, but how much freedom **we** [i.e., teachers] can handle.[28]

LOCAL SCHOOLS (1945-1977)

Bonekamp, on the other hand, like the proponents of the alternative public "value schools" in his community, showed the strong traditionalist "receptacle" view of learning. He claimed that the informal inquiry method was logically inconsistent with the necessity of teaching duty and obligation: "We as Christians do not search for the truth—we have the Bible . . . . The truth of the Bible is infallible and unchanging."[29] For Bonekamp, the inquiry approach was antithetical to his view of truth; the curriculum should consist of the basics taught in a straightforward, structured way.

However, De Vries' classroom differed less from Bonekamp's than the debates seemed to indicate. Although De Vries favoured De Graaff's personal relevance curriculum orientation (discussed in Chapter 7), his own classroom was fairly traditional. While his social studies and science projects demanded student initiative and creativity, he also taught the "basics" in a methodical and thorough manner. Today, De Vries admits that his personality influenced his teaching more than a carefully thought-out methodology or choice of content, and that his instruction did not differ all that much from a lively and warm traditional classroom.[30]

The Lynden, Washington, Christian schools displayed both differences and similarities with these Canadian schools. One of the two schools founded in Lynden in 1910 has grown into a system of three schools in the town itself with almost 1 000 pupils; and the other, Ebenezer, is still a small rural school of 75, two kilometres from the Canadian border. These schools always considered academic standards, especially in reading and arithmetic, important. Indeed, supporters have often given high standards as one of the reasons of existence for the schools. In the 1950s and 1960s the schools maintained such "standards" by means of a phonetic approach to reading, memorization and drill.[31] Paradoxically, while the school gave physical education little emphasis as a subject until the 1970s, athletic competition received considerable attention and effort. American individualism and the corresponding competitive instinct made interscholastic events, primarily in sports but also in debates and music festivals, highlights for the supporting community.[32]

The Canadian schools tried to move away from overt Dutch characteristics more quickly than their Lynden counterparts had. While the Lynden schools by 1913 taught all subjects in English except on Friday afternoons, the community remained quite Dutch for many years. Until 1936, the board secretary wrote the general society meeting minutes in Dutch. In Abbotsford, on the other hand, no Dutch was ever taught and after only four years the minutes were written in English.

253

The Abbotsford 1954-55 Annual Report stated that "we also want our schools to be national schools and not Dutch ones. A token of that is that the national flag will be flown." Speeches at school society meetings in the mid-1950s, when many immigrants were still arriving, stressed nationalistic themes: "Love to God and Country," and "How to Get Canadian Christians interested in Christian Education." Dutch influence was not easily eradicated, however. Especially in rural Abbotsford the Dutch Calvinists, like the Mennonites, were able to maintain a homogeneous, cohesive community. A school like Fraser Valley Christian High, in contrast to Vancouver, remained an ethnic community which "tolerated and welcomed others only if they remained in a minority." What continued to make the schools unique, after all, even where it wasn't Dutch ethnicity **per se**, was the way Dutch Calvinism had developed the Christian schools and their **modus operandi** on the basis of commonly-held beliefs, values, and social inclinations.[33]

To sum up, in the 1950s and 1960s both the Canadian and Lynden schools emphasized a traditional, structured education. High standards were important in Canada to prove educational legitimacy; in Lynden, as one of the basic reasons for operating Christian schools. While some Canadian classrooms in the 1970s emphasized open-ended project work, especially in social studies and science, the "open classroom" did not occur among the sample schools. Particularly rural Abbotsford, in sharp contrast with Lynden's emphasis on music, did little to promote the fine arts and creativity among pupils. The Canadian schools tried to shrug off their Dutchness more quickly than the Lynden schools had done, with varying degrees of success from one community to the next. Yet, even where the school communities remained ethnic enclaves, as the next section describes, the influence of public education on the Christian school curriculum was stronger than that mustered by the traditions of Dutch Calvinist thinking.

Curriculum Influences on Local Christian Schools

In 1966, the secretary of the Abbotsford Christian school society encapsulated an unresolved dilemma for the Christian school curriculum:

> In the instructions to the education committee we read as its task: to watch 1st that the requirements of the state are fulfilled
>
>> 2nd that the requirements of the school's own philosophy are satisfied.
>
> If our school . . . does not comply with the state requirements, we are doing a poor job and lose support, but if we cannot give

education according to our own philosophy, all the work is in vain, because we don't do our basic duties and the basis of our existence disappears.[34]

The secretary failed to address an obvious difficulty.   Where a disagreement arose between a Calvinistic viewpoint and government stipulations, which should take precedence?   How should schools resolve such conflicting claims?   The secretary assumed that his two requirements would always be compatible.   Yet if Calvinists were serious about their faith affecting all areas of scholarship, conflicts between the two requirements were bound to arise.

At the time the secretary wrote this report, not enough curriculum theory and materials had been developed by Canadian Christian schools for such questions to cause difficulties.   Except for the Biblical studies program, the "requirements of the state" could—and did—take precedence.   Both in Abbotsford and in Vancouver, "public school courses were used completely, entirely, without revision, and free textbooks from the B. C. government were gratefully accepted."[35] The schools took pride that they taught all courses "prescribed by the Department of Education,"[36]   even though in fact those prescriptions applied only to public schools.   Leaders assumed that meeting B.C. government guidelines and emphasizing "the Kingship of Christ in all areas of life" were mutually consistent intents.

The B.C. Christian schools did not debate the merits of the "liberal" versus the "practical" as U.S. Christian schools did in the 1950s.   Influenced by both their Dutch roots and by the Canadian push for technical and vocational courses in the 1960s,[37]   they assumed that Christian schools should provide practical courses paralleling those in public schools as staff, facilities, and funds became available.   The Vancouver Christian school taught home economics as early as 1952, and introduced industrial education in 1963.   While the founders of the Fraser Valley Christian High School wanted in the first place to educate "our future ministers, teachers, doctors, and lawyers," the board introduced a commercial course almost immediately and agreed "to move in the direction of additional vocational courses."   Abbotsford also soon purchased typewriters for a commercial program at the junior secondary school level, and aimed to extend its program to other vocational subjects.[38]

The Lynden schools similarly accepted public education trends and stipulations by introducing, for instance, civics and Washington State history.   The 1944 school by-laws stated that "the High School Curriculum shall fulfill as nearly as possible the requirements as prescribed for High Schools by the Washington State Department of

Education."[39]   In the 1950s accreditation became important for the high
school, especially to enable participation in county sports programs.
The state curriculum requirements were considered to be a common
denominator that the schools could easily accept since "they could add
as much as they wanted."[40]   Lynden also introduced the "new math"
and the modern science program recommended by the NUCS in the
1960s.   It taught vocationally-oriented courses when requested by
parents, as it found teachers and facilities.   In 1952, for example, the
high school offered typing and shorthand, home economics, general shop,
farm shop, and agriculture.   The superintendent's defense for these
courses did little more than state their existence:

> The school has continued to stress high academic standards, with
> an emphasis on the liberal arts, although not at the expense of
> the applied subjects for the general students.[41]

Theoretical analyses were not taken into consideration in decisions
about specific courses; practical considerations governed their choice
and content.

The Christian Reformed Church had surprisingly little influence on
the curriculum of British Columbia's Christian schools, at least directly.
While its clergymen gave important moral support (e.g., by means of
sermons and inspirational speeches), few were members of school boards
or education committees or even advisors except when the schools were
first founded.   Ministers and teachers held occasional consultative
meetings to prevent undue overlap between the schools' Biblical studies
courses and church education programs.   Of course, if a school had
wandered away from Calvinist doctrines or moral standards, the church
would have objected quickly.   As it was, school board members often
alternated their terms of office with ones on a church council.   This
created a unity of purpose that made direct supervision unnecessary.
People also assumed that principals, especially the older Dutch-trained
ones, knew what was best for the schools.   Such lack of direct
ministerial influence contrasted with Lynden where ministers, as the
community's guardians of religious and moral truth, at various times
were asked to construct—and also to teach—Biblical studies courses.
On occasion the community used them to resolve staff-board disputes as
well.[42]   The Canadian Dutch immigrants, on the other hand, respected
their ministers but believed that normally the spheres of school and
church must be kept distinct.   Schools were to be run by the parents
and their elected representatives, not by the clergy.

The National Union of Christian Schools affected local schools
mainly through its published textbooks.   The NUCS Biblical studies

manuals, John De Bie's **Story of the Old World, The Pilot Series in Literature,** and a book of Christian hymns were used consistently by all sample schools. Both the Canadian schools and Lynden used the limited number of student textbooks available from the NUCS as much as possible during the 1950s and 1960s. However, Canadian schools began to realize that cultural differences between Canadian and American Christian schools made some NUCS textbooks less than satisfactory for Canadian schools. Vancouver had joined the NUCS in 1952, and Abbotsford had contacted it even before its school began operation. A League of South West British Columbia Christian Schools was founded in 1960, but a 1964 attempt to form a Canadian organization independent from the U.S.-based NUCS received little support. Both attempts, however, reflected some dissatisfaction with the NUCS. Canadians felt that the NUCS had overemphasized Biblical studies books at the expense of social studies and science ones and that it often promoted a superficial pietism that failed to see the impact of Christianity on all of life. Canadians criticized school inspections made by NUCS personnel for being worthwhile technically but having "little or no Christian perspective," something they considered a general shortcoming of American Calvinists. The NUCS board member for B.C. in 1970 stated that NUCS materials lacked both a sound Christian and a Canadian national orientation and consequently were "not geared for our Canadian programs."[43]

Canadian Christian schools were beginning to define their own educational identity. They did so less in support of general moves for Canadian studies than in reaction against their American counterparts.[44] "The entirety of God's creation, the cosmos, is one coherent whole," wrote Frank De Vries. Integration became a key word for Canadian Christian education. But leaders did not make clear whether this meant integrating Christian faith and learning, or integrating the various subject areas into a coherent whole, or integrating skill development with the study of curriculum content. Many leaders (though not all) did believe that Canadian curriculum thinking and materials in the early 1970s succeeded in bringing about "integration," and hence the implementation of Christian perspective, better than the work of the NUCS.[45] The Vancouver school, for one, began to use the **Joy in Learning** integrated primary curriculum. However, it formed the basis of the social studies and science programs rather than leading to the integrated day intended by the authors.[46] By the mid-1970s, the Vancouver Christian School had developed a school curriculum guide that still followed Ministry of Education directives in most subjects, but that also tried to establish distinctiveness, especially in Biblical studies, social studies, and science. The aim of the guide was:

> Towards the joyfully unfolding
> of the Lord's world,
> together with the children
> entrusted to us,
> guiding them to obediently respond
> to the whole of God's Word
> in an integrated way.[47]

The next section discusses how and the extent to which the sample schools attempted to implement such aims in their programs.

Christian Characteristics of the Curriculum

In 1956, when little difference existed between public and Christian school course content, the Reverend Henry Van Andel, a recent Dutch immigrant minister and staunch supporter of Christian schools, spoke to an Abbotsford Christian School Society membership meeting advocating distinct approaches in all subject areas, especially in history and geography but also in arithmetic and writing.[48] Although quick to agree, British Columbia's Christian school supporters and boards during the 1950s and 1960s spent almost no time considering how such a goal could be attained, or even what it meant to promulgate a Calvinist Christian worldview in and through the curriculum.

Board members were not indifferent to curriculum issues. However, organizational problems and financial survival took precedence, and, being immigrants with limited educational backgrounds, they often felt incompetent to address curriculum issues. Unless complaints were lodged about, for instance, "negligence in the form of Bible study," they were content to leave program decisions to their principals and staffs. Principals and board members during the 1950s and 1960s agreed that, as one principal put it, "the principal had the trust of the board . . . the education committee had as yet little impact . . . the principal and staff went ahead and informed the community of changes and why." Vancouver's principal from 1956-61 was unique in presenting detailed curriculum plans to the school's education committee for discussion.[49] However, there, as elsewhere, the curriculum embodied the educational views of the principal and his staff with little or no input from boards. Even in Lynden, where the community was much more established, parents left key curriculum decisions to the superintendent and his faculty.[50]

Moreover, with principals giving little direction or supervision except for textbook choice, teachers made most curriculum decisions. They usually depended on public school textbooks and courses, limiting the "Christian" aspect of their courses to distinctive interpretations of concepts and phenomena in standard subject content. A principal who moved from a public school to Vancouver Christian in 1962 "felt huge relief in that I was able to give a Christian view of things." One teacher discussed how the Roman Empire served as a "necessary crucible" for the early growth of Christianity. Another considered the legitimacy of Christians being involved in revolutions. Many told students that arithmetic was a discovery of God's laws in His creation rather than an invention of human thought. At the high school level, teachers inserted "Christian perspective" when dealing with ethical, social and economic issues. Of course, the frequency and quality of such interpretations and discussions depended on the background, interest and insight of individual teachers.[51]

Students reflected and extended their teachers' interpretations in their own discussions and writings. Sociologist K. Ishwaran analyzed the content of an Ontario local Christian school paper in the mid-1960s, showing that seventy percent of the children's writings were devoted to religious topics or ones closely related (e.g., "Science in the Light of the Bible"). A reporter who visited the Houston, B.C., Christian school in 1968 remarked favourably on the "Christian aspect" of student projects and the emphasis "upon the Kingship of Christ" in the classrooms. Ishwaran failed to note that teachers likely chose the more explicitly religious writing for a paper for school supporters, and the reporter visited the school on a preplanned "open house" day. Nevertheless, teachers regularly asked pupils to consider how Christian ideology and Calvinist beliefs affected one's view of the world and its phenomena. The children thus learned to find their religious, moral, social and emotional security in the system of beliefs and traditions of the community.[52]

Biblical studies contributed most to creating a Calvinist mind-set. All sample elementary schools used recall-oriented NUCS books for this subject until the early 1970s. The dramatic telling of Bible stories characterized the primary grades; the memorization of Biblical facts and concepts, the intermediate. Unlike Lynden, the British Columbia schools did not teach specific Calvinist doctrines since this would prevent them from broadening their base of support to other church groups. Both in Lynden and in B.C., teachers emphasized Biblical concepts, especially that God, the creator and sustainer of the world, called all humans to live in obedient response to Him. Songs and hymns, sung both for devotions and for what, in Abbotsford at least, constituted the bulk of the music program, endorsed these themes, as did stories and books read to students.[53]

Parents concerned themselves with the Christian character of the curriculum only when controversies arose about specific issues. Most parents favoured some sex education but in 1967 Abbotsford parents requested the local head of the health unit to re-write his presentation "to reflect the teachings of the Bible" before he was allowed to address the grade 7 and 8 Abbotsford students. Three years later a minister of a denomination claiming direct roots to the Dutch 1834 Secession accused the Abbotsford teachers of being theistic evolutionists by interpreting the six "days" of creation as long periods of time. However, the parents backed the teachers and the controversy died down quickly.[54]

In 1970 tension between monastic and integrationist views of Christian education led to a major conflict in the Fraser Valley Christian High School. The principal had given a teacher permission to present the rock opera **Jesus Christ Superstar**, if analyzed from a Christian point of view, to grades 10, 11 and 12 students. The teacher handed out some notes which not only criticized but also praised the musical. An uproar followed. How could a Christian school teacher praise anything that did not present Jesus Christ as the divine Saviour of men? The event crystallized the opposition of parents unhappy with those staff members they considered "radical" and not having high regard for the church. These parents charged that "chapel is like a hippie joint," and "teachers are bringing the world into the school." The board, while agreeing with the intent of the teacher involved, apologized for the procedure and the method of presentation. The event resulted in a number of student withdrawals, shook community confidence, and contributed to the more conservative Canadian Reformed Church establishing a separate high school.[55] A fairly narrow framework of protectionistic expectations defined how teachers were allowed to help students explore a Christian worldview and its implications. Parents expected a measure of Christian indoctrination and protectionism to accompany the study of books, works of art, and events taking place in society.

Several other skirmishes occurred at the school five years later when some teachers began to develop and use outlines and units with a Kuyperian social relevance orientation. Fraser Valley offered a grade 12 "Christian perspectives" course (called "Man in Society" in Alberta and Ontario) that dealt with such issues as the Christian's task in promoting economic and social justice. The school's science outlines had deliberately moved beyond scientific theories and experiments to investigate how science and technology shaped and misshaped Western society. Parents voiced suspicions about the orthodoxy of some teachers and their course descriptions. Complaining that some teachers had concluded from Kuyper's "sphere sovereignty" that the church was on an equal footing with organizations such as schools and labour unions, they did not allow the "Christian perspectives" course to replace the grade 12 Biblical studies course as it had in most Canadian Christian High Schools. Parents on the education committee asked the staff to revise a science outline introduction for putting too much emphasis on God's common grace and not enough on sin and the need for personal salvation. Parental uneasiness focused on theological concerns. The teachers revised the introduction to the science outlines but left the courses themselves untouched except for greater caution in class discussions. The result was that parental misgivings affected the curriculum only slightly.[56]

Social relevance approaches were not limited to the high school level. In 1971, a time when educational change and innovation were welcomed in public and, to a lesser extent, also in Christian schools, three B.C. Christian school teachers, for instance, developed a grade 2 social science curriculum guide. A typical unit in this guide combined discussions of "man and his needs," "tools and machines," and the Inuit people in order "to show how man uses, develops, and preserves the creation God has placed him in to fulfill his needs. In doing this, man is carrying out God's order." Investigations of how the Inuit used their physical surroundings and how technology both improved aspects of life and led to mismanagement and exploitation were "to impress children that physical things, plants, and animals are to be used but not misused."[57] This guide contributed to the more extensive 1973 **Joy in Learning** publication.

Vancouver, for one, was impressed with this type of approach and in 1974 formally adopted **Joy in Learning** as its basic resource for primary social studies and science. Units such as "God's Plan—Man Task" and "Man: Living and Working Together" provided a program quite distinct in content and methodology. Through a variety of structured and open-ended learning activities, the school provided a Christian social relevance orientation to its pupils, at least in primary social studies and science and for selected units at higher grade levels. The school listed its social studies aims as follows:

a) trace the responses of man to the Words of the Lord
b) discern the spirits that motivated the rises and falls of civilizations, including our own

c) create a sense of wonder in the children with regard specifically to God's unending love, and the created reality which he upholds by his laws.[58]

Similarly science attempted to create a sense of wonder in God's handiwork and of caring for God's world. This contrasted with the science "learning outcomes" of the B.C. public school curriculum which considered identification and classification of physical properties, plants and animals, and the use of simple machines without a social relevance context.[59]

By the mid-1970s, British Columbia's Christian school parents and boards had become aware of the importance of curriculum policies and their impact on the schools. Education committees became actively involved in curriculum matters even when they still depended on the staff's expertise to provide direction and guidance. At the Fraser Valley Christian High School the committee's mandate included assisting the staff in developing "a more unified approach in teaching the students out of a Christian perspective." Education committee activities in 1974 included, for instance, a "workshop dinner" with the board and staff to discuss a social studies program revision, the implementation of a "non-academic programme," and the development of a more integrated and unified curriculum. The board subsequently asked the school's recently-appointed curriculum coordinator to make the social studies program his priority and requested the education committee to study the Biblical studies course outlines. By this time, the education committee as well as the school's administration gave a great deal of scrutiny to courses and programs. Indeed, one experienced teacher who came to the school in 1976 found that the curriculum was so tightly structured with defined objectives, content and units that he reacted somewhat against "the schemes in which humans have to fit."[60]

Even in the 1970s, the Lynden education committee and board seldom discussed curriculum issues. The staff's main concern was that the school covered course content adequately and that courses could be readily implemented in the classroom. That the school usually made curriculum decisions on pragmatic rather than theoretical grounds did not seem to bother Lynden supporters. Their lack of recent Kuyperian roots caused issues such as strict behaviour codes and interschool athletic competition to assume primacy over curriculum issues. The Lynden and British Columbia teachers viewed each other with some suspicion because of their differing approaches to curriculum and their diverse cultural backgrounds.

In British Columbia, boards and teachers by the mid-1970s wanted to appoint a provincial curriculum coordinator who would help the schools develop and implement a distinctive Christian curriculum:

Instead of a secular curriculum being used presently by our schools with Christian interpretation, the committee recommends that a new curriculum be designed [that is] basically Christ-centered. A coordinator-inspector was also recommended.[61]

The uniqueness of the schools, the supporters were convinced, had to move beyond the provision of a special socialization environment, the teaching of Biblical knowledge, and a Christian interpretation of facts and events. Most courses included content similar to that of public schools, as shown by the use of public school readers. At the same time, schools taught not only Biblical studies but also a separate "Christian perspectives" course. A number of the schools used social studies and science units developed during summer workshops or available in **Joy in Learning**. Schools like Vancouver and Fraser Valley Christian High School constructed course outlines that differed significantly from public school ones. Like Bennink around the turn of the century in the U.S., British Columbia Christian school communities looked forward to a golden age of Christian school curriculum development. Yet, the shift in public opinion calling for a more structured and "basic" education in the late 1970s also influenced Christian school parents and teachers. The new mood, a lack of support personnel to develop and implement new programs, and teacher inertia would blunt attempted curriculum reforms.[62]

Religious, Moral, and Social Motives

At the baptism of their infant children, Christian Reformed parents in both Lynden and Canada publicly promised to instruct their children in Calvinist doctrine, and "cause them to be instructed therein."[63] Many construed not sending children to a Christian school to be a denial of that promise, an act of disobedience to God. Often parents sent their children to a Christian school because of unquestioned tradition—or, not infrequently, because of both implicit and explicit pressure from fellow church members. Stock phrases defended the importance of the schools. They were "schools with the Bible," where all subjects would demonstrate "the Bible's demands on all of life," and where "Christian perspective would permeate all knowledge." But such phrases hid the unresolved tension between the parents' desire to protect children from an evil society on the one hand and their aim to prepare them to be reformers of that society on the other.

Parents often started Christian schools because of unarticulated and unproven perceptions that public schools were ungodly. Both their strong religious views and immigrant heritage-rejection fears contributed to the Dutch Calvinists' wish to protect their children in a separate setting. Despite sin and failure, the 1960 Vancouver **Annual** wrote, "the Christian atmosphere in our schools does prevail." The Abbotsford board refused a teacher permission to take students to non-Christian Reformed worship services because of parental objections that children might be influenced by non-orthodox notions about doctrine and worship.[64] Christian schools were to be Calvinist islands untouched by the seas around it.

Parents wanted a protected environment that inculcated Calvinist morality. Boards discussed and enacted behaviour and discipline policies, for example. Canadians did criticize "self-righteous" morality with "the golden rule on top"; for them, true morality would follow naturally from a genuine submission to Jesus Christ.[65] The Lynden parents showed much more explicit concern for strict moral standards among teachers and students. Smoking, dancing, card playing, pin ball machines, cosmetics, improper language, and skating parties—over the years all these led not only to discussions at the board level but also to disciplinary action and even the dismissal of teachers. The school banned library books because of profanity and descriptions of sexual scenes. Board members questioned the company teachers kept. More than in Canada, the Lynden Christian schools were to build character by keeping children from any untoward moral influences.[66]

Socializing children into the traditions and patterns of the Dutch Calvinist community was perhaps the most important role of the schools. Supporters wanted the schools to maintain a homogeneous and unified community. They were "good" environments to make relationships and friendships. Lynden designed its sports program to aid such socialization. Not only did interscholastic sports build a sense of identity and a pride of belonging, but the school expected athletes, as school representatives and student models, to keep a behaviour code that was stricter than for other students. The community extended honour only to those who were willing to serve its purposes and standards.[67]

These social and moral motives for Christian schools were closely interlinked with religious ones. Children must learn to recognize that God existed as sovereign over all of life. Christian schools must instill faith in God and "lead our children to the cross of Christ." Supporters also saw the Christian school as an essential institution "in the building of a healthy church." The home, church and school, united in common purpose, should work in unison to inculcate children with a thorough knowledge of the Bible as well as a Calvinist, Christian worldview.

Schools taught that a "life in Jesus Christ" was the only way to happiness and truth. If the curriculum was based on this and worked out according to integrationist views, the school would help children "to meet the issues of life in strong and constructive ways, and to claim areas for Christ in whatever they are doing."[68]

By the mid-1970s, however, a distinct difference in emphasis had arisen between Canadian Calvinist parents who gave leadership in the schools and the newer, non-Calvinist ones who were joining forces with the Christian school movement. The new supporters emphasized an isolationist rationale for Christian schools. How the interaction of these two groups will affect the programs of the schools in the long run remains unclear. Other parents have supported Christian schools for non-religious reasons. Especially in Lynden, parents perceived that Christian schools gave a better quality education, particularly in core subjects areas, and administered a welcome tight discipline. Such parents believed that the Christian school, more than its public counterpart, would boost their children's social and economic prospects. In Canada, Christian school leaders consistently rejected such a rationale, and admission committees would likely refuse entrance to children of parents who gave this as a major reason for seeking enrollment. For Canadians, Christian schools existed to provide an alternative to the secular cultural "religion" of the public school, not to provide a better quality of education.[69]

Indeed, most supporters have held that the religious setting and direction was the basic raison d'etre for Christian schools. To that end, often without being able to specify the reasons, parents would support the Christian school through thick and thin, even if the curriculum lacked distinctiveness. For ardent proponents of Christian education obedience to God was foremost. Shortcomings in the school should be corrected but could not be used as an excuse to withdraw support. Besides, the socialization of children into the Calvinistic community was too important for parents to risk sending their children to the heterogeneous and heterodox public schools.

NOTES

1.	Henry S. Lucas, **Netherlanders in America: Dutch Immigration to the United States and Canada, 1789-1950** (Ann Arbor: University of Michigan Press, 1955), p. 646; Adriaan Peetoom, "From Mythology to Mythology: Dutch-Canadian Orthodox Calvinist

Immigrants and Their Schools" (M.A. thesis, University of Toronto, 1983), p. 5.
2. Study by Watson Kirkconnell of the Canadian Census, quoted by Aileen Marilyn Van Ginkel, "Ethnicity in the Reformed Tradition: Dutch Calvinist Immigrants in Canada, 1946-1960" (M.A. thesis, University of Toronto, 1982), p. 124.
3. Christian Reformed Church **Yearbook 1945**; Van Ginkel, p. 58.
4. Calculated from the tables in Van Ginkel, p. 10. The number of immigrants joining the Christian Reformed Church was given by John Knight, **Calvinist Contact**, July 16, 1982, p. 7.
5. NUCS Christian School **Annuals** and **Directories**, 1945 to 1977-78.
6. For details, see Van Ginkel, pp. 16-28; Peetoom, pp. 54-64.
7. Vancouver Christian School **Minutes**, Jan. 9, 1959.
8. Van Ginkel, pp. 5-7; Peetoom, pp. 6-9; **Christian Home and School**, July-Aug. 1952, p. 12; **Christian School Herald**, May-June 1963, p. 8.
9. **Christian Home and School**, July-Aug. 1952, p. 4; Bill Hoogland, "The Development of Calvinistic Christian Day Schools in Canada 1943-1965," unpublished paper, 1981, p. 7; Van Ginkel, pp. 60-68, 113-114.
10. Henry Van Brummelen, "Indrukken over Canada" [Impressions of Canada], unpublished paper written in 1958, five years after his immigration to Canada, pp. 2, 10.
11. Ontario Alliance of Christian Schools, Statement on "Religion in Public Schools," Jan. 1966; **Christian Home and School**, July-Aug. 1965, p. 17.
12. Peetoom, pp. 106-110, 123-131. Peetoom based this conclusion on an analysis of articles in **The Christian School Herald** from 1957-1960. See also Van Ginkel, pp. 148-49.
13. Aris Haalboom, **Om het kind** [On account of the child] (Toronto: Pro Rege, 1957), pp. 20-21.
14. **The Banner**, April 10, 1919, p. 233. Neerlandia is still one of the very few Canadian communities where a majority of the residents are of Dutch extraction. Today, the community's public school continues to advertise in **Calvinist Contact** and similar magazines for Christian teachers (e.g., see **Calvinist Contact**, April 27, 1984, p. 15).
15. Paul De Koekkoek, **Calvin Forum**, Jan. 1946, pp. 123-24; P. Tuininga and Cecil W. Tuininga, **Calvin Forum**, March 1946, p. 170.
16. The other community was Nobleford, founded by Dutch settlers in 1905 near Lethbridge, Alberta. When the settlers proposed to

start a Christian school, the local public school board authorized them to choose their own teachers. In 1952 one observer reported that "the Christian Reformed people fell for this proposal and now realize that it was a mistake" (Public Relations Secretary **Report** to NUCS Board of Directors, Dec. 20, 1952).

17. **Christian Home and School**, March 1946, p. 21; Feb. 1950, pp. 12-13; July-Aug. 1952, p. 16; and July-Aug. 1971, p. 7.

18. **Calvinist Contact**, April 15, 1983, p. 11; and **Christian Home and School**, July-Aug. 1952, p. 4. For a sociological study of the Holland Marsh Dutch Calvinist Community, including the role of the Christian school, see K. Ishwaran, "Calvanism [sic] and Social Behaviour in a Dutch-Canadian Community," in K. Ishwaran, ed., **The Canadian Family** (Toronto: Holt, Rinehart and Winston, 1971) and **Family, Kinship and Community: A Study of Dutch Canadians** (Toronto: McGraw-Hill Ryerson, 1977). What Ishwaran said about the Christian schools in Holland Marsh must be used with care. First, the community was unique in that its heavy concentration of Dutch immigrants came prior to World War II. Second, the respondents' answers to questionnaires and interviews were affected by Ishwaran's failure to win the community's trust for either his motives or his methods. Finally, the factual inaccuracies in the study, also in the sections on education, while not invalidating his conclusions, detract from the study's usefulness.

19. Sidney Dykstra, "Report to NUCS Board on Visit to Ontario Schools," January 1958. He also noted that even though there were enough basic texts, supplementary reading books and libraries were lacking.

20. John A. Vander Ark, **22 Landmark Years: Christian Schools International 1943-65** (Grand Rapids: Baker, 1983), p. 95. Lynda Valerie Parker gave a descriptive survey of Ontario's Dutch Calvinist schools in "A History of Protestant Schools in Ontario" (Master of Christian Studies thesis, Regent College, Vancouver, 1982), Chapter 4.

21. Toronto District Christian High School Yearbook, **Heyday 1966**, n.p.

22. 1960 **Annual** of the Vancouver Christian School Association, pp. 3-4.

23. Enid Spruyt, Vancouver Christian School 1960 **Annual**, p. 17; Vancouver Christian School **Minutes**, May 7, 1960; interviews with Alie Munneke (March 27, 1984); Case Pel (April 3, 1984); Gerard Ensing (March 29, 1984); and Hank Van Huizen (April 3, 1984).

24. Interviews with John Dykshoorn, John Kampman and Peter

Brandsma (all on April 4, 1984); Abbotsford Christian School **Minutes,** June 13, 1955; Feb. 9, 1959; April 28, 1961; March 23, 1964; Oct. 20, 1969 and Feb. 9, 1970. The quote is from a report by NUCS' Ivan Zylstra to the Abbotsford Christian School board on Oct. 20, 1969. An emphasis on basics also occurred in many public schools, of course. The shortage of teachers of the late 1950s and early 1960s hit Christian schools especially hard. Enrollments were expanding rapidly. Yet among the immigrants relatively few students had the background or resources to go to university or teachers' college. As a result, many unqualified teachers were hired during these years.

25. Vancouver Christian School **Minutes,** Nov. 24, 1949 and Jan. 20, 1950.
26. Interviews with Walter Van der Kamp (March 28, 1984), John Kampman, Hank Van Huizen, and Gerard Ensing; written communication from N. De Regt, principal of the John Knox Christian School in Burnaby during the 1960s and 1970s (Jan. 30, 1981).
27. Vancouver Christian School **1960 Annual,** p. 21.
28. **Christian Educators Journal,** Sept. 1973, pp. 21, 22. Significantly, De Vries' articles on a more open approach, the publication of the integrated primary curriculum for Christian schools, and other Christian school writings on informal education all occurred between 1970-1975, about the same time that such writers as John Holt, Neil Postman and Ivan Illich were at the height of their popularity.
29. **Christian Home and School,** July-Aug. 1973, p. 18.
30. Interviews with Frank De Vries (March 29, 1984) and Gerard Ensing. De Vries was was a catalyst in stimulating discussions about educational issues in the Christian school teaching force and among the parents in his own community.
31. This was stated by almost all interviewees in the Lynden area and by the Lynden Christian School **Annual Reports.** The 1958-59 **Annual Report,** for instance, said, "In general, our program had never departed from the "discipline" concept of learning to the harmful extent to which typical American schools went." The annual reports also regularly boasted of excellent achievement test results and the strict phonetic approach used in reading.
32. See, for example, the Lynden Christian Schools 1968-69 **Annual Report,** p. 6. Also, interviews with Garris Timmer (April 2, 1984), and Peter Brandsma.
33. Lynden Christian School **Minutes,** Bylaw Art. 10 passed Feb. 26,

1913, and Annual General Meeting **Minutes,** July 8, 1936; Abbotsford Christian School 1954-55 **Annual Report; Minutes,** June 13, 1955 and April 8, 1957; Vancouver Christian School panel topic, Nov. 15, 1956; interview with Sam Van Randen (April 3, 1984).

34. Abbotsford Christian School 1965-66 **Annual Report,** Sept. 28, 1966.
35. Telephone interview with Alie Munneke.
36. See, for example, the Vancouver Christian School **1960 Annual,** pp. 9 and 21.
37. For a description of the 1960 Federal-Provincial Technical-Vocational Training Agreement and its effect on vocational education in Canada, see Chapter 21 in J. Donald Wilson, R.M. Stamp, and L. P. Audet, eds., **Canadian Education: A History** (Toronto: Prentice-Hall, 1970).
38. Vancouver Christian School **Annual 1960,** pp. 9 and 21; Vancouver Christian School **Minutes,** Oct. 21, 1952 and Jan. 9, 1963; letter from William Vander Beek and Walter Vander Kamp to supporters of a Christian High School Association (Feb., 1960); Fraser Valley Christian High School **Minutes,** Feb. 16, 1970 and Feb. 21, 1974; Abbotsford Christian School **Minutes** Aug. 8 and Sept. 28, 1966.
39. Bylaws inserted in **Minutes,** Nov. 6, 1944, Art. 6. The civics requirement was accepted on Dec. 9, 1926; the Washington State history during the 1962-63 school year (see 1962-63 **Annual Report,** p. 4).
40. Lynden Christian School **Minutes,** Nov. 23, 1948; Jan. 1950; March 21, 1957; June 25, 1957; and 1958-59 **Annual Report.** Interviews with Peter Bulthuis and Jelte Visser (April 2, 1984).
41. Lynden Christian Schools, **Golden Anniversary Book** (1960), p. 21.
42. Lynden Christian School **Minutes,** May 4, 1923; May 13, 1927; Jan. 22, 1946; July 22, 1947; Oct. 24, 1947; March 17, 1955; 1969-70 **Annual Report,** p. 6.
43. Abbotsford Christian School **Minutes,** April 21, 1951; Dec. 12, 1955; Nov. 14, 1960; Feb. 11, 1969; March 16, 1970; Vancouver Christian School **Minutes,** Oct. 24, 1949. June 11, 1957; Jan. 31.1958; Nov. 6, 1959; Jan. 15, 1964; June 1, 1966; Vancouver **Annual 1960,** p. 9; Lynden Christian School 1968-69 **Annual Report,** p. 5; interviews with Frank De Vries, Gerard Ensing, John Kampman, and Alie Munneke.
44. For example, there were no references to Hodgett's work, and not until the mid-1970s did Canadian Christian school leaders begin to demand that the NUCS develop Canadian social studies materials. For a description of the implications of Hodgett's **What**

LOCAL SCHOOLS (1945-1977)

Culture? What Heritage? for Canadian curriculum in general, see George S. Tomkins, "Stability and Change in the Canadian Curriculum", in J. Donald Wilson, ed., **Canadian Education in the 1980s** (Calgary: Detselig, 1981), pp. 145-46. The increasing number of Canadian studies publications becoming available in the late 1970s also affected the curricula of Christian schools, of course.

45. Frank De Vries, "Christian Education View," in the Smithers **Interior News** in the fall of 1970 (contained in a scrapbook kept by Frank De Vries); interviews with Conrad Van der Kamp (March 29, 1984), and Hank Van Huizen; Abbotsford Christian School **Minutes** Dec. 14, 1970; Feb. 8, 1970; and Dec. 13, 1972.

46. Arnold H. De Graaff and Jean Olthuis, **Joy in Learning: An Integrated Curriculum for the Elementary School** (Toronto: Joy in Learning Curriculum Development Centre, 1973); Vancouver Christian School **Curriculum Guide**, 1974-75, pp. 2 and 5.

47. Vancouver Christian School **Curriculum Guide**, 1974-75, cover.

48. Abbotsford Christian School society membership meeting **Minutes**, Jan. 13, 1956.

49. Vancouver Christian School **Minutes**, Nov. 18, 1949; June 28, Oct. 4 and Nov. 1, 1956; Biblical Studies Questionnaire completed by Hank Van Huizen for Harro Van Brummelen, "Biblical Studies in Member Schools of the Society of Christian Schools: Conformation or Transformation?," unpublished paper (1981); interviews with Frank De Vries, Gerard Ensing, Hank Van Huizen, John Dykshoorn, and John Kampman.

50. Lynden Christian Schools **Plan for Curriculum Study** (1956) and Board **Minutes**, Feb. 26, 1957; **Annual Reports** 1966-67, p. 4; 1967-68, p. 5; interviews with Jim Van Andel (April 9, 1984), Dan Bratt (March 30, 1984), Garris Timmer, Peter Bulthuis and Ben Boxum (April 10, 1984).

51. Interviews with Gerard Ensing, John Kampman, Conrad Vander Kamp, Walter Vander Kamp, Hank Van Huizen, and Sam Van Randen.

52. Ishwaran, **The Canadian Family** (1971), pp. 301-02; Smithers **Interior News**, Smithers, B.C., Nov. 13, 1968. Teachers who were not part of a Christian Reformed or closely allied church ran into difficulty when, for example, they emphasized secular celebrations such as Hallowe'en or when they did not teach a traditional Calvinist view of Christ's miracles (Abbotsford Christian School **Minutes**, March 15, 1962, and Nov. 14, 1966).

53. For sources see footnotes 49 and 51. Lynden put greater emphasis

270

on regular devotional chapel services than Canadian schools. The latter often felt that such mini-"worship services" were not in character with the nature of the school and that Christian views should permeate all instruction rather than be presented in separate "chapel" time slots. Canadian Calvinists believed that the schools should become more interdenominational. However, church groups with close theoretical affinity such as the Presbyterian Church showed little interest, and Fundamentalists looked askance at the approval Calvinists gave to smoking and moderate drinking. Only in the 1970s did the schools become successful in attracting non-Calvinist students. Of the twenty-six association-operated schools in 1983, half had a student population of which a majority was not Dutch Calvinist.

54. Abbotsford Christian School **Minutes**, Sept. 11, 1967; Feb. 19, 1970; interviews with John Dykshoorn and John Kampman.

55. Interviews with Conrad Vander Kamp, Walter Vander Kamp, Henry Van Andel, Sam Van Randen; Fraser Valley Christian High School **Minutes**, Dec. 7 and 17, 1970; "History of Fraser Valley Christian High School, 1963-1973," unpublished paper by Henry Van Andel.

56. Fraser Valley Christian High School **Minutes**, Feb. 4 and May 13, 1975; interviews with Sam Van Randen and Conrad Vander Kamp; submission of Ken Elgersma to the education committee, March 1975.

57. Jane Mulder, Trix Wikkerink, and Marianne Klein, "Social Science Curriculum (Grade 2)," written during the 1971 Christian Educators Summer School in Surrey, B.C., pp. 78, 91.

58. Vancouver Christian School **Curriculum Guide 1974-75**, p. 2. The "Words of the Lord" was a metaphor referring to (1) the Bible, (2) the revelation of God through Jesus Christ, and (3) God's revelation in nature and society.

59. See, for example, Ministry of Education, **Guide to the Core Curriculum** (Victoria, 1977), p. 20.

60. Fraser Valley Christian High School **Minutes**, Aug. 13, 1968; March 16, 1970; Oct. 9 and 16, 1973; Jan. 8, March 12, June 25, Sept. 10, Oct. 8, and Oct. 29, 1974; and Feb. 17, 1976; interviews with Henry Van Andel (March 28, 1984), Conrad Vander Kamp, Walter Vander Kamp, Hank Van Huizen, and Sam Van Randen.

61. Abbotsford Christian School **Minutes**, Jan. 26, 1970. The provincial association appointed such a coordinator in 1977.

62. Curriculum development did continue unimpeded and little opposition was expressed to innovative practices, partly because few controversial learning modes existed. Parents were more open

to project work, field experiences, and fine arts activities at the end of the decade than ten years earlier. The reaction against traditionalism in the early 1970s did not recede without leaving its mark.

63. Baptism of infants form, Christian Reformed Church **Psalter Hymnal,** "Liturgical Forms," p. 125 (Grand Rapids: Christian Reformed Church, 1976 edition).

64. Interview with Hank Van Huizen; Vancouver Christian School 1960 **Annual,** p. 13; Abbotsford Christian School **Minutes,** Jan. 15, 1969.

65. Interviews with Sam Van Randen, Frank De Vries, Case Pel; Abbotsford Christian School **Minutes,** June 28, 1956 and April 14, 1958.

66. Interviews with Ben Boxum, Dan Bratt, and Peter Bulthuis; Lynden Christian Schools, 1975-76 **Annual Report,** p. 5; Lynden Christian School **Minutes,** May 21, 1913; March 8, 1918; Jan. 14, 1929; May 20, 1930; May 2, 1941; Nov. 6, 1945; May 10, 1949; April 3, 1950; Feb. 24, 1953; Dec. 29, 1954; Sept. 17, 1962.

67. Interviews with Ben Boxum, Garris Timmer, Walter Vander Kamp, and George Yntema (April 4, 1984).

68. Interviews with Peter Brandsma, Ben Boxum, Dan Bratt, John Dykshoorn, Walter Vander Kamp, Hank Van Huizen, and William Verwolf (April 2, 1984); Abbotsford Christian School **Minutes,** Aug. 29, 1950 and Nov. 4, 1976; **Christian Home and School,** Dec. 1938, p. 12; Lynden Christian School **Annual Report 1968-69,** p. 6; and letter of W. Vander Beek and W. Vander Kamp to supporters for the establishment of Fraser Valley Christian High School, Feb. 1960.

69. See, for example, **"Cri de Coureur:** An Urgent Plea for Educational Justice in British Columbia," a brief prepared for the B.C. government by the Society of Christian Schools in B.C. (District 12 of NUCS), Fall 1975.

U.S. History

In grades I, II, III, IV, the Biblical History given in Story form every morning, will afford abundant opportunity for teaching concepts of government by Supreme Ruler, by officials (kings, presidents etc) placed and appointed by God through the people; its teachings will also give clear concepts of respect to God, and to officials in church, school, and state. Much history is given incidentally in Story-telling (for grades my to fours, a subheading of English or Language). Sacred and national anniversaries give material for making a closer acquaintance with history of human race and of nation. Form of government can be discussed when readers call for it.

Remember the following in teaching history:

God as Creator, Sustainer, (See Geog. notes) and Ruler of His whole creation is known as such to the children from Bible History lessons. In a special sense did he rule Israel, but all nations as well as individuals are governed by Him. In Him we live, move, and have our being. Nations also live, move, and have their being in Him. In the whole history of the Israelites (patriarchs,

A page from the handwritten school course outlines prepared by principal Henry Van Zyl between 1913 and 1922 for the Hull, Iowa, Christian School.

10 Isolation, Conformation, or Transformation?

Why Calvinist Christian Schools?

American immigrants have viewed the school as a central instrument in shaping character and promoting material progress. For Dutch Calvinist immigrants, the school was more important for religious and moral molding than for improving economic status. Already Albertus Van Raalte in his Holland, Michigan, colony emphasized schooling not for future material benefits but for spiritual vitality. The first Christian Reformed high school limited its enrollment to future ministers. In Grand Rapids, while the native-born Dutch school enrollment in 1910 for 6-to-14-year olds equaled that of other groups, high school enrollment fell off sharply.[1] Children had to learn to read and write, especially to study the Bible and the catechism. Opportunity and success came through hard work; schools existed primarily to teach basic skills and inculcate Calvinism. Since public schools could not do the latter, non-public Christian schools became necessary.

Until well into the twentieth century, American public schools, although officially nonsectarian, "were generally Protestant in orientation and often explicit in practice."[2] Many Protestant clergymen, including Dutch immigrant leader Hendrik Scholte in Iowa, believed that public schools provided the means to unify the nation through the transmission of a Protestantism closely aligned with the emerging American culture.[3] The more conservative Dutch Calvinists, however, refused, for historical, social and religious reasons, to participate in building such a consensus through the public schools.

The first wave of Dutch Calvinist immigrants in the 1840s and 1850s vividly remembered their oppression at the hands of Dutch public schools that promoted Enlightenment thinking and forbade Bible reading and prayer. Later immigrants left the Netherlands during the unfinished Schoolstrijd [School Struggle] that fought the public school establishment to gain financial government support for schools. Post-World War II Dutch immigrants saw public schools as bastions of political socialism

275

and religious free thought and therefore oppressive in their own way. Many immigrants, whether in the 1850s or the 1910s or the 1950s, found it difficult to accept public schools, making Christian schools, quite apart from the nature of North American public schools, the only viable alternative for their children.

One hundred years ago, the belief that Dutch was the only suitable language vehicle for Calvinism made Calvinist Christian schools—and some rural district ones—little more than "Dutch schools." Immigrants who joined the Christian Reformed Church rather than the Reformed Church came from areas in the Netherlands with a high degree of local particularism. As a result, they showed greater resistance to American assimilation and were more prone to start Christian school enclaves than their more cosmopolitan and accommodating Reformed Church counterparts.[4] That church groups theologically and ethnically close to the Christian Reformed Church (e.g., the Canadian Reformed Church) have established their own denominational schools has also demonstrated the importance of group identity in starting Christian schools. Parents have intended Christian schools to preserve the purity of the group.

Supporters formally justified their Christian schools on religious rather than historical or ethnic grounds. Orthodox Calvinists felt uneasy with a fundamentalism that denied the Calvinist doctrine of divine election and appeared to limit religion to personal morality. They rejected social gospel thinking which held that human effort could bring about a perfect social order without personal repentance and conversion as necessary prerequisites. But the Kuyperian Calvinists' own call for cultural transformation through separate Christian organizations found little sympathy among, for example, the doctrinally akin but much more enculturated Presbyterians. Religiously, Dutch Calvinists found themselves strangers in their newly adopted nations. Their faith could be preserved and begin to impinge on society, they felt, only if their children would attend non-public Christian schools.

Dutch Calvinist schools, then, served three goals, often contradictory in practice: religious and social isolation to preserve Calvinist beliefs and group identity; behavioural assimilation to enable students to function well in society economically; and the cultural transformation of society through Calvinist contributions. Schools served as guardians of the truth and, through their socialization function, as community anchors. Yet, at least since 1900, immigrants also wanted the Christian schools to help their children become part of North American society, and therefore aligned curricula close to the mainstream of American and Canadian education. Moreover, the

Kuyperian aim to transform culture often was transformed itself into American religious nationalism. Many Calvinists no less than other Americans believed that Christianity had fueled the remarkable advance of American civilization, and the march of progress would be restrained only if America deserted its Christian doctrinal and moral roots. Thus, especially after 1910, American Christian schools concurrently promoted Calvinist doctrines, a Methodist avoidance of "worldliness," and faith in American patriotism, pragmatism and progress. When Canadian Kuyperians as well as persons like Nicholas Wolterstorff in the 1960s once again began to emphasize that Christianity was a radical religion that ought to question and change the basic direction and structures of society, many school supporters and leaders no longer understood the call for Calvinists to be dissenters and reformers in society. The cultural transformation goal of the schools often faded because their supporters accepted the worldview of the overpowering American dream even while maintaining Calvinist doctrinal and moral purity.

Other Religiously-Oriented Non-Public
Schools in North America

In order to understand more completely the influences Calvinist schools belonging to Christian Schools International [CSI],[5] this section compares features of some North American religously-oriented schools with CSI ones.

Catholic schools. American Catholic schools, like Dutch Calvinist ones, were founded for both ethnic and religious reasons. With public schools promoting a Protestant consensus, religious education seemed indispensable for preserving the Catholic faith. But the schools also served separate German, Polish, French Canadian and Irish communities. Until World War I, similarities with Calvinist Christian schools were striking. Religious studies took place at the beginning of the day, including church history in the upper elementary grades. Religious interpretation in other subjects supplemented the direct teaching of religion. The schools cultivated piety and Christian virtues. Teachers wanted to use Catholic textbooks, but only a few were available. In a Polish Catholic school in Chicago in 1910, the time allotted to subjects closely matched that of Calvinist schools, except for a little more emphasis on drawing and a little less on nature study and science. Some schools taught the primary grades using the ethnic language; others taught subjects like religion and the history of the homeland in the native tongue. By 1920 the curriculum in most Catholic schools closely paralleled that of public ones, except that, as in Christian schools, the introduction of "progressive" subjects such as manual training, household arts, art and construction, and physical culture received little or no attention.

However, the Catholics, in the tradition of Thomas Aquinas, drew a much sharper distinction between sacred and secular subject material than did the Calvinists. As a result, they were more willing to adopt public school content and methodology (including progressivism) and their imbedded values in subjects other than religion. By 1970, for example, few Catholic science teachers wanted to use textbooks designed specifically for Catholic schools. In Canada, Catholics in several provinces accepted publicly-funded Catholic separate schools, although that required the schools' structure and organization, teacher qualifications and curriculum to be identical with those of public schools, religious studies excepted.

Catholic schools had some success in attaining three goals: advancing a knowledge of the Catholic faith; promoting religious behaviour and Catholic social attitudes; and helping minorities improve their socioeconomic status.[6] For Dutch Calvinist schools such goals proved insufficient; Calvinists did not want to limit Christ to a "religious" domain, but saw Him as the transformer of human culture. As such, faith must touch all subject areas and no "secular" subjects existed. Consequently, in contrast to Catholic schools, the Calvinist schools since World War II renewed their efforts to develop Christian curriculum materials. In practice, however, Catholic and Calvinist schools, especially in the U.S., continued to show many similar features such as a strong emphasis on the basic subject areas, with religious or Biblical studies contained, by and large, to its allotted time slot. The adoption of the American way of life by most Catholic and Calvinist immigrants often also led to an uncritical acceptance of public school curricula in most subject areas.[7]

The Amish schools. The Amish, like the Calvinists, wanted to maintain cultural continuity and integrity. However, they believed that Christ opposes most forms of contemporary human culture. Therefore, assimilation with society, including learning about the intellectual enterprises of "fallen humankind," must be shunned. The Amish curriculum contained only the basic three R's taught through drill, memorization and recitation. Christianity pervaded all subjects, largely through teacher modeling.

Teachers taught children to cultivate humility, self-denial, simple living, and resignation to the will of God, all in preparation for eternity. The curriculum avoided anything "worldly" such as fairy tales and myths, as well as most science and social studies content.

Calvinists, wanting to live in and contribute to the mainstream of society, have for that very reason been unable to adopt and implement a structure of education as unique as that of the Amish.[8]

Jewish education. Despite the Protestant bias of America's public schools, Jewish immigrants, with few exceptions, embraced the public schools to help themselves assimilate into American society and meet social and economic aspirations. Like other ethnic groups, they maintained a sense of identity through after-school education. Such Jewish education stressed religious beliefs, Biblical history and moral didacticism derived from Biblical examples. Reform Jews especially wanted to become fully integrated in American society, except for religious beliefs. They accepted, for example, John Dewey's conceptions of the scientific method and democracy as they applied to schooling much more readily than the Dutch Calvinists.

Both after-school Jewish education and the recently increasing number of Orthodox and Conservative Jewish day schools have maintained a sharp distinction between the secular and the religious curriculum. The religious curriculum was God-given, to be accepted in faith. The secular curriculum, based on rational and empirical examination and taught by different teachers, provided the pathway to vocational and academic aspirations. This dualistic approach helped the Jews integrate well into the American socio-political system and advance rapidly economically. However, the schools' presentation of two clashing views of reality also made it difficult for students to construct a coherent worldview.

Officially, CSI schools made no such distinction between religious and secular curricula, and used regular teachers for the Biblical studies program. However, in practice their programs often could be identified through their religious exercises and Biblical studies courses, with other courses closely paralleling public school ones. In what ways a formal lack of a sacred-secular distinction and the occurrence of differing conceptions of reality affected Calvinist students is beyond the scope of this book. A case study of the curriculum and instruction (and of "the hidden curriculum") in CSI schools would help reveal to what extent such conflicts have affected CSI students.[9]

The uniqueness of CSI schools. Protestant non-public schools in North America have shown significant similarities. A survey of the aims of the Seventh Day Adventist, Lutheran and Calvinist schools in Alberta showed responses that were "characterized more by their similarities than by their differences." Most schools and parents mentioned imparting Biblical knowledge, providing children with a Christian philosophy of life, promoting reverence for God and kindness and tolerance to men, and "good discipline." In the U.S., diverse Protestant schools have also shown affinity in goal statements.[10] Similarly, a 1967 study of the curriculum of schools in the interdenominational National Association of Christian Schools reported features resembling those of CSI schools. Teachers made individual attempts to integrate religious content in subjects like social studies, but none to correlate Biblical or religious studies with other subjects. Overtly religious content consisted of theistic elements (e.g., God is the creator and sustainer of the universe) and moral applications that the teacher deemed suitable for the topic at hand. On the whole, as in CSI schools, the curriculum closely resembled that of public schools except for the Biblical or religious studies classes.[11]

The goals given in the Alberta survey mentioned group cohesiveness only indirectly: the home and the school were to provide a unified educational direction. Yet ethnic and/or religious group solidarity played a major role in all religiously-oriented schools. For example, despite the desire of both the National Association of Christian Schools and CSI to develop more consistently Christian programs, they did not attempt to do so jointly. Group cohesiveness overrode the possibility of cooperation that could have taken place in subjects like science. In CSI schools, ethnicity strengthened isolationist tendencies, although in British Columbia ethnic identity has not been maintained quite as strongly as, for example, in Michigan and Iowa. In B.C., Dutch did not appear as the language of instruction or even as an optional subject; the study of Dutch culture did not receive a prominent place in the curriculum; and both the first and the most recently founded schools involved persons of various denominational and ethnic backgrounds.[12]

Despite curricular similarities in religiously-oriented schools, they differ in more than ethnic and religious backgrounds. Robert L. Smith, executive director of the Council for American Private Education, recently quoted a Lutheran statement as being representative of all religiously oriented schools: such schools want to be "a salt, a leaven, a light in society," since "Christianity is basically counterculture."[13] However, it is precisely the definition of "counterculture" that has led to disagreements affecting the schools and their curricula. For the Amish, it means separation from mainstream society and a curriculum that teaches little about that society. Most Catholics, on the other hand, accept the secular realm of society as long as the authority of the church is recognized in religious and moral matters. Therefore, the content and approach of most subjects can be identical to that of public schools. For recently-established fundamentalist schools such as those using the Accelerated Christian Education programmed learning materials, "counterculture" may mean a return to an idealized version of nineteenth century America, or a view that society is so corrupt that the focus of most of life is to proselytize and await the return of Christ. Such groups have resurrected the McGuffey readers and object to students studying much modern literature, including science fiction. For Kuyperian Calvinists and other socially-aware evangelical Christians, "counterculture" means analyzing modern societal structures and phenomena and influencing them on the basis of Christian norms. For them, the curriculum must be both socially and personally relevant, in a distinctly Christian way.

Influences on Curriculum and Instruction
in CSI Schools

A discussion of five main categories of influences on educational programs—religious beliefs and background, moral views, social and economic circumstances, general educational context, and political milieux—leads to a number of conclusions about thinking and development, decision-making, and implementation of curriculum and instruction in CSI schools.

Religious background and beliefs. Religious convictions have been the main source of power fueling the continued existence of Calvinist Christian schools. Christian schools have emphasized prayers, Bible reading and the singing of psalms and hymns. Biblical studies, often taught during the first period of each day, served as the foremost subject.

But the tenets of the Christian faith were supposed to do more than just provide the basis for devotions and a Biblical studies program. Especially the late nineteenth-century Dutch leader Abraham Kuyper had convinced Calvinists that neutral, objective scholarship did not exist and that the foundations of all subject disciplines rested upon faith presuppositions. The schools could prepare children to exert a beneficial Christian influence on society only if the whole curriculum disclosed "God's hand." The rhetoric outstripped the reality, however. Christian approaches to curriculum were usually limited to the insertion of religious and moral "truths," to Christian interpretations of historical and societal phenomena, and to literature selections helping students to understand a Christian worldview. During the last twenty years, some social studies and the **Man in Society** textbooks have tried to work out and apply Christian conceptions of justice, economic stewardship, and community living. Such publications, however, have underscored

281

disagreements about the implications of Calvinistic faith. For example, the CSI civics textbook **Under God** assumed that the underlying structure of American democracy was a Christian one, while **Man in Society** was critical of the North American way of life and its institutions.[14] Calvinists readily agreed that God's hand existed, but not about the direction in which it pointed.

The Christian Reformed Church gave the schools wholehearted support, but, with a few notable exceptions, did not try to influence curricula directly since the schools became association-controlled at the local level early in the century. Nonetheless, ministers or theologians sometimes served as writers or consultants for Biblical studies programs, and regularly addressed annual CSI conventions. Though respected, ministers assumed a limited place in Canadian Christian Reformed communities. The many informal links between school and church leadership, of course, resulted in a great deal of consensus on key issues, including curriculum ones. The Calvinist heritage, as interpreted by the Christian Reformed Church, indirectly continued to provide much religious and moral direction for the schools.

The moral purpose of the curriculum. A Calvinist worldview encompasses not only religious doctrines, but also a moral framework. Since Calvinists believe that true faith and obedience to God manifest themselves in "good works," the moral purpose of the curriculum has been important. Early twentieth century readers written for U.S. Christian schools, like many nineteenth century public school readers, presented a "moral truth" in every selection. Penmanship samples in the first published course of study similarly stressed a Calvinistic work ethic and a Methodist striving for personal holiness and perfection. In the interwar years, teachers frequently condemned "worldly" amusements and corruption, and, sometimes, usury and underpayment of labourers. In the 1970s, CSI developed a high school ethics course to help students make personal moral decisions on the basis of Biblical injunctions. In addition, the Canadian **Man in Society** course considered corporate moral responsibility in the political, social and economic realms. Schools consciously strove to use the curriculum to develop the students' moral perspicacity. At the same time, the total school structure and environment likely had more influence on the moral decisions and behaviour of students than did formal instruction.

Social and economic background circumstances. The social, educational and economic background of Dutch immigrants affected their curricular views. Almost all immigrants joining the Christian Reformed Church in the mid-nineteenth century—and many of those arriving between 1880 and 1914—came from rural areas in the Netherlands that promoted separatism and particularism. Suspicious of culture and intellectualism, they emphasized the antithesis between Christian and non-Christian (often, Calvinist and non-Calvinist) thought and action. They leaned towards a monastic ("Christ against culture") view of the role of Christian education. Christian schools must fight the forces of modernization and secularization, such as the evolutionistic and progressive education notions of the 1930s, by promoting religious and cultural isolation. The curriculum must include the three R's and traditional Calvinist doctrines and virtues taught mainly through memorization and recitation, but avoid "frills" like the fine arts. The Kuyperian integrationists ("Christ the transformer of culture"), however, manifested another side of the Dutch Calvinist tradition. For them, Christian schools were to educate students to understand the forces that shaped society, helping them contribute to modern culture as Christians. A broad curriculum based on sound pedagogical theories provided Biblical direction to students. Generally, persons with such views hailed from less localistic areas of the Netherlands or, at least, had been influenced by the urban and cultured Kuyper.

Leaders like principal B. J. Bennink promoted Kuyper's ideas early in the twentieth century. However, most, having come from small Seceder communities, soon reverted to their Seceder roots in curriculum work. After World War II, leaders recognized that the defensive Seceder stance had led to an ingrown, static school system. Those leaders who turned towards a traditional academic education had little influence other than to perpetuate straightforward receptacle learning. Others, more successfully, turned towards a dualist ("Christ above culture") view of the curriculum. Choosing what they considered best in modern secular curricula, they added Christian personal ethics through a moral or "decisional" dimension of learning. Not until the 1960s did the Kuyperians once again exert some influence, mainly through the post-World War II influx of Canadian immigrants.[15]

Of course, not all Seceders came from particularist rural areas, and their stance cannot be explained exclusively in terms of social background. Nor have the differing viewpoints always been clearcut. B. J. Bennink, for example, based his successful moves to wrest the schools from church control on Kuyper's theory of sphere sovereignty. In contrast, most of his curriculum work followed the pietistic, monastic Seceder tradition—but his strong push for Americanization was once again influenced by Kuyper. Nevertheless, the generally conservative, particularist social background of the majority of Dutch Calvinist immigrants has been an essential element in forging curriculum and instruction in Calvinist Christian schools.

ISOLATION, CONFORMATION, OR TRANSFORMATION?

Educational context. The handful of nineteenth century Calvinist Christian schools remained isolated from the American scene and were "Dutch schools" in language, content, and type of instruction given. Since 1900, however, the four educational and pedagogical forces in public education identified by R. Freeman Butts were also found in CSI schools, though often with modifications attributable to the group's conservative nature.[16]

First, a strong academic emphasis came to the fore especially with the calls for intellectual discipline around 1950 and with the introduction of new mathematics and science programs in the 1960s. Calvinist schools often participated in government examinations and administered standardized tests as a way of meeting or surpassing public school standards.

Secondly, Calvinist schools, though critical of child-centred progressivism, were not immune to demands for more learner-oriented methods. Some U.S. schools, for instance, implemented Pestalozzi's object lesson approach in the primary grades, and gave the project method limited promotion in the 1920s. Around 1970, several Canadian schools made moves towards a more informal approach and an integrated curriculum. However, the schools generally wanted children, though considered "image bearers of the Lord," to develop within narrow, well-defined parameters.

Thirdly, the schools occasionally resisted but always yielded to pressures for a more practical curriculum, at least at the high school level. CSI high schools established in the 1910s and 1920s immediately implemented commercial programs, and most schools gradually introduced, as funds and teachers became available, general industrial arts and, in rural areas, agriculture courses.

Fourthly, already in the 1910s several spokespersons for Calvinist schools promoted the notion that efficiency in "producing results" was a key to effective Christian education. However, not until the 1960s and 1970s did CSI approach curriculum in terms of functional efficiency. Then, especially in science and Biblical studies, writers defined behavioural objectives, found specific means to attain them, and developed test item banks to evaluate their achievement. A scientific approach to curriculum held sway for more than a decade.

The oft-conflicting calls for new directions in public schools, therefore, also influenced curriculum and instruction in CSI schools. The social mood of the times, the general educational milieu, and post-secondary entrance requirements all affected parents, board members and teachers. Also, the different curriculum orientations in public education—the academic, process, personal relevance, and social relevance ones—all had counterparts among CSI school leaders. However, the conservative and more homogeneous nature of the supporters, and the fact that dissatisfied parents could take their children elsewhere, meant that most schools steered away from any radical innovations.

Political context. The homogenizing power of the modern state affected CSI schools both directly and indirectly. A remarkable degree of freedom to implement the programs they saw fit may well have contributed to the U.S. schools' willingness to "Americanize" their curricula,[17] and later to accept, for instance, accreditation stipulations with respect to curriculum. Government curriculum guidelines for public schools, while seldom stipulated for CSI schools, affected them. During most of the twentieth century, teachers used them as references, or, at least, adopted textbooks written to fulfill state departments' expectations.

What about Canadian schools during the past thirty years? Ontario's Christian schools also generally followed the broad contours of public school courses, although some high schools use locally-developed alternative history programs. Western Canada presents two significant cases of political influence on non-public school programs. Alberta's Department of Education Act during the 1960s and 1970s authorized private schools to exist only if they offered "instruction in courses prescribed or approved by the Minister or courses substantially the same."[18] CSI schools, therefore, did not stray far from the prescribed curriculum, even before government grants became available in 1968. Indeed, during the 1970s, both because of decentralization trends in education and because of increasing confidence in CSI schools, the Ministry of Education interpreted "substantially the same" content quite liberally. Schools could offer even Biblical studies and **Man in Society** courses for religious studies and sociology high school credits respectively. The swing back to more accountability in the public sector, however, now affects CSI schools as well, particularly with the imposition of grade 12 final examinations applicable to both public and non-public schools.

In British Columbia, regulations have governed only those non-public schools that apply for government funding under the School Support (Independent) Act [often called "Bill 33"]. All eligible CSI schools receive the higher Group 2 level of funding requiring the schools to meet teacher certification, curriculum, and assessment criteria. Government funding and the accompanying monitoring had an immediate effect on the schools, although the long-term implications are far from clear at this time. When the Act was passed in 1977, many schools increased their fine arts and physical education emphasis, and took steps to improve programs such as elementary science. The introduction of government funding coincided with a high degree of interest in curriculum in Canadian CSI schools. The British Columbia schools had just appointed a coordinator to stimulate curriculum development and implementation. The provincial organization developed a Curriculum Handbook and teacher resource units that distanced the schools from the B.C. public school curriculum, particularly in social studies and science. The increasing distinctiveness of the schools' curricula soon led to continuing but amiable discussions with the first two Inspectors of Independent Schools, J. Phillipson and E. L. Bullen. As long as the schools demonstrated that their curriculum covered the B.C. Ministry of Education 1977 "core curriculum,"[19] the Inspectors allowed substantial curricular deviations.

However, the implementation of units and courses based on a Christian ideology resulted in a major confrontation with the B.C. government during the 1983-84 school year. In August 1983, the Minister of Education, Jack Heinrich, imposed senior secondary examinations based on public school courses and textbooks on Group 2 non-public schools. CSI schools protested that this action undermined their curricular independence. However, the Minister refused to accept the compromise the schools suggested, viz., to have students write the group's own examinations in English, social studies and biology, subject to prior government approval. In the three schools that took a vote, the parent members decided that to prevent a further erosion of independence the students would not participate in government exams. In May, 1984, the Inspector indicated he would cut grade 11 and 12 Group 2 funding to such schools. In addition, the universities and the B.C. Institute of Technology made the examinations an entrance requirement. As a result, the associations operating the three schools reversed themselves and all students wrote the government exams after all.[20]

Several tentative conclusions can be drawn. First, Canadian Christian schools, participating in government examinations without question in the 1960s and early 1970s, had developed enough distinctive curriculum thought and materials that their communities objected to Ministry courses and examinations found inconsistent with the schools' philosophy and goals. However, most Christian school parents declined to opt for a continued distinctive approach if, as a result, children would have difficulty gaining university entrance and the schools would lose funding. With Canada's centralized regulation of education, B.C. non-public schools receiving government funding must now, to a large extent, follow curriculum policies set by the Minister for public schools. At the senior secondary level, at least, British Columbia's Christian schools must in the future teach the public school curriculum to which some Christian interpretation and values have been added (a situation that, somewhat ironically, parallels what Christian schools do in the United States despite the latter's lack of government funding).

The American and Canadian national identities have also influenced the schools' curricula. American nationalism, as Allan Smith has pointed out,[21] demands the assimilation of all to a common way—a way accepted by most CSI communities by 1920. The approval of the American system as a Christian one led the schools to adopt most public school programs, adding only Biblical studies and, elsewhere, Christian interpretations. Dutch immigrants to Canada since World War II were less ready to identify Christianity with Americanism. Moreover, Canada has been more tolerant of differences, and Dutch Canadians, using their more recent Kuyperian perspective, felt freer to analyze critically the North American way of life. Canadian curriculum work, therefore, in line with the Canadian national identity, has called for a pluralism that values diversity and sets out Christian alternatives and proposals. Although the curriculum clashes of the late 1960s and 1970s between Canadian and American supporters have decreased with the more conservative social mood and an increasing Canadian influence in CSI, the two different national psyches continue to lead to differing approaches, particularly in the area of social studies.

The five categories of influences described—religious, moral, social, educational and political—are not all-encompassing, but do provide an explanatory framework for the types of learning that occurred in CSI classrooms. Especially the religious and social categories underscore how and why the schools have been distinctive. Educational and political contexts, on the other hand, have tended to steer the schools into the mainstreams of Canadian and American education. As in most educational situations, complex networks of interrelated influences resulted in certain directions or specific decisions being taken.

Implications for CSI and Other
Religiously-Oriented
Non-Public Schools

Curriculum and instruction in CSI schools have been distinctive only to a limited degree. The schools have taught Biblical studies at each grade level and have embedded a strict moral code in various program components.   Also, teachers have added their Christian exegeses in subjects like literature, science and social studies.   The schools welcomed the one major attempt to develop a Christian approach to pedagogy early in the century, but did not take steps to implement it.   Other than in Biblical studies, only an occasional "Christian" textbook was published that gained widespread acceptance. Most teaching differed only little from that in fairly traditional public schools, partly because religious rather than educational reasons usually led to the establishment of CSI schools.   Unlike the Waldorf schools, for example, founded explicitly to implement Rudolph Steiner's educational theories, CSI schools did not begin with a philosophically and psychologically defensible theory of education.   The North American movement attempted to develop some theoretical underpinnings around 1950 and in the 1970s.[22]   Not surprisingly, during these years the movement also developed its most distinctive curriculum materials, including some where authors chose both content and types of learning activities for their consistency with a Calvinistic worldview and theory of education.

However, even with a well-developed theoretical base and congruent courses and units, the schools would have had difficulty in implementing and maintaining notable curricular distinctiveness.   Small size prevented substantial curriculum development.   The teacher training programs at Calvinist colleges have, by and large, not been noted for their singular Christian approaches.   Until the 1970s, usually the only help given teachers in implementing new curricula and materials consisted of short sessions at regional professional conferences.   A lack of consensus about basic curriculum orientations aggravated the curricular inertia tendency that exists in all schools.   School boards, frequently not educationally perceptive and unable to pay teachers well, seldom required teachers to do the additional work necessary to implement a more distinctive approach.   Most parents were critical of society's religious and moral decadence but, wanting their children to do well in that society, nevertheless believed that the curriculum should not deviate too much from general societal expectations.   In addition, government departments of education as well as university and college entrance requirements have had a strong conforming influence on both public and non-public schools.   Only schools with a strong theoretical base and with knowledgeable parents committed to that base would be able to maintain their own unique approach to curriculum and instruction.   Otherwise, the unavoidable pressure to conform would not be withstood.

The effects of curriculum on children are real but should not be overrated, however.   As Bennink concluded later in his life, pedagogical approaches also have great impact. Wolterstorff in the late 1970s shifted his emphasis from curriculum to modeling a Christian lifestyle. Both expressed concerns about the socialization function of the schools. The so-called "hidden curriculum," i.e., the tacit teaching taking place in the context of schooling that socializes the pupils into a certain way of life, may well have had more influence on children than explicit curriculum and instruction. Beyond a few minor sociological studies that have drawn conflicting conclusions about the attitudes of Christian school students,[23] Calvinist schools have failed to investigate and address the issues about the structure and effects of schooling raised, for example, by the curricular reconceptualists. The school movement needs to investigate Christian approaches to the total "ecology" of the schools—including curriculum but also pedagogy, the structure of the school, how the school functions as a community, and so on.

Of course, the place of the school itself in the acculturation and education of children can also be exaggerated. It is significant that a city like Grand Rapids, Michigan, with a large Catholic and Calvinist non-public school population and many immigrants who stayed in school only a few years, nevertheless Americanized very rapidly in the 1910s.[24] The readiness of parents to become part of the American business and commercial world and the general societal forces for modernization likely had a greater impact on behavioural assimilation than the schools themselves.[25] Homes, the societal context, and, today, the media shape children as much as the schools. Certainly, as both John Dewey and Lawrence Cremin have pointed out, "in a modern industrial society, with its multiplicity of political and educative agencies, the school could never be the main determinant of political, intellectual, or moral change."[26] The best that Christian schools can do is to develop insights and tendencies that help students begin to work for some individual and social change based on Christian beliefs. For this, the schools are necessary. However, they are but one link—though an important one—in the chain that nurtures children.

Christian school supporters have recognized that socialization in a Christian way is difficult in a modern urban environment satiated with commercial media influences. How far they are willing to disconnect themselves from North American values and structures is a knotty problem for a minority group whose worldview differs from the one society takes for granted, but that must have roots in that society in order to contribute to it in a uniquely Christian way. Is Peter Berger right that such a minority's only effective remedy against the threat of cognitive collapse in modern society is for likeminded adherents to huddle in a ghetto-like "countercommunity"?[27] Christian school supporters need research to show how their schools have served as effective "retreats," and to what extent graduates have influenced society in a Christian way. This would help them establish in what ways they are willing to be a cognitive "countercommunity" in society, given the tendency for cognitive and social integration to increase over time.

Worldview and Curriculum

Does the Christian school have a legitimate place in society? Paul Hirst has argued that the logic of education excludes the possibility of theology making a distinctive contribution to educational theory or practice. Since for Hirst education must develop "a rationally autonomous person whose life is self-directed in the light of what reason determines," and religion has no objective, rational grounds for judging claims, Hirst concluded that religious or Christian education was a contradiction in terms.[28] However, Hirst has failed to recognize that his own view of education, based on the **belief** of rationality as the ultimate criterion of the goals of human life and of how education should be structured,[29] is one based on just one of many competing worldviews:

> One of the basic problems underlying the discussion of values and the future of education is the confusion caused by co-existing but divergent world-views. We could better appreciate the values perpetuated through the educational process if we came to terms with the world-views underlying what we value, how we value, and the manner in which we understand the very discussion of values. Everyone has a world-view or perspective on life. Not everyone, however, is aware of what this **Weltanschauung** is.[30]

Worldviews are based on certain assumptions and beliefs, most of which have not taken rationality as the ultimate justification. Ruth Miller Elson, for instance, has pointed out that "liberty" has been historically an assumed—and undefined—basic conception of the worldview embedded in and imparted through American textbooks. Others have described how an unquestioned, almost religious patriotism has been a basic tenet of American schools.[31] Werner has shown that if participants in a curriculum project do not share a common worldview, the implementation of such projects is often undermined.[32]

The point here is that worldviews undergird all approaches to education. Paul Hirst, Paulo Freire, and a Kuyperian Calvinist will develop different educational theories and practices because their basic worldviews differ. Christian educators—not theologians!—may well develop Christian theories of education that differ from Hirst even in their conception of education. Schools that try to implement such distinct theories have as legitimate a place within the North American educational landscape as schools based on Hirst's worldview.

Regrettably, within the Calvinist Christian school movement three difficulties have prevented the schools from making a mark as distinctive as its proponents envisioned. First, even where leaders tried to work out the implications of a Calvinist worldview for education, teachers and boards often did not give wholehearted support to such efforts and, as a result, the implementation of distinctive curriculum projects lagged. Secondly, and closely connected, differing religious and educational emphases in North American Dutch Calvinism have led to contrasting perceptions of the Christian school program. Thirdly, the positions of almost all Calvinists have been heavily influenced by the beliefs and values of the worldview underlying much of North American culture.[33] Consequently, the schools have failed to move in a unified direction. At a time when many are losing some of their religious and cultural cohesiveness, the schools have not yet demonstrated the possibility of fully implementing their leaders' vision of Biblical, Christian principles permeating the total program.

Between 1977 and 1984, a period beyond the scope of this study, some positive developments took place within the CSI Christian school movement. CSI's curriculum department's new materials moved away from a narrow process approach. In Canada, the emerging broad consensus among educational leaders about curriculum orientations and emphases resulted in much grass-root unit and course development and implementation, involving a large number of teachers, especially at the elementary level. In 1984 Christian Schools International itself recognized the value of such activity and organized a continent-wide coordinators' council to stimulate discussion of educational issues and new educational thrusts at both the regional and international levels.

But can such initiatives be sustained? As the last sections have shown, this will be difficult. First and foremost, the school movement needs to define more sharply how its Christian worldview determines the schools' curricular and instructional framework. A responsible uniqueness depends on the working out of such a definition and on the fortitude to move along an educational path that diverges from that of public education. The leadership must work consistently and constantly not only at setting out and implementing such new directions, but also at ensuring that the supporting community understands them and is willing to walk along the path, rocky though it may be at times.

Further, teacher training programs at Christian liberal arts colleges must also prepare teachers much more specifically for such a distinctive program. Boards must insist that teachers take such programs, either pre-service or in-service or both. Even then, it will be far from easy to maintain educational distinctiveness in an era when the mores and social climate of society-at-large impinges on those of sub-communities with increasing force.

However, a failure to build consistently on the foundations that have been laid will result in CSI schools becoming even less distinctive than they have been in the past. Then the schools, although still isolating children religiously and socially, will prepare them to conform to modern society rather than setting their minds and hearts on transforming it. And that, I believe, as a Christian in the Kuyperian Calvinist tradition, is not good enough. More is demanded if we are to work out our salvation with fear and trembling in nurturing children to act justly and to love mercy and to walk humbly with our God.

NOTES

1. Department of Commerce, Bureau of the Census, **Thirteenth Census of the U.S. Taken in the Year 1910, Vol. 1: Population 1910** [Washington: Government Printing Office, 1913], p. 1113.

2. R. Freeman Butts, **The Education of the West** (New York: McGraw Hill, 1973), p. 445.

3. David B. Tyack, "Onward Christian Soldiers: Religion in the American Common School," in Paul Nash, ed., **History and Education: The Educational Uses of the Past** (New York: Random House, 1970), chapter 8; David B. Tyack, "The Kingdom of God and the Common School," **Harvard Educational Review** 36 (1966): 468-69; Robert T. Handy, A **Christian America: Protestant Hopes and Historical Realities** (New York: Oxford University Press, 1971), pp. 103-115.

4. Robert P. Swierenga, "Local-Cosmopolitan Theory and Immigrant Religion: The Social Bases of the Antebellum Dutch Reformed Schism," **Journal of Social History** 14 (Fall 1980): 130-131.

5. See explanation, footnote 2, Chapter 1. This concluding chapter uses the present CSI name of the organization rather than the pre-1978 NUCS one.

6. For discussions of the economic success, occupational prestige and educational achievement of various Catholic ethnic groups, see

Andrew M. Greeley, William C. McCready, and Kathleen McCourt, **Catholic Schools in a Declining Church** (Kansas City: Sheed and Ward, 1976), especially p. 302. For Catholics in general, Greeley and Rossi concluded that in the 1960s there was a weak but persistent association between Catholic education and economic and social achievement (Andrew M. Greeley and Peter H. Rossi, **The Education of Catholic Americans** [Chicago: Aldine, 1966], pp. 220, 225-26). Research on such relationships for Dutch Calvinist schools in the U.S. and Canada has not been done.

7. For these paragraphs on Catholic education, the sources in footnote 6 as well as the following were used: James A. Burns, **The Growth and Development of the Catholic School System in the United States** (New York: Benziger Brothers, 1912); James S. Coleman, "Quality and Equality in American Education: Public and Catholic Schools," **Phi Delta Kappan**, Nov. 1981, pp. 159-164; Vincent P. Lannie, "Church and School Triumphant: The Sources of American Catholic Educational Historiography," **History of Education Quarterly** 16 (Summer 1976): 131-145; Marvin Lazerson, "Understanding American Catholic Educational History," **History of Education Quarterly** 17 (Fall 1977): 297-317; David R. Stronck, "Catholic Science Textbooks," **Science Education** 54 (July-Sept. 1970): 217-18; Timothy L. Smith, "Immigrant Social Aspirations and American Education, 1880-1930," **American Quarterly** 20 (Fall 1969): 527.

8. The information on Amish schools is based on John A. Hostetler and Gertrude E. Huntington, **Children in Amish Society: Socialization and Community Education** (New York: Holt, Rinehart and Winston, 1971); and John W. Friesen, **Schools with a Purpose** (Calgary: Detselig, 1983), Chapter 6. There are a variety of other Mennonite schools in North America, ones that tend to be more urban and modern but maintain distinctive religious beliefs. For a description of the various Mennonite schools in Ontario, see Lynda Valerie Parker, "A History of Protestant Schools in Ontario" (Master of Christian Studies thesis, Regent College, Vancouver, 1982), Chapter 3.

9. Sources for information on Jewish education were Lloyd P. Gartner, **Jewish Education in the United States. A Documentary History** (New York: Teachers College Press, 1969); Ronald Kronish, "John Dewey's Influence on Jewish Educators: The Case of Alexander M. Dushkin," **Teachers College Record** 83 (Spring 1982): 419-433; B. M. Bullivant, **The Way of Tradition: Life in an Orthodox Jewish School** (Victoria: Australian Council for

Educational Research, 1978).

10. John J. Bergen, "The Private School Movement in Alberta," **The Alberta Journal of Educational Research** 28 (Dec. 1982): 315-36, especially pp. 327-29; Robert L. Smith, "How Different Kinds of Private Schools View Their Purposes," **NASSP Bulletin** 66 (March 1982): 10-17.

11. John Allyne Burgess, "The Integration of Religious Content in Secular Subjects in Certain Church Related Schools" (Ed.D. dissertation, Harvard University, 1967), especially pp. 211-19.

12. As late as 1962 one American author in CSI's **Christian Home and School** (Dec. 1962, p. 20) still discussed the "transition to American culture" that U.S. Christian schools were making. In 1967 Ginn concluded that although Christian schools in B.C.'s Fraser Valley existed for religious reasons, they nevertheless isolated Dutch Calvinist children and accentuated intra-group relations (Edith M. Ginn, "Rural Dutch Immigrants in the Lower Fraser Valley" [M.A. thesis, University of British Columbia, 1967], pp. 85-86). This was true even though the Dutch accepted English for daily and worship use much more rapidly than, for example, the Mennonites of the same area, and the schools employed some non-Dutch teachers (pp. 85, 89).

13. Robert L. Smith, p. 11.

14. William C. Hendricks, **Under God** (Grand Rapids: CSI Publications, 1966, 1981); Ary De Moor et al., **Man in Society: A Study in Hope** (Grand Rapids, CSI Publications, 1980).

15. The Canadian immigrants themselves were not united either, as several sections in this book have indicated. Both the work of the NUCS and that of the Curriculum Development Centre, for instance, were opposed by different groups that also often opposed each other. Whether this was once again related to their local Dutch background is quite possible, but remains to be shown in a social historical investigation.

16. R. Freeman Butts, **Public Education in the United States: From Revolution to Reform** (New York: Holt, Rinehart and Winston, 1978), p. 263.

17. This theory, advanced by James A. Burns for Catholic schools in 1912, pp. 300-01, has been repeated by several authors since then.

18. Province of Alberta, **The Department of Education Act** (Edmonton: Queen's Printer, 1970), Article 8 (1).

19. Ministry of Education, **Guide to the Core Curriculum, 1977** (Victoria, B.C., 1977).

20. For a detailed investigation of these developments, see Donald A.

Erickson, "Victoria's Secret: The Effects of British Columbia's Aid to Independent Schools" (Los Angeles: Institute for the Study of Private Schools, 1984 Preliminary Draft), esp. pp. 14:29-14:48 and Chapter 16.

21. Allan Smith, "Metaphor and Nationality in North America," **Canadian Historical Review** 51 (Sept. 1970): 275.

22. John L. DeBeer and Cornelius Jaarsma, **Towards a Philosophy of Christian Education** (Grand Rapids: Christian Schools International, 1953); Henry N. Beversluis, **Christian Philosophy of Education** (Grand Rapids: Christian Schools International, 1971); Henry J. Triezenberg et al., **Principles to Practice** (Grand Rapids: Christian Schools International, 1973); Geraldine Steensma, **To Those Who Teach** (Terre Haute, Indiana: Signal, 1971); Geraldine Steensma and Harro Van Brummelen, eds., **Shaping School Curriculum: A Biblical View** (Terra Haute, Indiana: Signal, 1977); and Douglas G. Blomberg, "The Development of Curriculum with Relation to the Philosophy of the Cosmonomic Idea" (Ph.D. dissertation, University of Sydney, 1978).

23. **Christian Educators Journal**, May, 1972, pp. 8-9; March 1973, pp. 12-14; and Nov. 1973, pp. 8-12.

24. James A. Burns in his 1912 book on Catholic education indicated that in 1910 French-Canadian, Polish, and Lithuanian Catholic schools in Grand Rapids enrolled 5 408 students. This was in addition to German Catholic schools and about 2 000 students attending Dutch Calvinist schools, all in a city whose total student enrollment was 19 141 (**Thirteenth Census of the U.S. Taken in the Year 1910, Vol. 1: Population 1910**, p. 1113).

25. For a discussion of the role of the school compared with other acculturation factors, see Timothy L. Smith, "New Approaches to the History of Immigration in Twentieth Century America," **American Historical Review** 71 (July 1966): 1265-79.

26. Lawrence A. Cremin, "Public Education and the Education of the Public," in Donald R. Warren, **History, Education, and Public Policy** (Berkeley: McCutchan, 1978), p. 25.

27. Peter L. Berger, **A Rumour of Angels** (Hammondsworth, England: Penguin Books, 1969, 1970), pp. 31-34.

28. Paul H. Hirst, "Christian Education: a Contradiction in Terms?," **Learning for Living** 11 (No. 4, 1972): 6-11, quoted in Leslie J. Francis, "The Logic of Education, Theology, and the Church School," **Oxford Review of Education** 9 (1983): 149.

29. Paul H. Hirst, **Knowledge and the Curriculum** (London: Routledge and Kegan Paul, 1974), pp. 41-43.

30. Malloy-Hanley, Erin. "Some Thoughts on World-Views and Education," **McGill Journal of Education** 12 (Spring 1977): 153.

31. Ruth Miller Elson, **Guardians of Tradition: American Schoolbooks of the Nineteenth Century** (Lincoln: University of Nebraska Press, 1964), p. 285; D. W. Brogan, **The American Character** (New York: Vintage Books, 1956), pp. 163-67.

32. Walter Werner, "Implementation: The Role of the Belief," in Mike Daniels and Ian Wright, eds., **Implementation Viewpoints** (Vancouver: Centre for the Study of Curriculum and Instruction, University of British Columbia, 1980), pp. 54-65.

33. For a description of this worldview, see Wanda Avila, "Toward a Theory of American Culture," in Bernardo Bernardi, **The Concept and Dynamics of Culture** (The Hague: Mouton, 1977), especially pp. 541-44.

Bibliographical Notes

Much of the material in this book depends on interviews, personal papers, and manuscript materials such as minutes, conference proceedings, and unpublished biographies. I systematically scanned the personal papers of the following persons, many of whom were Christian school principals: Henry Beets, Andrew Blystra, Simon Dekker, Albert Hyma, Cornelius Jaarsma, B. K. Kuiper, Henry Ryskamp, John A. Van Bruggen, J. G. Vanden Bosch, Henry Van Zyl, and Dewey Westra. Principals George Bos and J. C. Lobbes wrote unpublished biographies. All these materials are available in Heritage Hall Archives, Calvin College, Grand Rapids, Michigan. I perused the minutes of the following Christian schools and related organizations: Abbotsford (1950-76); Baxter Street, Grand Rapids (1889-1906); Christian Reformed Church Acts of Synod (1857-1977); Classis Holland (1848-58); Franklin, Grand Rapids (1892-99); Fraser Valley High (1966-71, 1973-77); Holland (1911-23); Lynden, Washington (1910-77); Michigan Alliance of Christian Schools (1924-54); National Union of Christian Schools—Board of Directors, Executive Committee, Textbook and Education Committees, Annual Meetings (1920-78); and Vancouver (1944-71).

I also scanned most periodicals published for NUCS/CSI schools and their communities for articles about the schools' programs and related issues. These include **The Banner** (1866-1977); **Calvin Forum** (1935-56); **De Calvinist** (1911-18); **Christian Educators Journal** (1961-77); **Christian School Magazine/Christian Home and School** (1922-77); **Christian School Herald** (1957-69); **Christian Journal** (1918-20); **Church and Nation** (1956-69); **De Gereformeerde Amerikaan** (1897-1916); **De Gids** (1905-11); NUCS' **Yearbooks, Convention Papers, Annuals** and **Directories** from 1917-18 to 1977-78; **Torch and Trumpet/The Outlook** (1951-77); **The Reformed Journal** (1951-77); **Religion and Culture** (1919-25); **De Schoolbel** (1906-09; only a few issues are extant); **Vanguard** (1970-77); **De Wachter** (1868-1977); and **The Witness** (1921-25).

The first books and brochures about Christian education in North America appeared early in the century. Many tried to set out basic rationales for Christian day school education. These included Louis

BIBLIOGRAPHICAL NOTE

Berkhof's Het Christelijk onderwijs en onze kerkelijke toekomst [Christian education and the future of our church] (Holland, Michigan: H. Holkeboer, 1905); Louis Berkhof and B. J. Bennink, 'n Tweetal lezingen [Two lectures] (Grand Rapids: Michigan Alliance for Christian Education, 1917); J. W. Brink, Welke is de school voor onze kinderen? [Which is the school for our children?] (Holland, Michigan: Schoolraad and Holkeboer, 1904]; G. J. Diekema and F. Kniphuizen, Lichtstralen schijnende op onze schoolkwestie [Light rays shining on our school question] (Grand Rapids: Vereeniging voor Christelijk Onderwijs op Gereformeerde Grondslag, n.d.); J. Groen, Onze lagere school [Our elementary school] (Holland, Michigan: Holkeboer, 1903); Handwijzers: een vijftal referaten [Signposts: five lectures] (Grand Rapids: Eerdmans-Sevensma, 1911); G. W. Hylkema, The Free Christian School (Grand Rapids: Eerdmans-Sevensma, 1918); B. K. Kuiper, The Proposed Calvinistic College in Grand Rapids (Grand Rapids: Sevensma, 1903); and Six Lectures Delivered at the Michigan Christian Teachers' Institute (Kalamazoo: Dalm Printing, 1914). The last publication is the main one during this period that dealt with educational issues in some depth.

The interwar years saw several publications based on Dutch works in an attempt to maintain and develop the schools' uniqueness: J. Brederveld, Christian Education: A Summary and Critical Discussion of Bavinck's Pedagogical Principles, translated by two Calvin College faculty members (Grand Rapids: Smitter, 1928); A. G. D. Gerritsen, Christian Instruction, translated by P. Stam, Jr. (New Jersey: Eastern Schoolboards and Eastern Teachers Association, 1918); and Cornelius Jaarsma, The Educational Philosophy of Herman Bavinck: A Textbook in Education (Grand Rapids: Eerdmans, 1935). The curricular conflict in the Chicago Christian High School resulted in two publications: Herman Kuiper, The Chicago Situation: A Word of Warning to the Churches (Chicago: Calvin Press, 1935), and the response by the Chicago Christian High School Board, The Truth About the Chicago Situation (1936).

The post-World War II immigration to Canada led to two brochures setting out basic principles of Christian school education: Aris Haalboom, Om het kind [On account of the child] (Toronto: Pro Rege, 1957), and Albert Witvoet, ed., Learning Under the Lamp of God (Hamilton, Ont.: The Christian School Herald, 1965). Most publications during this period, however, dealt more specifically with philosophical, curricular, or pedagogical issues. Dealing specifically with Christian theories of learning were John De Beer and Cornelius Jaarsma's Toward a Philosophy of Christian Education (Grand Rapids:

NUCS, 1953) and N. Henry Beversluis' **Christian Philosophy of Education** (Grand Rapids: NUCS, 1971). Other books tackled a wide variety of curricular and pedagogical concerns: Cornelius Jaarsma, **Fundamentals in Christian Education** (Grand Rapids: Eerdmans, 1953); Henry Zylstra, **Testament of Vision** (Grand Rapids: Eerdmans, 1958); Nicholas Wolterstorff, **Curriculum: By What Standard?** (Grand Rapids: NUCS, 1966) and **School and Curriculum** (Grand Rapids: NUCS, 1969); John Vriend et al., **To Prod the "Slumbering Giant": Crisis, Commitment and Christian Education** (Toronto: Wedge, 1972); Henry J. Triezenberg, ed., **Principles to Practice** (Grand Rapids: NUCS, 1973); and Geraldine J. Steensma and Harro W. Van Brummelen, eds., **Shaping School Curriculum: A Biblical View** (Terre Haute: Signal, 1977).

Some publications discussed specific subject areas. These included, for example, Dennis Hoekstra and Arnold DeGraaff, **Contrasting Christian Approaches to Teaching Religion and Biblical Studies** (Grand Rapids: Calvin College, 1973); Russell Maatman and Gerald Bakker, **Contrasting Christian Approaches to Teaching the Sciences** (Grand Rapids: Calvin College, 1971); and Louis Vos et al., **Revelation-Response: Its Distinctive Approach** (Grand Rapids: NUCS, 1977). Unique was Geraldine J. Steensma's publication, **To Those Who Teach** (Terre Haute: Signal, 1971), widely used in teacher preparation in Christian colleges throughout the United States. Two recent publications analyze curriculum trends in Calvinist Christian schools in the post-World War II era: Peter P. De Boer, **Shifts in Curriculum Theory for Christian Education** (Grand Rapids: Calvin College, 1983), and Tony VanderEnde, "Conflicting Conceptions of Truth and Implications for Christian Curriculum" (unpublished major paper for M.A.T. degree, Calvin College, 1980).

The post-World War II period also revealed interest in the history of the Calvinist Christian school movement. Unpublished documents include Arthur H. De Kruyter, "The Reformed Christian Day School Movement in North America" (M.Th. thesis, Princeton Theological Seminary, 1952); George Stob, "The Christian Reformed Church and Her Schools" (Th.D. dissertation, Princeton Theological Seminary, 1955); Jack Talstra, "A Brief History of NUCS" (1958); Kay D. Rowe, "The Christian Day School Movement in America" (1978); William Hoogland, "The Development of Calvinistic Christian Day Schools in Canada 1943-1965" (1981); Herbert T. Brinks, "The Origins of Christian Education in the Christian Reformed Church" (1982); and Adriaan Peetoom, "From Mythology to Mythology: Dutch Canadian Orthodox-Calvinist Immigrants and Their Schools" (M.A. thesis, University of Toronto, 1983). All of these except the last are available in Heritage Hall Archives, Calvin

College. The best, though dated, short overview of the history of the Calvinist schools is Donald Oppewal's **The Roots of the Calvinistic Day School Movement** (Grand Rapids: Calvin College Monograph Series, 1963). Peter Y. De Jong, **The Story of the Schools** (Hamilton, Ont.: Christian School Herald, n.d.) is a lesser-known, more parent-oriented brochure, equally dated. John A. VanderArk, long-time executive director of the NUCS, more recently wrote **22 Landmark Years: Christian Schools International, 1943-65** (Grand Rapids: Baker Book House, 1983). This publication is descriptive rather than analytical. Louis Y. Van Dyke and James A. De Jong both wrote historical essays in the book they co-edited, **Building the House: Essays on Christian Education** (Sioux Center, Iowa: Dordt College Press, 1981). The first analyzes the NUCS Convention addresses from 1935-45; the second, Henricus Beuker's views of Abraham Kuyper (Beuker was a Dutch church leader in the **Afscheiding** tradition who moved to Michigan in 1893). Lynda V. Parker touched on the history of Ontario's Christian schools in her M.C.E. thesis, "A History of Protestant schools in Ontario" (Regent College, 1982). The history of Calvin College, including its original preparatory school, is described in John Timmerman's **Promises to Keep** (Grand Rapids: Eerdmans, 1975). A great deal of this book was based on Henry Ryskamp's unpublished manuscript found in the latter's personal papers in Heritage Hall Archives.

The classic reference on Dutch immigration to North America is Henry S. Lucas, **Netherlanders in America: Dutch Immigration to the United States and Canada, 1789-1950** (Ann Arbor: University of Michigan Press, 1955). Complementing this volume are the two volumes of Lucas' **Dutch Immigrant Memoirs and Related Writings** (Assen: Van Gorcum, 1955). Works of a similar nature include J. Van Hinte, **Netherlanders in Amerika**, 2 vols. (Groningen: P. Noordhoff, 1928); Arnold Mulder, **Americans from Holland** (Philadelphia and New York: Lippincott, 1947); and Gerald F. De Jong, **The Dutch in America 1609-1974** (Boston: Twayne, 1975). More recently Herman Ganzevoort and Mark Boekelman edited a collection of essays, **Dutch Immigration to North America** (Toronto: The Multicultural History Society of Ontario, 1983). Robert P. Swierenga wrote the article on the Dutch in the **Harvard Encyclopedia of American Ethnic Groups** (1980).

John H. Bratt's essay in W. Stanford Reid, **John Calvin: His Influence in the Western World** (Grand Rapids: Zondervan, 1982) gives a summary of Dutch Calvinism's development in North America. Much more extensive is James D. Bratt's insightful "Dutch Calvinism in Modern America: The History of a Conservative Subculture" (Ph.D. dissertation, Yale University, 1978; recently published by Eerdmans).

BIBLIOGRAPHICAL NOTE

Dealing with the Canadian scene is Aileen M. Van Ginkel's "Ethnicity in the Reformed Tradition: Dutch Calvinist Immigrants in Canada 1946-60" (M.A. thesis, University of Toronto, 1982). A noteworthy analysis of the pre-World War I years is Henry Zwaanstra's **Reformed Thought and Experience in a New World: A Study of the Christian Reformed Church and Its American Environment 1890-1918** (Kampen: Kok, 1973). A number of books exist by authors such as Henry Beets, John Kromminga, and Marian Schoolland that deal specifically with the history of the Christian Reformed Church.

Books that helped relate this study to general societal developments included Bernard Baylin's **Education in the Formation of American Society** (New York: Random House, 1960); Richard Hofstadter's **The Age of Reform** (New York: Alfred A. Knopf, 1955) and **Anti-Intellectualism in American Life** (New York: Alfred A. Knopf, 1963); J. Huizinga's **In the Shadow of To-Morrow** (London: William Heinemann, 1936); and Edward R. Tannenbaum's **1900: The Generation Before the Great War** (Garden City, N.Y.: Anchor Press, Doubleday, 1976). Of the numerous general histories of education, I used the following most frequently: James Bowen, **A History of Western Education, vol. 3: The Modern West: Europe and the New World** (London: Methuen, 1981); R. Freeman Butts, **Public Education in the United States: From Revolution to Reform** (New York: Holt, Rinehart, and Winston, 1978); Lawrence A. Cremin, **The Transformation of the School: Progressivism in American Education 1876-1957** (New York: Alfred A. Knopf, 1961); David B. Tyack, **Turning Points in American Educational History** (Waltham: Blaisdell, 1967); and Donald R. Warren, **History, Education, and Public Policy** (Berkeley: McCutchan, 1978). Ruth Miller Elson's **Guardians of Tradition: American Textbooks of the Nineteen Century** (Lincoln: University of Nebraska Press, 1964) has set a standard for the analysis of textbooks.

Useful references in Canadian educational history are W. G. Fleming, **Education: Ontario's Preoccupation** (Toronto: University of Toronto Press, 1972); Brian E. Titley and Peter J. Miller, eds., **Education in Canada: An Interpretation** (Calgary: Detselig, 1982); Robert M. Stamp, **The Schools of Ontario 1876-1976** (Toronto: University of Toronto, 1982); George S. Tomkins, ed., **The Curriculum in Canada in Historical Perspective** (Vancouver: Canadian Society for the Study of Education, 1979); J. Donald Wilson, R. M. Stamp and P. L. Audet, eds., **Canadian Education: A History** (Toronto: Prentice-Hall, 1970); and J. Donald Wilson, ed., **Canadian Education in the 1980s** (Calgary: Detselig, 1981).

A number of books that dealt with the history of Christianity in Western or American society in a way that, directly or indirectly, was relevant to some of the issues discussed in this study: Robert T. Handy, **A Christian America: Protestant Hopes and Historical Realities** (New York: Oxford University Press, 1971); George M. Marsden, **Fundamentalism and American Culture** (Oxford: Oxford University Press, 1980); Martin E. Marty, **A Nation of Behavers** (Chicago: The University of Chicago Press, 1976); Richard H. Niebuhr, **Christ and Culture** (New York: Harper and Row Torchbooks, 1951, 1956) and **The Social Sources of Denominationalism** (New York: Herry Holt, 1929); Richard Reinitz, ed., **Tension in American Puritanism** (New York: John Wiley, 1970); and Edwin H. Rian, **Christianity and American Education** (San Antonio: The Naylor Co., 1949). Of the many articles discussing the impact of immigration, ethnicity and religion on American education, the following were especially applicable: Michael R. Olneck and Marvin Lazerson, "Education," in the **Harvard Encyclopedia of American Ethnic Groups** (1980); Timothy L. Smith, "Immigrant Social Aspirations and American Education, 1880-1930," **American Quarterly** 21 (Fall 1969): 523-43; "New Approaches to the History of Immigration in Twentieth Century America," **American History Review** 71 (July 1966): 1265-79; "Protestant Schooling and American Nationality, 1800-1850," **Journal of American History** 53 (March 1967): 679-95; and "Religious Denominations as Ethnic Communities: A Regional Case Study," **Church History** 35 (1966): 207-26; and David B. Tyack, "The Kingdom of God and the Common School," **Harvard Educational Review** 36 (1966): 447-69.

Curriculum books published during the twentieth century in North America also influenced Calvinist Christian schools, sometimes directly, and sometimes because of the discussions the publication generated. Noteworthy among these were: W. H. Kilpatrick, **The Project Method** (New York: Columbia University Teachers College, 1918); Franklin Bobbitt, **How to Make a Curriculum** (Boston: Houghton Mifflin, 1924); G. M. Whipple, ed., **The Foundations and Techniques of Curriculum Construction. Part II: The Foundations of Curriculum Making,** Twenty-sixth Yearbook, National Society for the Study of Education (Bloomington: Illinois, 1927); Ralph W. Tyler, **Basic Principles of Curriculum and Instruction** (Chicago: The University of Chicago, 1950); Benjamin S. Bloom, ed., **Taxonomy of Educational Objectives, Handbook I: Cognitive Domain** and David R. Krathwohl, ed., **Taxonomy of Educational Objectives, Handbook II: Affective Domain** (New York: David McKay, 1956 and 1964); James Bryant Conant, **The American High School Today** (New York: McGraw-Hill, 1959); and Charles E. Silberman, **Crisis in the Classroom** (New York: Random House, Vintage

Books, 1971). In Canada, the so-called Hall-Dennis report also led to much deliberation (Report of the Provincial Committee on Aims and Objectives in the Schools of Ontario, **Living and Learning**, 1968). Elliot W. Eisner's **The Educational Imagination** (New York: Macmillan, 1979) provided a basis for categorizing curriculum orientations, though not without some revision.

For a complete bibliography, the reader may consult the author's doctoral dissertation, available in the University of British Columbia library as well as on microfilm through the National Library of Canada and University Microfilms International.

CURRICULUM MATERIALS DEVELOPED FOR NUCS/CSI SCHOOLS

Listed below are curriculum materials for Christian schools to which this book refers.

Aué, C. and Verhulst, H. C. **A Practical Guide for the Christian Instruction of United States History.** Sioux Center, Iowa: Roelofs Brothers, n.d.

Bennink, B. J. **Course of Study for the Elementary School for Christian Instruction.** Kalamazoo: Michigan Alliance of Christian Schools, 1915.

————. **First Lessons in Geography for the Fourth Grade of Christian Schools.** Grand Rapids: Grandville Christian School Board, n.d.

————. **Lessons in Geography for the Fifth Grade of Christian Schools.** Grand Rapids: Grandville Christian School Board, n.d.

————. **Sketches from Church History.** Grand Rapids: Eerdmans for the NUCS, 1925.

Berkhof, Louis. **Manual of Christian Doctrine.** Grand Rapids: Eerdmans, 1933.

Blystra, A.; Bosma, J.; Fakkema, M.; and Yff, N. **Bible Study Pupil's Manuals.** Grand Rapids: NUCS. Part I (1935); Part II (1936); Part III (1935); Part IV (1937); Part V (1940).

Boevé, Edgar. **Children's Art and the Christian Teacher.** Grand Rapids: NUCS, 1966.

Bos, George. **Practical Geography for Christian Schools, First Book.** Privately published, 1923.

Bos, Gerhardus, ed. **Excelsior Readers for Christian Schools.** Grand Rapids: Eerdmans-Sevensma. This series consisted of **Fourth Grade Reader** (1920); **Fifth Grade Reader** (1919); **Sixth Grade Reader** (1919); and **Seventh Grade Reader** (1920).

Bremer, A. **Eenvoudig leesonderwijs voor huisgezin en school**

[Simple reading instruction for family and school]. Grand Rapids: A. Bremer, 1910.

Bossenbroek, Edward. **Old Testament Studies.** Grand Rapids: NUCS. Part I, 1958; **Part II,** 1959; **Part III,** 1960.

Breisch, Francis. **The Kingdom of God** (Grand Rapids: NUCS, 1958).
_____. **The Ministry of Christ.** Grand Rapids: NUCS. **Part I,** 1961; **Part II,** 1962; **Part III,** 1963.

Bruinooge, Martha and Bruinooge, Jessie Mae. **My Bible Guide.** Grand Rapids: NUCS. **Book 4,** 1960; **Book 5,** 1961; **Book 6,** 1962.

Christian Educators Summer School, "Natural Science Outlines, Grades 6-10." Richmond, B.C., 1971.

De Bie, John. **The Story of the Old World.** Grand Rapids: NUCS, 1954.

De Boer, Bruce and Proper, Herman. "High School Science Curriculum." St. Catharines and London, Ontario, 1972.

De Graaff, Arnold H. and Olthuis, Jean. **Joy in Learning: An Integrated Curriculum for the Elementary School.** Toronto: Joy in Learning Curriculum Development Centre, 1973.

De Jong, A. S. **The Church in the World.** Grand Rapids: NUCS, 1936. This is the second edition of Bennink's **Sketches from Church History.**

De Moor, Ary; Oosterman, Gordon; Contant, Henry; Hull, John; Koole, Robert; Spoelstra, Fred; Van Huizen, Peter; and Williams, Stuart. **Man in Society: A Study in Hope.** Grand Rapids, CSI, 1980.

Fenenga, Alice; Haan, Gertrude; and Merizon, Beth, eds. **The Pilot Series in Literature.** Grand Rapids: NUCS. **Book 1** (1957); **Book 2** (1959); **Book 3** (1964).

Fernhout, Harry. **Of Kings and Prophets: A Study of the Book of Kings.** Toronto: Curriculum Development Centre, 1979.

Hendricks, William C. **Under God: A Government Textbook.** Grand Rapids: NUCS, 1966.

Heyns, Garrett and Roelofs, Garritt E. **Christian Interpretation of American History.** Chicago: NUCS, 1928.

Heyns, W. **Outlines and Notes on Bible History, Old Testament.** 2nd ed. Grand Rapids: Van Noord, 1921.

Hyma, Albert. **World History—A Christian Interpretation.** Grand Rapids: Eerdmans, 1942.

Institute for Christian Studies and Ontario Alliance of Christian Schools. "Biblical Studies, Grade 4, Part I." Toronto, 1970.

Jaarsma, C. R.; Postma, R. H.; and Tuls, J. **Outline of Sacred History for Christian Instruction.** Grand Rapids: Van Noord, 1920.

Kromminga, D. H. **A History of the Christian Church for High**

BIBLIOGRAPHICAL NOTE

Schools. Grand Rapids: Eerdmans, 1945.

Kuiper, B. K. **The Church in History.** Grand Rapids: NUCS and Eerdmans, 1951, 1964.

Laverman, Gerald. **Industrial Arts in the Christian School.** Grand Rapids: NUCS, 1970.

Mulder, Jane; Wikkerink, Trix; and Klein, Marianne. "Social Science Curriculum (Grade 2)." Surrey, B.C.: Christian Educators Summer School, 1971.

National Union of Christian Schools, **Bible Curriculum Guide, K-3.** Grand Rapids: NUCS, 1958.

_____. **Course of Study for Christian Schools.** Grand Rapids: NUCS, 1947.

_____. **Revelation-Response Bible Studies Series.** Grades K-3: **God's Great Love, God's Covenant, Judgment and Hope, Salvation and Service, Creation and Providence, The Church, Covenantal Learning and Living** (1974). Grade 4: **God's Witnesses** (1971, 1976); Grade 5: **God's Kingdom** (1971, 1976); Grade 6: **God's Community** (1971, 1976); Grade 7: **Student Book** (1974); Grade 8: **Student Book** (1974); Grade 9 and 10: **Orange, Yellow, Green,** and **Blue Books** (1974). A teacher's guide was published for each component, and test items with objectives for all components from grades 4-8.

_____. **A Uniform System of High School Credits.** Grand Rapids: NUCS, 1950.

NUCS Science Committee, **Manual for Teaching Science, Grades 5 and 6.** Grand Rapids: NUCS, 1957.

Oosterman, Gordon, ed. **Geneva to Geelong.** Grand Rapids: NUCS, 1974.

_____. **The People: Three Indian Tribes of the Southwest.** Grand Rapids: NUCS and Eerdmans, 1973.

_____. **Teacher's Manual for "Under God."** Grand Rapids: NUCS, 1971.

Oosterman, Gordon, ed.; Bosch, Chris; De Vries, Anna; Klapwyk, Ray; Prinsen, Peter; Oosterhuis, Alyce; and Tiemstra, Bertha. **A Difficult Journey: Blackfoot, Cree and Métis on the Western Plains.** Grand Rapids: NUCS, 1977.

Oosterman, Gordon; Guldemond, Adrian; Vandezande, George; and Vreugdenhil, James. **To Find a Better Life: Aspects of a Dutch Immigrant to Canada and the United States 1920-1970.** Grand Rapids: NUCS, 1975.

Schoolland, Marion. **God's Great Outdoors.** Chicago: NUCS. **Book Four** (1939); **Book Five** (1938).

Sinnema, Don. **Reclaiming the Land: A Study of the Book of**

307

BIBLIOGRAPHICAL NOTE

Joshua. Toronto: Curriculum Development Centre, 1977.

Teachers of the East. **Teacher's Guide for Bible Study.** Prepublication edition for grades one to four, 1936.

Vander Meer, Lewis; Snoeyink, Arnold; and Vander Zicht, Sandy. **Biblical Perspectives Series: Authority and the Bible; The Christian in the World; The Church; Decision Making; Freedom; and Sexuality and the Christian Home.** Grand Rapids: NUCS, 1975.

Van Ee, Yvonne and Triezenberg, Henry J. **Interpret the Sky.** Grand Rapids: NUCS, 1976.

Zuidema, Marvin. **Education Through Motor Proficiency.** Grand Rapids: NUCS, 1979.

_____. **Motor Proficiency for All.** Grand Rapids: NUCS, 1975.

_____. **Self-Respect Through Health Fitness.** Grand Rapids: NUCS, 1974.

Index

INDEX

Conant, James Bryant, 210
Constitution, U.S., 89, 90, 214
Council for American Private Education, 280
Countercommunity, 289
Counterculture, 281
Counts, G., 182
Course of study for Christian schools, 84, 87, 89, 106, 112-13, 117, 121, 125, 149, 158, 172, 173, 206, 212, 220
Court, U.S. Supreme, 88
Cousin, Victor, 19, 63
Creativity, 183, 186, 251, 253, 254
Cremin, L., 148, 289
Cubberley, E., 54
Cultural approach in learning, 155, 175ff., 179, 182, 188-92, 248
Culture: relation to faith, 13, 44, 81, 247; Christian transformation of, 81, 92, 116, 124, 182, 186, 187, 208, 276, 283
Curriculum: Canada, 188-92, 193, 209, 210, 215-19, 224, 226-27; Christian interpretation, 150-51, 178, 259, 263, 287; development, 136, 183, 184ff., 192; in Dutch Christian schools, 14, 28-33; in Dutch public schools, 18; effect on students, 288-89; emphasis on personal commitment, 180; influences on, 205-09, 281-87; integration, 114, 140, 145, 146, 157, 180, 257-58, 284; planning, 82-83, 105, 106, 259, 262-63, 285
Curriculum coordinator, 262, 263, 286
Curriculum Development Centre, 217, 227

Curriculum orientations, 173-94; academic, 173, 175, 175-79, 189, 192, 209ff.; eclectic, 182-84, 193; personal relevance, 173, 174-75, 178-81, 189, 192, 208, 209ff., 227, 253; process, 173-75, 186-87, 226, 228; social relevance, 4, 6, 175, 182, 188-92, 208, 223, 225, 227, 229, 256

Darwin, C., 147
De Boer, John, 151, 153
De Boer, Peter, 192, 200, 212
De Cock, H., 23, 117
De Graaff, A., 189, 191, 212, 216, 222, 226-27, 230-31, 253
De Jong, A. S., 93, 118, 136, 161
De Jong, D. C., 90
De Jong, John, 136
De Kruyter, A., 173
De Liefde, J., 30-31, 58, 120
De Moor, A., 240
Denominational schools **See** parochial schools
Depression, 137
Descartes, R., 17
De Vries, F., 252-53, 257
Dewey, J., 4, 112, 143, 146-47, 279, 289
Diekema, G. J., 86
Discipline, 51, 107, 265
District schools **See** public district schools
Dooyeweerd, H., 188
Dordt College, 190
Dualism as an emphasis in the curriculum, 150, 208, 214-15, 225, 229, 279, 283
Dutch influence on North American schools, 55, 57-58, 76-77, 80, 122-23, 143-46, 177

311

Holtman, P. R., 93
Home economics, 210
Hope College, 53, 59
Hughes, J. L., 100
Huguenots, 17
Hulst, L. J., 19
Humanist Manifesto, 147
Hutchins, R. M., 175, 179
Hylkema, G. W. 116
Hyma, A., 165-66

Illich, I., 268
Immigration: American, 2,
33-34, 48, 60, 73, 125, 275;
Canadian, 81, 188, 245-48,
275, 283; importance of
schooling for immigrants, 71;
social background, 33, 43-44,
73
Indoctrination, 149, 261
Indonesia, 246
Industrial arts, 152, 210-11,
255
Institute for Christian Stud-
ies, 189, 216-19, 242
Instruction and pedagogy:
American Christian schools,
56, 105, 107-11, 124, 143-46,
211-13, 253; Canadian Christian schools, 250ff.; Dutch
Christian schools, 13, 28-29;
instructional efficiency,
105, 109, 111, 112, 211, 284;
modeling, 149
Integrationism as an emphasis
in the curriculum, 208, 214,
216, 218, 229, 231, 258, 261,
283
Intermediate Science Curriculum
Study (ISCS), 187, 225
Inuits, 180, 261
Iowa, 28, 45, 52
Irish, 277
Ishwaran, K., 259, 267
Isolationism, 3, 6, 44, 60,
135, 250, 261, 276, 280, 283

Jaarsma, C., 146, 173, 175,
178-81, 182-84, 186, 192,
210-12
Jacobsma, H., 71
Jellema, W. H., 175-78, 182,
192, 211
Jesus Christ Superstar, 260
Jewish schools, 1, 279
Joosten, T., 71

Kalamazoo, Mich., 55, 111, 114
Kantian philosophy, 20
Kellogsville, 87
Kilpatrick, W. H., 147
Kindergarten, 83, 100
Kingship of Jesus Christ, 78,
115-17, 118, 248, 255
Klapwyk, R., 188-91
Klokkenberg, 12, 14, 31
Kniphuizen, F., 61, 86
Kohlberg, L., 200, 240
Kuiper, B. K., 120
Kuiper, H. J., 136, 140, 142
Kuiper, K., 27, 106
Kuiper, R. T., 49, 55, 61
Kuyper, A., 3, 8, 14, 71, 75,
77-81, 86, 92, 105, 107,
116-118, 124-26, 136, 143,
156, 177, 179, 182, 231, 247,
261, 281, 283
Kuyperianism, Kuyperians, 3-7,
77-79, 81, 86, 92, 140, 184,
188, 191-92, 194, 206ff.,
210, 215, 224, 247, 261, 263,
277, 281, 283, 287, 292

Lacombe, Alberta, 246, 249-50
Landverhuizing, 14, 33-34
Language arts, 113, 144, 177
League of Southwest British
Columbia Christian Schools,
257
Leeuwarden, 27, 76
Liberal vs. practical emphasis
in curriculum, 209-13,
255-56
Lincoln, A., 45, 93
Literature, 114, 208, 215